FIRST PRESBYTERIAN CHURCH.

Inscriptions on Tombstones and Monuments

in the Burying Grounds of the
First Presbyterian Church
and St. John's Church
at Elizabeth,
New Jersey,

1664–1892

William Ogden Wheeler
and
Edmund Drake Halsey

HERITAGE BOOKS
2010

HERITAGE BOOKS
AN IMPRINT OF HERITAGE BOOKS, INC.

Books, CDs, and more—Worldwide

For our listing of thousands of titles see our website
at
www.HeritageBooks.com

A Facsimile Reprint
Published 2010 by
HERITAGE BOOKS, INC.
Publishing Division
100 Railroad Ave. #104
Westminster, Maryland 21157

Originally published 1892

— Publisher's Notice —
In reprints such as this, it is often not possible to remove blemishes from the original. We feel the contents of this book warrant its reissue despite these blemishes and hope you will agree and read it with pleasure.

International Standard Book Numbers
Paperbound: 978-1-58549-441-5
Clothbound: 978-0-7884-8507-7

PREFACE.

The settlement of Elizabethtown was the first within the bounds of New Jersey made by New England people. The Purchase of the land from the Indians was made by John Baily, Daniel Denton and Luke Watson of Jamaica, L. I., October 28, 1664, and the Patent granted by Gov. Nicolls to Capt. John Baker, John Ogden, John Baily, Luke Watson "and their associates," confirming the Indian deed, bears date December 1, 1664. John Ogden of Northampton had bought out Denton's interest, and Capt. John Baker of New York was probably allowed an interest in consideration of his services as interpreter. Gov. Nicolls when he signed this patent was no doubt ignorant of the deed from the Duke of York to Berkley and Carteret made on the 24th day of June previous. Dr. Hatfield in his history of Elizabeth, thinks it probable that a formal occupation was made upon the land between October and December 1664, and that occupation by actual settlers soon followed. Mr. William A. Whitehead, in his last edition of East Jersey under the Proprietors, gives proof that when Gov. Philip Carteret arrived in 1665, but four English-speaking families were to be found in New Jersey, pioneers of the Jamaica Colony. The patent granted by Governor Nicolls and the Indian purchase were relied upon in after years by the citizens as giving them a good title independent of that of Berkley and Carteret, but the latter grant was prior to the Nicolls patent and a vast amount of litigation was caused by these conflicting grants, lasting until the Revolutionary war put an end to it.

The first meeting house was of wood and of a very humble style of architecture. It was replaced by a new church in 1724, fifty-eight feet in length and forty-two feet in width. An addition in the rear of sixteen feet was made in 1766. On the night of January 25, 1780, a party of British troops and refugees, numbering nearly four hundred, crossed on the ice from Staten Island to Trembly's Point and were led by three Elizabethtown tories by the nearest and most retired route to the town. Here they secured a few prisoners, plundered many of the inhabitants, burned the Court House and Meeting House, and retreated with haste by way of De Hart's Point without loss. Washington spoke of this event a day or two after as " the late misfortune and disgrace of Elizabeth Town." The erection of a new church was commenced in 1784, and completed in 1789. It forms a part of the present edifice, and was extended and improved many times before it reached its present dimensions.

Dr. Kempshall in his historical discourse, delivered January 25, 1880, in celebrating the Centennial Anniversary of the burning of the church says:

" The lot on which the house was built included the present burying-ground, and extended on the west to the river (so called), and contained about eight acres. When the church property was surveyed in 1766, the Trustees affirmed 'that the first purchasers and associates did give the aforesaid tract of land for the use of the Presbyterian Church, the record of which, on or about the year 1719, was either lost or destroyed.' This statement was admitted by the Town Committee, and has constituted the only title of record to the present church property for over a century and a half. The meeting-house occupied part of the site of the present church, but, as it was much smaller, it did not cover much, if any, more than the front half, the other half containing the graves of most of the first settlers. Graves were sometimes dug under the floor of the church, a custom familiar to the early settlers and made dear by association with the habits of their ancestors in England, so that nearly the whole area of this church in which we are now gathered, is probably occupied with the dust which awaits the archangel's trump, of the first two or three generations of the people of the town."

Some of the headstones, removed to give room for the additions to the church, were set in the walls, where they can still be seen. Among them are two old headstones bearing the date 1687, erected to the memory of two sons of the widow of Captain Lawrence, who married, as her second husband, Governor Philip Carteret. Dr. Kempshall says of the lands on which the church is built—

"It is probable that for a long time the church and adjoining burial-ground was not enclosed, or if at all, only in a rude way. In 1762, immediately after the settlement of Rev. Mr. Caldwell, it was voted by the Trustees that 'the burial-ground be enclosed with a close, cedar-board fence; also agreed that a neat pale-fence be built to enclose a court-yard in the front and south end of the church.'"

In this old churchyard lie the forefathers of Elizabeth, and of many whose names are known throughout the State. Here are buried Rev. Jonathan Dickinson, Dr. John McDowell, Rev. James Caldwell, Hon. Elias Boudinot, Robert Ogden, 1st, Gen. Matthias Ogden, Gov. Aaron Ogden, Dr. Nicholas Murray, Shepard Kollock and many others prominent in the history of the country. Many of the headstones are crumbling with age and their lettering will soon become illegible. It was with a view to preserve, as well as to place in a form more convenient to the historian and genealogist, these inscriptions, that the authors of this work caused copies to be carefully made and this book to be printed. The order of location, rather than that of the alphabet has been observed, believing that the "directions to the Sexton," made in 1766, that he is "carefully to observe in the burial of the Dead, to keep the Bodies of the Respective particular Families of the Congregation together as much as possibly can be done," has been generally observed and that relationship may in many cases be indicated by situation.

St. John's Church is nearly as ancient as the First Presbyterian. The corner stone of the first building was laid on St. John the Baptist's day, 1706, on ground given by Col. Richard Townley. This building was enlarged and re-consecrated in 1841, and in 1857 the corner stone of the present handsome structure was laid. In this church yard are buried many of the earliest inhabitants of the town, and copies of the inscriptions on the headstones and monuments were necessary to complete the work proposed by the authors.

W. O. W.
E. D. H.

MORRISTOWN, N. J., 1892.

INSCRIPTIONS.

Note.—The italic letters following the full face number at head of inscriptions indicate material, viz: *g* granite ; *m* marble ; *r* red sandstone ; *w* wood.

1 *r*
A. P.
In Memory of
ABIGAIL wife of
Elihu Price
who died
Jany 2nd 1817
In the 39th year
of her age.

Happy soul we now resign thee
Called by the great I am
Left thy troubles all behind thee
Gone to Glorify the Lamb

O my mourning friends below
Did you half his glory know
Daily would you stretch the wing
Here to fly with me to sing

2 *m*
MARY ANN PRICE
BORN
Dec 18th 1795
DIED
July 22^d 1870

"O : death : where is thy sting
O : grave : where is thy victory
Thanks be to God which giveth
us the victory"

3 *r*
E P
In memory of
ELIZABETH
widow of
Ralph Price
who died
Septr 14th 1817
in the 63^d year
of her age

Her months of affliction are o'er
The days and nights of distress,
We see her in anguish no more
She's gain'd her happy release.
No sickness or sorrow or pain
Shall ever disquiet her now,
For death to her spirit was gain
Since Christ was her life when below,

4 *r*
R P
In memory of
RALPH PRICE,
who died
Decr 2nd 1815,
in the 67th year
of his age.

By long experience have I known
Thy sov'reign power to save ;
At thy command I venture down
Securely to the grave.
When I lie buried deep in dust,
My flesh shall be thy care ;
These wither'd limbs with thee I trust
To raise them strong and fair.

5 r

R P

In memory of
ROBERT PRICE,
who died
July 20th 1843
Aged 61 Years

At rest in Jesus' faithful arms,
At rest as in a peaceful bead,
Secure from all the dreadful storms,
Which round this sinful world are spread.

Thrice happy souls who're gone before,
To that inheritance divine,
They labor, sorrow, sigh no more,
But bright in endless glory shine.

---

6 r

P P.   R P.   H R P.   P P.   R P.
In memory of
Five children of Ralph & Elizabeth Price, viz
Puah, their daughter died Feby 1st 1780: aged 8 mo^s & 7 days.
Ralph, their son died Feby 8th 1787, aged 10 mo^s & 23 days
Hedges Ralph, their son died Augst 25th 1793; aged 1 year 6 mo^s & 22 days
Phebe, their daugh^r died May 3^d 1798 aged 10 years 6 mo^s & 8 days,
Ralph, their son died July 21st 1799 aged 1 year 1 mo^s & 1 day
Reader by these victims you may know
Death strikes early oft, & sudden too,
Therefore, ask thyself, "Am I
Prepared, should I be call'd to die."

---

7 r

P P
In memory of
PAMELA,
daughter of Ralph
& Elizabeth Price:
who died
Decr 30th 1823;
in the 34th year
of her age.

Farewell! no more I tread your ground,
No more I need the gospel sound;
My feet have reach'd the heavenly shore,
I know no imperfection more.

Let friends no more my suff'rings mourn,
Nor view my relics with concern;
O cease to drop the pitying tear,
I've passed beyond the reach of fear.

8 r

M M
In Memory of
Mariah wife of
Henry Meeker died
March 9th 1806. In the
20th Year of her age.

9 r

H. M.
In Memory of
Henry Meeker died
Aust 11th 1807. In the
26th Year of his Age,

9½ m

In memory of
GEORGE W.
Son of John &
Abigail P. Davidson

who died March 30th
1840, aged 1 year
and 4 days.

Farewell my dearest parents,
No more on earth I stay;
For angels in their glory,
Have beckon'd me away.
Weep not for you shall meet me;
In that bright heaven above,
Where sorrow never enters;
And all is joy and peace.

10 *m*
OUR FATHER
CORNELIUS CLARK,
Died January, 5th, 1832,
Aged 48 years.

OUR MOTHER,
NANCY CLARK,
Died April, 3d, 1847,
Aged 62 years.

11 *m*
WM. M. KOLLOCK.
born Aug. 9 1839
died Feb. 15 1840.
SUSAN KOLLOCK,
born June 6 1843,
died July 18 1844,
CHILDREN OF
Rev. Shepard K. &
Sarah Kollock.
ELIZABETH H. KOLLOCK,
born Jan 3d: 1841
died March 3: 1848.

12 *r*
M. M. D.
In memory of
MATTHEW MC
DOWELL,
of Kentucky,
who died
Novr 1st, 1821;
Aged 31 years.

13 *m*
[This a Horizontal Stone]
IN MEMORY
OF
SHEPARD KOLLOCK ESQr
an Officer of the Revolution,
who, after having aided in the
establishment of the liberty of
his country, and for many years
filled with usefulness various civil
stations, died in the full assurance of
a glorious resurrection, & a blessed
immortality; July 28th 1839;
Aged 88 years.

ALSO
IN MEMORY OF
SUSAN,
WIFE OF
Shepard Kollock Esq
who died April 13th 1846;
Aged 90 Years
and 6 months.

14 *r*
[Horizontal Stone]
Sacred to
the memory of
Isaac Arnett
Who departed this Life
Novr 19th A D 1801,
in the 76th year of his
age.

Dear partner of my Life
And children who I love
Remember dying strife
Which you have got to prove.

Come learn the heavenly art
To improve the hours you have
Come act the wiser part
And live beyond the grave.

---

[13] Owner and Editor 1779 of "New Jersey Journal," at Chatham, N. J., 1783 "N. Y. Gazetteer and County Journal," etc. His wife was a daughter of Isaac and Hannah Arnett. *Hatfield's Elizabeth,* 554.

ALSO
In Memory of
HANNAH ARNETT, his wife
who departed this life
January 10th 1823 ;
Aged 90 years

Blessed are the dead, which
die in the Lord.

15 r
HERE lies the Bodies of three chil-
[dren
of Isaac & Hannah Arnett, ——
Elisabeth Ann, died April ye 6th,
A. D. 1758. Aged 3 Months, ——
Abigail, died December ye 1r A. D.
1766. Aged 11 Months.
John was Born & died Sepr 6th A. D.
1770.

16 r
[Broken]
S S
Sarah daughter of
Benjamin & Sarah
Stockton who di
ed Decemr 3d 179
aged 9 Years.

17 r
W A
Here lies
the body of
WILLIAM ARNETT,
who died
Septr 20th 1821 :
Aged 47 years,

"I know that my Redeemer liveth
In my flesh shall I see God."

18 m
MY BROTHER.
AGED 22 YEARS.

19 m
IN
Memory of
SARAH H KOLLOCK
wife of
The Rev Dr. S. K. Kollock
born at Norfolk Virgn on the 15th
of Sept, 1804, died at Greenwich
N. J. on the 21st of Nov. 1859.

She was an affectionate wife,
faithful mother, sincere friend,
and eminent christian :

"Precious in the sight of the Lord
is the death of his saints."

20 m
SACRED
To the Memory of
SHEPARD K. KOLLOCK, D.D.
Born in this place
JUNE 25th 1795
Died in Philadelphia
APRIL 7th, 1865

"Victory through our Lord Jesus
Christ."

21 m
D. O. BROWN
Co. K.
73rd N. Y. I N F.

21½
[Nothing but a stone cross]

---

[14] Her maiden name Hannah White. It is said of her, that when she heard her husband and several other dispirited patriots discussing the question of giving up the effort for national independence, she burst into the room and upbraided them with want of courage and said to her husband, "What greater cause could there be than that of country. I married a good man and true, a faithful friend and loyal Christian gentleman, but it needs no divorce to sever me from a traitor and a coward. If you take the infamous British protection which a treacherous enemy of your country offers, you—you lose your wife and I—I lose my husband and my home." *Dr. Tuttle's Revolutionary Forefathers of Morris County.*

22 *m*
JULIA ELYEA
Wife of
WILLIAM H. PRICE
DIED
October 5, 1872,
Aged 57 Years.

"Safe within the vail."

---

23 *m*
IN
Memory of
JOSEPH G.
Son of Wm. H. and
Julia Price,
who was drowned
July 22^d 1847.
Aged 10 Years
and 9 Months.

Seek unto God betimes
and make thy supplica
tion to the Almighty
                Job 8. 5.

---

24 *r*
IN
Memory of
JOHN ELYEA,
who died
June 15th 1841,
Aged 80 years.

Waken, O Lord, our drowsy sense,
To walk this dang'rous road :
And if our souls are hurry'd hence
May they be found with God.

---

25 *r*
In Memory of Sarah y^e
wife of Joseph Jelf
who departed this life
July 5th 1738
Aged 37 years.

26 *r*
E D
In memory of Eunice,
wife of Luther Dean,
& her two infant babes
who died April 1st 1796,
in the 23^d year of her
age.

Crop't like a flower she wither'd in
her bloom,
Though flattering life had
promis'd years to come.

---

27 *r*
Here lies ye Body
of Mary, Wife of
John Meeker who
deceas'd Novr 7th
A. D. 1773. In the
20th Year of her
Age.

---

28 *r*
In memory of
Catharine, wife of
Benjamin Haines,
who departed this
Life Septr 9th 1777 :
in the 48 year of
her age.

---

29 *r*
Here lies the Body of
Benjamin Hainds,
who departed this
Life Dece^r the 12th
A. D. 1774, In ye 53^d
Year his Age.

---

30 *r*
R. H.
In memory of
Rebekah, wife of
Benjamin Haines
who died May 30,
1798, in the 27th
year of her age.

INSCRIPTIONS IN FIRST PRESBYTERIAN

31 *r*
Sacred
to the memory of
BENJAMIN HAINES,
who died Novr 17^n
1808 in the 40th
year of his
Age.

His days are number,^{d} and his spirit fled
He's gone the Husband Father, Friend, is dead ;
Nor weeping friend, nor healing art could save
His body from the cold and silent grave.

32 *r*
In Memory of
Jean Ogden wife
of Thomas Ogden,
Died Decr 8 1760
In ye 66 year of
her Age

33 *m*
IN
MEMORY OF
SUSAN, WIFE OF
Tenrub Price,
WHO DIED
FEB 15, 1839
IN HER 75, YEAR

34 *m*
IN
MEMORY OF
TENRUB PRICE,
WHO DIED
OCT 11 1810
IN HIS 77 YEAR.

35 *r*
[Both on one stone]

In Memory
of Thomas Price,
who died
January 21st A. D.
1802 in the 79th
year of his
Age.

In Memory
of Abigail, widow
of Thomas Price,
who died January
the 30th A. D. 1802,
in the 77th year
of her Age.

36 *r*

Here lies ye Body
of Dinah, Wife of Mr
Thomas Ogden, Died
April ye 20 1731 aged 45 ye^{ars}

Here lies ye Body
of Thomas son of Mr
Thomas Ogden Died
April ye 20 1731 aged 19 ye^{ars}

Here lies ye Body of Abraham, Son of Mr Thomas
Ogden, Died August ye 29 1732 Aged 2 years,

37 *m*
EDWARD CORNWELL,
DIED
APRIL 24th 1840,
AGED 37.
JANE S CORNWELL,
DIED
JANUARY 1st 1850,
AGED 46

38 *r*
Here lyes ye Body of
Mary wife, of Mickel
Meeker & Dau^r of John
& Mary Ogden, who
Died Octr ye 10th 1757
In ye 30th year
of her Age.

39 r
Here lyes ye Body of Mary
wife of John Ogden who
Died April ye 15 1758
in ye 53 year of her Age.

Remember me laid Here in Dust
the Grave Shall Rott off all my Rust
Till ye last Trump Shall Rend ye Skeys
when Christ Shall Say ye Dead arise.

40 r
J. O.
In Memory of
Joanna
Widow of John Ogden
who died Sept 23^d
1797 in the 54th Year
of her Age

41 r
HERE lies ye Body
of Ezekiel Ogden.
who died Janu^r the 5th
A D 1766 In the 25th
Year of his Age.

42 r
Here lies ye Body of
Elizabeth wife of John
Ogden Junr who Died
Octr 6th 1763 in y^e
30th Year of her age.

43 r
Here lies ye Body of
John Ogden who de
parted this Life Feb^y
ye 5th A. D. 1777 In y^e
45th Year of his Age.

44 r
P. P.
In memory of Prudence
daughter of Elihu &
Rebekah Pierson who
died April 26th 1797
aged 2 years & 3 mon^s.

45 r
Here lies ye Body
of John Peirson
Who departed
this Life Feb^{ry} 10th
1774 in ye 55 Year
of His age.

46 r
Here lies what was Mortal
of Abigail Pierson the
Wife of John Pierson
who Departed this life
March 18th A. D. 1782.
In the 54 Year of
her Age.

47 r
HERE lies interred
The Body of Mr. John
Ogden, who died
Novr ye 15th Anno
Domini 1780 In the
LXXXth Year of his
Age ———

48 r
IN MEMORY OF
Mr Jonathan Ogden
who died March y^e
24th A. D. 1790 In
the XXXV Year of his
Age.

49 r
A. O.
In memory of
ABRAHAM OGDEN
son of Ezekiel and
Abigail Ogden died
July 8th 1812, aged 24
years 6 months & 9 days.

Here lies a lovely pleasant flower,
Cut down in early time ;
Death doth our fairest hopes devour,
And nips our joys in prime.

$^{41\ and\ 43}$ Sons of John, No. 47 and Mary, No. 39, Ogden.

50 *r*
In
memory of
MARTHA,
relict of William Ramsden
who died Jany 8th 1810,
Aged 48 years.

Dear friends who live to mourn & weep,
Behold the grave in which I sleep;
Prepare for death for you must die,
And be entomb'd as well as I.

51 *r*
In
MEMORY OF
WILLIAM RAMSDEN
who departed this life
Jan 15th 1807
aged 57 years.

[Note. This stone is scaled off so that only a faint trace of the inscription is discernible.]

52 *r*
In memory of
William Ramsden son
of William and Martha Ramsden
[Broken off] 1801 in the [ ] f his Age.

Sleep on dear Babe
And take your rest
We hope in Heaven
To see you Blesse'd.

53 *r*
Israel Ludlow, Son
of William & Martha
Ramsden, deceas'd
Aug ye 11 A. D. 1782,
In the 2nd Year of his
Age.

54 *r*

P. R.
In
Memory
of
Phebe wife of
Boynton Ramsden
who died Oct 9th
1802 in the 77th
year of her
Age.

B. R.
In
memory
of
Boynton Ramsden
who died Oct 9th
1804 in the 84th
year of his
Age.

55 *r*
In
Memory of
———— Ann daughter of
Stephen & Rhode Cumstick
died Septr 18th 1808 aged
1 year 4 months & 20 days.

Our first born child is gone to rest
God called her home he thought it best.

56 *w*
IN MEMORY
OF
Annie E. Huey
DIED
Sept 3rd 1854
In The 7th Y^r of her Age.

Charlotte E. Huey
DIED
July 14 1873
Aged 6 Mth's & 14 Dys
DEAR CHILDREN
Thou Art Asleep In
Jesus.

57 *r*
THIS
Stone is
Erected to
the memory of
PATTY LYON TODD,
who departed this life
Oct 24th 1816, in the
34th year of her age.

The victory now is obtain'd
She's gone her dear Saviour to see
Her wishes she fully has gained—
She's now where she longed to be.

58 *r*
T. B.
In memory of
JOHN BURNET
who died Augst 14th 1813
in the 27th year
of his age.

A pale consumption gave the fatal
blow;
The stroke was certain but the effect
was slow,
With wasting pain death found me
long oppress'd
Pityed my sighs & kindly brought me
rest.

59 *r*
B. H.
In memory of
BETSY
wife of
Stephen Harland;
who died
Dec 28th 1829:
in the 45th year
of her age.

60 *r*
B. T.
In Memory of
BAKER THORP
who died
June 27th 1809,
Aged 57 years.

My friends prepare to follow me,
Both old & young must die you see;
There's no discharge there's no delay.
When death demands we must obey,

61 *g*
MOSES HATFIELD
DIED
JUNE 3 1872

62 *m*
BENJAMIN H. WINANS
DIED
January 15th 1869,
Aged 43 years.

63 *m*
HARRIET C HATFIELD
Widow of
BENJAMIN H WINANS
DIED
April 3 1885,
Aged 59 Years.

There shall be no more pain.

64 *m*
JOB H HATFIELD
DIED
30th JANY, 1850
AGED 63 YEARS.

In life he was an humble and devoted
follower of Jesus, and died in the
triumphs of faith.

IN GOD IS MY TRUST.

INSCRIPTIONS IN FIRST PRESBYTERIAN

65 *m*
CHARLOTTE T
WIDOW OF
JOB H HATFIELD
DIED
Dec 18th 1856,
Aged 63 Years,

For we which have believed do
enter into rest.

66 *r*
IN
Memory of
Lewis & Charity
Son & Daughter of
Lewis & Phebe Mulford
She died
Nov ye 16th 1771 aged 1 MO
He died
March ye 5th 1779 aged 2 YS

67 *r*
HERE lies interr'd
the Body of Phebe
Wife of Lewis
Mulford who died
May ye 4th A D 1779
In the 28th Year of
her Age.

68 *r*
Michael Son of Lewis
& Phebe Mulford
died June the 12 1794.
in the 21 year of his
age.

69 *r*
In
Memory of
Mrs HANNAH CLARK
Who departed this
life on the 27th of May
1817 in the 43d year
of her age.

She's pass'd the waves of trouble here,
We trust beyond the reach of fear;
She hears no more the Gospel sound,
But lies here mouldering under
  ground.
Her dust and ruins that remain,
The Saviour will unite again;
Before the universe his power display,
At the great rising, glorious day.
All you who read this monument,
Behold here seal'd your last account;
For 'tis decreed: to dust you must
  return,
And all your works (unless in Christ)
  shall burn.

70 *m*
IN MEMORY OF
PHEBE M CLARK
Daughter of
HANNAH CLARK
DIED
January 10 1875
In the 76 year of
her age.

71 *m*
IN
Memory of
JAMES WILCOX,
WHO DIED
July 1st 1852
In the 68th Year
of his age.

Husband thou art gone to rest,
Thy toils and cares are o'er;
And sorrow pain and suffering,
Shall ne'er distress thee more.

72 *r*
M. J.
———
E. M. J.
———
In memory of
AARON JEWELL
who departed this
life May 11th 1824
Aged 26 years
& 4 months

Also of ELIHU M, son of
Aaron & Mary Jewell
who died Decr 11th 1823
Aged 5 months & 15 days.

Here in this narrow silent bed,
The father and his babe are laid,
How short their stay; their conflict's o'er
And have they reached fair Canaan's shore
Bless'd thought! and may we all prepare,
To leave this world, and meet them there

---

73 r
In Memory of
Capt Joseph Lyon
of Lyons farms who
Departed this life
August 26th A. D. 1772
In the 61st Year of his
Age

The liberal diviseth liberal things
& by liberal things shall he stand
Isiah xxxii^d 8th Verse

---

74 r
J. L.
In memory of
JOSEPH LYONS A. B.
who departed this life
May 14th A. D. 1821;
in the 81st year
of his age.

For thirty five years he was an Elder in this church, and exhibited in an eminent degree, a pattern of the most unaffected piety and of the christian virtues meekness and charity.
Mark the perfect man & behold the upright.

---

75 r
E. T.
In Memory of
ELIAS THOMPSON
who died
Octr 28th 1828;
in the 56th year
of his age
"There remaineth a rest
to the people of God"

---

76 r
F. T.
In Memory of
FANNY
widow of
Elias Thompson
who died
Jan'y 1st 1830;
in the 56th year
of her age
"Blessed are the dead
which die in the Lord,

---

77 r
V T.
In memory of
Vashti daugh^r
OF
Elias &
FANNY THOMPSON
WHO DIED
May 12th 1826
in the
10th year of
her age.

---

78 r
A. T.
In memory of
Abel son
OF
Elias &
FANNY THOMPSON
WHO DIED
Jan 22^d 1825
in the
18th year of
his age.

79 m
In
Memory
of
Ann T. Marsh
wife of
Caleb Price
who departed this life
April 15th 1817
in the 29th year
of her age.

Farewell friends parents children dear
No more I need your tender care:
My feet have reached the heavenly shore,
I know no imperfection more.

Charles Tooker
son of
Caleb & Ann Price
died June 1st 1814
Aged 2 years 5 months,
& 14 days.

80 m
HENRY M. BRITTIN
Born
February 22 1802,
Died
October 19 1877,
Aged 75 Years.

Asleep in Jesus.
ELIZA A.
wife of
HENRY M. BRITTIN,
Died Oct 26 1880,
Aged 73 Years.

"Though they sleep in the dust, they
shall rise to life Everlasting."

81 m
IN
Memory of
Hugh Mc Bride Brittin,
Son of
Henry M. & Eliza Ann Brittin
who died
May 6th 1827
Aged 1 Year 7 Months
and 6 days.

Beneath this stone an Infant lies,
To earth its ashes lent,
Who shall again more glorious rise,
But not more Innocent.

When the Archangels trump shall sound
And souls to bodies join,
Thousands on earth shall wish their lives
Had been as short as thine.

Catharine F. Brittin
died November 27th 1838
aged 7 years.

82 m
In
Memory of
four children of
Elihu and Mary A. Brittin.
Julia Ann died Sept 18th 1801
Aged 9 months.
Henrietta died Octr 21st 1803
Aged 7 months.
Maria died Jany 6th 1808
Aged 3 months.
Emaline died Oct'r 16th 1810
Aged 7 months.

83 r
Here lies ye Body
of Mary Daur of
William & Mary
Britton. She dy'd
March 31st 1773
in ye 6th Year of
her age.

84 *m*
IN
Memory of
CAPT WILLIAM BRITTIN
who died
July 22 1783,
Aged 45 Years
Also
MARY
widow of
Capt William Brittin,
who died April 5 1797,
Aged 53 Years.

85 *m*
AT REST
MARIA B. SILVERS
Daughter of
COL. ELIHU BRITTIN
Born
Nov. 10, 1808
DIED
Sept 2. 1882.

86 *m*
IN
Memory of
COL. ELIHU BRITTIN
who died
Novr 9th 1849,
Aged 71 Years.

86½ *m*
LUNA P.
DAUGHTER OF
Col. Elihu and Albina R. Brittin,
who died Sept 12 1851.
aged 3 years
and 1 month.
[This stone is at foot of 86]

87 *m*
IN
Memory of
MARY A.
wife of
Col. Elihu Brittin
who died
Jan 23 1843
Aged 62 Years.

88 *m*
SACRED
to the Memory of
ELIHU PIERSON,
Son of
John and Phebe Pierson,
who departed this life
February 23rd 1832,
in the 27th year
of his age.

With him
died the fondest earthly hopes of his
Mother, the dearest expectation of his
Brother, and Sisters, and much pleasing anticipations of the Church of
Christ.

89 *r*
E. M.
In memory of
ELIZA
wife of
Wm. M. Moore.
who died
June 1st 1834,
Aged 33 Years.

Thro' duty and thro' trials too,
I'll go at his command ;
Hinder me not for I am bound ;
To my Immanuels land

90 *r*
In Memory of
Rhoda, the wife of
John Pierson who
died October the
20th 1791, in ye 44th
Year of her age.

To God's unerring will
be eve'y wish resigned.

91 *r*
J. P.
In Memory of
John Pierson
who died Aug^st 11th 1811
in the 66th year
of his age

Go home dear friends and shed no tears,
I must lie here 'till Christ appears;
And at his coming hope to have,
A joyful rising from the grave.

---

92 *m*
TO
the Memory of
PHEBE,
Widow of
John Pierson;
who departed this life
April 7th A D 1834,
aged 74 years.

"Blessed are the dead
which die in the Lord"

---

93 *r*
C P
In memory of
Charlotte
daughter of Oliver
& Prudence Pierson
who departed this
life Aug^st 19th 1814,
in the 20th year
of her age

Jesus my love to glory's gone
Him will I go and see;
And you my breathern here below,
Will soon come after me.

---

94 *m*
IN
Memory of
JONATHAN PIERSON,
who died
March 13 1864
in the 73^d year
of his age

---

95 *r*
In Memory of
Jonathan Pierson, who
died January the 11th
1790, in the 39th year
of his age.

---

96 *r*
Sacred
to the
Memory of
Mary Chandler
daughter of Oliver
& Eliza Pierson
who died March 8th 1826
aged 2 years &
6 months

Tis done and lovely Mary yields her breath
But dies in peace to triumph over death
That choicest flower of Heaven's immortal love
Just buds on earth to bloom in worlds above.

---

97 *m*
MARY O HORTON
Died Sept 12th 1872
Aged 78 Years

"Blessed are the dead who die in the Lord"

CHURCH YARD, ELIZABETH, N. J. 19

98 r
O. P.
In memory of
Oliver Pierson
who died
Sept the 17th 1800
in the 31st Year of
his age.

99 r
A W
In Memory of
ABIGAIL
widow of
Michael Woodruff
who died
Sept 9th 1828
Aged 76 years.

100 r
M. W.
In memory of
MICHAEL WOODRUFF
who died
March 17th 1823
Aged 76 years.

101 r
M. W.
In Memory of
Morris Woodruff
who died Feb^{y}
the 23^{d} 1807; in
the 33^{d} year of
his Age.

Farewell my friends & loving wife
Since God has called me from this
life;
Go home and dry up all your tears,
I must lie here till Christ appears.

102 r
In memory of
Abner Woodruff
who died may the
28th 1792, in the 69th
year of his age

103 r
HERE lies the Body of
Rachel Wife of Abner
Woodruff who departed
this Life Nov the 30th
Anno Domini 1774 in
the 49th Year of her
Age.

104 r
In Memory
of Rachel Wife of El-
-ly Woodruff who di-
-ed Septr ye 24th 17-
-83 aged 28 Year & 6
Days.

105 m
In
Memory of
ELIAS GEORGE
son of Abner & Harriot
Woodruff, from Savannah
who died 29th July 1809.
aged 1 year 10 months
and 18 days.
also an infant son 5
days old died 15th
October 1808

106 r
HERE LIETH
the Remains of Mr
Daniel Meeker, who,
deceas'd Octr ye 1st
A. D. 1757 In ye 77th
Year of his
Age.

107 r
HERE LIETH
the Body of Rachel
Wife of Mr. Daniel
Meeker who died
June ye 22 A. D
1760. In ye 77th
Year of her
Age.

108 *r*
Here lies the Body of
Phebe Wife of Benjamin
Meeker Dec^d Nov^{er}
ye 11 : 1755 in the 75
Year of her age.

109 *r*
HERE lies the Body
of Samuel Meeker
who departed this—
Life Dece^r ye 11th Ann^o
Domini 1757 in ye 41st
Year of his Age.

110 *r*
HERE
Lieth the Remains of
Mrs. [or Miss] Charity Meeker
who departed this Life
Janua^y the 16th Anno–
Domini 1776 in the 22^d
Year of her Age

111 *r*
Charlotte, Daughter
of Nathaniel & Sarah
Meeker, died Augt y^e
27th A. D. 1771 aged
5 M^s & 2 D^s ——

112 *r*
Here lyes ye Body of
Mickel Meeker who
Died June ye 28th
1755 In ye 35th year
of his Age

113 *r*
Cumfort Wife of Moses
Price who died Nove^r
the 20th A. D. 1766
In the 34th Year of her
Age.
       call
As Loud as Thunder is the Solemn
        all
Prepare for Death Prepare survivors

114 *m*
OUR HENRY,
SON OF
James H. and
Harriet A. Thorp,
died July 13th 1856 ;
Aged 6 Years
& 11 Months.

Dear Son we miss thee
But hope to meet thee.

115 *r*
D. E.
In Memory of
Capt David Edwards,
who died
Feby 8th 1806 ;
in the 45th year
of his age.

Also Mary daughter of
David & Phebe Edwards ;
who died Octr 8th 1821 :
in the 18th year
of her age.

116 *r*
C. W.
In Memory of
CHARITY
daughter of James
& Elizabeth Willcock
who departed this life
Decr 19th 1831,
in the 39th year
of her age.

117 *r*
E W
In memory of
ELIZABETH WILLCOCK
who departed this
life Augst 18th 1803
in the 19th year
of her age.

118 *m*
IN
Memory of
ELIZABETH,
Wife of
JAMES WILCOX,
who died
Decr 17th 1836,
Aged 78 years.

"For this corruptible, must put on incorruption; and this mortal, must put on immortality"

119 *m*
IN
Memory of
Eld- JAMES WILCOX
who died
Oct 15th 1843,
Aged 80 years.

"There remaineth therefore a rest to the people of God,

ALSO
LYDIA ROSS,
Daughter of Elihu & Ann Eliza
WILCOX
who died Feby 19th 1846
Aged 1 year

120 *r*
S. W.
In memory of
SAMUEL WILLCOCK
who departed this
life Jan^y-12th, 1817;
in the 21st year
of his age.

121 *r*
Elener, Daughter of
Stephen & Martha
Willcock, died June
ye 6th 1761. In the 3^d
Year of her Age.

122 *r*
HERE lies the Body
of Stephen Willcock
who departed this
Life March ye 12th An^o-
Domini 1770 In ye 36th
Year of his Age.

123 *m*
THIS STONE
IS ERECTED AS A
MEMORIAL OF
GEORGE M.
JEWEL
WHO DIED
MAY 14 1824:
IN HIS 59th YEAR.

"The Lord is righteous in all his ways."

124 *m*
IN
MEMORY OF
MARY JEWEL
WIFE OF
George M. Jewel Dec'd,
WHO DIED
SEPT 22 1842
IN HER 74th YEAR.

"Blessed are the dead, which die in the Lord."

125 *m*
IN
MEMORY OF
SARAH WILBUR,
WIFE OF
JOSEPH WILBUR,
who departed this life
MAY 28th 1817;
IN HER 48th YEAR.

"The memory of the just is blessed,,

ALSO TWO SONS OF
Joseph & Sarah Wilbur,
JOSEPH LYON
DIED MAY 30th 1798 :
AGED 1 YEAR 1 MO & 4 DAYS
ERASTUS,
DIED JULY 18th 1817 :
AGED 3 YEARS 9 MO
& 21 DAYS.

126 *m*
J. W.
In memory of
JOSEPH WILBUR
a ruling Elder of
this Church,
who departed this life
Feb[y] 15th 1830,
in the 75th year
of his age.

"Blessed are the dead who die in the Lord from henceforth : yea, saith the Spirit, that they may rest from their labours, and their works do follow them."

127 *m*
J. L. W.
In memory of
JOSEPH L. WILBUR,
who departed this life
November 23[d] 1826
Aged 24 years.

Weep not for me, altho' the grave
My Mortal part contains,
My soul redeem'd by Jesus blood
With God forever reigns.

Also in Memory of
MARY WILBUR, daughter
of J. H. & R. W. Lambdin
who died Jan[y] 17th 1827
Aged 3 yrs & 5 months.

128 *m*
The Lord is my Shepherd.
SARAH
WIDOW OF
DANIEL COOPER,
died April 14th 1864
In the 86th Year
of her age.

129 *m*
SACRED
to the memory of
SUSAN M. PRICE
wife of
JOSEPH D. PRICE
who departed this life
May 1st 1838
Aged 30 years

ALSO WILLIAM DAYTON
Son of Joseph D & Susan M Price
who died Dec 11th 1841
Aged 5 Years 9 Months & 29 days.

130 *m*
SACRED
To the memory of
ABBY W PRICE
wife of Joseph D Price
who departed this life
August 17th 1830
in the 27th year
of her age.

131 *m*
SACRED
To the memory of
ELIZABETH W PRICE
wife of
JOSEPH D PRICE
who departed this life
May 13th 1824
in the 22d year of her age.

Also on the 15th Inst
her infant Child
aged 2 days

132 *m*
SACRED
to the memory of
RACHEL PRICE
wife of
Thomas Price
who departed this life
Jany 17th 1839
Aged 79 years.

133 *m*
SACRED
to the memory of
THOMAS PRICE
who departed this life
Sept 18th 1827
Aged 77 years.

134 *m*
S. F. E.
In memory of
SUSAN F.
wife of James Earl
who died June 25th 1826
Aged 26 years 7 months
& 9 days.

Also of JONATHAN
their son who died Augst 14th
1826 Aged 2 months
& 14 days.

"To me to live was Christ.
and to die is gain."

135 *m*
IN
Memory of
two Children of James
and Susan F Earl :
MARY LOUISA.
died April 4th 1822 :
aged 2 months & 14 days.

SARAH JERUSHA
died Novr 17th 1828
aged 5 years 6 months
and 21 days.

There is beyond the sky,
A heaven of joy and love ;
And holy children when they die
Go to that world above.

136 *r*
T. H. O.
In memory of
THEODORE H. OGDEN
who died
Jany 26th 1837,
in the 31st year
of his age.

"He shall return no more to his house, neither shall his place know him any more."

137 *r*
M. J. M. O.
In memory of
MARY JANE MAGIE
wife of
Theodore H. Ogden
who died
Septr 6th 1834
in the 24th year
of her age.

"There shall be no more death neither sorrow nor crying, neither shall there be any more pain."

138 *r*
R. O.
In memory of
RHODA wife of
Ichabod Ogden,
who departed this
life Novr 13th 1819
Aged 25 years.

The victory now is obtain'd ;
She's gone her dear Saviour to see ;
Her wishes she fully has gain'd—
She's now where she longed to be.

The coffin, the shroud, and the grave
To her were no objects of dread,
On him who is mighty to save
Her soul was with confidence stay'd.

139 r
H. O.
In memory of
HATFIELD, son of
Ezekiel & Abigail
Ogden, who died
Oct[r] 7th 1817:
in the 20th year
of his age.

Our brother nipt in early bloom,
Has left this scene of idle care,
Has reached his father's house in peace
We mourn but there's no mourning there.

140 r
A. O.
In memory of
ABIGAIL wife of
Ezekiel Ogden.
who died
May 14th 1820;
in the 55th year
of her age.

Blessed are they and only they,
Who in the Lord the Saviour die;
Their bodies wait redemption day
And sleep in peace where'er they lie.

141 r
E. O.
In memory of
EZEKIEL OGDEN
who died
Dec[r] 10th 1822;
in the 58th year
of his age.

Scarce had ceased the falling tear
Shed for a mother kind and dear,
E'er yet we feel still heavier woe,
And tears of deeper anguish flow:

The father's gone! our only hope,
Our counsellor and earthly prop.
Oh may the prayers which here he made
Descend in blessings on our head

142 r
HERE LIETH
Interred the Remains of
Doc[r] Ichabod Burnet, who
departed this Life
March the twelfth
Annoque Domini 1756
In the twenty-fourth
Year of his
Age.

143 r
HERE lies the Body of
Mrs. Hannah. Wife of
Doct[r] Ichabod Burnet
who departed this Life
Feby the 19th Anno-
Domini 1758 In the
57[in] Year of her Age.

144 r
HERE lies the Body
of Ichabod B. Barnet
obi[t] Sept[r] the 10th
Anno Domini 1783
Æ tatis Suæ XXXII.

Lean not on Earth, it will
pierce thee to the Heart.

145 r
In Memory of Doct[r]
William Barnet
who departed this
Life December the
1st 1790 In y[e] 63[d] Year
of his Age.

146 r
In Memory of
Mr Joseph Barnet
who deceas'd Sept[r]
y[e] 25th 1784 In the 88th
year of his age.

Ther's no Age nor Charact[r] but must
Repay to Earth its borrow'd Dust
In silent Slumbers there to lay
Till the last solemn Judgment Day.

---

[140] Born Oct. 3, 1765, dau. of Matthias Ogden and Margaret Megie.

CHURCH YARD, ELIZABETH, N. J.

147 *r*
In Memory of
Stephen Harrison
who died Dec^{br} 22^d
1793 In the 51st
Year of his
Age.

148 *r*
HERE lies ye Body
of Mrs Hannah
Relict of Deacon
Matthias Hetfield
who died June 13th
A. D. 1783 In the
84th Year of her
Age.

149 *r*
HERE lies the Body
of Deacon Matthias
Hetfield who died
Dece^r ye 10th A D. 1779
In the LXXXI Year of
his Age.

His loss was great
To Church & State.

150 *r*
J C
In memory
of Jacob Crane.
who died June 23
1799 in the 37 year
of his age.

151 *r*
In Memory of
Benjamin Crane Senr
who Departed this life
July 13 A. D. 1777
In the 72 Year of
his Age.

152 *g*
[Mc Dowell Monument (Granite Shaft)
North South & West faces blank]

[On East face]

TO THE MEMORY OF THE
REV JOHN Mc DOWELL D.D.

THE BELOVED AND HONORED PASTOR
OF THE FIRST PRESBYTERIAN CHURCH
OF ELIZABETHTOWN
FROM 1804 TO 1833

" The righteous shall be in
everlasting remembrance."

Mc DOWELL

153 *r*
Mary daughter of
Joseph & Eunice Bond
died Septr the 4th 1792
in the 2^d year of her
age.

154 *r*
Nathanael son of Jo-
seph & Eunice Bond
died Septr y 7 1792
in y 6th year of his
age

To Gods unerring will
be ev'ry wish resign'd

155 *r*
J. B.   M. B.
In memory of
two children of
Joseph & Eunice Bond
Joseph died May 24
1789. aged 3 days.
Maria died Novr 2^d 1804
aged 2 years & 2 days.

Our dear children Christ took & blest
We'll cease to mourn for there at rest.

156 r
A. B.
In memory of
AARON : son of
Elihu & Sarah
Bond who died
Septr 29th 1820
aged 5 years
& 21 days.

---

157 m
IN
Memory of
SARAH
Wife of
ELIHU BOND
WHO DIED
AUG. 26, 1857.
Aged 69 years.

Blessed are the dead which
die in the Lord.

---

158 r
S. B.   J. B.
In memory of
two children of Elihu & Phebe Bond
Sarah died Decr 11th 1790 aged 5 m^o
& 7 days
Jonathan died Septr 18th 1798 aged
5 m^o & 18 days.

Sleep sweet babes & take your rest
God call,^{d} you home he saw it best.

---

159 r
In
Memory of
Robert son of
Elihu & Phebe Bond
died Augst 1st 1794
aged 15 years 6 m^o
& 23 days.

---

160 r
In
Memory of
Robert Bond who
departed this life September
the 10th 1776 in the 23^d
year of his Age

---

161 r
A. S.
In memory of
Abigail wife of
Joseph Stackhouse
who died July 7th
1781 aged 36 years
11 months & 3 days

Joseph Stackhouse
died Sepr 16th 1805
in the 72^d year
of his age.

---

162 r
W. B.
In memory of
WILLIAM BROWN
who departed
this life
July 3^d 1803
in the 46th year
of his age.

---

163 m
PHEBE BROWN
DIED
June 6^d 1850
In the 92^d Year
of her age.

---

164 r
M. B.
In memory of
MARY DAUGHTER
of William and
Phebe Brown
who departed
this life
March 26th 1793
Aged 14 years
and 14 days.

165 *r*
[This is a Horizontal Slab]
ROBERT SMITH ROBERTSON
Born
Nov 4th 1779
died
April 20th 1866
" Jesus is THERE."

166 *m*
The Sepulchre
of
MARIA CALDWELL
wife of
Robert S Robertson
and daughter of
Rev James Caldwell
who fell asleep April 5 1852
in the 73d year of her age

HELEN MARIA BLAKEMAN
Grand daughter of
MARIA ROBERTSON
died Oct 6. 1837
Aged 1 year and 5 months.

" Precious in the sight of the Lord is the death of His saints "

167 *m*
ISAAC WATTS BLAKEMAN
Son of
Dr Wm N. and
Hellen R Blakeman
died Jany 31st 1861
aged 10 years 10 months
and 17 days

"Suffer little Children to come unto me,"

168 *m*
MARY LOUISA ROBERTSON
wife of
RUFUS PARK
and grand daughter of
REV JAMES CALDWELL
Born Dec 8. 1819
Died Nov 12. 1845

169 *m*
IN MEMORY
of
HELEN RODGERS
wife of
DR WILLIAM N. BLAKEMAN
Daughter of
ROBERT S. AND MARIA
ROBERTSON
BORN DEC 20th 1811
DIED MAY 11th 1870

" I shall be satisfied when
I awake with thy likeness,,

170 *m*
In memory
of
ELIZABETH BOYD
Daughter of
William N. and Helen R.
BLAKEMAN
Born in N. Y. Dec 27th 1838
Died in N. Y. Mch 11th 1873

" I'll sing with rapture and surprise
His loving kindness in the skies,,

171 *m*
MOTHER
HENRIETTA P THOMPSON
Died Jan 29 1882
Aged 63 Y'rs & 4 Mo's

CHARLES S THOMPSON
Died Feb 25 1864
Aged 28 Yr's & 7 Mo's

172 *m*
IN
Memory of
Sarah Lindsley
who died
May 23d 1853
In the 73d Year
of her age

" Blessed are the dead
which die in the Lord,,

173 *m*
[Horizontal Slab]
Here lie the Remains
of
Jane Daughter
of
Benjamin and Elizabeth Peach of
Westbury Wiltshire old England
and Wife of
the Revd John Giles
of
Elizabeth Town New Jersey
who departed this Life
on the 5th day of August
1799
Aged 36 Years
She lived deservedly beloved
and died sincerely lamented

174 *m*
The Twin Sisters
PHEBE AGNES
died June 13th 1848
aged 3 years & 2 months.
ALSO
MARTHA ALICE
died Septr 1st 1849
aged 4 years 4 months
& 16 days
Children of
Thomas H. & Elizabeth Price.

175 *r*
M P
In Memory of
MARTHA
wife of
John Price
who died
Decr 3^d 1831
Aged 43 years.

Hallowed be this spot
A Mother sleepeth here
Disturb not her repose
For angels hover near

Her spirit upward bourn
In heaven now's at rest
With God and saints above
With Jesus and the blest.

176 *r*
J. S.
In memory of
Jacamiah Smith
who died
Feby 16 1799
aged 66 years.

177 *r*
In Memory of
Doct^r John Clark
who died
April the 27th 1794
in the 37th year
of his age.

178 *r*
HERE lies ye Body of
John Clark who de-
parted this life March
the 24th A. D. 1771
in the 43^d Year of his
Age.

179 *r*
Here Lyeth ye Body
Of Henry Clarke j^{nr}
Dec^d Feb^{ye} 10th 1732
In ye 25th Year of his
Age

As you are now so once was i
In health & life now here I lay
As I am now so you must be
Prepare for death & follow me

180 *r*
MARY the Wife
of William Clark
who deceas'd Nov^r
the 18th A. D. 1762
In ye 21st Year of her
Age

181 *m*
IN
MEMORY OF
MARY
WIDOW OF
David Earl
WHO DIED
May 5th 1845
In the 87th Year
of her age.

All the days of my appointed time
will I wait till my change come.
Job 14. 14

182 *m*
IN
MEMORY OF
ABBEY
widow of
ISAAC MATTISON
who died April 20th 1862
AGED 78 YEARS 7 MOS.
& 6 DAYS

"Therefore be ye also ready: for in
such an hour as ye think not the
Son of Man cometh."

Also their daughter
ELIZA JOHNSON
who died Dec 23d 1805
IN HER 3d YEAR

Sleep on dear child and take thy rest
God called thee home he saw it best.

183 *m*
IN
MEMORY OF
MARY O MATTISON
WHO DIED NOV 3d 1862
AGED 57 YEARS 5 MO
& 21 DAYS

"Behold I have refined thee, but not
with silver; I have chosen thee in the
furnace of affliction."

184 *m*
IN
MEMORY OF
JULIA A MATTISON
WHO DIED JULY 13, 1880
IN THE 73d YEAR OF
HER AGE.

At Rest

185 *m*
IN
Memory of
THURSTON WHITEHEAD
who died
Jan 27 1843
in the 29 Year of
his age

Stop! passing stranger! drop one tear
A Husband, Father, Friend lies here.

186 *r*
Here lyeth ye body
Of Benjamin piers^{on}
Decesed A^o 1731 in
the 77 year of his
Age.

187 *r*
In memory of
Mrs Esther Baxter
who died
June the 18th 1789
Aged 24 years.

188 *r*
Here Lyeth
Interr'd ye Body
of John Thompson
Esqr who Died
April ye 25th 1734
Aged 61 years.

INSCRIPTIONS IN FIRST PRESBYTERIAN

189 m
IN
Memory of
JONATHAN M WHITEHEAD
who died
Sept 11th 1832
aged 32 years.

Let friends no more my suff'rings mourn
Nor view my relicks with concern
O cease to drop the pitying tear
I've passed beyond the reach of fear.

ALSO
ABBY, Daughter of
Jonathan M & Margaret Whitehead
who died
Aug 20th 1832
aged 7 months

God hath bereav'd me of my Child,
No more she visits me ;
My soul will mount to her at last
And I her face shall see.

190 m
In Memory of
JOHN WHITEHEAD
who died
August 25th 1828
Aged 55 Years, 7 Months
and 16 Days.

Go home dear friends, dry up your tears
I must lie here, till Christ appears.

191 m
OUR MOTHER
SARAH
WIDOW OF
JOHN WHITEHEAD
who died
Jany 25th 1858
Aged 82 Years 7 Months
and 3 Days

"There remaineth therefore a rest, to the people of God,,

192 m
OUR MOTHER
ELIZABETH
WIDOW OF
David Whitehead
died Novr 7th 1856
Aged 72 Years 7 Months
and 8 Days

Now in that land where christians rest
She bids her children seek for her
And meet her there among the blest
Before the throne a worshipper

193 m
IN
Memory of
DAVID WHITEHEAD
who was afflicted with a
cancer in his face 25 years
of which he died Sept 15th
1844.
Aged 66 Years 9 Months
and 20 days

His years of affliction are o'er
The days and the nights of distress
We see him in anguish no more
He has gained his happy release.

194 m
Erected to the Memory of 6 Children
of David & Elizabeth Whitehead

MARGARET
DIED
Sept 1st 1802
Aged 10 Months & 17 days.

Also
DAVID H
DIED
March 2nd 1815
Aged 6 Months & 18 days

ELIZA
DIED
Oct 27th 1810,
Aged 20 days

Also
ELIZABETH W
DIED
Feb 4th 1822
Aged 3 Years 3 Months & 17 days

Likewise
CALVIN L
DIED
June 4th 1825
Aged 4 Months & 24 days

Likewise
DAVID
DIED
Aug 14th 1825
Aged 3 Years 6 Months
and 19 days

Sleep on dear babes and take thy rest
For in Christ thou art forever blest.

195 r
In Memory of Dea-
-con David Whitehead
who deceas'd Sept^r
the 10th 1777 In
the 77th Year of
his age ———

Ee'n now the christians race is run
A glorious prize he now has won
And with angelic host's he's fix't
With joys celistial and unmixt

196 r
In Memory of
Margaret Wife of
David Whitehead
Junr she died Sept^r
the 26th 1 7 9 0
In the 55th Year
of her Age

The sweet remembrance of the just
Shall flourish when they sleep in dust.

197 m
IN
MEMORY OF
DANIEL PRICE
WHO
DEPARTED THIS LIFE
APRIL 10th 1824
IN THE 56th YEAR OF HIS
AGE

"Watch—Lest coming suddenly
he find you sleeping."

198 m
IN
MEMORY OF
. PHEBE
WIDOW OF
DANIEL PRICE
WHO DEPARTED THIS LIFE
MARCH 1st 1857
IN THE 85th YEAR
OF HER AGE

" Blessed are the dead who
die in the Lord,,

199 m
MARTHA

MARTHA TAYLOR
daughter of
William W & Elizabeth
PRICE
died Sept 12th 1858
AGED 22 YEARS &
8 MONTHS

200 r
In
Memory of
MATILDA
daughter of
George and Betsey Ball
who died Jan 1st 1801
aged 8 years.

May you rest in peace, Sweet babe.

201 r
SACRED
to the memory of
SAMUEL O SMITH
who departed this life
Sept 16th 1821
in the 43 year of his age

ALSO
CALEB H SMITH
who departed this life
Sept 3 1821
aged 4 years & 18 days.

202 r
A. S.
Here lies entom'd
ABIGAIL
wife of
Samuel Owen Smith
who departed this life
Octr 19th 1814
Aged 36 years.

The spider's most attenuated thread
Is cord, is cable, to man's tender tie
On earthly bliss ; it breaks at every
breeze

203 r
In
Memory of
JOANNA
daughter of Samuel Owen
& Abigail Smith
who died Novr 29th 1813
in the 5th year of her age.

Also of their daughter
ANNE HALSTED.
who died Aug 5th 1814
Aged 11 months.

Insatiate Archer ! would not one suffice !
Thy shaft slew thrice & thrice my peace was slain

204 m
IN
memory of
JANE S WADE
who died Dec 2^d 1848
Aged 62 Years

ALSO
W^m R SMITH
died April 29th 1846.
Aged 76 Years

205 r
[Horizontal Slab]
S. S.
In Memory of
Sarah daugh^r of Caleb & Rebecca Hal-
-sted & wife of Samuel Smith, who de-
-ceas'd Novr 29th 1803 in the 54th year of
her age
Also of her daughters Betsy died May 3^d
1777 aged 11 mon^s & 25 days.
Abigail deceas'd Septr 3^d 1778 aged 10 mon^s
& 22 days
Also of her son Caleb H who died March
26th 1785 aged 3 years 9 months & 18
days
Also of Julia who deceas'd Sept 2^d 1788
aged 10 months & 22 days
Also of Caleb H who deceas'd Sept 2^d
1794 aged 3 years & 8 mon^s
And of Fanny who deceas'd March 9th
1793 aged 10 mon^s
Also Sarah H. daugh^r of Owen Smith died June
29th 1805 aged 3 years &
7 mon's

206 r
S. S.
In memory of
Sarah widow of
Henry Smith
who died
Feby the 10th 1786
in the 92^d Year
of her age

Great God is this our certain doom
And are we still secure?
Still walking downward to our tomb
And yet prepare no more?

207 r
HERE lies the Body
of Henry Smith who
departed this Life
March the 28th Anno
Domini 1759. In the
60th Year of his Age.

208 r
HERE lies ye Body
of Henry Smith Junr
who died April ye 4th
Anno Domini 1777
In the 52 Year of his
Age.

Beneath this Stone, death's pris'ner lies
The Stone shall move, the pris'ner rise
When Jesus with Almighty word
Call's his dead Saints to meet y^r Lord

209 r
Here lies ye Body of
William Smith who
departed this Life
Novr ye 17th Anno
Domini 1750. In the
24th Year of his Age.

210 r
Jeffery Son of Henry &
Sarah Smith Aged About
21 years. Dec^d April y^e
23^d 1   7   4   3

211 r
Hannah Daugh^r of
Samuel & Margery
Smith, died Octo^r y^e
28th 1769. In the 2^d
Year of her Age

212 r
HERE lies the Body of
Margery, Wife of Samuel
Smith who departed this
Life April ye 25th Anno
Domini 1773. In the 32^d
Year of her Age ———

Here from all worldly joys I'm fled
To the dark Mansions of the dead
Prepare Spectator, for you must
Like me be turned into dust

213 r
S. S.
SACRED
To the memory of
SAMUEL SMITH
who died July 2nd 1821
in the 86th year
of his age

And of his daughter
MRS JANE WADE, who died
Septr 6th 1822 in the 59th
year of her age

Also of FRANCIS WADE
son of Mrs Jane Wade who
departed this life on the
same 6th day of Septr 1822
aged 37 years.

214 m
[No. 214 lies flat on grave No. 213]

Sacred to the memory of
Margery Ross Dill
Boorn Sept 17th 1792
Died April 5th 1880

215 r
M. S.
In memory of
Moses Smith who deceas'd
[2d fig. dug out] June 2-th 1778
aged 50 years

Likewise Phebe his wife
died Feb\[y] 17th 1799
aged 66 years

---

216 r
Here lies ye Body of
Hannah wife of Isaac
Meeker who Departed
this Life Sept\[r] 18 1764
In the 41 Year of her age

My Flesh shall slumber in the Ground
Till the last Trumpets Joyful Sound
Then burst the chains in sweet sur-
prise
To meet my Saviour in the skies

---

217 m
IN
Memory of
JACOB
SON OF
Pierce and Catharine Ogden
who died Nov\[r] 2d 1853
aged 5 years 8 months
and 17 days

When blooming youth is snatched
away
By death's resistless hand
Our hearts the mournful tribute pay
Which pity must demand.

---

218 r
Here lies the Body of
Job Son of James
& Martha Hains
Dec\[d], June ye 26th 1754
in the 20th year of his
Age.

---

219 r
Here lieth the
Remains of Est-
-her Hindes wife
of Stephen Hindes
who died M\[rch] ye
31st Anno Domini
1750 and in the 40th
y\[r] of her Age.

---

220 r
The Remains of
Phebe & Mary Daugh-
Ters of Stephen &
Esther Hindes. phebe
aged 9 months
Died Sept ye 2   1741
Mary died May ye 5th
1747 aged 7
months

---

221 r
Here Lyes ye Body of
Mary Wife of Stephen
Hindes Aged 24 years
Dec\[d] Dec\[r] ye 11th 1727
Stephen son of Stephen
Hindes 4 months
Dec\[d] March ye 25 1728

---

222 r
Here lies the Body of
Stephen Hanes who
departed this life
April 14th A D 1770
In the 66th Year of his
Age.

---

223 r
In memory of ye three
sons of Stephen and Jo-
-anna Haines
Daniel died Nov\[r] ye 24th
1764 aged 2 months
Stephen died Oct\[r] ye 19th
1788 in ye 29th year of his
age
David died Oct ye 31st
1791 in ye 19th year of his
age

224 r
J. H.
SACRED
To the memory of
JOANNA HAINES
daughter of
Stephen & Joanna Haines
who
was born Jany 14th 1763
and
died Septr 29th 1828
Aged
65 years 8 months
& 15 days.

225 r
J. H.
In memory of
Joanna wife of
Stephen Haines
who died
March 21st 1802
in the 66th year
of her age

---

226 r
S. H.
In Memory of
STEPHEN HAINES
who died July 1st 1810
in the 78th year
of his Age

---

227 m
[Haines Monument—On the North side]
SACRED TO THE MEMORY OF
ELIAS HAINES
WHO DIED OCTOBER 11 1824 IN THE 58th YEAR OF HIS AGE
A NATIVE OF THIS PLACE—A MERCHANT OF NEW YORK
BENEVOLENCE, ENERGY, AND ENTERPRIZE, CHARACTERIZED HIS LIFE
AFTER VARIOUS FLUCTUATIONS OF FORTUNE
HE FOUND OF A TRUTH
" NOTHING CAN WE CALL OUR OWN BUT DEATH ,,

[On East end]
MARY HAINES
SHE JUDGED HIM FAITHFUL
WHO HAD PROMISED
Hebrews XI. 11.

REJOICING IN HOPE ; PATIENT
IN TRIBULATION : CONTINUING INSTANT
IN PRAYER.
ROMANS XII. 15

[On South side]
SACRED TO THE MEMORY OF
MARY HAINES RELICT OF ELIAS HAINES. DAUGHTER OF ROBERT OGDEN
BORN JULY 3 1778—DIED MAY 5, 1852

WITH CONSCIOUS UNWORTHINESS   WITH GRATITUDE FOR REDEMPTION
SHE RENOUNCED HERSELF   SHE REPOSED UPON HER SAVIOUR
WITH THE TENDEREST CHARITY   WITH FILIAL LOVE SHE RESTED.
SHE WAS THE HELPER OF OTHERS IN A COVENANT GOD.
BY THE RENEWING OF THE SPIRIT SHE WAS RENDERED MEET FOR THE
[INHERITANCE OF THE SAINTS IN LIGHT

[On West end]
ELIAS HAINS
"WHATSOEVER THY HAND
FINDETH TO DO, DO IT WITH THY MIGHT;
FOR THERE IS NO WORK, NOR DEVICE, NOR
KNOWLEDGE, NOR WISDOM, IN THE GRAVE
WHITHER THOU GOEST,,"
ECCLES 9 CHAP 10 VER.

[Lying on the ground close against the monument on the north side is a head stone with the following inscription]

228 r
[See No. 227]
Sacred
To the memory of
Elias Haines
who died Oct 11th 1824
in the 58th year
of his age
He was the kind Husband
affectionate Father
and sincere Friend

229 r
In memory of
Margaret W. wife
of Job Haines who
departed this life
Sept the 13th 1792 in
the 24th year of her
age
To Gods unerring will be
ev'ry wish resigned

230 m
Sacred
to
the memory of
CAPT JOB HAINES
who departed this life
on the 28th of May 1807
in the 51st year of
his Age.

231 m
SACRED
TO THE MEMORY OF
ROBERT OGDEN HAINES
YOUNGEST SON OF
ELIAS AND MARY HAINES
BORN OCTOBER 16, 1809
DIED AUGUST 16, 1841

Reposing on thy Saviours breast
Thy sufferings o'er—rest, Brother rest.
"There shall be no more death, neither sorrow, nor crying, neither shall there be any more pain; for the former things have passed away,
Rev. XXI 4 Ver.

232 m
SACRED
TO THE MEMORY OF
HENRIETTA B HAINES
YOUNGEST CHILD
ELIAS AND MARY HAINES
BORN JUNE 24, 1816
DIED MAY 7 1879

"In my hand no price I bring
Simply To Thy cross I cling."
[All in Haines Plot enclosed with iron fence and red stone posts]
[Since copying this inscription there has been interred in this plot]

Camille
Died 25th May 1890

CHURCH YARD, ELIZABETH, N. J.

233 *m*
SACRED
To the memory of
MARTHA ANN
Wife of
Henry Meeker
and Daughter of
Jediah J & Abby
Baldwin
who died Feby 14th 1840
Aged 27 years
& 6 months.

" Father I will that they also whom
those hast given me, be with me where
I am, that they may behold my Glory
which thou hast given me,,

234 *m*
IN
Memory of
STEPHEN son of
Obadiah & Jerusha
Meeker who died
November 2nd 1810
Aged 11 months.

Alas how changed that lovely flower
That bloomed & cheered my heart
Fair fleeting comfort of an hour
How soon we're called to part.

235 *r*
D. M.
David son of Obadiah
& Comfort Meeker who
died Jan the 26th 1796
aged 19 years 9 months
& 12 days.

Farewell this body here
Both friends and parents dear
For god has called him home
To his eternal doom

God is a sovereign still
He orders all things best
O that we all may be prepared
For his eternal rest

236 *m*
SACRED
To the Memory of
Comfort wife of
Capt. Obadiah Meeker
who departed this life
April 14th 1812
Aged 71 Years
and 6 months

How happy are the souls above.
From sin and sorrow free;
With Jesus they are now at rest,
And all his glory see.

With wondering joy they recollect,
Their sins and danger past;
And bless the wisdom power & love
That brought them safe at last

237 *m*
SACRED
to
the memory of
CAPT OBEDIAH MEEKER
who departed this life
April 5th 1829
Aged 90 years
& 11 months

An affectionate Husband, a
kind Father, a zealous friend
to his Country during her
Revolutionary struggle for
liberty, and a liberal suppor-
-ter of the Gospel.

238 *m*
E. P. S.
ELIZABETH P SAYRE
Born Feb'y 23 1787
DIED
March 1, 1875
Aged 88 years

" Blessed are the dead
who die in the Lord,,

239 *m*
SACRED
To the memory of
THEODORE J SAYRE
who died at New Orleans
Augst 8th 1854
Aged 39 Years.

No relative near in his last hours but he had many kind friends in the land of strangers.

---

240 *m*
SACRED
To the memory of
JAMES C SAYRE
formerly of this place
who died at Louisville
Octr 5th 1847
In the 66th Year
of his age.

Thy will be done

---

241 *m*
SACRED
To the memory of
SIDNEY W SAYRE
WHO DIED
Feb 5th 1846
In the 28th Year
of his age

He was accidentally killed while in discharge of his duty as first Engineer on board of the steamer Alexander Scott upon her downward trip from Louisville to New Orleans

Alike kind, generous, and unfortunate.

---

242 *r*
This
Stone is
erected in
memory of two
beloved Children of
James C & Elizabeth
P. Sayre. formerly of
this Town. who died at
Louisville Kentucky
in the year of 1834
THOMAS M SAYRE
died Feby 4th aged
5 years and 4 months
ELIZABETH P SAYRE
died March 5th aged
25 years and 6 months

Almighty God thy will be done
To take them early to thy home
Thy chastening rod we humbly kiss
Nor would deprive them of such bliss.

---

243 *r*
T. J. S.
In memory of
Theodore James
son of James C & Elizabeth
P Sayre who died Feby 3^d
1814 aged 3 years
& 2 months

Dear parents do, with reverence bow
Before your great Creators throne
His wisdom has ordain'd the blow
And call'd me to my peaceful home

---

244 *r*
E. P.
In memory of
ELIZABETH
relict of
Joseph Periam
who died
April 5th 1808
Aged 61 years

Hear what the voice from Heaven
  proclaims
For all the pious dead
Sweet is the Saviour of their names
And soft their sleeping bed

245 r
Here lies interr'd
what was Mortal of
Mr Joseph Periam
who died Octr ye 8th
Anno Domini 1781
In ye 39th Year of his
Age
VALE! LONGUM VALE!

246 r
Here lies the Body of
Uzal Woodruff who
departed this life
March ye 16th Anno
Domini 1774 In ye 29th
year of his Age.

247 r
Here lies the Body
of Elias Son of
Uzal & Elizabeth
Woodruff, who
died November 18th
A.D. 1772, In the 2^d
year of his Age ------

248 m
J. C.
SACRED
To the
Memory of
JABEZ CRANE Esq
who departed this life
Feby 17th 1818 in
the 27th year
of his age.

When every pain and every joy is o'er
When fortune age, disease can wound
no more
Virtues like his, with radient lustre
glow
And breathe refulgent through the
clouds of wo

Could tenderest friendship or purest
love, disarm the King of terrors
he had not died.

249 m
IN
Memory of
JANE S HATFIELD
WIFE OF
the late Elis Noe;
Born Sept 9 1793
DIED
June 1. 1841

250 r
Beneath this
Monumental stone
is Intered the Remains
of Sarah daughter of
Oliver & Jane Hatfield
who died Nov 17th 1810;
aged 1 year 8 months
& 4 days

251 m
LAURA D. HATFIELD
FIFTH
DAUGHTER OF
OLIVER S AND JANE HATFIELD
BORN IN ELIZABETH
January 6th 1826
DIED AT MONROE N. Y.
July 30th 1881

Patient, long-suffering, kind—she
departed in the full assurance of a
blessed immortality.

Her memory is
dearly cherished by her friends.

252 m
EMILY A HATFIELD
First daughter of
OLIVER S. AND JANE HATFIELD
born in Elizabeth March 21 1805
died at Bayonne N. J.
August 19 1874
ALSO
CENOTAPH OF
SARAH HATFIELD
their third daughter

INSCRIPTIONS IN FIRST PRESBYTERIAN

born in Elizabeth Jany 4 1811
died at New York
May 21st 1836
Her remains were interred in a vault of the Seventh Presbyterian Church of that City.
Sweet is the memory of the beloved.

253 *m*
OLIVER S. HATFIELD
SON OF
AARON HATFIELD
and Decendent of Matthias
one of the Founders of Elizabeth
born in this town Oct 16th 1782
died at Hoboken N. J.
April 25th 1860

Jane Hatfield
wife of Oliver Spencer Hatfield
and daughter of Thomas Mann
born in this town Feby 10th 1787
died at Hoboken N. J
May 6th 1858
They rest in Peace.

254 *r*
D H
In memory of
DAMARIS
relict of
Isaac Hatfield
Who died Novr 3^d
1808, in the 73^d year
of her age

O glorious hour! O blest abode!
I shall be near, and like my God;
And flesh and sin no more control
The sacred pleasures of the soul

255 *r*
I. H.
In memory of
Isaac Hetfield
who died Febru^y 3^d
1807
in the 77th year
of his
age

My flesh shall slumber in the ground
Till the last trumpet's joyful sound
Then burst the chains with sweet surprice
And in my saviours image rise

256 *r*
Oliver Spencer, Son
of Isaac & Damaris
Hetfield, died Oct^r
the 8th A.D. 1780
In the 4th Year of his
Age.

257 *r*
H. N. H.
Harriot Novee
Daughter of Aaron &
Sarah Hatfield, died
Jan^r 4th 1796 aged XI
month's & 26 days

Farewell sweet child,
Thy day is come;
At Gods right hand,
You'll find a home.

258 *r*
IN
Memory of
SARAH BARNET
WIFE OF
AARON HATFIELD
Born April 17 1759
Died July 29 1824

259 *r*
IN
Memory of
AARON HATFIELD
BORN
July 30. 1757
Died May 15 1839

260 r
S. H.
In memory of
SARAH
Widow of
Silas Halsey
who died
May 18th 1833
in the 76th year
of her age

Her soul has now taken flight
To mansions of glory above
To mingle with angels of light
And dwell in the kingdom of love

261 r
S. H.
In memory of
SILAS HALSEY
who died
Octr 22 1819;
in the 79th year
of his age.

262 r
In memory of
Phebe wife of
Silas Halsey
who died Augt 9th 1794
in the 44th year
of her age
Also their son Jeremiah
died Septr 30th 1794 in
the 3^d year of his age

263 r
Betsy daughter
of Silas and Phebe
Halsey died Oct^r
ye 21st 1792 in the
5th year of her age

264 r
M. H.
In memory of
Mary Halsey
who died
March 14th 1806
in the 33^d year
of her age

265 r
D L
In memory of
DAVID LYON
WHO DIED
May 21st 1845
In the 85th year
of his age

The Memory of the just is blessed.
Prov 10-7

266 r
M. L
In Memory of
MARY
wife of
David Lyon
who died
Oct 25th 1833
Aged 74 years

267 r
S. T L
In memory of
Sarah Treat
the Wife of
Doct^r Matthias
Clark Lyon
She died April 10
1802
Aged 30 Years.

268 r
M L
In Memory of
Capt Matthias Lyon
died Novr 11th 1797
Aged 59 Years.

269 r
S. C. M.
In memory of
SARAH C Wife of
William Murphy
who departed this
life April 25th 1821
in the 32 year
of her age

270 r
In
Memory of
Rachel Lyon
who died Feby 28th
1802 Aged 19
Years

---

271 r
BENEATH
this
stone
is deposited
the remains of
PHEBE LYON
Widow of
BENJAMIN LYON
(of Lyons farms)
who died 3^d May 1815
in the 56th year of
her age

The raptures, Oh! beyond our thought
That her enamor'd soul hath got
Which by no tongue can be explained
The splendid gloryies she's obtained

Around the dazzling throne of God
Rejoiceing in redeeming blood
With all the bright seraphic band
In shineing seats at God's right hand

---

272 r
Beneath
This Stone
is deposited
the Remains of
Benjamin Lyon
Seignior of Lyons
Farms who died
Decr 8th 1803 Aged
49 Years.

The unremitting path I have trod
That leads to hapiness and God
In Christ alone I hope and trust
To rise in judgement with the just

273 r
Here lyes the Body of
Benjamin Lyon who
Died July ye 31st 1758
in the 39th year
of his Age

---

274 r
Here lies ye Body of
Mary wife of James
Carpntr who Died
Jan^ry 27 1763 In y^e
31 year of her Age

---

275 r
AARON Son of Sa-
-muel & Phebe Lyon
who died Octr ye 31st
A + D. 1768 In the 3^d
Year of his Age ———

---

276 r
Here lies ye Body
of Phebe Widow
of Samuel Lyon
who died Ma^r ye 14
A. D. 1781 In ye LIst
Year of her Age

---

277 r
Here lies the Body
of Mr Samuel Ly-
-on who departed
this Life Feby ye 9th
Anno Domini 1780
In the LIst Year of
his Age.

---

278 r
In memory of
Joanna Lyon who
died Novem^r the 11th
1791, in the 22^d year
of her age

CHURCH YARD, ELIZABETH, N. J. 43

279 r
Moses Son of
Moses & Mary
Lyon who died
May ye 5 1763
aged 2 years
5 Months & 22 D^s

280 r
M. L.
In memory of
Mary wife of
Moses Lyon
who died June
12th 1809 in the
77th year of
her Age.

281 r
M. L.
In memory of
MOSES LYON
who died
March 27th 1813
in the 82^d year of
his age.

282 r
Abe Hendrex daugh^r
of Richard & Sally
Lyon. died Feb 3^d 1798
aged 5 years 5 mon^s
& 29 days.
Our lovely child christ took and blest
We'll cease to mourn for she's at rest

283 r
S L
In memory of
SARAH
wife of Richard
Lyon who died
June 1st 1810 in
the 36th year
of her age.

Adieu vain world, my dearest friends
  farewell
Prepare with me in this dark house
  to dwell
Till the last trump my ruin'd frame
  repair
At Christ descent to meet him in the
  air

Unsmoothe'd was thy pillow of death
By a fond parting and tender adieu
From home and from kindred bereft
In an instent from the world she
  withdrew

284 r
S. L.
Sacred to the Memory
of Susan the much
love'd wife of
Samuel Lyon
who departed this
life Augst 17th 1809
aged 30 years 1 month
& 24 days
A partner kind & mother dear
A friend most constant & sincere

285 r
E O
In memory of
Elizabeth wife
of Elihu Ogden
who died Decr 8
1797 in the 44th
year of her Age.

286 r
In memory of Hetfield
Son of Matthias and
Margaret Ogden. He
died Septr ye 26th 1793
in the 13th year of his
age.

287 r
Here lies yᵉ Body
of Mrs Hannah
Relict of Mr Samuel
Ogden who died
Januaʸ yᵉ 26ᵗʰ Anᵒ
Domini 1782. In
the 59ᵗʰ Year of her
Age

288 r
HERE lies the Body
of Samuel Ogden, who
departed this Life Febrʸ
the 20ᵗʰ Anno Domini
1775. aged LXI Years.

289 r
M. O.
In memory of
MATTHIAS OGDEN
who died
March 7ᵗʰ 1818;
in the 76ᵗʰ year
of his age.

Our age to sev'nty years is set
How short the time! how frail the
  state!
And if to eighty we arrive,
We rather sigh and groan than live.

290 r
M. O.
In memory of
MARGARET wife
of Matthias Ogden
who died March 18ᵗʰ
1820 in the 75ᵗʰ year
of her age

The coffin the shroud and the grave
  To her were no objects of dread
On him who is mighty to save
  Her soul was with Confidence
    stayed

291 r
L. O.
In memory of
LEWIS OGDEN
who died
May 15ᵗʰ 1818
in the 43ʳᵈ year
of his age.

292 r
M. O.
In memory of
MATTHIAS OGDEN
who died
April 18ᵗʰ 1821
in the 37ᵗʰ year
of his age

Farewell thou world with all thy toys
  For thou hast been to me
A world of transitory joys,
  Of sin and vanity.

293 m
IN
Memory of
CHARITY
widow of
Benjamin Ogden
who died July 8ᵗʰ 1852
Aged 80 years

294 m
IN
memory of
BENJAMIN OGDEN
who died
May 19ᵗʰ 1844
In the 75; year of
his age

behold, my witness is in heaven,
and my record is on high.
    Job 16, C 19 V.

---

²⁸⁷ Daughter of Isaac Hatfield.
²⁸⁹ Son of 288 Samuel.
²⁹⁰ Daughter of Joseph Megie.
²⁹¹ Son of Matthias Ogden 289.
²⁹³ Daughter of Matthias Ogden 289.

295 *m*
IN
memory of
RHODA
widow of Moses Ogden
who died Jany, 16th 1861
Aged 83 years

" Blessed are the dead which die in the Lord, from henceforth; Yea, saith the Spirit, that they may rest from their labors ; and their works do follow them.,,

296 *m*
IN
Memory of
MOSES OGDEN
WHO DIED
June 9th 1847
Aged 73 Years

Farewell ye friends whose tender care
Has long engaged my love
Your fond embrace I now exchange
For better friends above.

297 *m*
IN
MEMORY OF
MOSES H OGDEN
who died in New York
Jany, 29th 1861
Aged 45 Years 5 Mos.
& 18 Days

298 *m*
IN MEMORY
OF
two children of
John & Joanna Ogden
SARAH ROSS
died Augst 25th 1826
aged 11 months
& 23 days
MOSES CONDIT
died Octr 6th 1834
aged 5 years 3 months
& 16 days

"The Lord gave, and the Lord hath taken away; blessed be the name of the Lord,,

299 *m*
[East face, other three blank]
ICI REPOSE
LE CORPS DE
JOSEPH F
COLLET
NE A ST GERMAIN
DE-LA COUDRE,
DEPARTEM^t DE-LA
SARTHE EN FRANCE
LE 25 FEV. 1770
MORT A
ELIZABETH TOWN
LE 12 DEC 1841

Priez Dieu pour-le
repos de son âme.

300 *m*
WILLIAM CARGILL
Born June 19 1767
Died December 10 1842
GEORGE HARRIMAN
KIMBALL
Born at
NEW YORK. N. Y.
March 20, 1846,
Died at
RAVENSWOOD L. I.
August 8. 1846

301 *m*
ABIGAIL CARGILL
Born February 29 1781
Died January 13. 1848
KATE NELSON
KIMBALL
Born at
RAVENSWOOD L. I.
June 19. 1850
Died at
NEW YORK N. Y.
September 1. 1852

302 r
In
memory of
MARY SEELY
who died Octr 8th 1807
aged 43 years & 3 months

Sleep, balmy sleep has clos'd her eyes,
And put an end to all her sighs;
Through great distress & wrecking pain
She's gone to learn that death is gain

303 r
D L H
In memory of
DAVID L. HUMES
who died
Septr 4th 1822;
Aged 22 Years
& 23 Days

Also MARY ELIZABETH DOW
daughter of David L &
Catharine Humes; who died
June 22 1821; Aged 10
Months & 20 Days

Sweet babe! by deaths cold hand in earliest bloom
Torn from thy mothers bosom to the tomb
You in your Saviours arms are blest
So sleep dear babe and take your rest

304 m
IN
Memory of
LAURENT JOUSSERANDOT
A Native of Paris
FRANCE
Born Decr 3^d 1796
Died June 21st 1854

Thy place on earth no more shall know thee
But t'will long remembered be;
In the hearts where grateful memory,
Oft will breath, it's sigh for thee.

But amidst our earthly sorrow,
The hope that thou art free from pain,
Shines to guide us to yon Heaven
Where we yet shall meet again
LOUISE JOUSSERANDOT
Died July 8th 1886
In the 80th Year of her life

305 r
Sacred to the Memory
of Damaris the beloved
Wife of Luther Halsey
who departed this Life
Sept ye 11th A. D. 1790. In
the 22^d Year of her Age

Farewell my dearest Heart
Since you and I must part
We hope in Heaven to meet again
Where Love & Joy & Peace shall reign

306 r
Sacred to the Memory
of Sarah, the beloved
Wife of Luther Halsey
who departed this Life
Augt the 2^d A × D. 1787,
In the XXVIII Year of
her Age ———

And Luther their son,
died ye 8th of Septr in ye 2^d
Year of his Age ———

The Wife most kind
A Parent dear
The Christians friend
And one Sincere

307 r
In memory of
Jeremiah, son of
Luther & Sarah
Halsey. He died
July 17th 1792 in y^e
9th year of his age.

308 r
Here lies ye Body
of Joseph Son of
Joseph & Elisabeth
Wheaton. Dec^d Augs^t
ye 20 1736 Aged 4
years & 4 months

309 r
Here lies the Body
of Margaret Wife
of Samuel Lee
who died Augt ye 8th
Anno Domini 1782
In the 35th Year of
her Age ————

310 r
S. L.
In Memory of
SAMUEL LEE
who died May 12th
1812 in the 68th year
of his age

311 r
Here lieth
ye Body of Nathaniel
Bonnel who Died
Sept ye 4 1736
in ye 67 year
of his Age

312 r
HERE LI'S
interr'd the Body of
Mrs Phebe, Wife of
Captn John Joline
who died Dece^r y^e
6th A. D. 1763
Et^s Suæ
49.

313 r

In Memory
of Matthias
Joline who
died Decem^r
ye 17th 1782
aged 37 Years.

In Memory
of Anthony
Joline who
died S^eptem^r
ye 11th 1783
aged 30 years

314 m
[Stone broken off just below inscription and top part gone]

315 m
ABBY G
widow of
DAVID JOHNSON
Died December 6th 1886
Aged 83 Years 9 Mo's
and 17 Days

316 m
Catharine C Lyon
Died April 5th 1878
Aged 81 Years and
13 Days

317 m
STEPHEN M LYON
DIED
June 25th 1864
Aged 72 Years
8 Mo's & 22 Days

318 m
SARAH
WIDOW OF
Obadiah Lyon
died March 1st 1852
Aged 87 Years

INSCRIPTIONS IN FIRST PRESBYTERIAN

319 *m*
OBADIAH LYON
Died
Septr 6th 1847
Aged 82 Years

320 *r*
M. P.
In memory of
Mary wife of
Abner Passels
who died
Jany 15th 1822
in the 51st year
of her age.

321 *r*
S. A. P.
In Memory of
Sarah Ann
daughter of Edward
& Rosetta Price, who
died Oct 12th 1812 aged
15 months.

Her charms began to take effect
And draw her parents' hearts from God.
he thought it best to take her home
& wean their hearts from earth again.

322 *m*
Our Mother
" Rest Spirit Rest "
CELESTIA
Wife of
ROBERT G PRICE
Died
July 24 1875
Aged 65 yrs

323 *r*
EN
[Broken]   died
17th 1827
in the 50th year
of his age.

[No doubt this is Samuel Ogden. Close beside it is Esther wife of Samuel Ogden]

324 *r*
E. O.
In Memory of
Esther
wife of
Samuel Ogden
who died
Augst 17th 1832
in the 51st year
of her age.

325 *r*
C. A. O.
In memory of
Charity Ann daughter
of Samuel & Esther
Ogden. who died Jany 14^{t}h
1819 Aged 7 Years
9 months & 27 days

The months of affliction are o'er
The days and the nights of distress
We see her in anguish no more
She's gained her happy release

326 *m*
W. O.
In memory of
William Ogden
who died
August 16th 1832
in the 24th year
of his age

Ye fleeting charms of earth farewell
Your springs of joy are dry
My soul now seeks another home
A brighter world on high

327 *m*
MARY OGDEN
Died
April 11st 1865
In the 51st year
of her Age

328 *m*
JOHN P CREE
DIED
Aug 28th 1869
Aged 55 yrs
10 mos & 7
days

329 *m*
JANE E CREE
Wife of
JOHN P CREE
DIED
May 11th 1869
Aged 54 yrs 8
mos & 10 days

330 *m*
FRANCES F. CREE
daughter of
JOHN P & JANE E CREE
DIED
Jan 4th 1862
Aged 18 yrs. 10
mos & 21 days.

Pause youthful stranger view my doom. Think not that youth can shun the tomb

331 *m*
in
Memory of
CAP*t* WILLIAM MELVIN
DIED
Sept. 12th 1870
Aged 92 years

He is ever near us
Though not seen.

332 *m*
IN
Memory of
ABIGAIL OGDEN
WIFE OF
William Milven
who died
Sept 5 1855
Aged 76 Years
and 10 Months.

There is rest in Heaven

333 *m*
IN
Memory of
ELIZA
WIDOW OF
Oliver Smith
daughter of William
and Abigail Milven
who died Aug. 29th 1849
Aged 43 Years

The Lords time has come

334 *m*
IN
Memory of
HARRIETE
Daughter of
William & Abigail
MILVEN
who died
June 18th 1846
Aged 24 Years

" In the midst of life we are in death "

335 *m*
In
Memory of
JAMES MELVIN
DIED
Oct 26th 1865
Aged 61 years

He Served 32 years
in the U. S. Navy.

336 *r*
Here Lyeth y*e* Body
of Phebe Morehous
Daughter of David
Morehous, Deceased
December y*e* 16th
1729 aged 5 months.

INSCRIPTIONS IN FIRST PRESBYTERIAN

337 *r*
Here Lyeth ye Body
of Rebecca Morehous
Wife of mr David
Morehous. Departed
April ye 27th 1728 in y^e
52^d Year of her
Age.

---

338 *m*
J. G. O.
In memory of
JOSEPH G. OGDEN
who died
March 23^d 1817
in the 37th year
of his age

He cometh forth like a flower
and is cut down. he fleeth alway as
a shadow and continueth not
" In the midst of life we are in death"

---

339 *r*
W. O.
In memory of
William Ogden
who deceas'd March
11th 1799 in the 33^d
Year of his age

Farewel my friends I'me going to dust
God sent the summons and its just
Prepare for death and weep no more
O hasten to this friendly shore

Sally & Wil^m daugh^{tr} & son of Wil^m &
Nancy Ogden. Sally died April 3^d 1798
aged 1 year & 9 mon^s. Wil^m died decem^r
11th 1798 aged 7 mon^s

---

340 *r*
J. C.
In memory
of
JAMES CHAPMAN
who died
March 31,
1822
Aged
87 years

341 *r*
M C
In memory of
MARY
Relict of
James Chapman
who died
Sept 24th 1845
in the 80th year
of her age.

[Halsey plot inclosed with granite posts and
iron pipe railing, and contains the next 8
graves]

342 *m*
M H
In memory of
MARY
wife of
Meline W Halsey
and Daughter of
James & Mary
Chapman : who
died Decr 23^d 1831
Aged 28 years.

---

343 *m*
THE GRAVES
OF
two children of
Meline W &
Henrietta P Halsey
CATHARINE PRICE
died March 26th 1841
Aged 2 years 1 month
and 7 days.
ISAAC CRANE
died July 3rd 1844
Aged 7 months
" Of such is the Kingdom of heaven."

---

344 *m*
HENRIETTA CRANE
DAUGHTER OF
M. W. AND H. P. HALSEY
DIED FEB, 17, 1854
AGED 2 YEARS
AND 11 MONTHS
" IT IS WELL WITH HER,,

345 m
NOAH CRANE
SON OF
M. W. AND H. P. HALSEY
DIED
APRIL 21st 1856
AGED 20 YEARS AND
11 MONTHS

" DEATH LOVES A SHINING MARK,,

346 m
MARY CHAPMAN
DAUGHTER OF
M. W. AND H. P. HALSEY
DIED
APRIL 9th 1859
AGED 21 YEARS AND
5 MONTHS

" FOR HER TO DIE WAS GAIN,,

347 m
MELINE W HALSEY
BORN
AUGUST 27th 1800
DIED
MARCH 6th 1873

" MY TIMES ARE IN THY HANDS,,

348 m
HENRIETTA PERLEE
WIDOW OF
MELINE W HALSEY
BORN JULY 16th 1810
DIED OCT. 25. 1883

" IT IS THE EVENING TIME WITH ME "

349 m
SARAH W
WIFE OF
JAMES C OGDEN
AND DAUGHTER OF
M. W. & H. P. HALSEY
DIED AUG' 15' 1878
AGED 36 YEARS

HER INFANT DAUGHTER
SARAH HALSEY
DIED OCT' 14' 1878
AGED 2 MON'S.

ASLEEP IN JESUS

350 r
In
memory of
JOHN AMORY son of
Samuel & Julia Gamage
who died Sept 3^d 1815
Aged 1 year 7 months
& 5 days.

I take these little lambs said he
And lay them in my breast
Protection they shall find in me
In me be ever blest

351 r
Maria daughter of
Nehemiah & Patience
Tunis died Augt the
18th 1792. in ye 4th year
of her age

Sleep lov'ly babe
And take thy rest
God call'd the home
He thought it best

352 r
Bernadus G Son of
Nehemiah & Patience
Tunis. died May the
11th 1794 in the 3^d
year of his age

Sleep lovly babe
Till we doe meet
Within the wals
Of zions street

353 r
David W. son of
Nehemiah & Patience
Tunis. died April 23^d
1800 aged (^{gone}) years 7
months & 15 days

INSCRIPTIONS IN FIRST PRESBYTERIAN

Why do we mourn, departed babe,
Or shake at deaths alarms
Tis but the messenger he sends
To take him to his arms

---

354 *m*
In
Memory of
NEHEMIAH TUNIS
who departed this life
June 8th 1817
Aged 64 years

Here lies a dutiful son
An affectionate husband
a kind Father

As you are now so once was I
In health and strength tho here I lie
As I am now so you must be
Prepare for death and follow me

---

355 *m*
SACRED
to the
Memory of
PATIENCE
Relict of
Nehemiah Tunis
who departed this life
June 21 1831
Aged 72 years

To those who knew her, all eulogium, is needless. To those who enjoyed not the privilege of her aquaintance no words can delineate the excellence of her virtues

---

356 *m*
In
Memory of
SUSAN B. wife of
Henry P. Landis
and daughter of Nehe-
-miah & Patience Tunis
who departed this life
October 17th 1820
Aged 26 years
& 9 months

The victory now is obtained
She's gone her dear Saviour to see
Her wishes she fully has gained
She's now where she longed to be.

Also in memory of
SUSAN LANDIS
daughter of John & Hannah
Trumbull who died
May 9th 1821 Aged 1 month
& 20 days

---

357 *m*
SACRED
to the
Memory
of
Mrs Hannah W Trumbull
wife of
John M. Trumbull
who died
August 21st 1823
aged 23 Years.

---

358 *m*
LOUISA METTIA
DIED MARCH 10th 1874
AGED 6 YEARS 3 MOS,
AND 23 DAYS.
ADA ESTELLE
DIED APRIL 1st 1874
AGED 1 YEAR 1 MO
AND 16 DAYS
Children of
MEEKER & SUSAN WOOD

They have left us and gone
With the angels of light
To thier parents on earth
A few short years they were given
Now they'r sleeping in death
But thier spirits so bright
Finds a home far more dear
With their Savior in heaven

359 *m*
The grave of
JOHN HARBECK
son of Meeker and
Susan Wood
died Dec 5th 1866
aged 1 year 1 month
and 13 days

We loved him, yes, no tongue can tell
How much we loved him or how well
God loved him too and he thought best
To take him home to be at rest

360 *m*
The grave of
Marietta
daughter of Meeker
and Susan Wood
who died Aug 3 1863
aged 7 months
Rest here sweet babe

361 *m*
The grave of
CLARA LINCOLN
daughter of Meeker
and Susan Wood
who died July 27 1861
aged 5 months
and 8 days

She blooms in heaven

362 *m*
JANE GIBSON
DIED JUNE 29th 1850
AGED 89 YEARS.

RETURN UNTO THY REST O MY SOUL.
FOR THE LORD HATH DEALT
BOUNTIFULLY WITH ME.

[The above and the next are in plot enclosed with iron fence]

[Marble shaft with 4 inscriptions]
[On east side]
363
SACRED
TO THE MEMORY OF
ALEXANDER OGILVIE
DECEASED
APRIL 12 1857
AGED 90 YEARS.

" Precious in the sight
of the Lord is the death
of his saints."

[On west side]
SACRED
TO THE MEMORY OF
JANE J. OGILVIE
DECEASED
JAN 29 1870
AGED 81 YEARS

" My Flesh and my heart
faileth, but God is the
strength of my heart and
my portion forever."

[On north side]
AGNES OGILVIE
DAUGHTER OF
ALEX^R & J J OGILVIE
DIED
AUGUST 15th 1848
IN HER 22nd YEAR

" I am the ressurection
and the life ,,

[On south side]
JANE M. OGILVIE
DAUGHTER OF
ALEX^R & J J OGILVIE
DIED
JULY 1, 1842
IN HER 24th YEAR

" Blessed are the dead which
die in the Lord ,,

INSCRIPTIONS IN FIRST PRESBYTERIAN

364 *r*
In
memory of
ABIGAIL CHANDLER
who died
Septr 1st 1833
In the 70th year
of her age

"Blessed are the dead
which die in the Lord,,

---

365 *r*
I, C.
In memory of
ICHABOD CHANDLER
who died
April 7th 1829
in the 67th Year
of his age

Be ye also ready

---

366 *r*
P. C.
In memory of
PRUDENCE
wife of
Ichabod Chandler
who died
Decr 9th 1831
Aged 66 years

Prepare to follow me.

---

367 *m*
OUR MOTHER
PRUDENCE CHANDLER
DIED MARCH 9th 1863
AGED 68 YEARS 7 MO'S
& 8 DAYS

Asleep in Jesus

368 *m*
In
Memory of
HENRY W. CHANDLER
WHO DIED
April 11th 1836
Aged 42 Years
& 5 Months
Also
His infant son
aged 1 day

Thus much and this is all we know
Saints are completely blest
Have done with sin and care and wo
And with their saviour rest

---

369 *r*
In
Memory of
ELIZABETH
wife of
William Price
who died with the
Cholera Septr 5th 1832
in the 41st year
of her age

"Watch therefore,,

---

370 *m*
MATTHEW W. WOODWARD
DIED
FEBRUARY 7th 1883
AGED 76 YEARS, 3 MOS.
& 25 DAYS.

"In thee O Lord, do I put my trust."

---

371 *m*
HARRIET VREDENBURGH
WIFE OF
DR. M. W. WOODWARD
DIED JULY 21st 1876
AGED 68 YEARS 11 MOS
& 7 DAYS

"The Lord is my Shepherd"

CHURCH YARD, ELIZABETH, N. J.

372 *m*
BROTHER,

DAVID LYON
AGED 47 YEARS

---

373 *m*
AARON LYON
DIED
SEPT^r 5th 1854
IN THE 85th YEAR
OF HIS AGE.

---

374 *m*
JOANNA
WIFE OF
AARON LYON
WHO DIED
OCT^r 30th 1845
AGED 75 YEARS

None knew her but to love her

---

375 *m*
In Memory
OF
WILLIAM HENRY
Son of
George & Joanna B
BRYAN
who died July 25, 1843
Aged 2 Years 5 Months

"I take these little lambs said he
And lay them in my breast
Protection they shall find in me
In me be ever blest.

---

376 *r*
I. W.
In Memory of
Isaac Woodruff
who decease'd
July 2^d 1804
in the 61st year of
his Age

Weep not for me my friends
For why my race is run
It tis the will of God
So let his will be done

---

377 *r*
In Memory of
Dr Aaron Woodruff
who departed this
Life Janua^y ye 12th
Anno Domini 1784
In the 25th Year of
his Age

---

378 *r*

Here lyeth Samuel
Son of mr Samuel
& Elisabeth Woodruff
Born march the 15th
1746. Dec^d Novr ye
12th 1747 Aged 7.
months & 28 days

Here lyeth Abigail
Daughter of Mr
Samuel & Elisabeth
Woodruff. born
Sepr the 14th 1736
Decs^d Sepr ye 27th
1736 aged 13 days

Sleep lovely Babe's Since God has Call'd thee hence
Let us Submit to his wise Providence.

379 r
HERE lieth the Body
of Ann ——— Wife of
Joseph Woodruff Junr
ob^t June ye 28th Anno
Domini 1757 In ye 23^d
Year of her Age———

Remember me as you Pass by
As you are now so once was I
As I am now so you must be
Therefore prepare to Follow me

380 r
HERE lies the Body of
Jane Wife of Nathan
Woodruff who deceas'd
June ye 18th A D 1758
In the 20th Year of her
Age———————

As you are now so once was I
In Health & Strength; tho here I lie
As I am now so you must be
Prepare for Death & follow me

381 m
IN
Memory of
NATHAN WOODRUFF
who departed this life
March 20th AD 1801.
Aged 71 Years

382 m
T. P.
SACRED
To the Memory of
THOMAS PRICE Junr
who died
June 14 1824
in the 52^d year
of his age

383 r
M P
In Memory of
MARY PRICE
who died
Augst 15th 1820
in the 54th year
of her age

384 r
J. P.
In Memory of
John Price died
Novr 6th 1806   In the
44th Year of his Age

Precious time is ever sliding
Brightest hours have no abiding
Life and time are worth improving
Seize the moments as they fly

385 r
J. P.
In Memory
of
John Price
He died Sep^{er}
25th 1790 in the
52th Year of his
age

386 r
Here lies the Body
of John Drewe who
Deceas'd Augt ye 6^t
1771 in ye 80th Year
of his Age

387 r
In Memory of
Elizabeth, widow
of David Pierson
who died January y^e
8th 1793 in ye 58th year
of her age

388 r
Mary daughter
of Lewis and
Abigail Pierson
died Augt ye 27
1793 aged 2 years
and 3 months

CHURCH YARD, ELIZABETH, N. J.

389 *r*
In Memory of
David Pierson who
departed this life Apr^l
the 2^d 1788 in the 52^d
Year of his age

390 *r*
[But little of the inscription left]
1800
of his
may dep
her is no m
o more prov
s at Jesus sid

391 *m*
IN
MEMORY
OF
LOUISA ANGELINE
DAUGHTER OF
John J & Ann Decker
who died May 7th 1844
Aged 1 year 1 month
and 11 days

Death may the bands of life unloose
But cant dissolve my love
Millions of infant souls compose
The family above

392 *r*
E. O.
In memory of
ELIZABETH
wife of George Ogden
who died July 4th 1817
Aged 27 years
& 24 days

How long shall we be lingering here
While saints around us take their
 flight
Smiling they quit this dusky sphere
And mount the hills of heav'nly light

393 *r*
E. O.
In Memory of
ELIZABETH
daughter of Jacob &
Elizabeth Ogden who
died May 17th 1812 in
the 31st year of her age

In faith she live'd! in dust she lies!
But faith for'sees that dust shall rise.
When Jesus calls while hope assumes:
And boasts her joys among the tombs

394 *r*
[Lies flat on 393]
Here Lieth the
Body of David
Morehouse of
Elisabeth Town
born the 16th Day
of July in the year
1710, Who depar
ted this life the
29 Day of June
Anno Domini
1715

395 *r*
E. O.
In memory of
ELIZABETH
wife of Jacob Ogden
who died May 8th 1812
in the 63^d year
of her age

When I walke'd thro' the shadow of
 death
Thy presence was my stay
One word of thy supporting breath
Drove all my fears away

396 r
J O
In memory of
JACOB OGDEN
who died
Octr 10th 1818
in the 76th year
of his age

Lord I commit my soul to thee
Accept the sacred trust
Receive this nobler part of me
And watch my sleeping dust

397 r
Here
Lieth y^e Body
of Rebekah Og-
den of Elizabeth Town
born in November
In the year 1648 who
Departed this Life
y^e 11 : Day Septemb^{er}
Anno Domini 1723

398 r
Here Lyeth y^e Body of
Mr Jonathan Ogden Dec.
Jan^r y^e 3^d 1732 in ye 86th
year of his Age

My Life was Chr$\overset{is}{t}$ my Death is gain
This bed giues ease to all my pain
My Dust is safe my Soul's at home
To meet with Joy when Christ shall
come

399 r
Here
Lieth the Body
of Captain Benjamin
Ogden of Elizabeth
Town. Who Departed this
life the 20th Day of Novem
ber, in the Year of our LORD
1722. Being in the 69th Year
of his Age

400 r
Here lies Interr'd the Body of Mrs
Elizabeth, Relict of Mr Patrick
Charlton who Dec^d Jan^r 17 1778
In the 76 Year of her Age

My panting sould ascends on high
To praise my God eternelly

Also their Son John who died in the
Year 1752 Aged 19 Years

And their Daughter Elizabeth who
died in the Year 1759 Aged 24 Years

In Christ alone we hope and trust
To rise in judgement witn the just.

401 r
Here lies ye Body of
Mr Isaac Whitehead
Who Died July ye 1
1724 Aged 71 years

402 r
Here   Lyeth
The Body Of
Benjamin Ogden
Deceased Novem^{br}
ye 4th Anno 1729
Aged 49 Years

403 r
Here lies the Body
of Hannah Wife of
Jonathan Gillet who
departed this Life
July ye 9th Anno
Dom— 1784 In ye 22^d
Year of her Age

404 r
HERE lies the Body
of Susanna, Wife of
Joseph Crane who
departed this Life——
Octr ye 22^d A D 1781
In the 32^d Year of her
Age——————— ——

405 *r*
W. C.
In Memory of
WILLIAM CRANE ESQ
who died
June 4th 1830
In the 53d year
of his Age

406 *r*
S. C.
In memory of
SARAH
wife of
William Crane esq
who died
Augst 18th 1832
In the 57th year
of her age

407 *m*
IN
memory of
DAVID ROSS CRANE
who died
Jan. 13th 1848
Aged 42 Years

O life what is thy breath?
A vapour lost in death.

408 *r*
Here lyes ye Body of
Jane Cahune wife of
Walter Cahune, Decd
June ye 14 1753
in ye 61st year of her
Age

409 *r*
Here Lyeth ye
Body of James
sayre deceased
The 16th of April
A° 1731 in the 55th
Year of his Age

409½ *r*
Here lies Interr'd ye Body of
John Ross Esqr who
Departed this Life Decbr
the 21 A. D. 1772
Æ XXXVIII

My Consort dear and Lovely babes
Remember me in these Cold Shades
In God alone do you Confide
The Widows Stay the Orphans guide

410 *r*
Here Lies the Mortal Part of
Mrs Sarah ROSS Relict of
JOHN ROSS Eqr Decd April
19: 1759   Aged 54 Years

A more pious Christian A more
   Faithful Wife
A more Tender Mother A Sincerer
   Friend
Or A kinder Neighbour
She has not left Behind her

READER
Consider That as the Possession
of the Highest Virtues
Cannot ward off the Dart of DEATH
Wee ought before the uncertain
STROKE comes to Make our
PEACE with GOD

---

411 *r*
Here lies the Body of JOHN ROSS Esq
who departed this life August 21 1754
Aged 56 Years

Few in these Days his Equal none Superior
Of Temper just, benevolent and human
        Given to Hospitality
          with Piety sincere
Reader pray stop, reflect, on this a While
And let no Worldly Care, Your Soul beguile,
An upright Man lies here, Consider where
When death shall lay thee low thou wilt appear

INSCRIPTIONS IN FIRST PRESBYTERIAN

412 r
Elizabeth, Daughter of
Thomas and Sarah Ross
deceas'd Janua^y ye 22^d
A. D. 1759. In the 31st
Year of her Age ———

Behold ye Place where I do lie
As you are now so once was I
As I am now so you must be
Prepare for Death and follow me

---

413 r
Here Lyes ye Body
of Samuel Ward Dec^d
Jan^{ry} ye 27th 1731
In ye 38th year of
His Age

---

414 m
JOHN W
SON OF
John W & Catharine M
BOYLSTON
died Aug. 13th 1852
AGED 5 YEARS 11 MO
& 6 DAYS

Fare thee well sweet bud of beauty
Stainless spirit fare thee-well
Thou wert to pure and lovely
In a world like this to dwell

---

415 m
In Memory of
ISAAC
WHEELER
son of
John W &
Catharine M
Boylston
who died
May 10 1841
Aged 9 months
& 15 days

Eer sin could blight or sorrow fade
Death came with friendly care
The opening bud to heaven convey'd
And bade it blossom there

416 r
In
Memory of
Susanna W wife of Cornelius
Hoagland who departed this life
Oct 24th 1809 : in the 24th year
of her age

Death calls the aged and the young
From earthly cares from eve'y rong
His summons seizes on the best
And God the righteous soul hath blest

My glass' is run my days is spent
My life is gon. it was but lent
And as I am so must you be
O then prepare to follow me
(Rest)

---

417 r
Here lies ye Body
of Jane Dau^{tr} of
Nath^{ll} and Joanna
Bonnel Dec^d Augst
ye 2 1735 Aged 9
years & 10 month^s

---

418 r
Here Lyes ye Body of
Catharin Donaldson Wife
of Wm Donaldson Marchant
In Elizabeth town. Who
Departed this Life At y^e
Pleasor of ye Almighty God
July ye 30th 1733 In ye 41
year of her Age. Mementomori

---

419 m
IN
MEMORY OF
HANNAH
WIDOW OF
SAMUEL CHANDLER
who died Sept 22^d 1849
In the 72^d Year
of her age

420 *m*
IN
MEMORY OF
SAMUEL CHANDLER
WHO DIED
April 7th 1821
In the 51st Year
of his age

---

421 *r*
M. C.
In memory of
Mary Chandler who
died augt the 13 1800
in the 68 year of her
age

---

422 *r*
In Memory of
Stephen Chandler
who departed this
life Octr 25th 1800
in the 56th year of
his Age

---

423 *r*
SACRED
to the
Memory of
Benjamin Chandler
Son of Abner &
Phebe Chandler
who died 3d Nov. 1815
in the 27th year of his
age.

This sad memento, humble stone,
Recalls a brother, only son;
The hope of age, solace of grief,
The enfeebled sisters kind relief.

Reader has thou a Benjamin
In whom thy eyes with joy have seen,
All thy desire, and all thy hope?
Prepare thy heart to give him up.

With him, died the fondest earthly
        hopes of his parents
The dearest expectations of his sisters
And much pleasing anticipation of
        the church of God.

---

424 *r*
S. C.
In Memory of
Samuel Chandler
who died Feb 12th
1804. In the 69th
Year of his Age

When this you see
Remember me.

---

425 *r*
E. C.
In memory of
Elizabeth widow
of Samuel Chandler
who died March 30th
1813 in the 79th year
of her age

Whether we will or not, we must.
Take the succeeding world on trust

---

426 *r*
SACRED
To the
Memory of
ABNER CHANDLER
who died 18th of June
AD. 1817. Aged 57 Years
5 Months and 11 Days

The tear of sorrow scarcely dry,
  Shed for a brother, only son,
Before is felt a heavier sigh
  And tears of deeper sorrow run.

Ah! why is our last pillar broke!
  Says a lone family, in grief—
Tis God inflicts the painful stroke;
  Begone ye clouds of unbelief.

The Lord is good; we bless his name
  For mercies left; and the fond hope
That we shall quickly meet again,
  Where the dear comp'ny ne'er
          breaks up.

427 *r*
IN
memory of
PHEBE CHANDLER
widow of
Abner Chandler
who died
Novr 27th 1831
Aged 68 years

Pass'd from the trials of this world,
She's found a bless'd abode
Of happiness ; replete with joy,
The dwelling of her God

428 *r*
In
memory of
MARY CHANDLER
Daughter of Abner
& Phebe Chandler
who died Decr 17th
1819 aged 23 years
& 5 months

Time, what an empty vapour tis,
And days how swift they are.

429 *r*
In
Memory of
ABBY CHANDLER
Daughter of Abner
& Phebe Chandler
who died
Sept 10th 1830
Aged 47 years

To God our Sister now hath gone
Her pains and tears are o'er ;
Safe near her heavenly Father's throne
She tastes of death no more

430 *r*
Susanna Daughter
of John & Joanna
Hardy, died Jany y^e
31st 1771 In ye 8th Year
of her Age.

Blessed are the Dead
That die in the Lord.

431 *r*
[On one stone.]

Here lyeth ye Body
Of cap^t Ebenezer
Lyon who departe^d
this life march y^e
31^t Anno Domini
1739. and in ye 69th
Year of his Age

Here lyeth ye Body
Of Elizabeth Lyon
Who departed
this life July the 1^t
Anno Domini
1739 and in ye 71^t
Year of her Age

[Caldwell Plot with iron fence around.]

432 *m*

REUBEN VAN PELT
BORN
JUNE 20 1803
DIED DEC. 19 1879

A kind and loving Husband and
Father ; a useful Citizen ; a
devout and exemplary Christian

" First the blade, then the ear,
after that the full corn in
the ear."
     Mark IV. 28.

433 *m*

HELEN W
DAUGHTER OF
Reuben & Catharine V
VAN PELT
died April 23ᵈ 1857
aged 3 years & 3 months

She's gone to that Happy Land
Of which she so sweetly sang.

---

434 *m*

IN
MEMORY OF
MARGARET S.
WIFE OF
REUBEN VAN PELT
WHO DIED
JANʸ 14ᵗʰ 1849
AGED 46 YEARS

SHE DIED IN THE FAITH AND HOPE
OF THE GOSPEL
"BLESSED ARE THE DEAD WHO
DIE IN THE LORD „

---

435 *r*

[Lying flat on south side of Caldwell monument]

John Dickinson
Son of the Revᵈ
James Caldwell
& Hannah Ogden
Was Born Juneᵉ 29 1765
Fell aSleep May 11 1766
on yᵉ Morn of yᵉ Lords Day
Aged 10 Months and 10 Days

                          & said
But Jesus called them unto him
                          me
Suffer little Children to come unto
And forbid them not
for of such is yᵉ Kingdom of God
Luke 18. 16

436 *m*

[Caldwell Monument, North side]
" The memory of the Just is blessed ,,
Be of good courage and let us behave ourselves
valiently for our people, and for the cities of our God
and let the Lord do that which is good in his sight

" The glory of children are their fathers"

[Front or East side Caldwell Monument]
(Caldwell)
THIS MONUMENT
IS ERECTED TO THE MEMORY OF THE
REV: JAMES CALDWELL:
THE PIOUS AND FERVENT CHRISTIAN ;
THE ZEALOUS AND FAITHFUL MINISTER ;
THE ELOQUENT PREACHER ;
AND
A PROMINENT LEADER
AMONG THE WORTHIES WHO SECURED THE
INDEPENDENCE OF HIS COUNTRY

HIS NAME WILL BE CHERISHED
IN THE CHURCH AND IN THE STATE
SO LONG AS VIRTUE IS ESTEEMED OR PATRIOTISM HONORED
[Near the top of shaft on this side is the word (Caldwell) enclosed by a wreath. See above]

[South side of Caldwell Monument]
JAMES CALDWELL
BORN IN CHARLOTTE C° VIRGINIA APRIL 1734
GRADUATED AT PRINCETON COLLEGE 1759
ORDAINED PASTOR OF THE
FIRST PRESBYTERIAN CHURCH OF ELIZABETHTOWN
1762
AFTER SERVING AS CHAPLAIN IN THE
ARMY OF THE REVOLUTION
AND ACTING AS
COMMISSARY TO THE TROOPS IN NEW-JERSEY
HE WAS KILLED
BY A SHOT FROM A SENTINEL AT
ELIZABETHTOWN-POINT
NOV: 24th 1781

[Caldwell Monument, West side]
HANNAH
WIFE OF THE
REV JAMES CALDWELL
AND DAUGHTER OF

CHURCH YARD, ELIZABETH, N. J.　　65

JOHN OGDEN OF NEWARK
WAS KILLED AT CONNECTICUT FARMS BY A SHOT
FROM A BRITISH SOLDIER
JUNE 25 1780
CRUELLY SACRIFICED
BY THE ENEMIES OF HER HUSBAND
AND HER COUNTRY

---

437 m

SACRED
To THE MEMORY OF
MARGARET MAGRUDER CALDWELL
CONSORT
OF
T ROBINSON RODGERS
DAUGHTER OF
JOSIAH F CALDWELL
OF
WASHINGTON CITY D. C.
WHO DIED
AUGUST 16th A D 1855

---

438 r
In memory of William
son of John & Mary Mills
died Octr 10th 1794 aged
1 year 9 mon^s & 9 days

439 r
M. M.
In Memory of
Mary widow of the
Revd William Mills
who died Apr^l 4th 1794
in the 57th year of her
age

440 m
M. K.
SACRED
To the memory of
MERRITT
son of James
& Martha Kellogg
of Litchfield Connecticut
who departed this life
April 5th 1827
in the 19th year
of his age

Pause youthful stranger view my
　doom
Think not that you can shun the
　tomb

441 m
M. K.
SACRED
To the memory of
MARTHA
WIFE OF
James Kellogg
of Litchfield Connecticut
who departed this life
Novr 27th 1844
Aged 80 Years

442 m
IN
Memory of
PHEBE T
WIDOW OF
AARON WOODRUFF
who died Novr 17th 1857
In the 60th Year
of her age

" For to me to live is Christ
　and to die is gain ,,

443 *m*
IN
Memory of
AARON WOODRUFF
WHO DIED
April 29th 1848
In the 66th Year
of his age

No more the weary Pilgrim mourns
No more affliction wrings his heart
The unfettered soul to God returns
Forever he and anguish part

Receive O earth his faded form
In thy cold bosom let it lie
Safe let it rest from every storm
Soon must it rise no more to die

444 *m*
IN
Memory of
HANNAH O
WIDOW OF
JOHN HIGH
who died Jany 12th 1846
In the 66th Year
of her age

Thus much and this is all we know,
Saints are completely blessed ;
Have done with sin and care below,
And with their Saviour rest.

445 *r*
L. W.
In memory of
Luther son of
Ezekiel and Sarah
Woodruff. died
Octr 14th 1806 in
the 14th Year of
his Age

446 *r*
HERE lies ye Body
of Elizabeth, Wife
of Ezekiel Woodruff
who died Septr ye 9th
Anno Domini 1779
In the XXXV Year
of her Age———

My Time is come
Next may be thine
Prepare for it
Whilst thou hast Time

447 *r*
E W
In memory of
Ezekiel Woodruff
who deceas'd
Jany 14th 1802 in
the 58th Year of
his Age

Press'd by the hand of sore disease
In pain I wander'd on
                      love
Till God my Saviour arm'd with
In mercy call'd me home

448 *r*
S. W.
In memory of
SARAH widow of
Ezekiel Woodruff
who died
April 8th 1822
Aged 73 years

Wait on the Lord ye trembling saints
And keep your courage up :
He'il raise your spirit when it faints
And far exceed your hope.

449 *r*
A. H. W.
In Memory of
ARCHIBALD H WOODRUFF
who departed this life
November 10th 1817
In the 22nd Year of his age

Read on this stone ye passers by
That are sinners born to die
I once had prospects most compleat
                      u
But now i am trod beneath yor feet
I'd health and friends most near & dear
But dont let fall for me a tear
                   u
Mourn for yor sin then mount on high
                   a
Tis sweet on Jesus brest to die

450 r
S. W.
In memory of
SILAS WOODRUFF
who died
July 9th 1819
in the 50th year
of his age

Farewell ye friends whose tender care
Has long engag'd my love
Your fond embrace I now exchange
For better friends above.

451 m
IN
Memory of
MARY
WIDOW OF
SILAS WOODRUFF
who died Nov r 16th 1853
In the 82d Year
of her age

" Blessed are the dead that die in the
Lord."

452 r
E. W.
In memory of
EZEKIEL WOODRUFF
who departed this life
Sept r 3d 1823
in the 46th year
of his age

Wife and children may deplore,
The husband father is no more:
His frugal hands no more provide,
We trust he rests at Jesus side.

453 m
IN
Memory of
ELIZABETH
WIDOW OF
Ezekiel Woodruff
Born Dec r 20th 1780
Died Nov r 17th 1871

" Blessed are the dead that
die in the Lord ,,

454 r
E. W.
In memory of
ELIZABETH
daughter of Ezekiel
& Elizabeth Woodruff
who departed this life
March 9th 1840
Aged 22 years
& 1 month

Now let each furrow'd cheek be dry
And the redeemer's grace adore
Soon shall you mount with me on high
To sing and praise, and part, no
more

455 m
IN
Memory of
ELIZA ANN
wife of
Elias Woodruff
who departed this life
Feb 23rd 1846
Aged 34 Years 2 Months & 17 days

No sickness or sorrow or pain
Shall ever disquiet her now
For death to her spirit was gain
Since Christ was her life when below

456 m
In
memory of
two Children of
Elias & Eliza A
Woodruff
EMMA F
died Aug 6 1834
Aged 6 mo & 26 d's
EZEKIEL D
died Oct 6 1838
aged 3 years
4 mo & 25 d's

Alas how chang'd these lovely flowers
Which bloom'd and cheer'd our
hearts
Fair fleeting comfort of an hour
How soon we're call'd to part

68   INSCRIPTIONS IN FIRST PRESBYTERIAN

457 *r*
IN
Memory of
Col. Ephriam L
Whitlock
who died Sep. 22 1825
Aged 70
Also of
Ann his wife
who died Sep. 21 1826
Aged 64.
Blessed are the dead which die in the
Lord

———

Also of their daughters
Peggy who died Aug 29
1799 A 5 ys
And Sarah who died Ap 1
1801 A 10 ys

458 *m*
AARON RICHARDS
Born
February 19; 1793
Died September 28 1876
Aged 83 Yrs. 7
Mos. & 9 Days

459 *m*
My Brothers Grave
JOHN C RICHARDS
Died
Feb 18th 1851
Aged 28 Years 1 Months
and 16 Days

———

As a Christian, Friend, and only
Brother his loss is deeply felt.
How sweet were the accents that rose
on his breath
When passing the valley and shadow
of death
When to God, his Redeemer his hope
and his stay
His glorified spirit passed swiftly
away

460 *m*
[Small marble block with cross on top]
Simply to thy cross I cling.
WILLIAM
DE HART OGDEN
only child of Alice
& the late
E B Dayton Ogden
Born
June 4th 1863
Died
Jan 12th 1878

———

461 *r*
[Ogden Monument]
[West side]
SACRED
to the
Memory of
E B DAYTON OGDEN
Born
MAY 22 1800
Died
FEB 24 1865

———

[On East side]
Her Hope

And her glory

———

[Ogden Monument, South side]
SACRED
to the memory
of
SUSAN DAYTON
Daughter
of the Reverend
FREDERICK BEASLEY D. D.
grand daughter of
JONATHAN DAYTON
& wife of
E B DAYTON OGDEN

SHE WAS BORN
ON THE 13th OF JUNE 1805
AND DIED
ON THE 7th OF APRIL 1848
IN THE FAITH AND PATIENCE
OF THE GOSPEL
SHE WAS
A TRUE DAUGHTER
OF THE CHURCH
AND
IN THE LANGUAGE
OF THE BISHOP OF THE DIOCESE
WHO KNEW HER FROM HER YOUTH
AND
WAS WITH HER
ALMOST TO THE LAST
"THE MODEL
OF A CHRISTIAN LADY
AND A CHRISTIAN MOTHER"

"Right dear in the sight of the Lord
is the death of his Saints,,

[North side blank]

---

462 r
[Col. Aaron Ogden Monument]
[On West side]
Col Aaron Ogden L. L. D.
ob April XIX,
MDCCCXXXIX an. æt. LXXXIII
And his Consort
Elisabeth Chetwood
ob Sept. XXVII
MDCCCXXVI an. æt. LX.
OGDEN

[On North side]
I am
The Resurection
and
The Life
saith
The Lord

[Ogden Monument]
[South side]
Their Children
E B Dayton ob Aug VIII
MDCCXCIX an. æt. II

Aaron ob Oct V
MDCCCOIII æt VI months

John Robert ob. Jan XXII,
MDCCCXLV an. æt LI.

[On East side]
Matthias ob July XVII,
MDCCCLX ; an æt LXVIII

Mary C. Wife of G C Barber
ob Mar. XXIII
MDCCCLXIII an æt LXXIV.

Phebe Ann ob Nov XXX
MDCCCLXV an æt LXXV.

[Horizontal slab]
463 r
Sacred to the Memory of
SARAH PLATT
Daughter of Zopher & Rebekah Platt
Wife of Robert Ogden Junior Esquire
Serjeant at Law
She died in Childbed January 21st 1782
In the 31st Year of her Age

In the Bloom of Life
Adorned with every outward Grace
Enriched with every Christian Virtue
She bid adieu to Earth and went to
Heaven
  Twas the Survivor died !
Grief worn traveller !
Go learn Submission to the Will of
God
Permanent Felicity is not
  For Man on Earth

INSCRIPTIONS IN FIRST PRESBYTERIAN

464 *r*

[Horizontal]
This Tablet is inscribed in memory of
Mary Barber
Wife of Francis Barber and Daughter
Of Robert and Phebe Ogden
Who died October 7th 1773 in ye 21st Year
Of her age

She adorned every character she sustained
In life and augmented the felicity of
All around her
In her you saw a Pattern of Fillial Duty
Fidelity to her Friends, Love to her Husband
And unfeigned Piety to her God
By him she had been divinely taught
That One Thing was Needful
So that
The intruding cares of Connubial Life
Interrupted not her Homage to the
Great Parent of All

Reader! E'er yet thou pass this Earthly scene
Revere her name & be what she has been!

---

465 *r*
Here lies interred the
Body of phebe Ogden
Dec'd Octr ye 14 1735
In ye 17th year of her Age
is this ye fate that all must die
will Death no Ages spair
then let us All to Jesus flie
and seek for refuge there

466 *r*
Here Lyeth The
Body of Mrs Hannah
Ogden, Wife of Robert
Ogden who Slept in
Jesus October 30th
1726 Ætatis Suæ 36

467 *r*
Here ly the
Remains of Robert
Ogden Esqr O b i j t
Novr 20th A. D.
1733 Æ t a t

46
One dear to God to Man most dear
A Pillar in both Church & State
Was he whose precious Dust lies here
Whose Soul doth with bright Seraphs mate
His Name immortal shall remain
Till this cold Clay revive again

468 *r*
[Horizontal]
To the Memory of
Mrs Hannah Ogden
Daughter of
Genl Elias Dayton
& Relict of
Genl Matthias Ogden
who died 11th Decr 1802
Aged 44 Years

Jane Chandler Ogden
her daughter
died 9th Sepr 1789
Aged 10 months

---

[466] Daughter of Jasper Crane.
[467] Son of Jonathan and Rebecca Ogden.

469 r

[Horizontal]

Sacred to the memory of
General Matthias Ogden
who died on the 31st day of March 1791
Aged XXXVI years

In him were united those various virtues
of the Soldier the Patriot and the Friend
which endear men to society.
Distress failed not to find relief in his
bounty.
Unfortunate merit a refuge in his
generosity.

If manly sense and dignity of mind
If social virtues lib'ral and refin'd
Nipp'd in their bloom deserve compassion's tears
Then reader Weep, for Ogden's dust lies here

Weed his grave clean ye men of genius
for he was your kinsman
Tread lightly on his ashes ye men of feeling
for he was your brother

---

470 r

[Horizontal]

Here lies entombed
In expectation of the resurrection
of the Saints
The Body
of Mary Stockton relict
of Job Stockton Esqr
of Princeton
She lived
A generous Benefactor to the poor,
A tender Parent of the orphan
In her friendship open and candid
Inculcating and practising virtue
She set an example of undesembled Piety
She died
In the hope of the Gospel of Jesus
on the 29th Day of January
A. D. 1795
Aged 65 Years & 7 Months

---

[470] Daughter of Robert and Phebe Ogden.

471 *m*
REV. THOMAS A. OGDEN
DIED
Dec. 8. 1878.
In the 77th Year of
his age

Also his Nurse
MARY DRAKE
Died Jan. 17. 1826.
In the 83d Year of
her age.

The sweet remembrance of the just,
Shall flourish when they sleep in dust.

472 *r*
Sacred to the Memory
of Stephen Crane Esqr who
departed this life July ye 1st
A. D. 1780. In the 71st Year
of his Age.

Having been
Elected for a series of Years
to ye chief Magistracy of ye Place
and to a Seat
in the Grand Council of ye State
He
discharged the Duties of those
important Stations,
with strict Integrity and
general Approbation.

473 *r*
HERE lies interr'd
the Remains of Mrs.
Phebe. the wife of
Stephen Crane Esqr
who departed this
Life Augt ye 28th Ano
Dom 1776 In ye 62^d
Year of her Age

474 *r*

Here Lieth ye Body
of Daniel Craine
Deceased February
ye 24 A^o 172¾
In ye 51 Year of his
Age.

Here Lieth ye Body
of Daniel Crane
Junr Deceased y^e
25 of February A^o
172¾ In ye 20 Year
of his Age.

475 *r*
HERE lies ye Body
of Phebe Wife of
Stephen Crane Esq
who departed this
Life March ye 10th
A. D. 1786 In y^o 38th
Year of her Age.

She was the Mother of
11 Children.

476 *r*
In memory of
Stephen Crane who
died Feb. the 11th 1796 in
the 59th year of his age

477 *m*
[Horizontal]
SACRED
To the Memory of
General WILLIAM CRANE
who died July 30 1814
Aged 67 years

One of the firmest patriots of
our revolution ; in the darkest period
of his country's oppression & danger,
he volunteered in her cause & was
wounded in her defence.
Probity, benevolence and patriotism
characterized his life.
He lived beloved & died lamented
———o———

---

471 Son of Elias and Mary Anderson Ogden.

CHURCH YARD, ELIZABETH, N. J.

His sons have caused this monument a
faint tribute of gratitude & affection
to be erected over his grave
———o———
Also of
ABIGAIL CRANE wife of
Gen¹ William Crane, who died July 22ᵈ
1825, Aged 62 years

478 *m*
IN
Memory of
JOANNA M
WIFE OF
John O. Mage, and
Daughter of William,
and Abigail Crane ;
who died Janʸ 30ᵗʰ 1820
In the 22ⁿᵈ Year
of her age

"Oh Mother! who is left to love as
thou hast lov'd ;
For the cold grave did veil thee early
from my sight
But I will strive as best such frail
one may,
To follow thee to Heaven."

A tribute of a Daughter's affection

479 *r*
P. M. C.
SACRED
To the Memory of
PHEBE M. daughter
of William & Abigail
Crane : who died
February 28ᵗʰ 1820 ;
in the 25ᵗʰ year
of her age

Also, three children of
William & Abigail Crane ;
MARIA, died Augˢᵗ 3ʳᵈ 1785
Aged 7 months.
SARAH died Augˢᵗ 7ᵗʰ 1786
Aged 3 months
CHARLES died Augˢᵗ 9ᵗʰ 1789
Aged 3 months

480 *r*
J. C
In memory of
JANE widow of
Stephen Crane Esqʳ
who died
Janʸ 29ᵗʰ 1822
Aged 61 years

Why was unbelieving I
Trembling so afraid to die
Now my feet in safety stand
Here within the promis'd land

481 *m*
IN
MEMORY OF
MARY
DAUGHTER OF
Stephen and Jane Crane
who died May 2ᵈ 1826 :
In the 38ᵗʰ Year
of her age

"For this corruptible must put on incorruption and this mortal must put
on immortality."

There is a world we have not seen
That wasting time can ne'er destroy
Where mortal footsteps hath not been ;
Nor ear hath caught its sounds of joy.

482 *r*
W. M.
In memory of
WILLIAM MILLER
who died
July 15ᵗʰ 1817 ;
in the 51ˢᵗ year
of his age.

Also two children
of William & Sarah Miller
MOSES died Janʸ 31ˢᵗ 1800
aged 7 months & 3 days
ESTHER C. died Octʳ 19ᵗʰ 1807
aged 5 years 11 months
& 3 days

INSCRIPTIONS IN FIRST PRESBYTERIAN

483 *r*
In memory of
Ann wife of
William Miller who
departed this life July
the 18th 1795 in the 28th
Year of her age

Susanna Daughter of William
& Anne Miller died Nov'
the 4th 1793 aged 16 months

484 *m*
JOANNA
WIFE OF
CHARLES MILLER
died Dec' 3d 1859;
Aged 46 Years and
6 Months

Farewell my Partner and my Friends,
Our sufferings here soon have an end
Farewell dear Children my life is past
My love to you while life did last
Then after me no sorrow take
But love each other for my sake

485 *m*
IN
MEMORY
of
STEPHEN O. MARSH
who died
Aug. 21, 1841.
Aged 29 Years
and 11 Months

Stop passing stranger drop one tear,
A Husband Father Friend lies here

486 *m*
IN
Memory of
JOHN MORSE
SON OF
Stephen O. & Joanna
MARSH
who died
July 30th 1843;
Aged 8 years 7 months
and 22 days

Oh what is life! tis like a flower
That blossoms & is gone
Death comes and like a wintry day
It cuts the lovely flower away.

487 *r*
HERE lies y^e Body of
Mrs. Elizabeth wife
of Mr. Saml Miller
who deceas'd Nov^m
the 13th A D. 1747,
In y^e 73^d Year of her
Age

488 *r*
Here Lyeth y^e Body
Of Sam^{ll} Miller Junr
Dec'd= March y^e 29th
1732 in y^e 27th year
Of his Age.

489 *r*
HERE lies y^e Body of
Mr. Samuel Miller.
who deceas'd March
the 14th A. D. 1759,
In the 85th Year of his
Age

490 *m*
EMELINE
DAUGHTER OF
SAMUEL MILLER
DIED NOVEMBER 27th 1864,
AGED 39 YEARS &
8 MONTHS

My Master calls me I must go
My friends weep not for me
Gladly I leave you here below
Hoping each one in heaven to see

491 *m*
MARGARET
WIFE OF
SAMUEL MILLER
DIED JANY 27th, 1862,
AGED 81 YEARS &
2 MONTHS

"I know that my Redeemer liveth,,

492 *m*
SAMUEL MILLER
DIED
JANY. 30TH, 1860
AGED 82 YEARS &
3 MONTHS

He sleepeth.

'I will keep him in perfect peace
whose mind is stayed on Thee,
because he trusteth in Thee.,,

493 *r*
D. C.
In memory of
DAVID
son of Finley &
Jemima Chandler
who died Feby 15th
1812 aged 18 years
7 months & 15 days.

My dear youth when you pass me by
Remember you must be laid as low
as I.

494 *r*
HERE lies the
Body of Abigail
Chandler who died
Septr the 9th
A. D. 1763. In ye 26th
Year of her Age—

495 *r*
HERE lies ye Remains of
Mary Wife of Samuel
Chandler who died
Novr the 4th A. D. 1763,
In ye 58th Year of her Age.

Tho' in the Dust I lay my Head,
  Yet gracious God, thou wilt not
   leave
My Soul forever with the Dead,
  Nor lose thy Children in the Grave.

496 *r*
HERE lies the Body
of Benjamin Chandler
who departed this Life
June the 14th A. D. 1767
In ye 28th Year of his
Age————

497 *r*
In memory of
Sarah Chandler who
died Jany the 9th 1794,
in the 47th year of
her age.

498 *r*
S. C.
In memory of
SARAH,
widow of
Deac. David Chandler.
who died
March 31st 1830.
In the 83^d year
of her age.

When christians part they have this
 joy
They soon shall meet again above
Where distance shall no more annoy
Nor sin obstruct their warmest love.

499 *r*
In memory of
Deac^n David Chandler
who died Janu^y the 3^d
1786, in the 44th year
of his age
When this you see, rememb^r me:

500 *r*
Here lies the Body
of Moses Winans
who died June ye 26
1788 In ye 43^d Year of
his Age

Weep not for me my frien^d
For why! my Race is run
It is the Will of God
And let his Will be done

INSCRIPTIONS IN FIRST PRESBYTERIAN

501 r
Here Lyeth ye Body of
Zeruiah Winance Wife
of Samuel winance
Who Departed this
Life September ye 13th
Anno Dom. 1737 in y^e
53^d year of her Age.

502 r
Here Lyeth ye body
of phebe Daf^{tr} of
Sam'll & Zeruiah
Winance who dec^{ed}
octob^r ye 30th 1735 in y^e
10th year of her age.

503 r
HERE lies interr'd
what was Mortal of
Mr. Samuel Winans
who departed this Life
Septr ye 27th A. D. 1747.
In the LXXVII Year of
his Age———
I'll take a turn among the Tombs,
And see whereto all Glory comes:
There the vile Foot of every Clown,
Tramples the Sons of Honor down.

504 r
HERE lies ye Body
of Samuel Son of
Samuel & Hannah
Winans who died
Octr ye 9th 1774,
In the 19th Year of
his Age———

505 m
IN
MEMORY OF
WILLIAM W WOODRUFF
WHO DIED
June 17th 1850
Aged 32 Years 4 Months
and 28 Days

506 r
[Horizontal Slab]

HERE lies the Body of
Mrs Hannah Winans
the much esteemed widow
of Mr Samuel Winans
who departed this life
March ye 14th A. D. 1783,
In the LXIX Year of her
Age.
A virtuous Woman is a
Crown to her Husband.

HERE lies the Body of
Mr. Samuel Winans
the Honour'd Husband
of Mrs. Hannah Ogden
who departed this life
Decem^r 22^d A. D. 1772.
in the LXIII Year of his
Age.
An honest man the noblest
work of God,

THEIR DAUGHTERS
Miss Frances Winans
deceas'd June the 20th
An^o Domini 1746 in ye 15th
Year of her Age———
Phebe died Octo^r 18th
A. D. 1745 in the 8th
Year of her Age———
Zeruiah died June 15th
A. D. 1746, in the 5th
Year of her Age———
Hannah died Augt 6th
A. D. 1754. in the 6th
Year of her Age———

THEIR SONS
Mr. Jonathan Winans,
died of the Small Pox,
Feby ye 22^d 1771, in ye 24th
Year of his Age———
Samuel, died Septr 28th
A. D. 1740, in the 6th
Year of his Age———
2^d Samuel died June 19th
A. D. 1746, in the 4th
Year of his Age———
John, died Septem^r 14th
A. D. 1746, in the 2^d
Year of his Age.

Eight lovely Flow'rs cropt off in early Bloom.
Are here interr'd around this mournful Tomb.

^{506} Daughter of Robert and Hannah Crane Ogden.

CHURCH YARD, ELIZABETH, N. J. 77

507 r
Here Is
Interr'd the Body of mr^s
Joanna Dickinson —— Obiit April 20th
1 7 4 5 . Anno Æ tat 63.
Rest precious Dust till Christ revive this Clay
To Join the Triumphs of the Judgement Day.

---

508 r
Here is interred
The Remains of Miss
Joanna Dickinson

Daughter of ye Revrd
Mr Jonathan Dickins^{on}
Nat. Feb. 27. 1716
Obijt May 9 1732.

---

509 r
[Horizontal Slab]
HERE
Lyes ye Body of ye Rev^d
Mr Jonathan Dickinson Pastor
of the First Presbyterian Church
In Elizabeth Town who Died Oct^r
ye 7th 1747, Æ tatis Suæ 60.

Deep was the Wound Oh Death & Vastly wide
When he resigned his Useful breath and dy'd
Y^e Sacred Tribe with pious Sorrows mourn
And drop a tear at your great Pastors Urn
  a
Concel'd a moment from our Longing Eyes
Beneath this Stone his mortal Body Lies
Happy the Spirit lives and will we trust
  c
In Bliss associate with his preious dust

---

510 r
Here lies the Body of
Elizabeth Wife of
Jonathan Miller
Dau^r of the Rev^d
Jonathan Dickinson.
Who departed this
Life Nov^{br} 27 1788
in the 68th Year of
her age

511 r
Joseph : Son of
George & Mary
Armstrong Aged 13
years.   Dec$^{d=}$
May y^e 14th 1737

512 r
Catharine Dau^r of
George & Mary
Armstrong Aged 1
year & 2 m^o Dec^d= Feb^{ry}
y^e 5th 1736 7

513 r
IN MEMORY OF
Miss Catharine Daughter
of the Revd Danl Thane &
Mrs Mary Clowes who
deceas'd July 12th Anno
Domini 1771 in the 20th
Year of her Age———
Tho : I am wraped in the Shroud
A forsaken Nymph alone
My Soul joins y^e triumphant Crowd.
Who bow before the Throne.

514 *r*
IN
memory of
MOSES MOORE
who died Oct 19th 1829
aged 31 years 8 months
and 9 days.

Let friends no more my sufferings
  mourn
Nor view my relics with concern
O, cease to drop the pitying tear
I've past beyond the reach of fear

515 *r*
IN
memory of
SARAH ELENOR
daughter of
Moses & Catharine
Moore,
who died April 21st 1830
aged 3 years 8 months
and 4 days.

In all she did
or spoke or sung,
A nameless spell
about her hung,
An air so sweet
it seemed to tell
She was not long
on earth to dwell.

516 *m*
IN
Memory of
CATHARINE
WIDOW OF
MOSES MOORE
who died
June 4, 1846:
Aged 45 Years
and 7 Months

517 *r*
S. M.
In memory of
SARAH
wife of
David Moore
who died
May 6th 1834,
Aged 68 years.

Sweet soul we leave thee to thy rest,
  Enjoy thy Jesus and thy God ;
Till we from bands of Clay releas'd
  Spring out and climb the shining
  road

518 *r*
D M
In memory of
DAVID MOORE
who died
March 12th 1835
Aged 63 years

This hour perhaps our friend is well,
The next we hear his passing bell ;
He dies, and then for aught we see,
Ceases at once to breathe and be.

519 *r*
In memory of
Ichabod Grumman
who died
December the 16th 1788
in the 65th year
of his age.

520 *r*
Here lies ye Body
of Bethiah wife
of Ichabod
Grommon   who
Died July 10: 1766
Aged 53 Year

521 *r*

In Memory of
Agar Arnett Son
of James & Jemima
Arnett Decd Janry
ye 30 1757 Aged
8 months & 2 Ds

In Memory of
David Arnett Junr
Son of James &
Jemima Arnett Decd
Augt ye 26th 1757 Aged
8 years & 8 mo

CHURCH YARD, ELIZABETH, N. J.

522 r
M. W.
In memory of
MARGARET
wife of
Benjamin M. Woodruff,
who died April 14th 1826
Aged 32 years

Cheerful I leave this vale of tears
Where pains and sorrows grow,
Welcome the day that ends my toil
And every scene of wo.

My dearest friends they dwell above
Them will I go to see,
And all my friends in Christ below
Will soon come after me.

523 m
IN
Memory of
MARY A
WIFE OF
Melvin D. Decker;
who died July 21st 1852,
In the 26th Year
of her age
Also
MARY ANN
their infant daughter
died Augst 12th 1852,
aged 3 months

524 m
IN
Memory of
WILLIAM BALDWIN
who died Septr 17th 1799
Aged 40 Years

ALSO
his two daughters,
PHEBE,
died Feby 25th 1800
Aged 2 Months.
CORNELIA,
died June, 1808;
Aged 20 Years

525 r
Here lies
the Remains of
Mr MATTHIAS BALD-
-WIN, who died July ye 1st 1759,
aged XL Years
He was a good Neighbour
A generous Friend
An earnest promoter of the
PUBLIC GOOD
A kind Father, a tender Husband
In short he was
A CHRISTIAN
PASSENGER
Imitate him & be forever
HAPPY.

526 r
Here lies ye Body of
Joanna Daur of
Matthias & Mary
Baldwin Decd ye 9th
of Decer 1753, aged
1 year 8 Mo & 12 Days

527 m
FANNY C BALDWIN
DIED
NOVEMBER 23rd. 1842
AGED 57 YEARS

528 m
ELIZABETH ALBEY
DIED
JANUARY 26th 1872
AGED 65 YEARS

529 m
ELIZABETH BALDWIN,
WIFE OF
DAVID ALBEY,
DIED
JANUARY 17th, 1807,
AGED 27 YEARS
THEIR DAUGHTER
PHEBE E. ALBEY
AGED 3 YEARS

530 *m*
ELIZABETH THOMPSON
WIFE OF
JOHN BALDWIN
DIED
DECEMBER 6th, 1842
AGED 88 YEARS

---

531 *m*
PETER BALDWIN
DIED
SEPTEMBER 3RD, 1826
AGED 50 YEARS

---

532 *m*
To the
Memory of
JANE PRICE
WIFE OF
RICHARD CAMPBELL,
who died
March 13, 1858:
Aged 57 Years.

---

533 *r*
M. P.
In memory of
MARY
wife of
William Price
who died Decr 3^d
1809 in the 22^d
year of her
Age

---

534 *r*
In memory of
Nathaniel Price who died
Septr 7th 1807. Aged 25 years
Also
Abigail his wife who died
Septr 17th 1807 Aged 25 years
Likewise
their only child Wm Erastus
died Septr 22^d 1807, Aged 8 mon^s

O pencive mourner stay thy footsteps
  here,
And on these graves pour forth a
  grateful tear
Such as fond memory, on these be-
  stow,
Who whilst they lived could feel for
  others woe;
If sympathy at sorrows shrine can bow
A threefold cause demands that trib-
  ute now,
For o beneath this monumental stone,
Lies a fond husband wife & only son.

---

535 *r*
  ory of
  T. Price
[Broken off] ed April 22^d
  06 in the
  47th year of
  his age

---

536 *m*
S. C. M.
In memory of
SARAH C.
daughter of
William T. Price
and wife of
John R. Marsh
of the City of New York
who died
April 19th 1831
Aged 32 years 11 months
and 20 days

Go home my friends and dry your
  tears
I must lie here till Christ appears,
A few more days and you must lie
In the cold grave as well as I.

---

537 *r*
ANNA,
YOUNGEST DAUGHTER OF
MARY CHETWOOD
& GEORGE CLINTON
BARBER
BORN, FEB. 22nd 1829,
DIED AUG. 8th. 1861.

CHURCH YARD, ELIZABETH, N. J. 81

538 *m*
IN
MEMORY OF
GEORGE C. BARBER
an Elder of this Church
who died Octr 29th 1828
Aged 49 Years.

"A good and faithful servant he has
entered into the joys of his Lord,,

Children of
George C. and Mary C. Barber

GEORGE C. BARBER
Lieut. U. S. Army died of yellow
fever Octr 11th 1853, in Indianola
Texas, where his remains now
rest, aged 26 years

GEORGE CLINTON
died July 31, 1826 aged 4 years

PHEBE ANN OGDEN
died Feb. 20, 1816 aged 21 days

539 *r*
IN MEMORY OF
Moses Ogden
who was killed at
Connecticut Farms
June ye 7th A. D. 1780
In the 20th Year of his
Age

This lovely Youth
Adorned with Truth
A brave commander shone
His Soul emerging from its Dust
With his Progenetors we trust
Shall shine in Realms unknown

540 *m*
IN
Memory of
M^{rs} ANN BARBER
who died
July 17th 1825,
Aged 67 years

Relict of
Lt. Col. FRANCIS BARBER
who died
February 11th 1783,
in the 33^d year
of his age

541 *r*
HERE LIETH
the Remains of Mr Moses
Ogden who departed
this Life Octr y^e 14th
Anno Domini 1768
In the 46th Year
of his Age

542 *r*
D. O.
Here lieth in hope of a joyful
resurection. the body of
David Ogden who was born
Oct 26, $^{o. s.}$ 1726, and who died in
the triumphs of faith Nov. 28, N. S.
1801, for 57 years he adorned
the Christian profession by a
holy & exemplary life ; & for 15
years discharged the duties
of a Deacon to the first Pres-
beterian Church in this Town
with prudence fidelity &
acceptance,

Softly his fainting head he lay
Upon his saviours breast
His saviour kiss'd his soul away
And laid his flesh to rest,

543 *r*
In memory of
Hannah wife of
David Ogden. She
died May the 17th
1793, in the 74th
year of her age.

---

[540] Dau. of Moses Ogden, No. 541, and Mary Cozzens.
[542] Son of Robert Ogden ; married Hannah Woodruff, No. 543.

INSCRIPTIONS IN FIRST PRESBYTERIAN

544 *r*
HERE LIETH
interr'd ye Body of
Mr Joseph Ogden
who deceas'd April
the 29th A. D. 1761.
In the fifty third
Year of his
Age.

545 *r*
Here lies ye Body
of Sam^{ll} Scott dec^d
October ye 29. 1723
Aged 30 years.

546 *r*
Here lieth ye Body
of Martha Thompson.
Wife of Mr John Thompson.
who departed this life
July the 16th A^o 1728
Aged in her 50 Years.

547 *m*
IN
Memory of
JOB CRANE,
WHO DIED
DEC^r 17th 1848,
IN THE 62^d YEAR
OF HIS AGE

548 *m*
IN
Memory of
MARY B. CRANE
WIFE OF JOB CRANE
WHO DIED
AUGUST 15th 1873
IN THE 86th YEAR
OF HER AGE

549 *m*
IN
memory of
three daughters of
Job & Mary Crane

ELIZA died
Decr 16th 1832 Aged 4
years & 8 months
SARAH W. died
Jany 8th 1836 Aged 13
years & 10 months
JULIA ANN died
Feby 7th 1838 Aged 4
Yeas & 8 months.

550 *m*
IN
MEMORY OF
JOHN WOOD
WHO DIED
NOV. 26. 1727,
AGED 24 YEARS & 2 MO.

550½ *r*
[Is right against 550]
Jeremy Wood
Disceased May
the 21 A^o 1729
Aged 2 Years 7
Months & 21 Days

551 *m*
SACRED
To
THE MEMORY OF
JOHN WOOD
WHO DIED
APRIL 25th 1846
AGED 85 YEARS
1 MONTH AND
3 DAYS

552 *m*
SACRED
To
THE MEMORY OF
SARAH WOOD
wife of John Wood
WHO DIED JULY 17, 1841;
AGED 76 YEARS 8 MO.
& 23 DAYS

CHURCH YARD, ELIZABETH, N. J.   83

553 m
In
memory
of
NATHAN MORSE
son of Job and
Amy C. Winans;
who died
Feby 9th 1835,
Aged 1 year 3 months
and 18 days

Life is like a flower
That blossoms & is gone
We see it flourish for an hour
With all its beauty on
But death comes like a wintry day
And cuts the pretty flower away.

554 m
JOB WINANS
DIED
Aug. 26th 1872,
Aged 67 yrs.
6 mo. & 20 days.

555 m
AMY C WINANS
DIED
April 21st 1880
Aged 70 yrs.
8 mo & 10 days

556 m
IN
Memory of
JOB WINANS
SON OF
John & Phebe K. Force
who died Augst 19th 1848
Aged 5 Years and
8 months.

He had no mother's tender care
To soothe his dying cries, but he
Who heard her dying prayer
Has taken him to the skies.

557 m
IN
Memory of
SUSAN LEE
DAUGHTER OF
John & Phebe K. Force
WHO DIED
Septr 14th 1843 :
Aged 2 Years 11 Months
and 25 Days

Sweet blossom evermore adieu :
A Seraph bright calls thee away
Thou'll bloom again with brighter hue
In realms of bliss and endless day.

558 m
IN
Memory of
PHEBE KING
WIFE OF
JOHN FORCE
who died Novr 8th 1844
Aged 23 Years 1 Month
and 13 Days

Dear friend thou hast left us,
Here thy loss we deeply feel :
But 'tis God that hath bereft us
He can all our sorrows heal.

558½ m
[This stone is set close against the back of
558 & 559]
In
memory
of
ABBY WOOD
daughter of Joseph
& Polly Morse
who died May 15th
1827, Aged 3 years
& 5 days

Alas how changed that lovely flower
Which bloom'd and cheer'd my
  heart
Fair fleeting comfort of an hour
How soon we're call'd to part.

559 *m*
IN
Memory of
POLLY
WIFE OF
JOSEPH MORSE
WHO DIED
Septr 25th 1847
Aged 57 Years.

She has past the waves of trouble here
She has gone beyond the reach of fear
No more she hears the gospel sound
But lies here mouldering under
ground

560 *m*
JOSEPH D MORSE
DIED
April 11th 1852.
Aged 70 years. 2 m^{os}
& 7 days.

561 *r*
IN
memory of
Esther widow of
Cooper Woodruff
who died Jany 15th 1802
in the 63^d year of
her Age

Dear Father if thy lifted rod
Resolve to scourge us here below
Still we must lean upon our God
Thine arm shall bear us safely thro^{ugh}

562 *r*
In memory of
Cooper Woodruff
who died Apr^l the
2^d 1792 in ye LXXXth
year of his age.

563 *r*
M. W.
In Memory of
Mary Wife of Cooper
Woodruff & Daughter
of Nathaniel and
Elizabeth Mitchel
died June 7th 1766 In
the 41st Year of her Age

Death is a debt to mortals due
I've paid that debt and so must you.

564 *r*
S. W.
SACRED
To THE MEMORY OF
SARAH WOODRUFF
who died
Octr 7th 1824
in the 67th year
of her age

565 *m*
JOHN S MILLER
DIED
AUGUST 26th 1871.
AGED 56 YEARS

'For I know that my Redeemer
liveth and that he shall stand
at the latter day upon the earth,,

566 *m*
RACHAL ANN
WIFE OF
JOHN S MILLER
and daughter of
WARREN & MARY C. BROWN
DIED FEB. 12th 1865
AGED 35 YEARS 6 MO.
& 2 DAYS

Oh! Death where is thy sting
Oh! Grave where is thy Victory.
1 Cor, XV. 55.
Thanks be unto God who hath
given us the Victory through
our Lord Jesus Christ
1 Cor XV. 57.

567 *r*
Here lyes ye Body of
David Olliver Dec^d
Novr ye 12th 1747.
in ye 55   year
of his Age.

568 *r*
Here lyeth ye Body
of Samuel Oliver
Who Departed this
Life May ye 15th 1744.
In the 58th year of
His age.

569 *r*
Here lies ye Body of
Sarah wife of M^r
Samuel Oliver who
Died April ye 9 1735
Aged 47 years

570 *r*
Here lies ye Body
of Hannah wife of
David Oliver Dec^d
Feby ye 29 1735-6
Aged 43 years

571 *r*
Here lies ye Body
of Jonathan Oliver
who died Decem^r
ye 28 1733
Aged 34 years

572 *r*
Here lyes ye Body of
Mary Wife of Samuel
Oliver Aged 62 years
& 6 m^o Dec^d Jan^{ry}
ye 23^d 1729

573 *r*
S. O.
In memory of
SARAH
widow of
John N. Oliver
who died
June 22^d 1835
Aged 73 years

574 *r*
J. N. O.
In Memory of
JOHN N. OLIVER
who died
Novr 11th 1813
in the 61st year
of his age

575 *r*
J. O.
In Memory of
James Oliver
who died Dec^r
22^d 1809
in the 30th year
of his
Age

576 *r*
J. O.
In memory of
James son of
James & Elizabeth
Oliver. died
Jany 2^d 1809
aged 3 months

577 *r*
Rhoda daughter
of John N. & Sarah
Oliver died Aug^t
ye 2^d 1782 aged 4
months

INSCRIPTIONS IN FIRST PRESBYTERIAN

578 r
John Nicholas son
of John N & Sarah
Oliver died March
the 23 1793 in y^e
4th year of his age

---

579 m
L W
SACRED
To the memory of
LEWIS WOODRUFF
who departed this life
February 1st 1827
in the 32^d year
of his age

Ah! could affection, admiration save
So dear an object from the untimely
  grave
This transcript faint had not essay'd
  to tell
The loss of one beloved, revered so
  well

---

580 r
W. W.
In memory of
Whitehead son of
Baker & Mary
Woodruff, died
Septr 28th 1806
in the 29th year
of his age

Therefore be ye also ready
Matthew 24 & 44.

---

581 r
S. H. W.
In memory of
SARAH HENRY
daughter of Baker &
Sarah Woodruff, who died
Jany 29th 1816 aged 11 years
4 months & 8 days

And is the lovely shadow fled
  The blooming wonder of her years
So soon enshrin'd among the dead
  She justly claims our pious tears

582 r
S. W.
In memory of
SARAH widow of
Baker Woodruff
who died
Decr 21st 1816
in the 54th year
of her age

Insatiate archer! could not one suffice?
Thy shaft slew thrice and thrice
  our peace was slain

---

583 r
B. W.
In memory of
BAKER WOODRUFF
who died Decr 12th 1813
in the 63^d year
of his age

Wife and children may deplore
The husband, father, is no more
His frugal hands no more provide
We trust he rests at Jesus side

---

584 r
Sacred to the Me-
-mory of Mary
Wife of Baker Wood-
ruff. who died Dec^r
ye 7th 1790. In the
XXXIX Year of her
Age

Return unto thy Rest, O my
Soul, for the Lord hath dealt
Bountifully with Thee. Psal.
CXVI. 7th

---

585 r
J. W.
Jabez Son of Baker
& Mary Woodruff. died
Novr IV 1799. In the
XII Year of his Age

CHURCH YARD, ELIZABETH, N. J. 87

586 r
Whitehead, Son of
Baker and Mary
Woodruff, died Sep^t
the 29th 1776, aged
1 Year & 4 Months.

587 m
To the Memory
of
MARY ANN
wife of
John J Bryant
who died
Feby 14th 1838
Æ 40

588 m
To the Memory of
JANE V
wife of
John J Bryant
and daughter of
Baker & Sarah Woodruff
who died April 5th
1829 Æ 30

There remaineth therefore
a Rest to the people of God
Heb. IV. 9.

589 m
JOHN JAY BRYANT
DIED
JUNE 29th 1859
AGED 60 YEARS

SARAH JANE
WIFE OF
JOHN JAY BRYANT
DIED
DEC^r 26th 1865

[The last 11 are in Woodruff plot]

590 r
Jane Daughter of
Nathaniel & Mar^y
Woodruff, who
died March the
26th A D. 1758
Age^d 7 Months

591 r
[Face of stone all scaled off and gone]

592 r
In Memory of
Aaron Woodruff who
died Augt ye 29th 1780
In the 22^d Year of his
Age.

593 r
Mary Ann Daughter
of Nathaniel & Mary
Woodruff. died March
the 28th 1771 In ye 18th
Year of her Age———

594 r
Mary Wife of
Nathaniel Woodruff
died June ye 14th
A. D. 1770. In ye 48th
Year of her Age———

595 r
Here lies the Body
of Nathan^l Woodruff
who died Jany ye 17th
A. D. 1777. In the 59th
Year of his Age———

596 r
Here lyeth Seth son of
Timothy & Elizabeth
Woodruff. who died
Novr ye 12th Anno
Domini 1740 aged
3 months & 23 days

INSCRIPTIONS IN FIRST PRESBYTERIAN

597 *m*
In memory
of
CHARITY
daughter of
Enos and Charity Woodruff
who died April 12th 1845
In the 53 Year
of her age

598 *m*
In Memory
of
CHARITY
widow of
Enos Woodruff
who died Septr 5th 1828
In the 76th Year
of her age

599 *m*
In memory
of
ENOS WOODRUFF
who died
Decr 5th 1821
In the 72^d Year
of his age

600 *r*
T. W.   H. W.   P. W.
In memory of three Children, of
Enos and Charity Woodruff
Timothy died Sept 3^d 1776, aged
III Years X months and XXV days
Hannah died Sept 18th 1776 aged 2
Years 2 months and 28 days
Phebe died Sept 30th 1792 aged
1 Year 10 months and 25 days

601 *r*
E. W.
In memory of
Elizabeth wife of
Timothy Woodruff
who died Sepr 16th
1776 In the LXIVth
year of her age

602 *r*
T W
In memory of
Timothy Woodruff
who died
April 26 1798 in the
83^d year of his age

Cut by
Stewart & Ross
E—— Town

603 *m*
IN
Memory of
MARY
wife of
Timothy Woodruff
who died
March 16th 1818
Aged 39 Years

Also
MARY
daughter of
Timothy & Mary Woodruff
who died
Aug. 3rd 1823
Aged 15 Years
" The Lord reigneth,.

604 *r*
A. M. C.
In memory of
Ann M. wife of
William Christy Jun
who died March 25th
1822 Aged 25 years

Also
John Wesley their son
who died March 15th 1821
Aged 15 months

Around the azure throne of God
The soul now takes its high abode
To dwell in heavenly peace ;
Among the saints & angels blest.
It shall partake of endless rest
In joys that ne'er decrease

605 r
Elias R. son of
Elias and Jane
Sayre died June
the 28th 1793 aged
6 months

---

606 r
HERE lies the Body
of Anna, Wife of
Daniel Sayre who
deceas'd April yᵉ 2ᵈ
A. D. 1773. in the 26th
Year of her Age——

---

607 m
IN
Memory of
JANE
widow of
Matthew Decker,
who died
March 21st 1839
Aged 38 Years 4 Months
and 17 days

I leave this world without a tear,
Save for the friends that linger here,
To heal their Sorrows Lord decend
And to the friendless prove a friend

---

608 m
THOMAS O SAYRE
Died
Oct 20th 1864
Aged 63 years.

For ten years a faithful elder in this
church
"For to me to live is Christ and to
die is gain"

---

609 r
In Memory of
Hepzibah wife
of John Potter
Who Departed this
Life March 23
1779 Aged 30
Years

---

610 r
H. P.
In Memory of
Hannah Price, died
Mar XII 1799 in the
29 Year of her age

Behold in yᵉ cold Ground my Body lies
As you do pass along
Remember & prepare to dy
Before the Summons come.

---

611 r
HERE lies the Body of
Miss Mary Alleson,
who departed this Life
April the 7th AD. 1772
In the XXXII Year of her
Age——— ————

My Flesh shall Slumber in the Ground
Till the last Trumpets joyful Sound
Then burst yᵉ Chains in sweet surprise
And in my Saviour's Image rise

---

612 r
J. P.
In memory of
Jonathan son of Jonathan
& Polly Price died March
1st 1809 aged 3 mo & 1 day

Our dear child Christ took & blest
We'll cease to mourn for he's at rest

613 *r*
M. H. C.
―――
M. H. P.

In Memory of
MARY H wife of
Daniel D Conditt
and Daughter of
Ephriam & Chloe Price
who died April 25th 1822
in the 22d year
of her age

Also of MARY H daughter of
Thompson & Elizabeth Price
who died April 10th 1825
in the 10th year of her age

When Blooming youth are snatch'd
   away
By death's resistless hand
Our hearts the mournful tribute pay
Which pity must demand

614 *r*
D. W. P.
In memory of
DAVID W PRICE
son of Ephriam
& Chloe Price
who on a Journey
in the Republic
of Mexico was
asassinated in
the night by his
servant Oct 1825
Aged 34 years

615 *r*
Marian Daughter of
Ephriam & Chloe Price
died Sept 17, 1799 in
the 2d year of her age

Also her sister Phebe
died Augt 7th 1799
aged 5 weeks & 1 day

616 *r*
Jane Smith daughter
of Ephraim & Chloe
Price. died May 1st
1796. aged 15 months.

617 *r*
Anne, daughter of
Ephraim & Chloe
Price, died Octr ye
1st 1792 in ye 3d year
of her age

618 *r*
HERE lies interr'd
what was Mortal of
Mr Nathanael Price
      Life
who departed this
Novr the 7th Anno
Domini 1776 In
the LXXVI Year of
his Age―――

619 *r*
HERE lies ye Body
of Jane. Wife of
James Smith who
departed this Life
May ye 30th Anno
Dom. 1779 In the
XXIV Year of her
Age―――

620 *r*
In Memory of Mary
wife of Nathaniel
Price who died May
the 24th 1797 in the
62d Year of her age

621 *r*
N. P.
In memory of
Nathaniel Price
who died
Jany 10th 1809 in
the 76th Year of
his Age

622 r
E. P.
In Memory of
EPHRAIM PRICE
who died
Sept' 14th 1824
in the 58th year
of his age

Farewell ye friends whose tender care
Has long engag'd my love
Your fond embrace I now exchange
For better friends above

623 r
C. P.
In Memory of
CHLOE
wife of
Ephraim Price
who died
May 9th 1829
Aged 64 years

Hallowed be this spot
A Mother sleepeth here
Disturb not her repose
For angels hover near
Her spirit upward bourn
In heaven now's at rest
With God and saints above
With Jesus and the blest.

624 m
TO
THE MEMORY OF
MARGARET ANN
Daughter of
John and Eunice Hindes
Born June 14th 1824
Died Jany 20th 1852

O, ye mourners cease to languish
O'er the grave of her you love
Far removed from pain and anguish
She is chanting hymns above

625 m
TO
THE MEMORY OF
RACHEL ELIZABETH
Daughter of
John and Eunice Hindes
Born Nov' 11th 1818
Died Sept 11th 1851

Why should we mourn for those who die
Who rise to glory's sphere
The tenants of that cloudless sky
Need not our mortal tear

626 m
IN
Memory of
SARAH A. D.
Daughter of
John and Eunice Hindes
who died Oct' 27th 1850
Aged 28 Years

Her work on earth soon done
She passeth hence
A friend from loving friends
A Sister from her Sisters

627 m
IN
Memory of
JOHN HINDES
WHO DIED
Sept' 14th 1843
Aged 51 Years

Friends our span of life is fleeting
Hark ! the harps of angles swell
Think Of that eternal meeting
Where no voice shall say farewell

628 m
IN
Memory of
EUNICE
wife of
John Hindes

and daughter of
Henry and Rachel Freeman
who departed this life
Jan 6th 1841
In the 47th year of her age

Also their Children
WILLIAM JOSIAH
aged 3 years & 2 months
HENRY JOSIAH
aged 1 year & 27 days
LOUISA HOLDRIDGE
aged 9 months & 7 days

---

629 *m*
OUR BROTHER
JOHN J HINDES
DIED
March 27th 1861
Aged 33 Years
1 Month and
8 Days

---

630 *r*
Here Lieth ye Body
of James Hindes
Deceased October
ye 7th A° 1731 In ye 51st
Year of his Age

---

631 *r*
Here lies ye Body
of Irene Wife of
James Hindes Junr
Dec^d Feb^r ye 19 1733
Aged 26 years

---

632 *r*
H. H.
In memory of
HENRY HINDES
who died
May 21st 1836
in the 35th Year
of his age

633 *r*
C. H.
In memory
OF
CHARLOTTE
wife of
William Hindes
who died May 16th
1814, in the 53^d year
of her age

---

634 *r*
W. H.
In Memory
OF
WILLIAM HINDES
who died
Septr 28th 1820
in the 60th year
of his age

---

635 *r*
HERE lies intomb'd ye
Mortal part of Jerusha
Daughter of Oliver &
Anna Spencer, who
died Octr ye 9th 1787
aged 22 Years

I bid adieu to Earth.
For all things here are vain.

---

636 *m*
SACRED
TO THE
MEMORY
OF
M^{rs} ANN TRUMBULL
WIFE OF
JOHN M TRUMBULL
WHO DIED
JUNE 1st 1817
Aged 27 years

ALSO
OF
HER INFANT SON
JOSEPH
Aged 3 months

637 *m*
IN
memory of
CHARLES LATHROP
son of Noah and
Sarah Ann Norris
who died
August 2ᵈ 1836
aged 1 year 6 months
and 17 days

This lovely bud so young and fair
Call'd hence by early doom
Just came to show how sweet a flower
In paradise would bloom

638 *r*
Simeon son of
Jonathan & Sarah
Acken died Augᵗ
24ᵗʰ 1793 aged 1
month & 3 weeks

639 *m*
SACRED
To
the memory of
two Children
of John D &
Elizabeth T Norris
CERINTHA
died July 26ᵗʰ 1826
Aged 2 months
LAURA ANGELINE
died Decʳ 27ᵗʰ 1828
Aged 4 months

Alas! how changed these lovely flowers,
Which bloom'd and cheer'd our hearts;
Fair fleeting comfort of an hour,
How soon we're call'd to part!

640 *m*
SACRED
To
THE MEMORY OF
CATHARINE
MARIA DAUGHTER OF
JOHN D & ELIZABETH T
NORRIS: WHO DIED SEPTʳ
2ᵈ 1831 AGED 10 MONTHS
AND 17 DAYS

" I take these little lambs said he
" And lay them in my breast
" Protection they shall find in me
" In me be ever blest.

641 *m*
THE GRAVE
OF
CHARLOTTE
WIDOW OF
ELIAS NORRIS
WHO DIED
MARCH 26ᵗʰ 1878
IN THE 85ᵗʰ YEAR
OF HER AGE.

642 *m*
THE GRAVE
OF
ELIAS NORRIS
WHO DIED
Novʳ 27ᵗʰ 1853,
IN THE 60ᵗʰ YEAR
OF HIS AGE

643 *m*
SACRED
To the memory of
NOAH NORRIS,
who departed this life
August 29ᵗʰ 1828;
in the 60ᵗʰ year
of his age

The time is short the season near,
When death will us remove
To leave our friends however dear
And all we fondly love.

644 *m*
SACRED
To the memory of
REBECCA
WIDOW OF
NOAH NORRIS
who departed this life
Octr 22nd 1854
In the 81st Year
of her age.

Her months of affliction are o'er,
 The days and the nights of distress,
We see her in anguish no more,
 She has gained her happy release.

645 *r*
M. S.
Of paternal Affection
and
universal Benevolence
this Monument
is erected by filial Affection
to testify to after ages
that here lies the Body of
Elias Boudinot,
who died July ye 4th A D 1770
aged LXIII Years

This modest Stone, what few vain
 Marbels can
May truly say, "Here lies an honest
 Man

646 *r*
M. S.
Of Catharine ye Wife
of Elias Boudinot
who departed this Life
November ye 1st 1765
aged 51 Years

In Testimony
of whose Maternal
Affection & pious Care
this Monument is erect
ed by her gratefull
Children

647 *r*
HERE lies the Body
of Richard Stockton
Son of Abner & Mary
Hetfield, who died—
Febr^y ye 4th 1767 In y^e
3^d Year of his Age

Sleep lovely Babe & take your
 peaceful rest,
God call'd you home because
 he thought it best.

648 *r*
J. P.
In memory of
Jonathan Price
who died sept^r 12
1799. In the 72^d
Year of his Age

649 *m*
P. P.
In memory of
PERIAM PRICE
Died October 2, 1880
Aged
87 Years 4 Months

Them which sleep in Jesus
will God bring with him.

650 *m*
IN MEMORY OF
PHEBE
ANNA
DAUGHTER OF
JESSIE D & HARRIET
ELIZA PRICE
WHO DIED IN THE
CITY OF NEW YORK
JAN. 24, 1844:
AGED 10 MO.
& 7 DAYS

The Lord gave and the Lord
hath taken away, blessed be
the name of the Lord.

651 *m*
J. D. P.
IN MEMORY
of the
REV JONATHAN D
PRICE M. D. SON OF
David & Rachel Price
who died at Ava in
Burmah Feb. 14th 1828
after 7 years missionary
labour in that empire
Aged 32 years

In Burmah's sand from kindred dust
    afar
On thy cold stone looks down the
    Eastern Star

652 *r*
A. O. P.
In memory of
Aaron Ogden
son of David &
Rachel Price
died Octr 31st 1805
in the 20th year of
his age

What he was once forbear to say,
T'will best appear on that great day,
When you and I & every one
Must give account for what we've done

653 *r*
J. P.
Joseph Peream Son
of David & Rachel
Price, died July 26
1792. Aged I Year
& III Mon^s

654 *r*
D P
Daniel Son of
David & Rachel
Price, died Feby X
1785 Aged 4 Mon^s
& 6 days

655 *r*
D. P.
Daniel Son of
David & Rachel
Price died Nov^r
XIII 1783, aged IV
Months & 14 days

656 *r*
R. P.
In memory of
Rachel daughter
of David & Rachel
Price died March
8th 1809 aged 18
months & 9 days

657 *m*
OUR MOTHER
PHEBE
WIFE OF
ENOS PRICE
DIED SEP^t 12th 1861
AGED 76 YEARS

There is rest for the weary
There is sweet rest in Heaven

658 *m*
OUR FATHER
ENOS PRICE
DIED
July 1st 1872
Aged 90 Yrs
& 6 Months

"Thou shalt come to thy grave
in a full age, like a shock of
corn cometh in his season."

659 *r*
IN
memory
of
JONATHAN
Son of Enos &
Phebe Price, who
died March 9th 1831

aged 2 years &
6 months

Liv'd to wake each tender passion
Our delightful hopes inspire
Died to try our resignation
And direct our wishes higher,

660 r
In
Memory
of
Mary
daughter of Enos
& Phebe Price
who died
Feby 18th 1827
hs
Aged 1 year 4 mont
& 9 days

661 m
IN MEMORY
OF THE
REV JOHN HARRIMAN
The first Pastor
of the
First Presbyterian Church
of Elizabethtown
He was born in New Haven
Graduated in Cambridge college
in 1667 :
Was installed in Elizabethtown
in 1687 ;
And after faithfully serving the
church, and in the state, he died
in 1704,
" The memory of the just is blessed "

662 m
IN MEMORY OF
WILLIAM HARRIMAN
who was born
April 28, 1718 ;
Died
March 9, 1811
Also of
SUSANNA
His wife
who died
March 2, 1791.

Death like a narrow sea divides
That heavenly land from ours.

663 m
In Memory of
JOANNA E. LYONS
Grand daughter of
Capt SAMUEL HARRIMAN
Died April 20th 1879
in the 80th year
of her age

Blessed are the pure in heart
for they shall see God.

664 m
In
Memory of
JOHANNA
daughter of
Capt Samuel Harriman
Born Jan. 18th 1773.
Died Aug. 9th 1852.

A bright example of filial and sisterly
affection—her record is on high.

665 m
In memory of
CAPT SAMUEL HARRIMAN
who was born
Jan. 18. 1752,
and died Aug. 21. 1824.
Aged 72 years.
He was one
of the noble band of worthies
contributed by Elizabethtown
to the war of the Revolution,
among whom he obtained
a distinguished name
by his fearless courage

Also of
SUSANNA
his wife
who was born Nov. 8. 1752
And after
a blameless and useful life
through 46 years of which
she was a member of the church
died Nov. 2, 1830
aged 78 years

666 *m*
IN
MEMORY OF
four children
of
SAMUEL & SUSANNA
HARRIMAN.
EATON
was born May 7th 1778,
died July 5th 1779
SUSAN
was born Sep. 21st 1786
died Aug. 8th 1839
MARGARET
was born June 8th 1780
died Sep. 29th 1844
MARIA
was born Sep 3d 1774
died Sep. 31st 1844.

667 *r*
P W
SACRED
to the Memory of
PHEBE
WIFE of
JONATHAN WINANS
who died
Nov. 3. 1823
aged 25 years 6
months & 18 days

No chilling winds nor pois'nous breath
Can reach that healthful shore :
Sickness and sorrow pain and death.
Are felt and fear'd no more.

668 *m*
IN
Memory of
MARY
WIFE OF
Jonathan Winans
WHO DIED
Octr 29th 1844
In the 49th Year
of her age

Ye pleasing scenes, adieu,
Which I so long have known
My friends, a long farewell to you
For I must pass alone.

669 *m*
[This stone faces the west]
SARAH ANN MEEKER
HINDS.
the adopted Daughter of
SAMUEL & CHRISTIANA
MEEKER
of Philadelphia

MARY wife of ABNER
HINDS
died March 1st 1835 :
Aged 61 Years

Here lays an affectionate Mother and
an only Sister

670 *r*
E. B.
In memory of
EZEKIEL BAKER
who died May 15th 1810
aged 62 years 8
months & 15
days

Ye pleasing scenes adieu
Which I so long have known,
My friends a long farewell to you
For I must pass alone.

671 *m*
SACRED
To the memory of
PHEBE
widow of
Ezekiel Baker ; who
died March 21st 1840,
Aged 77 years,
4 months, &
18 days.

The time is short ! the season near,
When death will us remove
To leave our friends however dear
And all we fondly love.

672 r
[One stone]

Here lies the Body
of James Ross, who
departed this Life Janu^y
the 27th Anno Domini
1752. In the 29th Year
of his Age———

Here lies the Body
of James Son of Jame^s
& Rebekah Ross, who
died Dece^r ye 3^d A. D.
1769. In the 19th Year
of his Age———

673 r
Here lies ye Body of
Jehiel Son of Andrew
Hampton. Died Feb:
26 1734 in ye 6 year
of his Age

674 m
IN
memory of
WILLIAM SCHENCK
who died
March 5th 1841,
in the 21st year
of his age

675 m
IN
memory of
EPHRAIM
Son of Elias &
Catherine Hatfield:
who died
Decr 28th 1836.
aged 1 year 5 months
and 26 days

This lovely bud, so young and fair
Call'd hence by early doom;
Just came to show how sweet a flow^{er}
In paradise would bloom.

676 m
In
Memory
of
MARIA, wife of
Cornelius Storm

who departed this life
May 29th 1817;
in the 26th year
of her age.

Ye fleeting charms of earth farewell!
Your spring of joys are dry;
My soul now seek another home
A brighter world on high

677 m
IN
Memory of
CAP^t DAVID LYON,
who departed this Life
on the 30th March 1802,
Aged 57 Years

678 r
S. P. W.
Stephen P. son of
Person and Mary
Woodruff, died Feb^y
9th 1809 aged 6 years.

Lord it was thy will to take my son,
Teach me to say thy will be done.

679 r
P. W.
In Memory of
Parsons Whoodruff
who departed this
life the 1st day of
Nov^{br} 1803. In the
40th Year of his Age.

As you pass by Remember me,
For as you are now, so once was I.
For as I am now, so you must be.

680 *m*
OUR MOTHER
WHO WAS BORN
JULY 20th 1769,
AND
WHO SWEETLY FELL ASLEEP
OCT. 23d 1853,
"I shall be satisfied, when
I awake in thy likeness."

"Blessed are the dead
who die in the Lord."
MARY WOODRUFF
AGED 85 YEARS

681 *r*
IN
Memory
of
Seth Woodruff
who departed this life
Oct. 7th 1814, in the 73d
year of his age.

How sudden was the stroke of death,
That did me from my friends remove;
I in an instant lost my breath,
And wingd my flight to worlds above.
Farewell no more I tread your ground,
No more I need the gospel sound,
My feet have reached the heavenly
 shore,
I know no imperfection more.

682 *r*
In
Memory
of
PHEBE, wife of
Seth Woodruff:
who departed this
life Septr 8th 1823;
in the 82d year
of her age.

Great God I own the sentence just
And nature must decay,
I yield my body to the dust
To dwell with fellow clay.

683 *m*
[Horizontal Slab]
THE GRAVE
OF
STEPHEN H WOODRUFF
who died April 27th 1850
Aged 80 Years

"I know that my Redeemer liveth."
IN MEMORY OF
JANE L WOODRUFF
wife of Stephen H Woodruff
who died April 17th 1831;
Aged 58 years

"The grave is mine house, my bed is in the darkness
My flesh shall rest in hope."

"My Saviour shall my life restore,
And raise me from my dark abode,
My flesh and soul shall part no more,
But dwell forever near my God."

Died July 10th 1838. an infant Son of
S H Woodruff, aged 9 days.

684 *m*
[Horizontal Slab]
A. M.

ABBY MEEKER
WIFE OF
STEPHEN H WOODRUFF.

BORN SEPT. 14, 1798,
DIED APRIL 13, 1887.

---

685 *m*
IN
Memory of
ELIZABETH,
WIDOW OF
OGDEN WOODRUFF
who died
May 12th 1848;
Aged 66 Years.

Thou art gone to thy rest, but no longer we mourn thee,
Though deep in our hearts we had shrined thee in love;
For death and the grave with new bloom shall return thee,
To meet us again in the mansions above,

---

686 *m*
IN
Memory of
OGDEN WOODRUFF,
who died
Nov. 21st 1833;
Aged 56 Years.

Weep not for me, but weep for yourselves, and for your children."

687 *m*
IN
Memory of
PHEBE WOODRUFF,
Daughter of
OGDEN WOODRUFF,
who died
April 23rd 1829:
Aged 24 Years
Also EMELINE, Daughter of
OGDEN & ELIZABETH WOODRUFF,
who died Sept. 23rd 1824;
Aged 15 Months.

To faint is language to express
The moral worth of this lov'd friend:
Her life was one of usefulness
Tranquil submission marked her end.

688 *m*
IN
Memory of
BENJAMIN WOODRUFF
Son of
OGDEN WOODRUFF, DEC^d,
who died
June 5th 1846,
Aged 21 Years,

Press'd by the hand of sore desease,
In pain I linger'd on,
Till God my Saviour arm'd with love
In mercy call'd me home,

689 *m*
IN
Memory of
Joann B
WIFE OF
Jacob Thompson
who died May 18th 1848
Aged 27 Years

An affectionate Wife and tender
Mother
ALSO
SAMUEL,
their son, died Jany 12th 1849,
aged 8 months

He had no Mother's tender care
To soothe his dying cries
But he who heard her dying prayer
Has taken him to the skies.

690 *m*
IN
Memory of
STEPHEN T,
SON OF
David & Martha
Osmun
who died
Augst 15th 1833;
Aged 24 Years

691 *m*
IN
Memory of
MARTHA,
WIFE OF
David Osmun;
who died
Novr 24th 1846;
In the 63d Year
of her age.

Mother thy name I still revere
No earthly name to me so dear,
My first, my best, my long tried friend,
My love for thee will never end.

692 *m*
To the
Memory of
CAPT. JOHN FOSTER,
WHO DIED
in New York City;
Decr 16th 1841,
In the 68th Year
of his age

ALSO
SARAH
HIS WIDOW
died in Elizabeth City;
Novr 25th 1848
In the 69th Year
of her age

693 *m*
EDMUND
SON OF
Alfred & Elizabeth
LOACH;
DIED FEB. 29, 1856,
AGED 1 YEAR & 7 MO,
ALSO HARRY
SON OF
Alfred & Elizabeth
LOACH;
DIED APRIL 26, 1857,
AGED 8 MONTHS
The only and loved ones.

694 *m*
IN
memory of
SARAH
WIDOW OF
JOHN P WELLS
who died
Octr 17th 1845
Aged 65 Years

695 *m*
WILLIAM HENRY WILLIS
DIED
April 10. 1852
in the 23^d year of his age

In the midst of life we
are in death

SARAH LOUISA WILLIS
DIED
August 4. 1848,
in the 13 year of her age.

Earth has a mortal less
Heaven an Angel more

---

696 *r*
IN
memory
of
JOHN JAMES
son of James &
Sarah B Willis
who died
Augst 21st 1831 ;
Aged 7 months

---

697 *m*
JOHN O JARVIS
DIED
JULY 27th 1841,
AGED 33 YEARS

Return unto thy rest, O my
soul ; for the Lord hath dealt
bountifully with thee
116 Ps 7.v.

---

698 *m*
IN
Memory of
BENJAMIN J JARVIS
BORN
March 17th 1775
DIED
Octr 8th 1862

---

699 *r*
P. J.
In memory of
PHEBE
wife of
Benjamin J Jarvis
who died
Feby 26th 1830;
in the 61st year
of her age

Farewell ye friends whose tender care
Has long engag'd my love
Your fond embrace I now exchange
For better friends above,

---

700 *r*
R. P.
In memory of
Rachel widow of
Ebenezer Price
who died March 17th
1806 aged 79
years

To all surviving friends
Hears a loud call.
Prepare to meet your God,
I speak to all.
The old the middle aged,
And the youth.
Must all submit to death,
This awfull truth.

---

701 *m*
SIMEON PRICE
52 years,
a devoted and consistent member
of the M. E. church
in N. Y. city
Died Dec. 13th 1848,
in the 75th year of his age.

SARAH,
wife of
Simeon Price
Died in full hope
of a blissful immortality
Dec. 14th 1845,
aged 48 yrs. 7 mos & 16 days.
" Precious in the sight of the Lord
is the death of his saints."

702 *r*
IN MEMORY OF
M̄ Ebenezer Price, who
departed this Life De-
-cember the 23ᵈ 1788,
In the LXᵗʰ Year of his
Age
"Seek ye' the Lord
while he may be found."
Wife and children may deplore
The Husband Father is no more
His frugal hands no more provide
We trust he rests at Jesus side

703 *m*
IN
MEMORY OF
AARON WOODRUFF
WHO DIED
Septʳ 17ᵗʰ 1851 :
Aged 73 Years
and 12 Days

704 *m*
IN MEMORY OF
ANZONNETTE PRICE
WHO DIED
MARCH 18ᵗʰ 1842 ;
AGED 3 YEARS 6 MO. 19 DAYS.
ALSO
LOUISA WOODRUFF
WHO DIED JAN. 11ᵗʰ 1844
AGED 5 MO. 17 DAYS.
DAUGHTERS OF
PULASKI & MARY S. JACKS.

705 *m*
There is rest in Heaven
FILIAL AFFECTION
HAS ERECTED THIS STONE
TO THE MEMORY OF
MARY,
WIFE OF
AARON WOODRUFF
WHO DEPARTED THIS LIFE
in the City of New York
FEB. 28ᵗʰ 1842 :

AGED 61 YEARS
& 6 MONTHS

Weep not for me but weep for
Yourselves and your Children

706 *m*
IN MEMORY OF
LOUISA,
DAUGHTER OF
AARON & MARY
WOODRUFF,
WHO DIED IN THE
CITY OF NEW YORK ;
JULY 24. 1845 ;
AGED 29 YEARS 9 MO.
& 6 DAYS

Blessed are the dead who die in the
Lord, from henceforth ; Yea, saith the
spirit that they may rest from their labours and their works do follow them.

707 *m*
IN
Memory of
MARTHA WOODRUFF
WIFE OF
ISAAC HINDES
who died Nov. 15ᵗʰ 1843
Aged 43 Years 6. Months
and 7 Days

ALSO
SARAH JANE
their Daughter
died March 10ᵗʰ 1845.
Aged 6 Years 5. Months
and 12 Days

708 *m*
IN
Memory of
ISAAC HINDES,
WHO DIED
August 18ᵗʰ 1848.
Aged 54 Years,
4, Months and
5 Days.

INSCRIPTIONS IN FIRST PRESBYTERIAN

709 *r*
M. W. H.
In memory of
Moses W Hindes,
who died
Augst 15th 1831,
in the 42^d year
of his age.

Also two children of
Moses W & Betsey Hindes:
Ann Elizabeth,
died Augst 30th 1824,
aged 2 years, & 6 months,
Betsey Ann
died Augst 13th 1826,
Aged 2 years, 2 months,
& 22 days.

710 *m*
IN
Memory of
JOSEPH B. HINDES,
who died Feby 19th 1849;
aged 29 years 1. month
and 15 days.
Also
His twin brother
BENJAMIN W HINDES
died at Trenton N. C. Dec. 11. 1846
aged 26 years 11 months
and 7 days

Our youthful friends as you pass by:
stop a moment and think, that you too
may shortly die.

711 *m*
MARGARET H.
Daughter of
Jacob J & Janet
Van Doren
Died Feb. 9th 1852.
Aged 1 year 10 mo.
& 9 Days

712 *m*
ROBERT H
Son of Jacob J. &
Janet Van Doren,
Died July 5th 1849,
Aged 1 year 6 mo
& 10 days

713 *r*
HERE lies the Body
of Mr Isaac Scudder
of Eliz^h Town who died
ye 7th of April 1783
In ye 48th Year of his
Age————

Thou givest me the lot
of those that fear thy name
If endless life be there reward
I shall possess the same.

714 *r*

Eanock Son
of Benjamin &
Elizabeth
Scudder, died
Nov 12 1794
Aged 4 weeks.

Charlot Daug^r
of Benjamin &
Elizabeth
Scudder. died
Aug 7 1799
aged 1 year
& 9 months

715 *m*

TO
The memory of
ELIZA STACKHOUSE,
WHO DIED
March 22ᵈ A. D. 1853:
Aged 48 years

This Tablet is most affectionately inscribed, by the Teachers and Children of the Sunday School of St, Johns Episcopal Church, of which she was at her death and for many years previous thereto, the faithful Superintendent,

---

716 *m*

IN MEMORY OF
ABBY M. MUNSON,
WHO DEPARTED THIS LIFE
March 20ᵗʰ 1846,
AGED
48 years 5 months 3 days

"Blessed are the dead that die in the Lord"

---

717 *m*

IN
MEMORY OF
HALLSEY MUNSON,
BORN
Ocrʳ 22ᵈ 1787,
DIED
Janʸ 9ᵗʰ 1865.

---

718 *m*

IN
Memory of
ELIHU J CRANE
WHO DIED
Janʸ 8ᵗʰ 1853,
IN THE 56ᵗʰ YEAR
OF HIS AGE

---

719 *m*

ELIZA CRANE
DIED
AUG, 19, 1878,
AGED
76 Y'ʀs, 3 Mo, 22 D's,

"ASLEEP IN JESUS"

---

720 *m*

IN
Memory of
SARAH ELIZABETH
Daughter of
Elihu J. and Eliza Crane,
who died June 4ᵗʰ 1850,
Aged 20 years 3 Months
and 12 Days,

"Blessed are those servants whom the Lord when he cometh shall find watching"

ALSO
WILLIAM EDWIN
their infant son
died March 18ᵗʰ 1839,
Aged 19 days

---

721 *m*

[Little Monument in Genung Plot]
[On East side]
WILLIAM MILLER
ONLY SON OF
CHARLES H & ANNA
GENUNG
DIED AUG. 24. 1850
IN HIS 3D YEAR

[On South side]
WILLIE
He shall gather the lambs with his arms and carry them in his bosom

[North & West side blank]

722 *m*
THE GRAVE
OF
HORATIO E ROBERTS
WHO DIED MAY 19, 1852;
AGED 34 YEARS 6 MONTHS
AND 12 DAYS

---

723 *m*
THE GRAVE
OF
LUCY M. ROBERTS
CONSORT OF
JESSE ROBERTS
WHO DIED JAN. 21, 1853;
AGED 61 YEARS 2 MONTHS
AND 18 DAYS

May Angels twine a wreath for thee
A wreath of Immortality

---

724 *m*
THE GRAVE
OF
JESSE ROBERTS,
who departed this life
MAY 4th, 1829;
aged 43 years

He was a kind and affectionate husband a dear and beloved father

Come follow to that happy place,
Our master's joy to see,
For O! in one short moment's space
Ye all shall rest with me.

---

725 *r*
A. E. W.
Abert Eaton
son of Morris &
Susan Woodruff
died June 8 1805
aged 3 years
& 2 months

---

726 *r*
M. E.
Maria B. daughter of
Thomas & Sarah
Eaton died May
30th 1789 aged 3
years 4 months.

---

727 *r*
S. E.
Sarah the 2^d daughter
of Thomas & Sarah
Eaton died March
16th 1785 aged 2 mo.

---

728 *r*
S. W. E.
Samuel Wonton son
of Thomas & Sarah
Eaton, died Oct 10
1795 aged 1 year

---

729 *r*
Sar [Stone broken off]
Thoma
Eaton died
26th 1783 aged
13 months

---

730 *r*
[Stone broken off]
ow of
Joseph Eaton
died Oct 9th 1779
aged 59 years

---

731 *r*
S. E.
In memory of
Susanah wife of
Thomas Eaton
died Novr 12th
1774 aged 17
years

---

⁷²⁹ Sarah dau. of Thomas Eaton, died Aug. 26.
⁷³⁰ "Mother of Thomas Eaton," buried Oct. 11, 1779.

732 r
In Memory of
Abigail Wife of
Lewis Miller Died
Augt 9 1762
In ye 22^d year
of her Age

733 r
In Memory of
Flauiel Rossiter
Miller. Died Nov^r
6th 1761 Aged
1 year & 5 months

734 r
W. W.
In memory of
WILLIAM WOODRUFF
who died Feby 23^d 1811 in
the 69th year of his age

Farewell ye friends whose tender care
Has long engaged my love
Your fond embrace I now exchange
For better friends above

Eliza daughter of W^m and Mary
Woodruff, died Octr 20th 1793 in
the 4th year of her age

735 r
M. W.
In memory of
MARY
widow of
William Woodruff
who died
December 8th 1836.
Aged 88 years

736 r
D. W.
In memory of
David Woodruff,
who died July 29th 1804;
Aged 58 years.

His will and mind was well adorn^d
with fruit
But deaths destroying worm, at at
the root.
Farewell dear friend.—we trust thy
mouldering clay
Will rise triumphant in the last great
day.

737 r
J. W.
In memory of
JOANNA,
wife of
David Woodruff:
who died
June 20th 1830:
Aged 83 years.

Blessed are they and only they
Who in the Lord the Saviour die
Thier bodies wait redemption's day
And sleep in peace where'er they lie

738 m
BELCHER WOODRUFF
DIED
February 10' 1851,

Aged 70 Years

& 6 Months

739 m
JANE WOODRUFF
Widow of
BELCHER WOODRUFF,

Died May 3' 1876,

Aged 89 Years

& 3 Months

And there shall be no night there.

INSCRIPTIONS IN FIRST PRESBYTERIAN

740 r
Here lies the Body
of Anne Wife of
Abraham Woodruff
who died July ye 14th
Anno Domini 1784
In the 35th Year of
her Age————

741 r
D. W.
In memory
of
Daniel Woodruff
who died
April 15th 1812,
in the 70th year
of his age

742 r
W. B.
In memory of
William Brown
who died
Septr 15th, 1817,
in the 79th year
of his age,

743 r
L. G.
In memory of
Lydia
widow of
Alexander Gale,
who died
April 2^d, 1817,
in the 64th year
of her age.

744 r
Here lyeth ye Body of
Hannah Wife of
Elnathan Smith
Dec^d July ye 16th 1749
in ye 26th year
of her Age————

745 r
Here lyeth the Body of
Dauid Morehouse who
Departed this life Decem^r
The 12th Anno Domini
1739 and in the 51^t year
of his Age————

746 m
In memory of
MARTHA HINDS
Died
December 10, 1885.
Aged 88 Yr's & 5 Mo's
Also
Abner Hinds
Her Father.

747 r
In Memory of
Mrs Sarah Widow
of Mr Joseph Hines
who departed
this Life March
the 11th 1791, aged
81 Years

748 r
HERE lies the Body
of Mr Joseph Hinds
who departed this
Life February ye 25th
Anno Domini 1774
In the 70th Year of
his Age————

749 r
HERE lies the Body
of David Hinds,
who departed this
Life Septr ye 5th An^o.
Domini 1778 In ye 37th
Year of his Age————

750 r
Benjamin Son of
Joseph and Anna
Haines, departed
this Life June y̅ᵉ 8ᵗʰ
A. D. 1763, In y̅ᵉ 20ᵗʰ
Year of his Age——

751 r
A. H.
In memory of
Abigail widow of
David Hinds
who died
March 29ᵗʰ 1805
in the 64ᵗʰ year of
her age

Weep not for me my friends
For why my race is run
It is the will of God
So let his will be done.

752 m
JOHN CROZIER
Departed this life
MAY 4ᵗʰ, 1859,
Aged 75 years

753 r
D. M.
In memory of
David Mulford
who deceas'd
May 24ᵗʰ 1798:
in the 22ᵈ year
of his Age

754 r
Here lies the Body
of Moses, Son of
Joseph & Mary Cory
who deceas'd June
the 1ˢᵗ A. D. 1750
In the 13ᵗʰ Year of
his Age———

755 r
M. H.
In memory of
Mary Wife of
Benjamin Hinds
who deceas'd
May 24ᵗʰ 1801,
in the 22ᵈ year
of her Age

756 r
IN Memory of
Phebe Daughʳ of
Benjaⁿ. & Hannah
Cory, who died
July yᵉ 6ᵗʰ 1778
In the 3ᵈ Year of
her Age———

757 r
Abigail Daughtʳ. of
Benjamin & Hannah
Cory died March
the 31ˢᵗ A. D. 1786.
In the 16ᵗʰ Year of
her Age———

758 r
Jonathan, Son of
Benjamin & Hannah
Cory— died Januʸ.
the 17ᵗʰ A D 1787.
In the 14ᵗʰ Year
of his Age———

759 r

HERE lies interr'd
The Body of Mrs
Mary, Wife of
Joseph Cory who
deceas'd June yᵉ 4ᵗʰ
Anno Domini 1778
In the LXVII Year
of her Age————

HERE lies interr'd
the Remains of
Mr Joseph Cory
who departed this
Life March yᵉ 8ᵗʰ
Anno Domini 1782
In the LXXIV Year
of his Age————

760 *r*
Daniel Son of
Benjⁿ. & Hannah
Cory died Jan^y
the 28th A.D. 1768
aged 1 Month &
8 Days——

761 *r*
A K
In memory of
Anna wife of Daniel
Keyt who died July
the 15th 1806 in the 19th
year of her age

Farewell my dear husband said she
  Now from your kind bosom I leap
With Jesus my bridegroom to be
  My flesh in the tomb for to sleep

Why do we mourn departing friends
  Or shake at deaths alarms
Tis but the voice that Jesus sends
  To call them to his arms

Also Benjamin C son of
  Daniel and Anna Keyt died
                      days
March 31st 1807 aged 8 m^o & 28

Our lovely child Christ took & blest
We'll cease to mourn for he's at rest

762 *r*
M C
In Memory of
MULFORD CORY
who died
Jany 14th 1813
in the 48th year
of his age

As you are now, so once was I ;
As I am now, so you must be.

763 *m*
B. C.
In memory of
BENJAMIN CORY ESQ
who died Oct 8th 1821 :
Aged 80 : For 35 years
a faithful ruling elder
& deacon of this
church

"Well done good and faithful servant
enter thou into the joy of thy Lord."

764 *m*
H. C.
In Memory of
Mrs HANNAH CORY
wife of
Deac. Benjamin Cory
who died
November 8th 1826
Aged 80 years

"Precious in the sight of the Lord
is the death of his saints."

765 *m*
MARIA CORY
Wife of
MULFORD CORY
DIED
Dec 8th 1868
In the 82^d year
of her age

766 *m*
A. C. C.
Here repose
the ashes of
AARON C
son of Mulford &
Maria Cory
who died
Sept 1st 1829 :
Aged 19 years

Dear Mother, Brothers, do not weep,
Since in Jesus I sweetly sleep :
My days their dreary course have run.
And I my heaven, my all have won.

Oh ! stranger, lightly, lightly tread
As you draw near my grass grown bed
View the spot with a thoughtful eye
Where I calmly, solemnly lie.

A tribute of brotherly affection

767 *m*
IN
Memory of
DRAKE CRANE
who died
Sept 8th 1833
Aged 52 years

---

768 *m*
IN
MEMORY OF
DRAKE CRANE,
WHO DIED
Sept 8th 1833:
Aged 52 Years.
ALSO OF
ELIZABETH,
HIS WIDOW
who died Jany 11th 1858;
Aged 74 Years and
5 Months

769
[Small Marble Monument]
[East side]
IN
MEMORY OF
MARY C WOOD
DAUGHTER OF
JONAS & CHARITY
WOOD
AGED 21 YEARS
DIED AUGUST 13. 1839

Mourn not for me when I am gone
Nor shed one tear
Around my bier
But meet me, meet me, round the
Throne

[South side]
DIED
AT NEW ALBANY
INDIANNA
JOSEPH P WOOD
SON OF
JONAS & CHARITY
WOOD
AGED 26 YEARS

AND 6 MONTHS
March 1 1836

Boast not thyself of to morrow;
for thou knowest not what a
day may bring forth.
Prov XXVII 1

[North and West side blank]

---

770 *m*
MY MOTHER
CHARITY
WIFE OF
JONAS WOOD,
BORN FEB. 6th 1789,
DIED APRIL 8th 1867,
IN THE 79th YEAR
OF HER AGE

PATIENT AND ENDURING, SHE
DIED WITH FAITH IN JESUS

---

771 *m*
JONAS WOOD
DIED
MAY 18th 1852
AGED 64 YEARS.

---

772 *r*
In
Memory of
MEHETABLE
daughter of Elias
& Rebecca Whaley
who died
March 24th 1825:
in the 8th year
of her age

---

773 *m*
GEORGIANA V. WILLIS
Wife of
THOMAS BERRY,
Died Feb. 22 1881
in the 40th year
of her age.

"Thy will be done,"

INSCRIPTIONS IN FIRST PRESBYTERIAN

774 *m*
JAMES WILLIS
DIED
AUGUST 16th 1877
AGED 72 YEARS

Hark the glad refrain
Home at last,
Wandering toil and pain
All are past

SARAH B. JARVIS,
Wife of
JAMES WILLIS,
DIED MAY 13 1884,
IN THE 79th YEAR OF
HER AGE

At Rest

775 *m*
HANNAH O JARVIS
DAUGHTER OF
BENJAMIN J JARVIS
DIED MAY 10th, 1876,
AGED 72 YEARS.

No sin, no grief, no pain ;
Safe in my happy home ;
My fears all fled, my doubts all slain,
My hour of triumph come.

MARGARET M. WILLIS,
DAUGHTER OF
BENJAMIN J JARVIS
DIED NOV, 10th 1865.
AGED 54 YEARS

Affliction sore long time she bore,
Physicians art in vain,
Till God it pleased to give her ease,
And take her from her pain.

776 *m*
The Grave of
JAMES WARREN
son of
ELIAS & ADALINE C.
BONNELL
died Oct. 8, 1851
aged 8 months

777 *m*
The Grave of
ELIAS BONNELL
WHO DIED
Feb. 13. 1852.
In his 22^d year

Not lost, blest thought, but gone before,

778 *r*
P. M.
In memory of
PHEBE MOREHOUSE
who died
Septr 27th 1824 ;
in the 69th year
of her age

779 *r*
S. M.
In memory of
Samuel Morehouse
who died Decr 10th 1790.
in the 51st year
of his age

Like a frail leaf before the storm
I fly to worlds unknown
I have fulfil'd my weeks below
And leave my friends to mourn

780 *r*
S. M.
In memory of
SUSANNAH, widow of
Samuel Morehouse,
who died Feby 3^d 1819
in the 73^d year
of her age

Though in the dust I lay my head,
Yet gracious God thou will not leave
My flesh forever with the dead,
Nor lose thy children in the grave

CHURCH YARD, ELIZABETH, N. J. 113

781 *m*
AARON MOREHOUSE
BORN
JULY 5th 1785
DIED
MAY 13th 1849

Jesus can make a dying bed,
Feel soft as downy pillows are,
While on his breast I lay my head,
And breathe my life out sweetly there.

782 *m*
EMELINE WINANS
Wife of
WILLIAM G WARD
& daughter of Benjamin Frazee
Died Dec. 6th 1853
in her 31st year

Soon she followed her dear mother
Whom tenderly she loved
We trust they rest with Christ together
In paradise above.

Also their Daughter
HENRIETTA MARIA
Died Dec. 22d, 1853
in her 5th Year

The flowers you loved so well mother
And want placed o'er our grave
Will blossom in the spring mother
Where heavenly flowers are safe

783 *m*
IN
Memory
of
SARAH MARIA
daughter of Benjn
& Susan Frazee:
born August 16th 1830
died Novr 9th 1831

Liv'd to wake each tender passion
And delightful hopes inspire
Died to try our resignation
And direct our wishes higher

Rest sweet babe in gentle slumbers
Till the resurrection morn
Then arise to join the numbers
That its triumph shall adorn

784 *m*
IN MEMORY
OF
SUSAN OGDEN
wife of
BENJAMIN FRAZEE
Born May 14 1790
died Dec. 15 1852.

You are gone though we will not,
Cannot forget you
Our tears of affection fall far from your grave
You are gone but we hope once more we shall meet you
When time blends its streams with eternity's wave.
The months of affliction are o'er,
The days and the nights of distress;
We see her in anguish no more,
She has gained her happy release:
This languishing head is at rest,
Its thinking and aching are o'er:
This quiet immovable breast,
Is heaved by affliction no more.

785 *m*
IN
Memory of
ESTHER HUNT
WIDOW OF
JOSIAH HUNT
who departed this life
March 1st 1862;
Aged 76 Years 10 Months
and 16 Days

Our Mother
Dear as thou wert and justly dear,
We would not weep for thee:
One thought would check the falling tear
It is that thou art free.

786 *m*
IN
Memory of
JOSIAH HUNT
who departed this life
May 22ᵈ 1841 ;
Aged 81 Years 2 Months
and 5 Days

He was in the armies of Washington
through the Revolutionary War
Survived many severe wounds
and died as he lived a Christian
and a Patriot

I'll praise my Maker with my breath
And when my voice is lost in death
Praise shall employ my nobler pow'rs
My days of praise shall ne'er be past
While life and thought and being last
Or immortality endures

---

787 *r*
In
memory of
SARAH
wife of Josiah Hunt:
who departed this life
october the 6th 1806 :
Aged 33 years

---

788 *r*
In
Memory of
three only sons of
Josiah & Sarah Hunt,
JOHN D HUNT
died May 13th 1802
Aged 15 Months.
Jonathan D Hunt,
died Octʳ 11th 1802.
Aged 6 Years.
Josiah Hunt
died Feby 6th 1803
Aged 4 days,

---

789 *r*
D H
in Memory of
Mr Davis Hunt who
died May 15th 1801 in the
82ᵈ Year of his Age

---

790 *m*
Sacred
TO THE
MEMORY OF
MARGARET HAMILTON
WIDOW OF
JAMES B CLARK
WHO DIED
JANUARY 9th 1862.
AGED 62 YEARS

" Precious in the sight of the Lord
is the death of his saints "

Dearest Mother thou hast left us
Here thy loss we deeply feel
Yet tis God that hath bereft us
He can still our sorrows heal.
But again we hope to meet you
On that bright celestial shore
There with rapturous joy to greet you
There we meet to part no more

---

791 *m*
Sacred
TO THE
MEMORY OF
JAMES B CLARK
WHO DIED
DECʳ 21st 1844
IN THE 47th YEAR
OF HIS AGE
ALSO OF
MARGARET BISHOP
DAUGHTER OF
James B & Margaret H
CLARK
who died Decʳ 11th 1841 ;
Aged 2 Years
& 4 Months

CHURCH YARD, ELIZABETH, N. J. 115

792 m
ELIZA VOY
daughter of
ROBERT & CHRISTIAN
YOUNG
Died Dec 13 1856
In her 55th Year

Asleep in Jesus

793 m
Sacred to the memory of
CHRISTIAN
wife of Robert Young
who departed this life
on the 20th of Augst 1815
in the 41st year of her age
Also
to the memory of
JENNET VOY
daughter of Robert and Christian
Young. who departed this life on the
30th of May 1796 aged 1 year & 8
months

794 m
R. Y.
SACRED
To the memory of
ROBERT YOUNG

who departed this life
August 3d 1832;
in the 61st year
of his age

"The memory of the just
is blessed."

795 m
IN MEMORY OF
JAMES YOUNG
who departed this life
December 20th, 1851.
Aged 33 years 4 Months
& 14 days

796 m
ELIZA Y.
WIFE OF
SEAMAN P RICHARDS
DIED JAN, 29, 1867;
AGED 27 YEARS.

797 r
In Memory of
William Haviland
Who died the 20th of
April Anno Domini
1788 In the 43d Year
of his Age

798 r

In Memory of
Isaack Son of
William and
Jane Haviland
he Departed
this Life Septr 15
1774
Aged 2 Yars
and 7 Months

In Memory of
Sarah Daugr of
William and
Jane Haviland
She Departed
this Life Oct 10th
1774
Aged 5 Years

799 r
A. H.
In memory of
Abigail daughtr of
John & Sarah Havi
land who died Novr

17th 1797 in the 33d
year of her age

Why do ye mourn departing friends
Or shake at deaths alarm
Tis but the voice that Jesus sends
To call us to his arms.

800 *r*
Luke Heaviland Son of John
and Sarah Heaviland
was Born Jan^{ry} 26 : 1770
and Died Octr 16 1777
Sleep Lovely Child
and take your Rest
God Call'd you home
He thought it Best

---

801 *m*
IN
MEMORY OF
THOMAS HAVILAND
DIED
DEC. 25th 1825
IN THE 51st YEAR
OF HIS AGE

---

802 *r*
R. H.
In Memory of
Rhode wife of Tho-
mas Haviland who
died Octr 5th 1797
in the 20th year of
her age——

The brightest things below the sky
Give but a flattering light
We should expect some danger nigh
When we possess delight

---

803 *r*
S. H.
In Memory of
SARAH widow of
John Haviland
who died
June 26th 1812
in the 74th year
of her age

Let heav'nly love prepare my soul
And call her to the skies
Where years of long salvation roll
And glory never dies.

[Stone broken off]

---

804 *r*
Luke son of John
& Sarah Haviland
died May the 19th
1789. in the 8th year
of his age

To God's unerring will
Be ev'ry wish resigned

---

805 *r*
J. H.
In Memory of
Jacob son of
Benjamin & Sarah
Haviland died
Decr 5th 1806 in the
11th year of his age

Let all that's hear behold and see
This child, and wonder why
That wer'e alive while he is gone
Into Eternity

---

806 *r*
B. H.
In memory of
Mr Benjamin Haviland
who deceas'd
March 27th 1803 in
the 50th year of
his Age——

Wife and children dont deplore
A loving husband & kind father is no more
No more for us will he provide
We hope he'll rest at Jesus side

---

807 *r*
S. H.
In memory of
SARAH widow of
Benjamin Haviland
who died
March 7th 1826
in the 65th year
of her age

So then every one of us shall give
account of himself to God
ROMANS XIV. 12th

808 *r*
J H
In memory of
JANE wife of
Jotham Hand
who died
May 27th 1817;

in the 32d year
of her age
———
Also JANE HAVILAND,
their daughter died June 6th
1817 Aged 13 days

---

809 *m*
Sacred
To the memory
of
Capt THOMAS CROWELL
who died in London Decr 14
1799 in the 74th year of his age

Christian his wife departed
this life June 4th 1790 in the
61st year of her age
Also
Agness daughter of Capt Thomas
Crowell Junr and Esther his wife
who departed this life July 10th 1794
Aged 10 years 7 months and 13 days

What in others is usually the effect of
Education and Habit seemed born with her.
from a very Babe the utmost regularity
was observable in all her actions, what
ever she did was well done, and with an
apparent reflection far beyond her years.

---

810 *r*
F. W.
In memory of
FANNY
daughter of
David & Joanna
Woodruff
who died
Octr 17th 1824;
Aged 52 years.

Precious time is ever sliding,
Brightest hours have no delay
Life and time are worth improveing,
Seize the moments as they fly

811 *m*
IN
Memory of
HARRIET E.
Daughter of
Benjamin & Mary Ann Brown
who died Augst 25th 1838:
Aged 28 Years 2 Months
and 19 Days

Also
BENJAMIN,
their son
died Augst 25th 1815
Aged 9 mos. and 25 d's

812 *r*
M. A. B.
In memory of
MARY ANN
wife of
Benjamin Brown ;
who died
Decr 11th 1832,
in the 60th year
of her age

Ye fleeting charms of earth farewell !
Your springs of joy are dry ;
My soul now seeks another home
A brighter world on high.

---

813 *m*
IN
Memory of
BENJAMIN BROWN
WHO DIED
June 14th 1852,
Aged 83 Years
1 Month &
23 Days

---

814 *r*
L. B.
In memory of
LYDIA BROWN
who died
Octr 11th 1826 ;
in the 47th year
of her age.

The voice of this alarming scene
May ev'ry heart obey
Nor be the heav'nly warning vain
Which calls to watch and pray

---

815 *r*
E. M.
In memory of
ELIZABETH,
wife of Henry Martin
& daughter of Moses &
Phebe Connet, who
died Augst 25th 1811, in
the 27th year of
her age.

Stop passengers and O be wise
Hope not for bliss below the skies,
Here in this dark and silent bed
The mother and her babes are laid ;
Sweet babes, and mother short was
thy sta^y
A soul prepar'd, needs no delay.

---

816 *r*
M. C.
In memory of
Moses Connet,
who died June 19th
1785, in the 40th year
of his age.

Betsy, daughter of
Moses & Phebe Connet
died Augt 15th 1777, in
the 4th year of her age.

---

817 *r*
P. C.
In Memory of
PHEBE,
widow of
Moses Connet,
who died May 2^d
1813, in the 63^d
year of his age

Go home my friends dry up your tears
I must lie here till Christ appears,
Repent in time while time you have
There's no repentance in the grave.

---

818 *m*
IN
Memory of
MARY
WIDOW OF
Thomas Gorman
who died Novr 24th 1860 :
In the 85th Year
of her age

" Blessed are the dead that die in
the Lord ,,

819 m
IN
Memory of
RHODA
WIDOW OF
Major Denman
who died April 5th 1862 :
Aged 80 Years and
9 Months

"Father I will that they also whome thou hast given me be with me where I am."

820 m
IN
Memory of
MAJOR DENMAN
WHO DIED
March 22d 1851 :
Aged 75 Years

"So teach us to number our days that we may apply our hearts unto wisdom.",

821 m
IN
Memory of
Capt WILLIAM H
DENMAN
who died
June 2d 1847
Aged 44 Years

"Then shall the dust return to the earth as it was, and the spirit shall return unto God who gave it."

822 r
S. M.
In memory of
SOPHIA
daughter of Aaron
& Sarah Meeker
who died
April 29th 1814
Aged 17 years 8 months
& 21 days

Here lies a lovely pleasant flow'r
Cut down in early time
Death doth our fairest hopes destroy
And nips our joys in prime

823 r
Zeuiah Daughr
of David & Sarah
Meeker deceas'd
April ye 18th 1787
In the 19th Year
of her Age——

824 r
Here lyes ye Body of
Rebekah wife of Jona.
Meeker Junir Dec'd
Janry ye 12 1745-6
in ye 25th year
of her Age

825 r
I. M.
In Memory of
Jonathan Meeker
died June 10th 1805
In the 62d Year
of his Age

Be still and know that
I am God   Psalms XLVI, 10.

In Memory of Abigail C
Meeker Daur. of Jonathan &
Martha Meeker. died March
16th 1806. Aged 2 Months & 1 Day.

826 r
HERE lies the Body
of Mary Wife of
Jonathan Meeker
who departed this
Life May ye 30th Ano
Domini 1773 In ye 30th
Year of her Age

827 r
In
Memory of
Rachel Daur of
Jonathan & Rachel
Meeker. died Augst
15th 1804. Aged 11
Years 1 Month & 20 Ds.

A lovely Child & active two
Is gone & bid this whorld adieu

INSCRIPTIONS IN FIRST PRESBYTERIAN

828 r
In
Memory of
Polly Dau[r] of
Jonathan & Rachel
Meeker died April
7th 1805. In the 19th
Year of her Age.

She lived deserv'd belov'd
And died sincerely lamente[d],

829 r
In
Memory of
Elly Son of Jonathan
& Rachel Meeker
died June 7th 1797
Aged 11 Years 10
Months & 9 Days

To Gods unerring will
Be every wish resin'd

830 m
In
Memory of
JOB SAYER
who died
MAY 22 1843
In the 53. year of
his age

More quickly and shorter I breath—
 The dew is o'er spreading my cheek
I feel the approaches of death
 My heartstrings beginning to break
A struggle or two and tis done
 From earth and its anguish I fly
The Palm of the conquer'or won
 I live by submitting to die.

831 m
In
Memory of
Mrs PHEBE MULFORD
who died
June 30th 1857
in the 63[d] year
of her age

Farewell Dear Children my life is past,
My love to you while life did last:
Then after me no sorrow take
But love each other for my sake

832 m
In
memory of
MARY   CRANE
wife of
John Crane
who departed this life
March 5th 1837
in the 74th year
of her age

A virtuous woman, prudent and sincere,
A tender wife and mother slumbers here:
With Martha's care she still had Mary's part,
The world employ'd her hands but heav'n her heart.

833 m
In
memory of
JOHN CRANE
who departed this life
April 7th 1840
in the 80th year
of his age

The year rolls round and steals away
The breath that first it gave
What e'er we do, where e'er we be
We're trave'ling to the grave

834 m
[Stone broken]
In
Memory of
ABBY W.
widow of
David O Harrison
who died
March 30th 1844
In the 29th Year
of her age

also
DAVID, O.
their son who died
March 3 1842 Aged 2 Yeas
& 7 months

835 *m*
[Stone broken]
In
Memory of
ELIHU CRANE
WHO DIED
Dec 23rd 1845
Aged 41 Years

"In the midst of life we are in death
Death is a debt to mortals due
I've paid that debt and so must you."

836 *m*
IN
Memory of
JOANNA
daughter of
JOHN & HANNAH WINANS
WHO DIED
Dec 5th 1842
Aged 20 Years & 6 Months

The victory now is obtain'd
  She's gone her dear Saviour to see
Her wishes she fully has gain'd
  She's now where she longed to be
Then let us forbear to complain
  That she has now gone from our sight
We soon shall behold her again
  With new and redoubled delight.

837 *m*
S. A. W.
In memory of
SARAH ANN
daughter of John
& Hannah Winans
who died Dec'r 11th 1824
Aged 14 years
& 3 months

Farewell no more I tread your ground
No more I need the gospel sound
My feet have reached the heav'nly shore
I know no imperfections more.

838 *m*
IN
memory of
AARON LITTELL
who died
Dec'r 15th 1831
Aged 65 years

839 *m*
IN
memory of
SARAH
wife of
Aaron Littell
who died
Dec'r 10th 1831
Aged 60 years

840 *r*
W. J. B. J. M. J.
In memory of three children
of Herbert and Elizabeth Jewells
William died June 16th 1803 aged 1 year
10 months & 3 days. Betsy L. died
Oct'r 25th 1806 aged 1 year 2 m°. & 6 days
Matthew H. died Aug'st 21 1807 aged 16 days

841 r
P. B. S
———
J. M. S
In memory of
Phebe B wife of
William W Smith
who died Octr 22nd 1820
in the 33rd year
of her age

The months of affliction are o'er
The days and the nights of distress
We see her in anguish no more
She's gained her happy release

Also of James M their
son who died Augst 10th 1814
Aged 10 months & 5 days

842 r
S. S.
In Memory of
Susan
widow of
William Smith
who departed this life
February 25th 1813
Aged 67 years

My friends prepare to follow me
Both young and old must die you see
There's no discharge, there's no delay
When death demands we must obey

843 r
W S
J S
In Memory of
William Smith
who departed this Life
August the 6th 1788
in the 46th Year of his Age
Also
In Memory of
James Smith
who departed this life
July the 15th 1790
in the 14th Year of his Age

844 r
In memory of
Sarah, Susanna,
and Elizabeth
daughters of
William and Susanna
Smith
Sarah died Augt 20th 1773
aged 5 days
Susanna died Octr 4th 1778
aged 1 month
Elizabeth died Decr 3^d 1778
in the 8th year of her age

My parents dear weep not for me
When in this yard my grave you see
My time was short but blest is he
That call'd me to eternity,

845 r
In
memory of
Addeline
daughter of
Oliver and Susanna
Smith
who departed this life
April 24th 1808
aged 1 year 9 months
and 24 days——
May she rest in peace

846 r
In
memory
of
Oliver Smith
who died
Decr 24th 1823
in the 47th year
of his age
Also
Thaddeus M
Son of Oliver & Susan
Smith who died at
Nashville Tennessee
Septr 16th 1836
in the 22^d year
of his age

847 m
THE
GRAVE
OF
MARIA HINCHMAN
WIDOW OF
James A Hinchman
who died at Brooklyn N. Y.
Feby 4th 1857 :
Aged 56 Years

848 m
THE
GRAVE
OF
ANN LYON
DAUGHTER OF
Levi and Martha Lyon
who died at Osage Illinois
Feby 15th 1857
Aged 47 Years

849 m
IN
Memory of
JAMES STUART
SON OF
James & Harriet H
ROLLO
Born July 11th 1844
Died April 3^d 1845
Aged 8 months
& 23 days

850 r
W. O. H.
In memory of
WILLIAM OLIVER
son of Wm H. & Eliza
Hinchman who died
June 21st 1822
Aged 10 Months
& 13 Days

Vain world, how transien^t is its joys
Its pleasures soon will end in pain
But where I'm gone there's no alloy
Who would not die this Bliss to gain.

851 m
THE GRAVE
OF
ANN ELIZA
Daughter of
William H. and
Eliza Hinchman
who died
Decr 18th 1847 ;
Aged 24 Years
7 Months and
25 Days

852 m
THE
GRAVE
OF
WILLIAM H. HINCHMAN
who departed this life
in the City of New York
July 13th 1825 :
In the 31st year of his age

853 m
THE
GRAVE
OF
ELIZA DOANE
WHO DIED
at Osage Illinois
Jany 4th 1857
Aged 58 Years

854 m
THE
GRAVE
OF
AUSTIN PLATT
who departed this life
in the City of New York
November 30th 1830
In the 32 year
of his age

INSCRIPTIONS IN FIRST PRESBYTERIAN

855 *m*
The
Grave
of
HENRY DOANE
who departed this life
Augst 3^d 1849
In the 59th Year
of his age

856 *m*
JAMES ROLLO
Born
Jan. 15th 1816
Died
July 20th 1870

857 *m*
THE
GRAVE
OF
THOMAS ROLLO
who died
May 15th 1852 :
Aged 32 Years

858 *m*
IN
Memory of
Mrs DOLLY VAIL
from Orange County N. Y.
who departed this life
at Elizabeth Port N. J.
April 25th 1845
Aged 65 Years
2 Months
& 23 Days

859 *m*
IN
Memory of
CHARLES H. G.
son of
Gilbert B & Dolly M Gale
who died at Elizabeth Port N. J.
Sept 17th 1850
Aged 16 Years 7 Months
and 12 Days

860 *m*
GILBERT B GALE
Born
at Goshen Orange Co. N. Y.
April 14th 1797 :
Died
at Elizabeth Port N. J.
Novr 14th 1860.

861 *m*
IN
memory of
Phebe
wife of
Silas Ward
who departed this life
Septr 23^d 1831 ;
in the 63^d year
of her age

" There remaineth a rest
to the people of God."

862 *m*
IN
Memory of
SILAS WARD
born at Morristown
Octr 19th 1767 ;
and died
May 12th 1862 :

863 *m*
IN MEMORY OF
ELIZABETH CAROLINE
WARD
Daughter of
SILAS AND PHEBE WARD
Born September 21st 1803.
at Chatham N. J.
Died
May 26th 1882

864
[Marble Monument]
[North side]
ELIHU MORTON,
BORN
Nov. 13th. 1775.
DIED
April 28th 1863

Also his Wife
AMELIA MORTON
BORN
Aug. 5th 1781,
DIED
Nov 4th 1853.

[On West side]
ELVIRA MORTON,
DIED
Nov. 8th 1871,
In the 70th, Year
of her age

"In the world to come
Life everlasting."

[East side]
LEWIS M MORTON,
BORN
April 30th 1812,
DIED
Feby 2nd. 1834.

AMELIA KELLOGG,
BORN
March 10th 1810.
DIED
Nov. 24th 1849

ANNA D. HUNT,
BORN
Jan'y 29th, 1806,
DIED
Aug. 12th 1854

[South side blank]

865 *m*
[In plot enclosed by iron fence]
ARCHIBALD McCULLUM
DIED JULY 25th. 1843,
AGED 89 YEARS & 9 MOS.

REBECCA BALLARD
HIS WIFE
DIED SEPTr. 23rd. 1854,
AGED 74 YEARS & 6 MOS.

OUR LABORS DONE, SECURELY LAID
IN THIS OUR LAST RETREAT
UNHEEDED, O'ER OUR SILENT DUST,
THE STORMS OF LIFE SHALL BEAT.

THESE ASHES TOO, THIS LITTLE DUST,
OUR FATHER'S CARE SHALL KEEP,
TILL THE LAST ANGEL RISE, AND BREAK
THE LONG AND DREARY SLEEP

ELIZABETH BALLARD
DIED SEPTr, 11th 1858.
AGED 68 YEARS.
"BECAUSE I LIVE
YE SHALL LIVE ALSO."

866 *m*
J. T.
In memory of
JOANNA
wife of
Thomas R Thompson
who died Novr 24th 1826,
in the 36th year
of her age

Farewell ye friends whose tender care
Has long engag'd my love
Your fond embrace I now exchange
For better friends above.

867 *m*
SACRED
to the Memory of
ZURVIAH OGDEN
WHO DIED
April 11th 1836;
Aged 62 Years

"Blessed are the dead
that die in the Lord."

868 *m*
SACRED
to the Memory of
ELIZABETH QUIGLEY
WHO DIED
May 7th 1827;
Aged 61 Years.

"In such an hour as ye think not
the Son of man cometh."

869 *r*
J. Q.
In memory of
John Quigley
who died Septr. 22^d
1796 in the 28th
year of his Age

also John son of
John & Elizabeth
Quigley died Augst
13th 1797 aged 9 mon^s.

---

870 *r*
HERE lies the Bodies of two Sons of
Robert & Jane Quigley
Viz

Daniel who died
March the 25th
A. D. 1785 aged
7 Weeks.

Thomas who died
March the 7th
A. D. 1787 aged
8 Weeks

---

871 *m*
IN
MEMORY OF
SARAH C.
WIDOW OF
SAMUEL K. MILLER,
WHO DIED
May 5th. 1862;
In the 82^d Year
of her age

872 *m*
IN
MEMOBY OF
SAMUEL K MILLER,
WHO DIED
Decr. 27th 1850;
In the 75th Year
of his age

873 *m*
IN
MEMORY OF
HANNAH MILLER

BORN
March 22, 1804.
DIED
August 9, 1881

874 *r*
Here lies Intarr'd the
Body of Benjamin Hunt
who was Born In Rehoboth
In New England May 4th
1715 and Departed this
Life Jany. 17th A D 1763
In ye 48th. Year of his age

875 *r*
E. M.
In memory of
Eliza J daughter of
Isaac & Abigail
Matteson, died Dec^r.
25th. 1803; in the 3 year
of her age.

Sleep on dear child & take your rest
God call'd the home, he saw it best.

876 r

[Lies flat on the ground in front of 874 and 875]
Here lyeth ye Body of Mr Thomas
Johnson who Departed this Life Aprill
The 1st 1732 in ye 67 year of his Age
How vain this World in all its pompous Show
How soon will this vain Scene quite dissappear
When towering Expectations highest grow
The pale fac'd Conqueror is often near
Grim Death with ghastly Mein serves his Arres^t
The proudest Monarch prostrates in ye Dust
Nor Wealth, nor Power, nor humblest Reques^t
Bribes, awes, or softens him submit we must
Since it is so prepare for this dark Home
By making Christ your true and lasting Friend
That you may rise with joy when he shall come
And join in Hallelujah^s without End.

Here lies ye Body of Mrs Elizabeth Balm late
Relict of Mr Thomas Johnson Dec^d. Sepr. 22
1735   Aged 58 years

---

877 r
HERE lies the Body
of Mrs Abigail, wid°
of Mr Joseph Hallcy
who departed this
Life January ye 18th
Anno Domini 1777
In the LXXII Year of
her Age———————

878 r
Here lies ye Body
of Mr Joseph Hallcy
who departed this
Life Dece^r ye 16th An°
Domini 1771. In ye 76th
Year of his Age
Is this ye Fate. that all must die
Will Death no age's Spare?
Then let us àll to Jesus fly
And seek for Refuge there

879 m
JOHN CHANDLER
Born Apr 25 1756,
Died May 17, 1824
Æ 68

880 m
MARY
Wife of
JOHN CHANDLER,
Born June 3, 1757,
Died May 15, 1829
Æ 72

881 r
M. C.
In memory of
Mary widow of Mr
John Chandler
died May 10th 1801,
in the 70th year of
her age

882 r
J. C.
In memory of
John Chandler
------ ug ------ [Date gone]
1800 in the 68th
Year of his age

INSCRIPTIONS IN FIRST PRESBYTERIAN

883 r
HERE lies yᵉ Remains
of Mr Joseph Chandler
who died June the 1ˢᵗ
Anno Domini 1755
In the 87ᵗʰ Year of
his Age———

884 r
Here Lyeth yᵉ Body
of joseph Chandler
Who Departed
This life August yᵉ 5
Anno Domini 1738
in yᵉ 29ᵗʰ year of his
Age———

885 r
HERE LIETH
interr'd the Body of
Mr John Chandler
who died March yᵉ
24ᵗʰ A. D. 1758

In yᵉ 58ᵗʰ Year
of his
Age

886 r
Jemima
Daughᵗʳ of Jameˢ
& Jemima Chandlʳ
died Septʳ yᵉ 4ᵗʰ
A. D. 1746 In yᵉ 3ᵈ
Year of her Age

887 r
In memory of
James Chandler Junʳ.
who died
Janʸ 7ᵗʰ 1808
aged 55 years

The year rolls round and steals away
The breath that first it gave
What e'er we do where'er we be
We're trav'lling to the grave.

888 r

In
memory of
James Chandler
who departed
this life
April 30ᵗʰ 1791
in the 74 year
of his Age

In
memory of
Jemmiaˢ. I Chandler
wife of
James Chandler
who departed
this life
August 19ᵗʰ 1807
in the 88ᵗʰ year
of her Age

889 m
IN
Memory of
JONATHAN CHANDLER
WHO DIED
Feb'y. 9ᵗʰ 1836
Aged 73 years

The time is short the season near
When death will us remove
To leave our friends however dear
And all we fondly love.

890 m
IN
Memory of
MARY
WIDOW OF
Jonathan Chandler
who died Octʳ 20ᵗʰ 1851
aged 83 years

Mother thy name I still revere
No earthly name to me so dear
My first, my best, my long tried friend
My love for thee will never end.

891 *r*
IN
memory of
SAMUEL LOCKER
who died
Sept 7 1831
aged 41 years 1 month
and 7 days
ALSO
Two children of Samuel
& Maria C. Locker
DAVID CHANDLER
died Augst 24th 1826
aged 1 month
and 22 days
SAMUEL MERRIT
died Feby 24th 1836
aged 3 years 11 months
and 21 days

892 *m*
IN
Memory of
PAMELA P.
daughter of
JONATHAN & MARY
CHANDLER
who died
Feb. 10. 1844
In the 33, Year of
her age

Happy soul, thy days are ended
All thy mourning days below
Go, by angel guards attended
To the sight of Jesus go.

893 *m*
JANE SQUIER
WIDOW OF
JACOB G. CRANE,
BORN
JAN^y 14th 1809,
DIED
MAY 10th 1869,
"ASLEEP IN JESUS"

894 *m*
JACOB G CRANE
BORN
AUGst 13th 1806
DIED
DEC^r. 3^d 1864,

"IN THE MIDST OF LIFE WE ARE IN
DEATH"

895 *r*
Abigail Daughter of
Matthias & Susanna
Crane died Augst. 11th
Anno Domini 1774
in the 17th Year of her
Age————

896 *m*
HANNAH
WIFE OF ANDREW CRANE
DIED FEB. 28th 1852
AGED 45 YEARS

Stop my friend ! O take another view !
The dust that moulders here
Was once belov'd like you !
No longer then on future time rely
Improve the present—
And prepare to die.!

897 *m*
IN
Memory of
GEORGE CRANE
WHO DIED
Feby 24st 1848
Aged 51 Years
also 5 Children of
George and Susas Crane
SEAREN
died Novr. 16th 1821 aged 9 days
FANNY
died Oct 25 1825 aged 1 yr & 11 mo
ROBERT
Born & died Jan. 5 1825
FANNY
died April 5 1828 aged 11 months
MARY
died Oct 6 1838
aged 8 y'rs 10 mo's & 23 d's

898 r
D B C
David B son of
Matthias and
Phebe Crane
died March 19th
1797 in the 12th year
of his Age———

899 r
P C
In memory of
PHEBE
widow of
Matthias Crane
who died Oct[r] 26th
1825 in the 86th year
of her age

Great God I own thy sentence just,
And nature must decay!
I yield my body to the dust.
To dwell with fellow clay.

900 r
HERE lies y[e] Body
of Mr George———
Williams. who died
May y[e] 26th Anno
Domini 1774 In y[e]
51st Year of his Age

901 m
IN
Memory of
JOHN C CRANE
WHO DIED
Sept 13th 1840
Aged 26 Years 5 months
and 3 days
Also
EDWIN B.
Son of
John C & Catharine Crane
who died Dec 25th 1840
Aged 1 Year & 10 Months

Dear as thou wert and justly dear
We will not weep for thee
One thought shall check the starting
tear
It is that thou art free

902 m
In
Memory of
P R U D E N C E
Wife of Matthias Crane
who departed this Life
December 23rd 1804
In the 21st Year of
her age

903 m
M. C.
In Memory of
Maj. MATTHIAS CRANE
who died
July 3[d] 1825
in the 45th year
of his age

An affectionate husband, a ten-
-der father, a kind brother, a good
neighbour, a useful citizen, and an
humble diciple of Christ
" The memory of the just is blessed."

904 m
OUR DEAR MOTHER
SARAH LUM
Widow of
MAJ. M CRANE
Deceased Sep. 5th, A. D. 1868 ;
IN HER 87th YEAR.

OUR ONLY SISTER
JANE ELIZ. CRANE,
DIED SEP. 24th A. D. 1864 ;
IN HER 44th YEAR

905 *m*
IN
Memory of
ELIZABETH S.
daughter of
Jacob & Sarah Crane
Who died Dec. 8th 1837
Aged 36 Years
Also
Elizabeth S.
daughter of
William A & Ann F Crane
who died Dec. 18th 1844
Aged 15 Months & 13 days

Benevolence with grace combin'd
Were characteristic of her mind
She's gone to dwell in Heaven above
Where all is joy and peace and love

" Except ye become as little children ye shall in no wise enter the Kingdom of Heaven "

---

906 *m*
SACRED
to the Memory of
JACOB CRANE
who died
July 4th 1847
IN THE 73RD YEAR OF HIS AGE

A devoted Husband, an affectionate Parent, and a faithful Friend. His integrity ; his honor and his love of Justice made him uni- -versally esteemed and beloved by all the friends of good order, and his death brought sorrow to many loving hearts.

Father thou art gone ! but the remembrance of your kind and generous heart will live in our memory while we sojourn here on earth

---

907 *m*
IN
Memory of
SARAH SAYRE
Wife of Jacob Crane
who died Dec. 6th 1863
Aged 84 Years 11 Mo's & 22 Days

A beloved wife, A kind and faithful Mother, whose prayers are answered in the conversion of all her children to God

908 r

HERE lies ye Body of
Esther Wife of John
Donington, who died
June ye 8th 1785 in the
25th Year of her Age
In the bloom of life She bid farewell
To Parents Friends and all
And willingly resigned her breath
At Jesus sovereign call

909 r

Jane wife of John
Donington died Aug
20   1803,
in the 23^d year of
her age

John Donington
Died Aug
28   1803
in the 48th year of
his age

910 m

In
Memory of
JOB SAYER
son of Elias B &
Maria Crane
who died
April 5th 1847
aged 2 years
8 months &
11 days

We miss him O how sadly
He whom we loved so well
But we know that he is happy
For he is gone with God to dwell.

911 m

JACOB D. E.
Son of
Col James W, &
Martha A, Woodruff

DIED
May 29th 1875,
Aged 33 Yrs &
9 Months

He responded to his Countrys
Call. and fell asleep in the
arms of his Saviour

912 m

LIZZIE B.
WILLIS
Daughter of
Col James W. &
Martha A. Woodruff,
DIED
May 16th 1875,
Aged 25 Yrs &
11 Days

There is sweet music in Heaven.

913 m

[Marble monument, stone coping and wood picket fence around it]
[South Side]

Col JACOB D
EDWARDS,
Died at Boston Mass
June 24th 1847,
Aged 47 years.
—o—
"In the midst of life we are in death,,
"I have finish'd my work upon earth,
"And there's rest for me
in Heaven"

[East Side]

MARTHA
WIFE OF
J. D. EDWARDS
DIED MARCH 26th 1845
AGED 40 YEARS
———o———
HUSBAND, CHILDREN, FRIENDS,
MOURN NOT FOR ME
MOURN FOR YOURSELVES
"FOR DEATH CAN BRING TO ME NO STING,
THE GRAVE NO DESOLATION
TIS GAIN TO DIE WITH JESUS NIGH
THE ROCK OF OUR SALVATION."

[North Side]

MARY ALICE WOODRUFF
BORN AUG 5 1843
DIED NOV 6 1878

COL. JAMES W. WOODRUFF
BORN NOV. 16 1814
DIED JULY 8 1877

MARTHA A.
WIFE OF
JAMES W WOODRUFF
DIED
SEPT 27th 1853,
AGED 28 YEARS
& 27 DAYS

LOVED ONES
MEET ME IN HEAVEN

[West Side]

JACOB
DIED
March 4th 1825
Aged 18 Months
HANNAH ELIZABETH
DIED
April 28th 1832
Aged 4 Years

INSCRIPTIONS IN FIRST PRESBYTERIAN

914 *r*
Here lies the Body
of Phebe Wife of
Jesse Woodruff who
departed this Life
Oct ye 10th Anno
Domini 1776 and
in the 27th Year of her
Age

915 *m*
FRANCIS PIERSON
BORN
August 18th 1818,
DIED
March 22nd 1883

916 *m*
ALBERT A PIERSON
DIED
JULY 13th 1848
AGED 44 YEARS

917 *m*
CATHARINE A
Wife of
WILLIAM PIERSON
DIED
April 6th 1866
In the 88th year of
her age

918 *m*
WILLIAM PIERSON
DIED
May 22^d 1871
Aged 93 yrs 10
mo's & 11 days

919 *m*
W^M ROCKWELL
Son of
John H & Harriet
ROLSTON
BORN
Dec 23^d 1852
DIED
May 7th 1853

920 *m*
DOLLY M GALE
Wife of
GILBERT B GALE
Born at Goshen Orange
Co. N. Y. Oct 1st 1798
Died at Elizabethport
N. J. March 27th 1868.

921 *m*
MATILDA WOODHULL
Daughter of
JAMES G & MATILDA G,
NUTTMAN,
DIED FEBRUARY 21st 1875
AGED 30 YEARS

My spirit hath rejoiced in God my
Saviour

922 *m*
IN
Memory of
JAMES GARDINER
SON OF
JAMES G & MATILDA G
NUTTMAN
WHO DIED
MAY 12th 1858,
AGED 16 YEARS

"Be still and know that I am God"

---

918 Son of Elishabe Wood by her first husband. She was sister of Clement Wood and was b. 1738. Md., 1st, Pierson, 2d, Moses Johnson and d. Sept. 23, 1831.

923 *m*
IN
Memory of
OLIVER CRAIG
SON OF
JAMES G & MATILDA G
NUTTMAN
who died
July 3^d 1855,
Aged 15 years & 9 months

"Peaceful in death
Asleep in Jesus."

924 *r*
J B D
This stone is
Erected to the
memory
of
Jonathan B Dayton
who died
May 15th 1832.
Aged 48 years

As a Friend, he was firm & sincere;
As a Husband, kind & affectionate.

925 *m*
TO THE MEMORY
OF
MARY DAYTON
WIFE OF
SMITH HALSEY,
Died March 20th, 1866
In her 71st year

926 *m*
The
grave of
MY MOTHER.
ELIZABETH DOW.
died Jan, 3. 1858,
aged 82 years
& 6 mo's

927 *r*
S D
Samuel Son of
Samuel & Elizabeth
Dow. died June ye 28
1799. aged 4 months
and 17 days

928 *r*
S. D.
In memory of
Samuel, son of
Samuel & Eliza^h
Dow. died Oct^r
15th 1806 aged
1 year 9 months
& 16 days

929 *r*
Martha, daughter
of Daniel & Desire
Ross died July y^e
13th 1793, aged 2
days

930 *r*
David
Osborn
Aged 9 m
1731

931 *r*
W. B. H.
In memory of
William Brown, Son
of Isaac and Hannah
Higgins, died Oct^r
30th 1802 in the 3^d
year of his
Age

932 *r*
D. H.
In memory of
Deborah Halsted
daughter of Isaac &
Hannah Higgins, died
Feby 11th 1807; aged
8 years 11 months
& 1 day

933 r
[Stone broken]
iggin
who died
Mar^h the 2^d 1808
in the 41st year of
his age

A husband dear a father kind
A social faithful friend
Has gone to that world above
where joys shall never end

---

934 r
H. H.
In memory of
Hannah widow of
Isaac Higgins
who died
April 17th 1811
aged 36 years

Pressed by the hand of sore disease
In pain I wandered on :
Till God my Saviour arm'd with love
In Mercy call'd me home

---

935 m
ERECTED
For my Husband
RICHARD KETTLEWELL,
who departed this life
March 2nd 1848 :
Aged 62 Years and
11 Months

Asleep in Jesus ! far from thee,
Thy kindred and thier graves may be.
But sweet the thought ; the grave
can't sever ;
Earths broken ties will in Heaven
unite forever,

---

936 m
THEODORE A,
SON OF
Charles A &
Abby C Kiggins
died Sept, 16th 1850,
In the 3^d Year
of his age

---

937 m
[Monument]
[East Side]
EVERT MARSH
BORN
FEB^y 28th 1783
DIED
OCT^r 11th 1843
MARY D CHANDLER
WIFE OF
EVERT MARSH
Born May 8th 1786
Died Feby 24th 1838

[North Side]
EVERT MARSH
SON OF
EVERT & MARY MARSH
BORN
DEC^r 15th 1824
DIED
AUG^st 15th 1827

[South Side]
CHESTER E MARSH
SON OF
EVERT & MARY MARSH
BORN
OCT^r 8th 1826,
DIED
JULY 17th 1849.

[West Side blank]

---

938 m
IN
memory of
ELIZABETH KILBORN
WIFE OF
ISAAC CHANDLER,
Born August 8th 1790,
Fell asleep May 25th 1875.

" Her children arise up and call
her blessed."

Also of
COMFORT
WIDOW OF
MOSES CHANDLER,
Jan, 4. 1835,
Aged 69.

939 m
IN
Memory of
ISAAC CHANDLER,
WHO DIED
Nov, 10, 1865,
Aged 75 years.
Also of
MOSES CHANDLER
a Ruling Elder of the First Church
for Thirty years,
WHO DIED
JAN, 25, 1834,
AGED 68 YEARS.
ELIZABETH P WILSON
DIED SEPT, 6, 1866
AGED 8, MONTHS.

940 r
Mary Daughter
of Jonathan and
Sarah Crane.
who died March
ye 6th A D. 1769 Ag^d
3 Years & 11 Months

941 m
IN
memory of
ABBY CLARK.
daughter of
Robert & Anna Clark.
who died
March 4th 1845.
Aged 24 Years 11 Months & 18 days,
———o———
The months of affliction are o'er
The days and the nights of distress
We'll see her in anguish no more
She's gain'd her happy release.

942 m
IN
MEMORY OF
ANNA L.
WIDOW OF ROBERT CLARK,
WHO DIED
DECEMBER 4th 1851:
AGED 58 YEARS 3 MO &
15 DAYS

943 r
IN
memory of
ROBERT CLARK
who died
Novr 12th 1835,
in the 48th year
of his age
The year rolls round and steals away,
The breath that first it gave ;
What e'er we do, where e'er we be,
We're trav'ling to the grave.

943½ r
[This Stone is set close against back of
No. 943]
Here lies ye Body
of Phebe Stanbro
who Departed
this Life Sepr ye 22
1736 in ye 59 year
of her Age

944 r
IN
memory of
MARY ANN
daughter of Robert
& Anna Clark
who died
Augst 23^d 1835,
aged 17 years
and 5 months.
Stop my friend, O take another view ;
The dust that moulders here,
Was once belov'd like you ;
No longer then on future time rely.
Improve the present
And prepare to die !

945 r
James ye Son of
Sovereign & Joanna
Sybrandt. who
deceas'd Decem^r
ye 28th 1762. In y^e
2^d year of his Age

946 r
In memory of Joanna & Mary,
wives of James Carmichael.
Joanna was Daughter of Matt^a
Hetfield Esqr & died Septr 27th
A x D. 1756. in the 25th Year
of her Age———
Mary Daughter of George
Badgley died July the 30th
A x D. 1759. in the 21st Year
of her Age———

947 r
[This Stone lies flat in front of Nos. 945 and 946]
Beneath this Stone
Rests
Phebe, once Miss Chandler
and the late amiable consort
of Capt Saml Hendry
With her infant Daughter
Ob^{nt} 22^d June 13th Augt 1781
Ann Ætat 20 & Mense 4.

Quando ullam invenies parem
Guiltless alike chaste spirits wheresoe'er
Ye bask irradiate in the beams of love
Oh bid one ray of comfort gild dispair
Till blest reunion shall the cloud remove

948 m
IN MEMORY OF
SARAH
WIFE OF
NEHEMIAH CRANE
who died Septr 28th 1828.
In the 36th Year
of her age
———o———
Almost the last I heard her say.
Come kind Jesus take me away

949 m
IN MEMORY OF
NEHEMIAH CRANE
who died Dec, 31st 1833 ;
Aged 48 years

Survey me well, ye youthful, and believe
The grave may terrify but can't deceive
On beauty's fragile base no more depend,
Here youth and pleasure, age and sorrow end.

950 m
MARTHA CRANE
RELICT OF
NOAH CRANE
DIED
MARCH 31st 1862,
IN HER 85th YEAR

My flesh and my heart faileth : but God is the strength of my heart, and my portion for ever.
Psalms LXXIII, 26,

951 m
To
the memory of
NOAH CRANE
who died suddenly
Feby 25th 1831
Aged 57 years

He maintained through life the character of an honest man and for some years a consistent christian

Death like an overflowing stream
Sweeps us away our life's a dream
An empty tale: a morning flower
Cut down and withered in an hour

Reader!
Boast not thyself of to morrow
for thou knowest not what a day
may bring forth.

952 m
JONATHAN SQUIER
SON OF
JACOB G AND
JANE S. CRANE,
DIED OCT. 4th 1859,
AGED 7 YEARS
11 MONTHS AND
13 DAYS

"It is well"

953 m
NOAH
SON OF
JACOB G. AND
JANE S CRANE
BORN NOVr 15th 1836–
DIED APRIL 18th 1861

"THY BROTHER SHALL RISE AGAIN"

954 m
THE GRAVE
OF
ABRAHAM W CRANE
SON OF
NOAH & MARTHA CRANE,
WHO DIED
JUNE 27th 1847,
IN THE 27th YEAR
OF HIS AGE

"WHAT IS YOUR LIFE? IT IS EVEN A
VAPOR THAT APPEARETH FOR A LITTLE
TIME AND THEN VANISHETH AWAY."

955 m
[Horizontal Tomb, 2 feet high]
THE GRAVE
OF
JONATHAN CRANE
who died in the City of Mobile
October 12th 1837
Aged 37 years.

"Death loves a shining mark."

Here also sleep two children of
Jonathan & Henrietta M Crane
GEORGE LEWIS
died Jan– 29th 1836 Aged 5 years
and 2 months

HENRIETTA MIDDLEBROOK
died June 20th 1839 Aged 2 years
and 5 months

"of Such is the Kingdom of heaven."

956 m
THE GRAVE
OF
ISAAC CRANE
SON OF
NOAH & MARTHA CRANE
WHO DIED
IN MOBILE
OCTr 1st 1843:
AGED 26 YEARS,

DEAREST SON THOU HAST LEFT ME
HERE THY LOSS I DEEPLY FEEL
BUT TIS GOD WHO HAS BEREAVED ME
HE CAN ALL MY SORROWS HEAL

957 m
PHEBE
DAUGHTER OF
NOAH AND MARTHA CRANE
WIFE OF
JOHN J VAN DERVEER,
BORN FEB. 17th 1798
DIED JAN. 29th 1874.

She hath gone to her rest

INSCRIPTIONS IN FIRST PRESBYTERIAN

958 *r*
A. C.
In memory of
ANNA
wife of
Ezekiel Crane,
who died
Dec[r] 2[d] 1816
in the 44th year
of her age.

959 *m*
IN
MEMORY OF
THOMAS CRANE
BORN
August 7th 1778,
DIED
August 22nd 1855

960 *r*
In
memory
of
THOMAS BOYLSTON
who died
January 1st 1834
In the 60th year
of his age
———o———
All thy tears are wip'd away,
Sighs no more shall heave thy breast:
Night is lost in endless day,
Sorrow in eternal rest.
Happy spirit,
Now with Jesus thou art blest.

961 *m*
IN
memory of
Mrs LYDIA ROSETTE
WHO DIED
in the city of New York
Dece[r] 23rd 1842
In the 83rd Year
of her age
———o———
Tis done the debt of nature now is paid
On memory's urn be my last offering laid
My Mother! here with solemn step I tread
To trace thy name amongst the silent dead
Up to yon Heaven where parting is unknown
Thy spirit seeks eternal bliss before my Father's throne
Bliss bought by the blood of his beloved son.

A sweet remembrance of the just
Will flourish when they sleep in dust.

SUSAN ROSETTE
daughter of
LYDIA ROSETTE Died Sep.
23[d] 1866 Aged 66 yrs

Her bosom was the hallowed shrine
Of justice charity truth And piety
with ray divine. Serenely shone
in age and youth

962 *r*
In
Memory
of
ABRAHAM ROSETTE
who died
April 8th 1815
in the 35th year
of his age

Also
two children
of Abraham
& Susan Rosette
FRANCIS PETER
died Augst 27th 1812
Aged 1 year & 6 months
LOUISA died Octr 17th 1813
Aged 7 months

963 *r*
J. B.
In memory of
JEMIMA

widow of
Caleb Boylston
who departed this life
August 27th 1817
Aged 79 years
& 10 months

There is a calm for those who weep
A rest for weary pilgrims found
They softly lie and sweetly sleep
Low in the ground

964 *r*
C. B.
In memory of
CALEB BOYLSTON
who departed this
life April 14th 1810
aged 80 years &
14 days

Joyful I lay this body down
And leave the lifeless clay
Without a sigh, without a groan
And stretch & soar away.

965 *r*

J. W. B.
In memory of
John Wood son
of Nathaniel &
Abbey Boylston
who died Decr
28 1804 aged
one month &
twenty eight
days

S. W. B.
In memory of
Susan Wheeler
daughter of
Nathaniel &
Abbey Boylston
who died April
26th 1812, aged
three years nine
months & sixteen
days

Sleep on sweet babes and take your rest
In Jesus arms I hope you'r bless'd

966 *r*
C. W. B.
In memory of
CALEB WHEELER
son of Nathaniel

& Abby Boylston
who died
Oct 11th 1814
Aged 3 months
& 29 days

967 *r*
IN
Memory
of
ISAAC BALL
son of Nathaniel
& Abbey Boylston
who died Septr 25th
1828 Aged 3 years
11 months & 2 days

Happy Infant, early bless'd,
Rest in peaceful slumber rest,
Early rescu'd from the cares
Which increase with growing years

968 *m*
NATHANIEL BOYLSTON
DIED
OCT^r 15th 1860
IN HIS 82D YEAR

Come to Jesus

969 *m*
ABBY WOOD
WIFE OF
NATHANIEL BOYLSTON,
Died Sept. 1st 1855
in her 71st year

" Be ye also ready "

970 *r*
Magdalene daughter of
Moses & Ruth Winans
died Feb^r 10th 1796 aged
8 years 11 months & 2 days

Psal 90th 12.
So teach us to number our days that
we may apply our hearts unto wisdom

971 *m*
IN
Memory of
RUTH WINANS
WIFE OF
Moses Winans
WHO DIED
Jan 26th 1817

Aged 58 Years
5 Months
& 20 Days

972 *m*
IN
Memory of
MOSES WINANS
WHO DIED
Jany 28th 1822 :
Aged 69 Years
2 Months
& 29 Days

973 *m*
IN
Memory of
DEBORAH
DAUGHTER OF
Moses & Ruth
WINANS
who died
April 29th 1817 :
In the 34th Year
of her age

974 *m*
IN
Memory of
MOSES
SON OF
Moses and Ruth
WINANS
who died
April 30th 1823
In the 35th Year
of his age

975 *m*
IN
Memory of
MARGARET
WIFE OF
John Wood
WHO DIED
Feb. 3^d 1826 :
Aged 75 Years
1 Month
& 6 Days

CHURCH YARD, ELIZABETH, N. J. 143

976 *m*
[Broken stone]
IN
Memory of
ELIZABETH WINANS
WHO DIED
Jan. 8th 1840 :
Aged 80 Years
5 Months
& 5 Days

977 *m*
IN
Memory of
ISAAC WINANS
WHO DIED
May 20th 1846
Aged 66 Years
4 Months
& 14 Days

My flesh shall slumber in the ground
Till the last trumpets joyful sound
Then burst the chains with sweet surprise
And in my Saviours image rise

978 *m*
IN
Memory of
SUSANNA WINANS
WHO DIED
Novr 27th 1846 :
Aged 89 Years
——o——
The victory now is obtained
She's gone her dear Saviour to see
Her wishes she fully has gain'd
She's now where she longed to be

979 *m*
IN
Memory of
MALINE
son of Jonas W. &
Sarah Winans
who died Jany 12. 1845.

Aged 11 Years
10 Months
& 28 Days

The dead are like the stars by day
Withdrawn from mortal eye
But not extinct they point the way
In glory through the sky.

980 *r*
[Inscription all gone]

981 *r*
J. R.
In memory of John
Richards. who died
Octr 1 1799 in the
XXII Year of his age

982 *r*
HERE lies the Body
of Joseph Conkling
who departed this
Life Febry ye 24th Ano
Domini 1779. In the
fiftieth Year of his
Age————

The Grave in Silence teach
More than Divine can preach

983 *r*
M. C.
In memory of
Mary widow of
Joseph Conklin
who died
Feby the 7th 1805.
in the 72d year of
her age

Death is the debt to mortals due
I have paid that debt & so must you.

984 *r*
[Broken off and inscription gone]

985 *m*
MOTHER
In
memory of
ANN. B.
wife of
STEPHEN PIERSON
Died
September 6th 1876.
In the 78 Year
of her age

Trust in Christ

986 *m*
FATHER
In
memory of
STEPHEN PIERSON
For 40 years sexton of the
First Presbyterian Church
DIED
June 18th 1876,
In the 75 Year
of his age

"Let God's will be done."

987 *m*
STEPHEN EDWIN
Son of
Stephen & Ann B Pierson,
DIED
Apr. 7th 1867
In the 37 year
of his age

988 *r*
IN
Memory
of
Susan Whitewr-
-ight, daughter
of Stephen &
Ann B Pierson
born
August 15th 1828
died
February 8th 1831

989 *r*
IN
memory
of
Albert Riley
son of Stephen &
Ann B Pierson
born
August 16th 1826
died
August 9th 1827

990 *r*
W. R. J.
In memory of
William R Jones
who departed
this life
Decr 27th 1825;
in the 56th year
of his age

991 *r*
P. J.
In memory of
PHEBE
wife of
William R Jones:
who departed
this life
Novr 30th 1834
Aged 63 years

992 *m*
S. W.
In memory of
Susannah
wife of
William Whitewright
who departed this life
on the 14th Augst 1828
in the 36th year
of her age

Also of
their two infant Children
James died Octr 1816
aged 10 weeks
John died Augst 1828
aged 7 weeks

993 *m*
IN
Memory of
JAMES F MEEKER
WHO DIED
OCT^r 12th 1854
AGED 62 YEARS

HE WAS FOR 31 YEARS AN ELDER OF THIS CHURCH, AND PROMINENT IN ADVANCING HER WELFARE.

"AND THE FRUIT OF RIGHTEOUSNESS IS SOWN IN PEACE OF THEM THAT MAKE PEACE."

994 *m*
REBECCA C MEEKER
WIDOW OF
JAMES F. MEEKER
Died August 15th, 1872
Aged 76 Years

995 *m*
S. E. M.
SACRED
To the memory of
SARAH E
daughter of James F.
& Rebecca C. Meeker;
who died on the eve of her
birth day July 14th 1827
Aged 7 years

"Jesus said suffer little children
to come unto me."

Beloved child, to Jesus go
Yet o'er thy Tomb our tears shall flow
We would love Jesus too and trust
That when our frames return to dust
On wings of love our souls may rise
And meet thy spirit in the skies

996 *m*
JOHN T HALSEY
SON OF
James R Meeker
and Anna H. his wife,
died April 22^d 1851;
Aged 3 Years
& 10 Days

The One in Heaven

997 *m*
ANNA HALSEY
WIFE OF
JAMES R MEEKER
died March 30th 1863,
Aged 40 Years

There is rest for the weary

998 *m*
JAMES R MEEKER
DIED
January 10th 1865
Aged 47 Years

"It is well"

999 *m*
MATILDA GRISWOLD
widow of
JAMES G NUTTMAN
DIED
DEC. 7th 1885
Aged 72 years
——o——
In thy presence is fullness of joy.

1000 *m*
JAMES G. NUTTMAN
For 17 years an Elder
of this church
DIED
MAY 27th 1869,
Aged 58 years
——o——
There remaineth therefore
a rest to the people of God

1001 *m*

Lavinia   Matilda
Children of J. G. & M. G. Nuttman
Lavinia   Matilda
died Feb 10th 1848   died Sept 23^d 1841
aged 2 years & 3 months   aged 6 months & 3 days

1002 *m*
IN
Memory of
OLIVER NUTTMAN,
a Ruling Elder of this Church,
and a Magistrate of this County;
WHO DIED
JANUARY 27th 1833,
AGED 44 YEARS
———o———
"Blessed are the dead which die in the Lord

1003 *m*
IN
Memory of
A W NUTTMAN
WIDOW OF
OLIVER NUTTMAN
WHO DIED
FEB 1st 1858,
IN THE 68th YEAR
OF HER AGE
———o———
"Precious in the sight of the Lord is the death of his saints."

1004 *m*
IN
memory of
OLIVER CRAIG
SON OF
OLIVER & A W NUTTMAN
WHO WAS drowned
JULY 20th 1835,
AGED 16 YEARS
Also of his Brother
JOHN McDOWELL
WHO DIED
Nov 8th 1817
AGED 2 YEARS & 6 MONTHS

1005 *m*
IN
memory of
JANE GREEN
Daughter of
Selah S and Cornelia
WOODHULL
who died September 5th
1840
Aged 22 Years

"The less of this cold world, the more of heaven
The briefer life, the earlier immortality."

1006 *m*
IN
Memory of
CORNELIA
Widow of the late
Selah Strong Woodhull, D.D.
WHO DIED
January 3d 1841;
Aged 53 Years

"Them also which sleep in Jesus will God bring with him."

1007 *m*
IN
Memory of
ELIZABETH
DAUGHTER OF
OLIVER & A. W. NUTTMAN
who died
May 16th, 1853,
aged 23 years

"Our days are as a shadow."

1008 *m*
IN
Memory of
SARAH
DAUGHTER OF
OLIVER & A W NUTTMAN
who died
May 30th 1854,
aged 29 years

"There is rest in Heaven."

CHURCH YARD, ELIZABETH, N. J. 147

1009 r
W. B. H.
In memory
of
WILLIAM B HIGGINS

who died
Novr 17th 1827
in the 66th year
of his age

1010 r

Here lyes
ye Body of
Gershom Higgins
Dec^d Augt y^e
25th 1729
in ye 6 year
of his Age

Here lyes
ye Body of
Nathaniel Higgins
Dec^d Sep^t y^e
1st 1729
in ye 2 year
of his Age

Ye Children of Gershom Higgins

1011 r
In memory of
Wm Higgins son of Robt
& Hannah Gibbons who
died Feb. 5. 1798 aged 2
Mon^s & 10 days. Also Ann his
sister who died Jan. 9 1800 aged 4
months & 15 days.

1012 r
IN MEMORY
of Elizabeth the
wife of Nathaniel
Higgins who died
Jan^r 31st 1784 in the
43^d Year of her Age

1013 m
IN
MEMORY OF
FANNY
WIDOW OF
LUKE H HIGGINS
WHO DIED
OCT. 26th 1849
AGED 68 YEARS 11 MO
& 26 DAYS

"Blessed are the dead which die in
the Lord

Mother peace to thy spirit
Tis all thy children cry
And when they leave this terrestrial
world
May dwell with thee on high.

1014 m
IN
MEMORY OF
LUKE H HIGGINS
WHO DIED
SEPT. 27, 1822
AGED 53 YEARS 4 MO
& 21 DAYS

Wife and children may deplore
The Husband, Father, is no more
His frugal hands no more provide
We trust he rests at Jesus side

NATHANIEL
SON OF LUKE H, AND
FANNY HIGGINS
DIED AUG 17 1805
AGED 5 WEEKS

1015 *m*

IN
MEMORY OF
LUKE T HIGGINS
WHO DIED
FEB 28. 1818
AGED 25 YEARS 1 MO
& 4 DAYS

Friends nor Physicians could not save
His Mortal body from the grave
Nor can the grave confine him here
When Christ shall call him to appear

1016 *r*

S. B.
Sarah Butler daughter
of John & Susannah
Higgins died sept^r 19th
1801 in the IV year of
her age

Sleep dear child till Christ
Shall bid the rise, with wings
of Glory to the skies.

1017 *m*

His word was a lamp to their feet
And a light unto their path

SACRED
TO THE
MEMORY OF OUR PARENTS
JOHN HIGGINS
WHO DIED
IN THE CITY OF NEW YORK
SEPTEMBER 29th 1848;
AGED 77 YEARS

SUSAN HATFIELD
HIS WIFE DIED
July 18th 1838
AGED 62 YEARS & 11 MONTHS

Sweet be thy sleep dear Father and
Mother
Until the morning of the Resurrection
For Christ hath given a glorious
hope
To meet them mid the blest;
Where parting tear was never shed
And where the weary rest's

1018 *m*

GOD GAVE HE TOOK
HE WILL RESTORE

SACRED
TO THE
MEMORY OF
GEORGE S. KETTLEWELL
WHO DIED
IN THE CITY OF NEW YORK
DECEMBER 26th 1845:
AGED 32 YEARS & 4 MONTHS

Also to the memory of
SARAH W KETTLEWELL
DAUGHTER OF
GEORGE & ABBY KETTLEWELL
WHO DIED IN THE CITY OF NEW YORK
APRIL 29th 1846.
AGED 5 YEARS AND 4 MONTHS

Gentle spirit sweet be thy rest
Peaceful sleeping on thy Fathers breast
This changeful world twill thus be ever
Earth hath no ties too dear for death to sever.
How happy thus to sink to rest
So early numbered with the blest
A revelation to us so sweetly given
To meet thy Father and thee in Heaven

CHURCH YARD, ELIZABETH, N. J. 149

1019 m
THE GRAVE
OF
JOSEPH LATHAM,
who departed this life
November 29th 1848 ;
Aged 29 Years
6 Months and
13 Days
Mother, Sister, Friend,
I am not lost but gone before.

1020 m
T. L.
THE GRAVE
of
THOMAS LATHAM
who departed
this life
January 17th 1829,
in the 36th year
of his age
Also of
ISAAC MORSE
Son of Thomas & Joanna
Latham : who departed this
life March 7th 1837.
in the 21st year
of his age

1021 m
IN MEMORY
of
JOANNA BROWN
Daughter of
Isaac & Amy Morse
Died Feby 14 1873
Aged 74 Yrs. 7 Mo. 13 Days

1022 m
[Small Monument]
[On East side]
OUR
EDDY

EDWARD M
SON OF
GEORGE & MARY F
WHITEFIELD

[On West side]
DIED
AUG. 8. 1852.
AGED 1 YEAR
6 MONTHS
& 5 DAYS

1023 m
JAMES WADE
DIED
July 10th 1838
In the 65th Year
of his age
ALSO
NANCY
WIDOW OF
James Wade
died Augst 27th 1851
In the 72d Year
of her age
" In the midst of life we are in death."

1024 r
In memory of
JOSEPH M
son of James and
Nancy Wade who
departed this life
Septr 28th 1803
aged 1 year 10 months
and 6 days

1025 m
N. S. M.
In memory of
Nathan Stewart son
of John T and Margaret
Marsh, who died
April 24th 1813
Aged 7 months
& 14 days

1026 r
Elizabeth Morse
born
March 23d 1787,
died
August 1st 1792
aged 5 yrs, 4 mo, 8 ds,

10

INSCRIPTIONS IN FIRST PRESBYTERIAN

1027 r
Mrs Phebe Wife of
~~Capt~~ Ephraim Terril
departed this Life
June ye 24th A D 1762
In the 43^d Year of
her age————

[The word Capt (before Ephraim) has been cut out as above]

1028 m
[Horizontal tomb 2 feet high]
THE GRAVE
OF
DOCT ISAAC MORSE
FOR MORE THAN FORTY YEARS
A RESPECTABLE PHYSICIAN
OF THIS TOWN
WHO DIED JULY 23^d 1825
IN THE 67th YEAR
OF HIS AGE
——o——
ALSO OF
AMY MORSE
WIDOW OF DOCT. ISAAC MORSE:
WHO DIED APRIL 17th 1832
IN THE 73^d YEAR
of her Age.

MARY JAQUIS
Daughter of Thomas
& Joanna Latham died Augst 16th 1826
Aged 2 years 1 month & 8 days

1029 m
IN
memory of
ELIZABETH
daughter of
John and Catharine
Ballard & relict of
Isaac Watson
who deceased
Oct, 5th 1828
in the 75th year
of her age,

1030 m
[Horizontal tomb 2 feet high]
SACRED
To the memory of
Jeremiah Ballard Esqr
who died Septr 4th 1825 aged 75 years

Mayor of the Borough
A Pillar in the Church
A Captain in the Revolutionary Army
And for more than thirty years
A Magistrate of the County
A Christian & a Patriot
He sustained his various relations
with great fidelity
to the honor of religion
and the advantage of his country

———

He was a good man

——— ——— ——— ———

Also to the memory of
MARY
daughter of James & Jemima Arnett
relict of Caleb Crane
and wife of Jeremiah Ballard Esq
who died in the faith and hope of the
gospel Decr 3rd 1822 aged 79 years

———

" Blessed are the dead
who die in the Lord."

1031 r
N. C.
In memory of
NATHANIEL CRANE,
who died
Augst 31st 1825
in the 63^d year
of his age
——o——
Also
Henry, his son
died Septr 19th 1813,
in the 10th year
of his age

1032 *r*
S. C.
In memory of
SARAH
wife of
Nathaniel Crane;
who died
May 17th 1832,
in the 64th year
of her age
———o———
" For I recon that the suff-
-erings of this present time
are not worthy to be compa-
-red with the glory which
shall be revealed in us."
                   The Text.

1033 *m*
OBADIAH MEEKER CRANE.
OF
Sumpter, S. C.
Died Nov. 17, 1881,
In the 68, Year
of his age

1034 *r*
M. P. C.
In memory of
Moses P Crane
son of Jacob &
Jennet Crane, who
died Decr 28th 1826,
in the 23d year
of his age.

When blooming youth is snatched
    away
By death's resistless hand,
Our hearts the mournful tribute pay
Which pity must demand.

The voice of this alarming scene
May ev'ry heart obey,

1035 *m*
IN
MEMORY OF
MY MOTHER
WIDOW OF
JACOB CRANE 3rd
WHO DIED
Novr 6th 1831,
IN THE 32d YEAR
OF HER AGE

Rest from thy labours Mother dear
Only thy mouldering dust lies here:
The immortal past hath wing'd its
    way,
From Earth, to realms of Endless Day.

1036 *r*
J. C.
In memory of
JACOB CRANE 3d
who died
Feby 14th, 1826;
in the 45th year
of his age
———o———
Farewell ye friends whose tender care
Has long engaged my love,
Your fond embrace I now exchange
For better friends above

1037 *r*
J. C.
In memory of
JENNET wife of
Jacob Crane 3d
who died
Augst 21st, 1824;
in the 40th year
of her age

The months of affliction are o'er
The days and the nights of distress
We see her in anguish no more
She has gained her happy release.

1038 *r*
O. C.
In memory of
three children of
Jacob & Jennet Crane;
OBEDIAH, died Sept 28th
1805; aged 7 months.
OBEDIAH, died July 10th
1811: aged 4 years & 7 months
OBEDIAH, died Augst 10th
1812; aged 28 days.
———o———
I take these little lambs said he
And lay them in my breast
Protection they shall find in me
In me be ever blest.

1039 *r*
J. C.
In memory of
JACOB CRANE
who died
June 11th 1817;
in the 69th year
of his age

———o———

The time is short the season near,
When death will us remove ;
To leave our friends however dear
And all we fondly love.

1040 *r*
P. C.
In memory of
Phebe Wife of Jacob
Crane, who departed this
life July 23d 1806 in the
58th Year of her Age

A wife most kind a parent dear ;
Of Christ & poor a friend sincere

There remaineth therefore a rest
to the people of God. Heb. IV. 9th

1041 *r*
M. C.
In Memory of
Mary Wife of Nathaniel
Crane who departed this
life Sepr 12th 1793 In the
28th Year of her Age

Elihu their Son died
Sepr 12th 1793 In the
5th Year of his Age

1042 *r*
Here lieth ye Body
of Damaris Wife of
Nathal. Crane, who
died Oct ye 9th
AD. 1745 In ye 61st
Year of her Age

1043 *r*
HERE lieth ye Body
of Nathaniel Crane
who deceas'd January
ye 13th Anno Dom:i
1755. In the 75th
Year of his Age

1044 *r*
In Memory of Mary
ye wife of Caleb
Crane who Departed
this Life April ye
2 1758 in ye 36th
year of her Age

1045 *r*
Here lies the Body
of Elizabeth, Wife
of Caleb Crane ———
who died March ye
20th 1772 in ye 47th
Year of her Age

1046 *r*
Here lies the Body
of Caleb Crane
who died Decer ye 19th
A.D. 1773 in the 58th
Year of his Age———

1047 *r*
Here lies ye Body
of Caleb Crane Jur
who departed this
Life April the 9th
Anno Domini 1777
In the XXXVIII Year
of his Age———

1048 *r*
N. C.
In Memory of
Nehemiah Crane
who departed this life
April 14th 1777   In the
34th Year of his Age

1049 r
In memory of
ABIGAIL
wife of Amos Clark,
who departed this life
March 29th 1827, in the
67th year of her age

How much beloved it matters not,
Cold death is sure the common lot;
Be wise to day to Jesus fly
He'll give you rest above the sky
To morrow it may be too late!
For death may end your mortal
state.

1050 r
A. C.
In memory of
Amos Clark
who died March 31st
1791, in the 35th year
of his age

Dear partner of my life,
And children who I love;
Remember dying strife,
Which you have got to prove.

1051 r
HERE lies ye Body
of Rebekah wife of
Henry Garthwait
who died Novr ye 1st
Anno Domini 1773
In the LXXIII Year of
her Age———

1052 r
Here lies interr'd
the Body of James
Crane who depart-
-ed this Life Sept^r
the 2^d A * D 1777
In the 65th Year of
his Age———

1053 r
S. C.
In memory of
Sarah wife of
James Crane
who died March
21st 1805 in the 61st
year of her
Age.

1054 r
J. C.
In memory of
JAMES CRANE
who died
Octr 17th 1819
in the 80th year
of his age

1055 r
S. C.
In memory of
SARAH CRANE
who died
March 4th 1825
in the 49th year
of her age
——o——
Our life is ever on the wing
And death is ever nigh
The moment when our lives begin
We all begin to die.

1056 r
R. C.
In memory of
RACHEL CRANE
who died
March 27th 1825
in the 57th year
of her age
——o——
Attend dear friends as you pass by
As you are now so once was I;
As I am now so you must be,
Therefore prepare to follow me.

1057 *r*
P. C.
In memory of
PHEBE
wife of
Stephen Crane
who died
April 29th 1829,
in the 46th year
of her age

1058 *r*
S C
In memory of
STEPHEN CRANE,
who died
Feby 14th 1846,
in the 65th year
of his age

1059 *m*
IN
Memory of
JEREMIAH CRANE
WHO DIED
April 12th 1842,
In the 71st Year of
his age

How still and peaceful is the grave,
Where lifes vain tumult past ;
The appointed house by heaven's decree
Receive us all at last

1060 *m*
IN
memory of
MARGARET
wife of
Jeremiah Crane
WHO DIED
July 3rd 1825,
In the 41st Year of
her age.

There remaineth therefore a
rest to the people of God.
Heb. 4 c. 9 v.

1061 *r*
A. C.
In memory of
ANN CRANE
who died
Novr 6th 1828,
in the 64th year
of her age

1062 *m*
IN
memory of
JEREMIAH G. CRANE
WHO DIED
June 25th 1837,
In the 23rd Year of
his age
ALSO
ROBERT M CRANE
WHO DIED
Dec. 31st 1840
In the 25th Year of
his age

1063 *r*
In memory of Jen-
-net, daughter of John
and Jennet Taylor
She died Augt the
29th 1792, aged 5
years and 25 days

1064 *r*
In memory of Ra-
-chel daughter of
John and Jennet
Taylor. She died
decr ye 6th 1790 Ag
ed 5 years and 3
Months.

1065 *m*
IN
memory of
ELIZABETH H
WIFE OF
James Erwin

who died Feby 7th 1851;
Aged 39 years 5 months
and 3 days

1066 r
IN
Memory
of
LYDIA MORRELL
daughter of
Benjamin W.
& Elizabeth Tucker
who died Octr 11 1824
Aged 11 months
& 24 days

1067 r
J. T. H.
In memory of
Jason T. son of
Mars & Mary Hart
died July 14 1811
aged 2 months

All Heaven received him
With immortal love
And sung he's welcome
To the courts above

1068 r
In Memory of
John Potter
who Departed this
Life Sepr 12 : 1780
In the 75 Year
of his Age

1069 r
B. W.

1791

1070 r
IN
Memory of
Mrs CATHARINE
Chapman
Daughter of

Mrs Lydia Rosette
who died in New York
Jany 27th 1843.
in the 56th year
of her age

No pain nor grief invade thy bounds
O Grave. No mortal woes
Can reach the peaceful Sleeper here
While Angels watch the soft repose

There is Rest for thee in Heaven my
Sister
S. Rosette

1071 m
Blessed are the pure in heart for
they shall see God

IN
memory of
FURMAN ROSETTE
of Delaware Ohio who died
in New York of Consumption
May 29th 1849
In the 24th Year
of his age

Of modest Deportment, stainless pur-
-ity of Life, and Character. refined
manners, and Cultivated Intellect,
He lived without reproach, and died
lamented when best known.

1072 m
C. J. C.
SACRED
To the memory of
CALEB J CONKLIN
who departed this life
June 3rd 1826;
Aged 37 years 3 months
and 8 days

Hark from the tombs a doleful sound
My ears attend the cry,
Ye living men come view the ground
Where you must shortly lie

1073 *m*
IN
Memory of
JOHN CONKLIN
who departed this life
Octr 20th 1843
in the 85th year
of his age

"Blessed are the dead who
die in the Lord."

1074 *m*
IN
memory of
JERUSHA
wife of
John Conklin
who departed this life
Novr 12th 1824
in the 62^d year
of her age

Farewell, no more I tread your ground
No more I need the Gospels sound
My feet have reached the heaven'ly shore
I know no imperfection more.

1075 *m*
IN
Memory of
JOHN CONKLIN Jun
who departed this life
Novr 2nd 1838
Aged 49 Years.

Let friends no more my sufferings mourn
Nor view my relicks with concern
O cease to drop the pitying tear
I've passed beyond the reach of fear

1076 *m*
IN
Memory of
CATHARINE H
daughter of John Junr
& Abigail Conklin
who departed this life
Novr 2^d 1849
Aged 21 Years 8 Months
and 22 Days

She said her trust was in the Saviour

1077 *m*
IN
Memory of
ABIGAIL
WIDOW OF
JOHN CONKLIN JUN^r
who departed this life
March 20th 1854
Aged 52 Years 9 Months
and 22 Days

Thou'rt gone to the grave, but we will
not deplore thee
Though sorrows and darkness encompass the tomb
The Saviour has passed through the
portal before thee
And the lamp of his love is thy guide
through the gloom

1078 *m*
IN
Memory of
HANNAH
DAUGHTER OF
John and Jerusha Conklin
who died
Augst 5th 1855
Aged 57 Years

"O death where is thy sting. O grave
where is thy victory."

1079 *m*
CATHARINE CONKLIN
BORN
MAY 31 1791
DIED
MAY 16 1872

Many are the afflictions of
the righteous, but the Lord
delivereth him out of them
all   Ps 34-19

1080 *m*
J. C.
SACRED
to the memory of
JAMES CONKLIN
who departed this life
October 21st 1833 ;
aged 41 years 7 months.
and 15 days

When my Saviour call's me home
Still this my cry shall be ;
Hinder me not come welcome death
I'll gladly go with thee.

1081 *r*
M. J.
In memory of
MARY
wife of
Moses Johnson
who departed this
life Oct 14th 1815
in the 49th year
of her age

1082 *m*
[Horizontal, 2 feet high]
SACRED
to the memory of
CHARLOTTE HALSEY
wife of
Isaac T Ludlam
of the City of New York
who died 29th Jan 1825
aged 20 years 7 months & 19 days

ALSO
of her Infant son
STEPHEN
who died 24th Jan 1825
aged 2 months & 16 days

1083 *m*
M. H.
In memory of
MARY wife of
Isaac Halsey who
departed this life
Decr 21st 1823 in
the 59th year
of her age

But do not weep or grieve for me.
You know I must go home :
I was upon a visit here,
And now I must return.

1084 *r*
In
Memory of
ELIZABETH
Wife of Wm Clark
who departed this life
January 11th 1813 in
the 70th Year of her age

1085 *r*
HERE lies the Body
of Mr Abraham
Tucker who departed
this life Octr the 30th
1792 in the 61st
Year of his Age

My friends that live to mourn & weep
To see the grave wherein I sleep
Remember well that you must die
And be en'tombed as well as I.

1086 *r*
C. T.
Charles son of Lewis
& Elizabeth Tooker
died April 9th 1793 in
the 4th year of
his age

1087 *r*
J. W. T.
In memory of
Jonathan Wade
Son of Lewis & Eliza
beth Tuker, who
died July 7th 1805
aged 14 days

1088 *r*
L. T.
Lewis 2^d son of
Lewis & Elizabeth
Tooker, died Sept^r
16 1803 aged 6
months & 16 days

1089 *r*
L. T.
Lewis son of Lewis
& Elizabeth Tooker
died Augst 24th 1800
in the 2^d year
of his age

1090 *r*
S. B
Susannah Brant
daughter of Lewis
& Elizabeth Tooker
died aug 17th 1800 in
the 5 year of her age

1091 *r*
C. T.
Charles 3^d son of
Lewis & Elizabeth
Tooker, died aug^t :
[date gone] 1798 aged 28
days

1092 *r*
C. T.
Charles 2^d son of
Lewis & Elizabeth
Tooker. died dec^r 21
1795 aged 2 months
& 20 days

1093 *r*
P. C.
Phebe Clark daugh'r
of Lewis & Elizabeth
Tooker. died oct^r 6
1788 aged 10 days

1094 *r*
In memory of
Charles Tucker who
departed this life Sep^r
the 27th 1791 in ye 61st
year of his age

1095 *r*
In memory of Phebe
wife of Charles Tuck
er who departed this
life Augst y^s 26th 1791
in the 59th year of her
age

1096 *r*
S. T.
In memory of
Sarah widow of
Wessel Tucker,
who died
Augst 30 1808
in the 61st year
of her age

Prest by the hand of sore disease
In pain I wandered on
Till God my Saviour armed with love
In mercy call'd me home

1097 *r*
W. T.
In memory of
Wessel Tucker
who died
Jany 30th 1803
in the 64th year
of his age

My glass is run my days are spent
My life is gone it was but lent
And as I am so must you be
Therefore prepare to follow me

1098 *m*
IN MEMORY
OF
ABBY. C.
WIDOW OF
LUKE TUCKER
WHO DEPARTED THIS LIFE
AUGst 31st 1873
IN THE 82nd YEAR
OF HER AGE
" Return unto thy rest
O my soul."

1099 *m*
IN MEMORY
OF
LUKE TUCKER
WHO
departed this life
March 20th 1865;
in the 80th year
of his age.

"Mark the perfect man and behold the upright; for the end of that man is peace."

1100 *r*
A. T.
In memory of
ABBY wife of
Luke Tucker
who died Decr 26th
1824 in the 40th year
of her age

Also of their children
HENRY P died Octr 20th 1815
Aged 1 year & 2 months

MARGARET died Sept 27th 1819
Aged 7 months

JAMES H died Augst 15th 1826
Aged 3 years

Kindred and friends farewell
I am no more with you on earth
In sorrows or in joys to share
But faith looks up to view
The land of promise o'er
Where all in Christ will meet to part
no more

1101 *m*
IN
Memory of
JANE
daughter of
Luke & Abby Tucker
who died
Sept 21 1838
Aged 21 Years

Farewell dear parents you will grieve
Brothers and Sisters you I leave
And you must follow me
O look to Christ and seek relief
He reigns Eternally

1102 *r*

Here lies ye Body
of Mrs Elizabeth
Widow of Charles
Tooker who died
Decr ye 16th 1770
in the 65th year of
her Age———

Here lies ye Body
of Mr. Charles
Tooker who de
parted this life
Augst ye 14th 1769
in the 65th year of
his Age———

INSCRIPTIONS IN FIRST PRESBYTERIAN

1103 *m*
IN
Memory of
ELLEN S.
who died
Aug. 13, 1834
Aged 11 Months
and 20 days
ALSO
JACOB M.
who died
Sept, 12, 1841,
Aged 6 Years 4 Months
and 2 days
Two Children of
Abram & Eliza Tooker

1104 *m*
MARY ELIZABETH
WIFE OF
George Parmalie
died April 28th 1860.
Aged 27 Years

GEORGE W.
THEIR SON
died Feby 2d 1861
aged 11 months
& 15 days

1105 *m*
IN
Memory of
ABRAM TOOKER
WHO DIED
Nov. 16. 1834
In the 73. Year of
his age
Also
MARY
widow of
Abram Tooker
WHO DIED
Feb 18, 1836,
In the 73, Year of her age
" Blessed are the dead who die in the
Lord."

1106 *m*
F. D.
In memory of
FOSTER DAY
WHO WAS BORN
March 6th 1781:
AND DIED
June 26th 1845:
In the 65th Year
of his age

1107 *m*
S. R. D.
In memory of
SUSAN R.
WIDOW OF
FOSTER DAY
WHO WAS BORN
April 21st 1781
AND DIED
Jany 10th 1854
In the 73d Year
of her age

1108 *m*
N. B. D.
In memory of
NANCY B.
Daughter of
Foster & Susan Day;
who died
June 18th 1833
Aged 18 years

Reader o'er this ground I've often trod
But now I lie beneath its sod :
In youthful bloom I'm called away
'Gainst death, youth's no security

Dear friend are you afraid of death ?
To lie you down? yield up your
breath ?
Sin is its sting from it be free,
Believe in Christ, and follow me.

1109 *m*
IN
Memory of
PETER S
son of Foster and Susan
Day, who died April 14
1812, aged 11 months
and 11 days

Sleep on sweet babe & take your rest
You in your Makers arms are blest
And now to you we bid adieu
God fit us all to follow you

1110 *m*
C. J. D.
In memory of
CAROLINE J.
Daughter of Foster
& Susan Day, who
departed this life
April 15th, 1822:
Aged 17 Years 2 Months
& 26 Days
——o——
In early bloom death me invade
Translate my body to the shade
Both young and old by this may see
That they must quickly follow me

1111 *m*
E. B. D.
In memory of
ELIZA B.
daughter of
Foster & Susan Day
who died
Feby 26th 1831,
Aged 24 years

"Weep not for me but weep
for yourselves and for your
children."

"My Father calls me to his arms
And willingly I go
With cheerfulness I bid farewell
To every thing below.

1112 *m*
In
Memory of
FREDERICK JULIAN
son of
Isaac C. & Lavinia E.
DAY
died Augst 21st 1849,
aged 10 mo & 5 days
"Of such is the Kingdom
of Heaven

1113 *r*
Here lies ye Body of
Elizth Radley Shute,
Dau^r of Barnaby &
Mary Ann Shute
who Departed this
Life Sep^t 16th 1763
Aged 1 year & 11 m^o

1114 *r*
Here lies ye Body
of Deborah Wife of
Robert Spencer who
departed this Life
Septr ye 20th Anno
Dom 1785 in ye 27th
Year of her Age

1115 *r*

Here lyeth ye Bod
y
Of Isaac Winans
Obij^t Mar 6th 1730
Æ tat 25

Here lyeth ye Bo
Dy of Hannah wife
Of Isaac Winans
Dec^D April ye 10th 1731
In ye 26 yer of h^{er}
Age

Here lyeth ye Bo
Dy of Remember
Winans Obijt Feb
10 1722 Æ tat 42

1116 *r*
HERE LYES
Interr'd ye Body of John
Winans who Departed
this Life Novr ye 5th
1734 in ye 62 year
of his Age

1117 *r*
HERE LYETH
interred the Body of
Benjamin Trotter who
departed this Life July
the sixteenth Annoq^e
Domini 1754 In
the fiftiseventh
Year of his
Age

1118 *r*
S. W.
In memory of
Sarah Ward
relict of
Abner Ward
who died
Octr the 3^d 1801
in the
92^d year of
her age

1119 *r*
Here lieth the
Body of Charles Allen
who departed this life
the 10th Day of August
Anno Domini 1717

1120 *r*
Here lyeth
The Body of Mrs
Mary Allen Wife
Of Jonathan Allen
Dec^D April ye 25th
1732 Aged 31 Year^s

1121 *r*
Here Lies the Remains
of John Radly Esqr
who Departed this Life
February ye 22 1760
Aged 52 years
2 Months & 12 D^s

1122 *r*
HERE LIETH
Interred the Remains of
Mr Jonathan Allen, who
departed this Life Feb^y
the 11th Annoque
Domini 1758. And
in the 61st Year
of his
Age

1123 *m*
JOHN PEASON
DIED
JULY 11th 1860,
IN THE 67th YEAR
OF HIS AGE

"THE MEMORY OF THE JUST IS
BLESSED."

1124 *m*
EDMUND HARVEY
son of
Joseph T. & Susan C
Higgins
Died Oct. 26th 1854
Aged 8 years & 22 days

See the kind shepperd Jesus stands
With all engaging charms
Hark how he calls the tender lambs
And folds them in his arms

1125 *m*
JOSEPH T HIGGINS
DIED
MARCH 19th 1858
AGED
40 YEARS
AND 4 MONTHS

CHURCH YARD, ELIZABETH, N. J.

"Blessed are the dead which die in the Lord, yea saith the spirit that they may rest from their labors and their works do follow them."

1126 *m*

[Monument with iron fence around plot and 4 head stones]

[South side]

JACOB DONINGTON
DIED MAY 11th, 1810 :
AGED 45 YEARS

ELIZABETH
WIDOW OF
JACOB DONINGTON
DIED AUGUST 10th 1819
AGED 50 YEARS

[East side]
ANN A. DONINGTON,
DIED JULY 19th 1817,
AGED 23 YEARS.

SARAH DONINGTON
DIED JUNE 28th 1832
AGED 34 YEARS

[North side]
HENRY DONINGTON,
DIED SEPT. 10, 1862.
AGED 54 YEARS

MARY A BADGLEY,
WIDOW OF
HENRY DONINGTON,
DIED NOV, 2, 1887
AGED 77 YEARS,

[West side]
WILLIAM DONINGTON
DIED JANUARY 16th 1796
AGED 4 YEARS

ELIZABETH DONINGTON
DIED OCTOBER 6th 1810
AGED 7 YEARS

1127 *m*

[Headstone at foot of grave]
In memory of
two children of
Henry & Mary Ann
Donington
SILAS HAYS
died Novr 15th 1835
aged 1 year & 5 months
SARAH E.
died Feby 1st 1840

These lovely buds so young and fair
Call'd hence by early doom
Just came to show how such flowers
In paradise would bloom

1128 *m*

MARY ELIZABETH
DAUGHTER OF
Henry and Mary Ann
DONINGTON
died April 14th 1850 :
Aged 8 years & 10 days

She faded, not like sunlight gone,
From out the west at even ;
Her smile was yet the smile of morn,
'Twas quenched in morning's heaven.

Soft shadows wooed her youthful bloom
And folded it to rest ;
But left the dwelling dark with gloom
Which late her presence blessed.

1129 *m*
JOHN S DONINGTON
DIED
OCT. 1st. 1862.
IN THE 25th YEAR
OF HIS AGE

CARRIE K DONINGTON
DIED
JUNE 12th 1863.
IN THE 15th YEAR
OF HER AGE

1130 *m*
SAMUEL BRADBURY
A native of England
DIED
March 31st 1861
Aged 65 Years

I am the resurrection and the life saith the Lord ; he that believeth in me, though he were dead yet shall he live ; and whosoever liveth and believeth in me shall never die

MARY A DONINGTON
widow of
SAMUEL BRADBURY,
Died October 21, 1885,
Aged 89 Years

1131 *r*
In memory of
Doc^tr Jonathan Dayton
who died October the 17th 1794
in the LIst year of his age

Of Margaret his wife
who died
December the 2d 1789
in the 41st year of her age

1132 *r*
Here lyes ye Body
of Martha Wife of
Nathaniel Pard'w
Aged 42 years
Dec^D Jany 11 1742

1133 *m*
ELIZABETH
wife of
Thomas O Crane.
Died Dec. 1837,
aged 30 years

Alonzo De La Vergne
son of Thomas O &
Elizabeth Crane

Died Oct. 22 1854,
aged 22 years

THOMAS
son of Thomas O & Bethia Crane
Died Oct. 5 1848

1134 *r*
I. C.
A. C.
In memory of
ISAAC CRANE,
an Elder of this church
who died Feb. 5. 1831 :
Aged 65 years.
Also of
ABIGAIL his wife
who died May 4, 1832 :
Aged 65 years

By glimm'ring hopes and gloomy fears
They trac'd the sacred road
Through dismal deeps and dang'rous snares
They made their way to God.

There on a green and flow'ry mount,
Their weary souls now sit,
And with transporting joys recount
The labours of their feet.

Also
MARY ELIZABETH
daughter of Thomas O
& Elizabeth Crane
who died March 27 1832
Aged 18 months

1135 *m*
IN
Memory of
JEREMIAH B CRANE
who died
August 8th 1829,
Aged 37 Years

"Therefore are they before the throne
of God, and serve him day and night
in his temple."

1136 *m*
IN
memory of
MARY B. D.
daughter of Isaac
and Abigail Crane
who died Oct. 24. 1824
Aged 24 years

She proved the truth of the religion she professed, by her humble walk with God, her earnest endeavours to do good her resignation under sufferings and her peaceful end

Also in memory of
their infant children
CALEB who died Dec 31 1796
Aged 3 m & 16 d.
and
THOMAS O who died Aug. 18
1803 Aged 1 m. & 14 d.

1137 *m*
JONATHAN E CRANE
DIED
OCT. 4th 1828,
AGED 34 YEARS 2 MO.
& 12 DAYS

MARY P CRANE
DIED
OCT 5th 1834
AGED 37 YEARS 11 MO
& 6 DAYS

1138 *m*
IN
Memory of
MARY
WIDOW OF
Samuel Crane
who died Octr 28th 1850
In the 79th Year
of her age

Farewell ye friends whose tender care
Has long engaged my love
Your fond embrace I now exchange
For better friends above

1139 *r*
In memory of James
Wilson Son of Mr
James Wilson in Ire
land who died Sep^r
ye 28th 1781 In y^e
31st Year of his Age
He lived beloved, he died lam
ented.

1140 *r*
IN
Memory of
JOANNA
widow of
Waters Burrows
who died
March 30th 1833
in the 73rd year
of her age
Mourning friends weep
not for me
prepare for death
& eternity

1141 *m*
SACRED
TO THE MEMORY OF
ELIZABETH
WIFE OF
ANDREW PARCELL.
WHO DIED
OCT. 7th 1823
IN THE 46th YEAR
OF HER AGE
Cheerful I leave this vale of tears
Where pains and sorrows grow
Welcome the day that ends my toil
And every scene of woe

1142 *m*
SACRED
TO THE MEMORY OF
ANDREW PARCELL
WHO DIED
JULY 7th 1854
IN THE 69th YEAR
OF HIS AGE
Is there not an appointed time
to man upon earth
Job vii. 1,

1143 *m*
SACRED
To the memory of
ELIZABETH
wife of
ANDREW PARCELL
who died
December 7, 1844,
In the 47th year
of her age

Jesus, O, when shall that blest day
That joyful hour appear
When I shall leave this house of clay
To dwell amongst them there.

1144 *m*
HANNAH SPINNING
widow of
Abraham Spinning
Born Nov. 20th 1784,
Died Oct. 31st 1874
Aged 89 years 11 mo
& 10 days
The law of the Lord was her delight

1145 *m*
Our Mother
HESTER MARSAY
widow of
John Spinning
Died
Aust 29th 1855
In the 72d Year
of her age

ABRAHAM FRANCIS
Their son
Died at New Orleans
Decr 15th 1856:
In the 34th Year
of his age

1146 *m*
IN
Memory of
JOHN SPINNING
who died
Jany 5th 1841
In the 65th Year
of his age
Also
THEODORE SARON
son of
John and Hester Spinning
died Feby 15th 1826
aged 5 months and 7 days

1147 *m*
IN
Memory of
SARAH
widow of
DANIEL WINANS
who died
Feby 22^d 1853
In the 76th Year
of her age

1148 *r*
[Top broken off]
Farewell terrestrial joys
I in the Grave must lie
Adieu to glittering toys
Death will not pass me by

1149 *r*
In Memory of
Benjamin Spinning
who died March 11
1802. In the 56th Year
of his Age

Also Abigail wife of Benjamin
Spinning who died Oct^{br} 3^d
1803. In the 51st Year of her Age
Also Polly & Abby Daughters
of Benjamin & Abigail
Spinning

1150 *r*
IN
Memory of
JOHN SPINNAGE
who died 15th of Sep^r
1817. in the 67th year
of his age

Also of Isaac Spinnage
who died Novr 25th
1803 aged 17 years
& 22 days

Also of Mary Spinnage
who died March 6th
1785

1151 r
IN
Memory of
MARY widow of
John Spinnage
who died
March 24th 1824
in the 77th year
of her age

1152 r
J. R. W.
In Memory of
Job R Winans
Son of Daniel &
Sarah Winans
who died
Octr 6th 1811
Aged 13 Years
6 Months & 9 Days

1153 m
A. W. T.
SACRED
To the memory of
Abby W. wife of
Benjamin W Tucker Junr
who died April 6th 1827
Aged 26 years 7 months
& 29 days

Also of
AMELIA H. their daughter
who died March 11th 1827
Aged 2 months
& 10 days

The sweet remembrance of the just
Shall flourish when they sleep in dust

1154 r
B. W.
In memory of
BETSEY widow of
Elijah Woodruff
who died
Augst 31st 1821
in the 47th year
of her age

She's passed the waves of trouble here
We trust beyond the reach of fear
She hears no more the gospel sound
But lies here mouldering under

1155 m
SACRED
TO THE MEMORY OF
MRS SARAH WINANS
WHO DIED
DEC. 15th 1848,
AGED 67 YEARS

She lived the life and died the death
of a christian.

1156 r
J. W.
In memory of
Job Winans
who died
Jany the 22^d 1808
in the 26th year of
his age.

My friends that left to mourn & weep
Do see the grave where in I sleep.
Remember all that you must die,
And be entombed as well as I.

1157 r
H. W.
In memory of
HANNAH
widow of
John Winans
who died
Octr 17th 1830
in the 77th year
of her age.

The sweet remembrance of the just
Shall flourish when they sleep in dust.

1158 r
J. W.
In memory of
John Winans
who died
Feby the 2^d 1802
in the 52^d year
of his age

Death is a debt to mortals due
I have paid that debt & so must you

1159 r
B. W.
In memory of
Jun
Benjamin Winans
who died
Septr 20, 1805
in the 42^d year of
his age

The midnight snares lay thick around
Unthought of and unseen
Death seiz'd the moment gave the
   wound
Which closed this mortal scene

My friends bedew with tears my fate
Remembering you must die
And e'er alas it be too late
To God for mercy cry.

1160 r
In memory of
HESTER
widow of
Jun
Benjamin Winans
who died
Septr 2^d 1821
Aged 56 years

Deep was the wound, O death and
   vastly wide
When she resign'd her useful breath
   and dy'd,
Ye sacred ones with pious sorrow
   mourn,
And drop a tear at your great Parents
   urn,

Conceal'd a moment from our longing
   eyes,
Beneath this stone her mortal body
   lies,
Happy the spirit lives and will we
   trust,
In bliss associate with her pious dust.

1161 r
In memory of
Susanna daughter
of Joshua and Mary
Winans. She died
Novr ye 4th 1788 in y^e
18th year of her age

1162 m
SACRED
to the
Memory of
Abby W wife of
Robert Rindell and
daughter of Benjⁿ Winans
who died April 14th 1825
in the 25th year
of her age

Farewell farewell my partner dear
My parents and my friends
This call of God to you is near
Oh! hear the voice it sends

1163 r
Son, and Daughter, of
John and Hannah Winans
Benjamin died Octr the
28th 1773 aged 14 days
Hannah died Augst ye 12th
1791 in ye 2^d year of her age

Farewell our dearest hearts
Since we with you must part
We hope in heaven to meet again
Where love, joy, and peace shall reign

CHURCH YARD, ELIZABETH, N. J.

1164 *r*
A. W.
In memory of
ABBY
wife of
Jobe Winans
who died Augst 20th
1803 in the 37th
year of her age

Also Jobe, son of
Elias and Abby Winans
died June 24th 1815 in
the 5th year of his age

1165 *r*
J. W.
In
memory of
Job Winans
who died Febru^y 8th
1803
in the 40th year of her age

1166 *r*
J. W.
In
memory of
Jacob Winans
who died Dece^r 23^d
1799
in the 58th year of
his age

1167 *r*
In memory of
Betty wife of Jacob
Winans who depart
ed this life Feby the
6th 1791, in ye 46th year
of her age

Tho' I walk thro the gloomy vale,
Where death and all its terrors are;
My heart and hope shall never fail
For God my shepherd's with me there.

1168 *r*
MARY Daughter of
Jacob and Betty
Winans died Janua^y
the 30th A^{x}D. 1775
aged 6 Years 11 Mont^s
and 22 days.

1169 *m*
IN
Memory of
JACOB WINANS

1170 *m*
IN
Memory of
SUSAN WOODRUFF
WIFE OF
Jacob Winans
who died Decr 20th 1817
Aged 35 years & 7 months

Also two of their children
MARY PERINE
died Feby 11th 1819
Aged 9 years 4 months
& 24 days
ANN MARIA
died Septr 18th 1815
Aged 8 months & 24 days

Life how short

1171 *m*
IN
memory of
JOHN WINANS
who died June 18th 1842
Aged 58 years
ALSO
two children of
John & Catherine Winans
JULIA died Novr 5th 1821
Aged 5 years &
7 months
UJENIA died Novr 11th 1829
Aged 2 years &
10 months

1172 *r*
In memory of
Mr. Benjamin Winans
who departed this life
March the 24th 1793
in the LXXI year
of his age.

Wife and children may deplore
The husband father is no more
[Cross on stone]
His frugal hands no more provide
We trust he rests at Jesus side

1173 *r*
In Memory
of Jane wife of Ben
jamin Winans who de
parted this Life
Septr ye 6th 1776
In ye 55th Year of
her Age

A loving Wife
A Mother dear
And faithful friend
Lies buried here

1174 *m*
In
Memory
of
HENRIETTA
daughter of John
and Catherine Winans
who died
Feby 28th 1818
Aged 4 years 1 month
and 29 days

No more the pleasant child is seen
Her parents joys to crown;
The tender plant so fresh and green,
All withered is and gone.

Until the last loud trumpet's sound,
And christ appears again;
And calls the dead from under ground,
We'll surely see her then.

1175 *m*
OUR MOTHER
DAMARIS N.
WIDOW OF
Lewis Woodruff:
died Augst 26th 1870
In the 81st Year
of her age

"The weary are at rest."

1176 *m*
IN
Memory of
AARON WINANS
WHO DIED
May 13th 1810;
In the 57th Year
of his age

Wife and children may deplore
The husband father is no more
His frugal hands no more provide
We trust he rests at Jesus side

ALSO
the birth and death of a daughter
April 23^d 1806.

1177 *m*
IN
Memory of
PRUDENCE
WIDOW OF
Aaron Winans
who died May 19th 1851
In the 90th Year
of her age

"For I know that my Redeemer liveth
And though after my skin worms dest
roy this body yet in my flesh shall I see
God."

ALSO
PRUDENCE
their daughter died Nov. 16, 1802
aged 4 weeks.

1178 *m*
JANE TUCKER
DIED JUNE 23rd 1856.
AGED 72 YEARS 7 MONTHS
AND 14 DAYS

Her faith and patience, love and zeal
Still make her memory dear :—
And Lord ! do thou the prayer fulfill,
She offered for us here.

1179 *r*
J. W.
Sacred to the memory of
Mrs JANE WINANS
wife of
Capt. Benjamin Winans
who departed this life
May 30th 1812, in the 63^{d}
year of her age

What e'er the wife and friend should be,
In this imperfect state was she,
What e'er the christian's promised prize,
She now possesses in the skies.
This prize eternity alone,
To kindred spirits can make known,
Reader aspire, earth's not thy home,
Seek here by faith a heaven to come.

1180 *m*
CAPT BENJAMIN WINANS

1181 *m*
PHEBE T WOODRUFF
DIED
Dec. 23^{d} 1869
in the 81st year
of her age
——o——
This stone erected by her
Brother, Job Woodruff.

1182 *m*
SACRED
to the
Memory of
Job Woodruff
who departed this life
Jany 17th 1794 :
in the 41st year
of his age

Also of
ELIZABETH
his wife, who was called
from her scene of troubles
Novr 21st 1824
in the 61st year
of her age

1183 *m*
LOUIS T. WOODRUFF
BORN
May 13, 1813.
DIED
March 10, 1864

"He giveth his beloved sleep."

1184 *m*
JACOB GEIGER
DIED
JANUARY 3rd 1870
IN THE 82nd YEAR
OF HIS AGE

1185 *m*
ABIGAIL T.
WIFE OF
JACOB GEIGER
DIED
Novr 3^d 1860
IN THE 70th YEAR
OF HER AGE

1186 *m*
IN
Memory of
SOPHIA CRITTENTON
Infant daughter of
Jacob and Abigail T.
GEIGER
who departed this life
April 2nd 1831
Aged 7 months & 13 days

"Suffer little children to come unto me.

1187 *m*
IN
Memory of
JAMES WOODRUFF
Infant son of
Doct James and Elizabeth T.
Bryan
of Philadelphia
who departed this life
July 2nd 1843
Aged 7 Months & 13 days

"Of such is the kingdom of heaven."

1188 *m*
IN
Memory of
AARON J. WOODRUFF
who departed this life
Novr 20th 1827,
in the 43rd year
of his age
Also
MARY LYON
daughter of Aaron J. &
Abigail T. Woodruff
died Octr 20th 1820
aged 1 year 7 months
and 14 days.

"Blessed are the dead
who die in the Lord."

1189 *r*
L. T.
In memory of
LEWIS TOOKER
who departed this life
June 1st 1830
Aged 63 years
Also
NEHEMIAH W. TOOKER
Son of
Lewis & Elizabeth Tooker
who departed this life
Sept 1st 1825
Aged 30 years

1190 *r*
E. T.
In memory of
ELIZABETH
wife of
Lewis Tooker
who departed this life
March 27th 1824,
in the 54th year
of her age

No sickness or sorrow or pain
Shall ever disquiet her now
For death to her spirit was gain
Since Christ was her life when below.

1191 *m*
IN
memory of
My Sister
SUSAN M TOOKER
WHO DIED
Feby 24th 1835,
In the 19th Year
of her age

None knew her but to love her
None named her but to praise

1192 *m*
SACRED
To the memory of
USELNA LEONARD
Son of
Samuel and Elizabeth
OLLIVER
who departed this life
January 30th 1846
Aged 1 year

We lay thee in the silent tomb
Sweet blossom of a day
We just began to view thy bloom
And thou was't called away

1193 *m*
JACOB G. OLIVER
DIED
Novr 29th 1856,
AGED 19 YEARS
AND 4 MONTHS

1194 *m*
MARGIE W. GRIER
WIFE OF
DR. PHILLIP H. GRIER
DIED JULY 11, 1868,
IN THE 28TH YEAR
OF HER AGE

1195 *m*
[On North side. Other three sides blank.]
MARGARET M.
WIFE OF
MATTHIAS B. CRANE
DIED JULY 19th 1867
AGED 55 YEARS

JOHN W.
THEIR SON
DIED AUG^st 26th 1850
AGED 2 YEARS
9 MONTHS
& 1 DAY.

1196 *m*
In
Memory of
HANNAH
daughter of
Thompson & Susan Bell
who died
August 3rd 1825 ; aged
29 Days

O murmur not my struggling breath
Twas call'd as soon as given
There's nothing terrible in death
To those that go to Heav'n.

1197 *m*
In
Memory of
JULIA ANN D.
daughter of
Thompson and Susan Bell
who died
July 7 1825 aged 2
Years 6 Months &
20 Days

Alas how chang'd that lovely flow'r
Which bloom'd & cheer'd my heart
Fair fleeting comfort of an hour
How soon we're call'd to part.

INSCRIPTIONS IN FIRST PRESBYTERIAN

1198 *m*
In
memory of
SMITH
son of
Thompson and Susan Bell
who was drowned
August 29th 1824 aged 3
Years 9 Months &
22 Days

Like the fair flower that's cropt in
  early spring
Hush'd is thy heart and dim'd thy
  beauty's bloom
But mem'ry still around thy dust
  shall cling
Affection haunt thee e'en beyond the
  tomb.

1199 *m*
In
memory of
THOMPSON
son of Thompson
& Susan Bell
who died Jany 28th
1829: Aged 1 year
& 29 days

Transient and vain is every hope
A rising race can give
In endless honour and delight
My children all shall live.

1200 *m*
IN
memory
of
HANNAH MOUNT
daughter of Matthias
& Matilda Mount
and Neice of
Thompson Bell
who died
Feby 23d 1832:
in the 25th year of
her age

Cheerful I leave this vale of tears
Where pains and sorrows grow,
Welcome the day that ends my toil
And every scene of woe

1201 *r*
Here Lyeth ye Body
Of Richard Miller
Junr DecD Janry ye 5th
1732 In ye 29th year
Of his Age

1202 *r*
Here lyeth ye Body
Of Mr. Jonathan Miller
DecD August ye 29th 1727.
In ye 46 year of his age.

1203 *m*
[Horizontal 2 ft. high and stands on graves Nos. 1201 and 1202]
BENEATH THIS MARBLE
LIE INTERRED THE REMAINS OF
MRS SARAH WILLIAMS
Widow of the late
REV. THOMAS F WILLIAMS
Of Georgia
WHO DEPARTED THIS LIFE
SEPTr 11th 1824
AGED 45 YEARS
ALSO
THE REMAINS OF HER DAUGHTER
HANNAH P WILLIAMS
WHO DIED SEPTr 3d 1824
AGED 8 YEARS

Thy way is in the sea and thy path in the
great waters, and thy footsteps are not known.
The Lord reigneth, let the earth rejoice
Our flesh shall rest in hope. It is
sown in corruption, it is
raised in incorruption. It is sown in
dishonor it is raised in glory
This corruptible must put
on Incorruption
and this mortal shall put on immortality
Then shall be brought to pass the
saying, Death is swallowed up
in victory.

1204 r
Benjamin Son of Benjn
and Hannah Miller
deceas'd June ye 22^d
AD 1770, In the 10th
Year of his Age

Sleep lovely child & take your Rest
God call'd you Home he tho^t it best.

1205 m
[Horizontal 2 ft. high]
Ici Repose
SUSANNE LENORE VINCENT
EPOUSE DE
MESSIRE AUGUSTIN TESSIER
DECEDEE LE 9^e 8bre 1801
AGEE DE 36 ANS.

1206 r
E. S.
In memory of
Ephriam Sayre
who deceas'd
July 22^d 1804:
in the 66th year
of his Age

Unshaken as the sacred hill,
n
And firm as mountains stad.
Firm as a rock the soul shall rest,
That trust th' almighty hand.

1207 r
M. S.
In memory of Ma-
ry wife of Ephriam
Sayre who deceas'd
Aug 7th 1797 in the
58th year of her age

Here I dismiss my carnal hope
My fond desires recall
I give my mortal interest up
And make my God my all

1208 r
Here lies ye Body of
Ezekiel, the Son of
Ephriam & Mary Sayre
who died Octr 12th 1773
in ye 5th Year of his Age

1209 r
H. S.
Hannah daugh^r
of Ephriam & ——
Mary Sayre died
Feby 25th 1771 in
the 7th year of her
age

Suffer little children to come
unto me and forbid them not
for of such is the kingdom of
God

1210 *m*
IN
Memory of
My Mother
MARY SAYRE
WHO DIED
Sept 6th 1846;
Aged 82 Years
9 months
& 13 Days

There is rest in Heaven.

1211 *m*
HANNAH A.
Wife of
FRANCIS BARBER
and daughter of
Stephen & Phebe Barton
Died Dec. 2, 1886
Aged 62 Years

O how love I thy law! it is my
meditation all the day.
" She hath done what she could."

1212 *m*
MARIA M. BARTON
DIED
Feby 11th 1861.
In the 57th Year
of her age

"Not the death we die
But the life we live."
The way of the Lord is perfect.

1213 *m*
MOTHER [on top of stone]
To my precious Mother
Mrs.
PHEBE W. BARTON
Who slept in Jesus
Apr. 26. 1865,
Aged 82 Yrs.
Erected by her loving daughter
Mrs. William T. Nichols.

1214 *m*
STEPHEN BARTON
BORN
SEPT. 17th 1773
DIED
JUNE 27th 1863,

1215 *r*
In memory of Barnaby
Shute who died
March 25th 1797 in the
70th year of his age

1216 *r*
[Broken off]
M. P.
In mem
Margery.
Price, died D
in the 54th y
also Jacob
& Margery Price
26th 1803 aged 12 year

My friends one hour in health
The next in the simtoms of death
This was my lot reader prepare
The same call, you may sudanly hear

1217 *m*
E. M.
In memory of
ELIZABETH MAGIE,
daughter of
DAVID MAGIE
who departed this life
April 26, 1880,
in the 80th Year
of her age

1218 *m*
D. M.
In memory of
DAVID MAGIE
for 52 years an Elder
of this Church
who departed this life

Novr 6th 1854.
In the 90th Year
of his age

"Mark the perfect man, and behold the upright, for the end of that man is peace."

1219 *m*
P. M.
In memory of
PHEBE
wife of
David Magie
who died
April 26th 1842
Aged 73 years

Tis finished! the conflict is past
The heaven born spirit is fled
Her wish is accomplished at last
And now she's entombed with the dead

1220 *r*
Here lies the Body
of Rachel Wife of
Benjamin Magie
who died March 20th
A.D. 1783. In the 40th
Year of her Age

1221 *r*
In
memory of
Benjamin Megie
who died Octr th 27th 1807
in the 72nd Year of his
Age

Most sudden was his call to Death,
By a raging beast resign'd his breath,
Yet high above among the blest,
Tis hop'd his soul doth sweetly rest.

1222 *r*
M. M.
In memory of
MARY wife of
Jonathan Magie:
who departed this
life Octr 2nd 1819;
in the 24th year
of her age.

Also their children

MARY died Decr 8th 1817, aged 7 mont^{hs}
ELIZABETH died Septr 16th 1819;
aged 2 months:

Tis God that lifts our comforts high
Or sinks them in the grave,
He gives and blessed be his name
He takes but what he gave.

1223
HERE lies ye Body
of Mrs Margaret
Wid^o of Mr Joseph
Magie who died
July ye 10th Anno
Domini 1783 I y^e
72nd Year of her age

1224 *r*
HERE lies ye Body
of Mr Joseph Ma
gie who departed
this life March ye 9th
Anno Dom: 1783
In the LXXVIII Year
of his age

1225 r

Here lies ye Body
of Anna Megie
Dec'd June 3 1735
Aged 61 years

Here lies ye Body
of John Megie
Dec^d Feb^r 3 1735
Aged 76 years

Since it so plainly doth Appear
We ware not made for to stay here
But that we all must goe this way
Let us prepare without Delay.

1226 r
Here lyeth ye Body
of phebe Daughter
of Joseph & Elizabeth
Marsh Dec^et June y^e
17th Anno Domini
1736 in ye 10th year
her Age

1227 r
Here lyeth the body of
John Megie who died
January ye 5th AD 1741
and in ye 42^t year
of his age

1228 r
Here lies ye Body of
Jonathan Megie, Son
of Joseph & Margaret
Megie who Died
July 14th 1763
In ye 23^d year
of his Age

1229 r
HERE   LIES
the remains of Phebe
widow of John Magie
who died July the
10th 1798. In the
64th year of her
age

1230 r
HERE   LIES
the Remains of Mr.
Jonn Magie, who
departed this Life
September ye 26th
1781 In ye 49th
Year of his
Age

1231 r
HERE lies ye Body
of John Magie Junr
who died April ye 28th
Anno Dom 1782
In the 28th Year
of his Age

1232 m
IN
Memory of
JOHN O. MAGIE
WHO DIED
Dec^br 26th 1825;
In the 30th Year
of his age

"And so ye say he died
But all the glorious company of
Heaven
Do say, he lives, for he was a good
man."

A tribute of a Daughter's affection

---

^1229 Daughter of John Ogden.

1233 *m*
IN
Memory of
SOPHIA MAGIE
widow of
Ezekiel Magie
WHO DIED
Jany 23 1844;
in the 78th year
of her age

Without a sigh
A change of feature, or a shaded smile
She gave her hand to the stern messenger.
And as a glad child seeks its Father's house
Went home.

1234 *m*
IN
Memory of
EZEKIEL MAGIE
WHO DIED
Decr 3^d 1826;
in the 68th year
of his age

If he hath entered first what then? be still
And let the few brief sands of time roll on
And keep your armour bright and waiting stan^d
For his warm welcome to a realm of bliss.

1235 *r*
M. M.
In memory of
MARY
relict of
Michael Magie
who died
Septr 20th 1829;
aged 57 years

Father I will that they also whom thou hast given me be with me where I am

1236 *r*
M. M.
In memory of
Michael Megie
who died
Jany 6th 1810
aged 53 years

Wife and children may deplore
The Husband Father is no more
His frugal hand no more provide
We trust he rests at Jesus side

1237 *r*
In memory of Catherine wife of Michael Megie. She died Janu^y ye 25th 1793 in the 35th year of her age

Their son^s
Michael. died Augst ye 5th 1782 aged 1 year and 7 mon^s

Hainds, died Septr ye 18th 1791 aged 11 mon^s & 8 days

1238 *r*
P. M.
In memory of
Phebe daughter of
Michael and Katharine
Megie died Sept^r
the 5th 1807 in the
20th year of
her Age

Though young and blooming as we are
Prepare for death, its always near
Both young and old by this may see
That they must quickly follow me.

---

^{1231}, ^{1234}, ^{1236} Sons of John Magie No. 1230.

INSCRIPTIONS IN FIRST PRESBYTERIAN

1239 r
In
Memory of
Jane Wife of David
C. Brown and Dau^r of
Michael Megie. died
Sepr 29th 1807 in the
24th Year of her Age
Also Michael their son
died Oc^r 22^d 1807 Aged 1 Year.

Stop passenger and O be wise
Hope not for bliss b°low the skies
Here in this dark and silent bed
The Mother and her babe are laid
Sweet babe and Mother short was thy stay
A soul prepared needs no delay

1240 m
In Memory of
MOSES M. CRANE
WHO DIED
Novr 27th, A, D. 1874.
Aged 74 Years 11 Months
and 11 Days

" He doeth all things well."

1241 m
In Memory of
PHEBE T CRANE
WIFE OF
MOSES M CRANE
WHO DIED
Feby 5th A. D. 1868,
Aged 68 Years and 24 Days

" Blessed are the pure in heart
for they shall see God."

1242 m
[Little square shaft]
ANNA IRENA
DAUGHTER OF
ABRAHAM C &
ANNA W. MILLER
DIED

MAY 8. 1853,
AGED 1 YEAR
9 MONTHS &
20 DAYS

Sleep on sweet babe
And take your rest
God called you home
He thought it best

1243 m
IN
MEMORY OF
ANNA W.
WIFE OF ABRAHAM C.
MILLER
& eldest Daughter of
Moses M. & Phebe S. Crane
WHO DIED OCT. 12th 1854
AGED 26 YEARS 5 MO
& 27 DAYS

Adieu my friends a long adieu
I leave the joys of earth with you :
I seek a heavenly prize :
May you in Jesus yet be found
And when the trump of God shall sound
In his blest image rise.

1244 m
In memory of
two Sons of Moses M.
& Phebe S Crane :
ELIAS SPENCER
died Feby 16th 1840,
Aged 14 years
and 19 days.
CHARLES HENRY
died Feby 13th 1840
Aged 2 years 1 month
and 13 days

Not in cruelty, not in wrath,
The reaper came that day
Twas an angel visited the earth
And took the flowers away.

1245 *m*
In memory of
AARON
Son of Nathan M &
Mary Ann Winans
who died Septr 30th 1841
aged 1 year 10 months
and 27 days

This lovely bud so young and fair,
Call'd hence by early doom :
Just came to show how sweet a flower
In paradise would bloom

1246 *m*
HANNAH C WINANS
Daughter of
Benjamin & Anabel
WINANS
Born May 28, 1807,
Died March 24, 1885,
Aged 77 Y'rs 9 Mo's
& 27 Days

" I shall be satisfied, when I awake,
with thy likeness."
Psa. 17–15.

1247 *r*
B W
In memory of
BENJAMIN WINANS
who died
March 12th 1852
in the 56th year
of his age

" The night cometh when
no man can work."

1248 *r*
A. W.
In memory of
ANNABLE
WIDOW OF
Benjamin Winans
who died aug, 30, 1854
In the 72^d year
of her age

Verily verily I say unto you
if a man keep my sayings
he shall never see death.

1249 *m*
IN MEMORY
OF
MY MOTHER
MARY
WIFE OF
JACOB B. ANGUS
AND DAUGHTER OF
Job & Abby Winans ;
who died Novr 27th 1824
In the 41st Year
of her age

Dearest Mother, thou hast lift us
Here thy loss we deeply feel
But tis God who hath bereft us
He can all our sorrows heal

1250 *m*
THE GRAVE
OF
JACOB ANGUS
son of Henry K. &
Abby W. Woodruff
who died Decr 21st 1847
aged 6 years 2 months
& 15 days

Could'st thou his gentle voice now hear
Sweetly he'd whisper in thine ear
Fond Mother weep no more for me
I'm now from every suffering free

1251 *m*
IN MEMORY OF
AMELIA A.
wife of
THEADORE W WINANS
Born Nov, 19, 1829
DIED
Sept, 15, 1880

Dearest Mother thou hast left us
And thy loss we deeply feel
Tis our God who hast bereft us
He can all our sorrows heal

Also
David R Winans, Died Sept 10, 1851
W^m O Winans, Died Nov'r 3, 1854

1252 *m*
IN
Memory of
OLIVER W. WINANS
son of Benjamin and
Fanny Winans
who died
March 24th 1839:
Aged 20 Years
& 10 Months

Brothers, Sisters, Farewell,
I pass to immortality
In Jesus breast to dwell
And spend a blest eternity

1253 *r*
F. W.
In Memory of
FANNY
Wife of Benjamin
Winans Junr who
died Feby 22^d 1832
Aged 40 years

Press'd by the hand of sore disease
In pain I wandered on
Till God my Saviour arm'd with love
In mercy call'd me home

Also their Son
AARON T WINANS
Died Sept 29th 1815 Aged 1 year
1 month and 27 days

1254 *r*
B. W.
In memory of
BENJAMIN
WINANS Junr
who died
June 1st 1832
Aged 45 years

Affliction sore long time I bore
Physicians art was vain
Till God alone did hear me mourn
And free'd me from my pain

Farewell dear friends I leave this
world
Of sorrow sin and pain
If I am washed in Jesus blood
I shall a crown obtain

1255 *r*
E. D.
In memory of
Elias Darby
who died July
27 1798 in the
26 year of his
Age

1256
S D
In memory of
SALLY
widow of
Elias Darby;
who died
June 26th 1839
in the 63rd year
of her age
" The just shall live by faith."

1257 *r*
[Horizontal slab]
In memory of
George Ross Esq
who died
on the 22^d day of February 1794
in the 54th year of his age
He was an affectionate husband, a
tender parent, a kind neighbour, a
faithful friend and much esteemed
by all who knew him: in his death
the public have lost a worthy citizen
and useful member of society

1258 *m*
IN
Memory of
LEWIS RIVERS
who died
Aug. 11, 1828
Aged 64 Years 9 Months
and 10 days

1259 *m*
IN
Memory of
RACHEL RIVERS
who died
July 14, 1843.
Aged 54 Years 7 Months
and 7 days

1260 *m*
IN
Memory of
JANE ELIZA
daughter of
Lewis & Rachel Rivers
who died
Sept. 16. 1827,
Aged 13 Years 8 Months
and 16 days

1261 *r*

HERE lies the Body
of Jane the Wife of
William Bonner Jelf
who departed this
Life March ye 20th
Anno Domini 1773
In the 19th Year of her
Age

1262 *r*
In memory of
Mrs Jane, widow of
William Ross
She died Augt the 25th
1772 aged LIX years

1263 *r*

Here lies interred y^e
Body of William Ross
who departed this Life
Feby the 15th Anno
Domini 1764 aged 54
Years & 4 Months

1264 *m*

LEWIS T WOODRUFF
Son of
JOB AND SARAH WOODRUFF
DIED
May 17th 1867,
Aged 22 Years and
10 Months

1265 *m*
IN
Memory of
JOB WOODRUFF, JR.
WHO DIED
Novr 30th 1859
Aged 38 Years and
10 Months
Also
FRANCIS WADE
son of Job and Sarah Woodruff
died Septr 28th 1848 ;
aged 20 months

1266 *m*
IN
Memory of
three Children of
James F and
Catherine N Stansbery
JAMES F
died Octr 31st 1843
aged 2 years 1 month
and 13 days
HARRIET A
died Feby 17th 1850
aged 2 days
WILLIAM A
died July 16 1852
aged 1 year 5 months
and 8 days

1267 *m*
IN
Memory of
HENRY STAGG
WHO DIED
August 18th 1822
Aged 38 Years
ALSO
PHEBE
WIDOW OF
HENRY STAGG
who died Octr 25th 1843
Aged 56 Years and
9 Months

Dearest Parents thou hast left us
Here thy loss we deeply feel
But tis God who has bereav'd us
He can all our sorrows heal

1268 *r*
In
Memory of
Mary the wife of
Abr^m Stagg who
departed this life
August 29th 1808
in the 23^d year of
her age

1269 *m*
SARAH H.
WIFE OF
AARON WINANS
DIED NOV. 23^d, 1860
AGED 49 YEARS

Life's duty done, as sinks the clay,
Light from their load the spirits fly.
While heaven and earth combine to
say.
How blest the righteous when they
die.

1270 *r*
T. C.
In memory of
Susan daughter of
Edward & Phebe
Clark
who died Octr 13 1801
aged 9 months &
6 days

1271 *r*
D. W.
David son of
Nehemiah & Phebe Wade
died Octr 22^d 1813, aged
6 years 1 month
and 5 days

Our life is ever on the wing
And death is ever nigh
The moment when our lives begin
We all begin to die.

1272 *r*
J. H. W.
In memory
of Jonas H. Wade
Son of Elias &
Elizabeth Wade
died Ap^r XII 1797
in the 2^d year of
his Age
Also of Jonas H. Wade
their second son who
was drowned in a ciste-
-rn Nov. 15th 1805 : aged
4 years 9 months & 6
days

1273 *m*
IN
memory of
HENRY KOLLOCK WADE
son of
Elias & Elizth Wade
who died
Nov 29th 1828
Aged 17 y. 4 m. & 18 d.

He was universally beloved & died
deeply lamented.
"He being dead yet speaketh."
A tribute of brotherly affection

1274 *m*
IN
MEMORY OF
ELIAS WADE
who died
April 27, 1844,
In the 78, Year of
his age

1275 *m*
LIEUT
E. W. BRANT
Co. B
30TH
N. J. INF,

1276 *r*
H H
SACRED
To the memory
of
HANNAH
widow of
William Hunt
who died
April 24th 1826;
Aged 70 years

1277 *r*
H. M.
In memory of
HANNAH widow of
Benjamin Miller
who died Octr 28th
1819 in the 84th
year of her age

Blessed are the dead
which die in the Lord

1278 *r*
In memory of
Benjamin Miller who
died March the 12th
1795 in the 65th year
of his age

1279 *m*
[Monument. N & W side blank]
[East side]
STILMAN E
ARMS M. D.
DIED
July 10, 1877,
In his 74th year
At Rest

[South side]
HENRY MARTYN
son of
DR. S. E. & R ARMS
DIED
Sept 3, 1850
Æ 12 yrs

1280 *m*
IN
MEMORY OF
EDWARD SANDERSON
who departed this life
April 25th 1852;
Aged 60 Years 1 Month
and 13 Days

"Go thou thy way till the end be for
thou shalt rest and stand in thy lot
at the end of the days."

1281 *m*
HANNAH
RELICT OF
EDWARD SANDERSON
Born Nov. 20th 1796
Died at Newark N. J. April 5th
1867
AGED 70 YEARS
4 MONTHS AND 15 DAYS

"I shall be satisfied when I awake
with thy likeness."

1282 *m*
IN
MEMORY OF
MARY CHAPMAN
DAUGHTER OF
EDWARD & HANNAH SANDERSON
WHO DIED
July 1st 1847
Aged 25 years

"Thanks be to God whe giveth us the victory through our Lord Jesus Christ."

1283 *m*
IN
Memory of
EDWARD
Son of Edward &
Hannah Sanderson
who departed this life
Dec 7th 1827
Aged 3 years 9 months
& 10 days

The Lord gave and the
Lord hath taken away
blessed be the name of
the Lord.   Job i. 21.

1284 *m*
IN
Memory of
SARAH BLISS
daughter of Edward &
Hannah Sanderson
who died
Feb. 4th 1832:
Aged 1 year
and 15 days

" Is it well with the child
It is well."

1285 *m*
IN
Memory of
ANNA MULFORD
WHO DIED
Septr 21st 1870,
In the 76th Year
of her age

1286 *r*
In
Memory of
three children of
Lewis & Charlotte Mulford
JANE HENDERSON died
May 21st 1822. Aged 1 year
5 months and 25 days
MARY MILLER died
Sept 12th 1823   Aged 4
years & 10 months
MOSES WILLIAMS died
July 8th 1824   Aged 1 year
1 month & 5 days

I take these little lambs said he
And lay them in my breast
Protection they shall find in me
In me be ever blest,

1287 *m*
IN
Memory of
SARAH W.
DAUGHTER OF
Lewis & Charlotte
MULFORD
who died June 23rd 1843
in the 15th Year
of her age
ALSO
MARY E.
who died Oct. 20th 1831
Aged 5 months & 5 days

1288 *m*
IN
Memory of
EMELINE
DAUGHTER OF
Lewis & Charlotte
MULFORD
who died
Oct 15th 1846
Aged 13 Years

1289 *m*
IN
Memory of
PATIENCE
WIFE OF
BENJAMIN MULFORD
WHO DIED
Decr 28th 1827
In the 67th Year
of her age

1290 *m*
IN
Memory of
BENJAMIN MULFORD
a Patriot of the Revolution
WHO DIED
July 27th 1840
In the 89th Year
of his age

1291 *r*
Here lies ye Body of
Elijah Davis Died n°ve^r
ye 26 1733 in ye 49
year of his Age

     sound
Hark from ye Tombs a Doleful
Mine Ears attend ye Cry
ye Living men Come view ye ground
Where you must shortly ly

Great God is this our Certain Doom
and are we still secure
still walking Downward to our Tomb
and yet prepare no more?

1292 *r*
Here Lyeth ye Body
of Mary Wife of
Jacob Hatfield who
Departed this Life
January ye 5th Ann°
Domini 1738
in the 32^d year of
Her Age

1293 *m*
MY FATHER
ELIHU PRICE JR
DIED
MAY 10th 1863
AGED 55 YEARS

1294 *m*
IN
Memory of
MARY W.
DAUGHTER OF
David and Phebe Price
who died April 23^d 1851
Aged 44 Years 11 Months
and 27 Days

1295 *m*
IN
Memory of
NOAH MEEKER
who died
April 14th 1807
In the 34th year
of his age

Children come view my bed of clay
And pillow of the ground
Where your fair bodies soon must lay
And clods must wrap you round

1296 *m*
IN
Memory of
NEHEMIAH
SON OF
Stephen & Charity
Meeker
WHO DIED
Sept 2^d 1845
In the 52^d Year
of his age

"Blessed are the dead who die
in the Lord."

1297 *r*

E. M.
Esther daughter
of Stephen &
Charity Meeker
died Sept 30th 1798
Aged 10 days

E. M.
Esther daughter
of Stephen &
Charity Meeker
died Sept 3d 1803
Aged 3 years
and 32 days

Our time is come, near may be thine
Prepare for it while thou hath time.

1298 *r*
C. M.
In memory of
CHARITY WIFE
OF STEPHEN
MEEKER
WHO DIED
Aug 23d, 1825;
in the
55th year of
her age

My dearest friends they dwell above
Them will I go to see
And all my friends in Christ below
Will soon come after me.

1299 *m*
IN
MEMORY OF
STEPHEN MEEKER
WHO DIED
JULY 17th 1857
AGED 89 YEARS
3 MONTHS AND
13 DAYS

Our age to seventy years is set
How short the term how frail the state
And if to eighty we arrive
We rather sigh and groan than live

1300 *r*
M. M.
In memory of
MARY WIFE OF
STEPHEN MEEKER
WHO DIED
Septr 30th 1827,
in the
54th year of
her age

Ye pleasing scenes adieu
which I so long have known
My friends a long farewell to you
For I must pass alone

1301 *m*
IN
Memory of
ESTHER
WIDOW OF
NOAH SAYRE
who died Sept 5th 1858
Aged 81 Years 8 Months
and 26 Days

"All the days of my appointed
time will I wait till my change come."

1302 *m*
IN
memory of
NOAH SAYRE
WHO DIED
Octr 11th 1848
Aged 77 Years
1 Month and
21 Days

Affliction sore long time I bore
Physicians art were vain
Till God alone did hear my moan
And ease me from my pain

1303 *g*
JOHN WINANS
BORN DEC. 7, 1813
DIED JULY 20, 1844
SUSAN BOYLESTON WOOD
WIFE OF JOHN WINANS
BORN APRIL. 9, 1821
SUSAN BOYLSTON
THEIR DAUGHTER
BORN MAR. 20. 1840

DIED APR. 1. 1840
WINANS.

1304 *r*
In memory of
Stephen Passel who
died March the 29th
1796 in the 22^{d}
year of his age.

1305 *r*

In Memory of
Phebe Widow of
Stephen Passel
who died Sept^r
the 26th A D 1787
In the LVI Year of
her Age

In Memory of
Mr. Stephen Pas-
-sel, who deceas'd
April the 8th An-
no Domini 1786
In the LXth Year of
his Age

1306
Price, son of Abner
and Elizabeth
Passel died June
18th 1795 in the 3^{d}
year of his age

1307 *m*
IN MEMORY
OF
SARAH
WIDOW OF
HAMPTON WOODRUFF
WHO DIED MAY 12th 1833
IN THE 55th YEAR OF HER AGE

"Prepare to meet thy God."

1308 *r*
M. T.
Mary Mitchel
Daughter of Job
and Sarah Smith
died Jany 24th
1779 in the 5th
year of her age

1309 *r*
SACRED
To the Memory of
SARAH
widow of Job Smith
who died May 11th 1827
in the 76th year
of her age

Blessed are the dead who
die in the Lord

1310 *r*
In memory of
Job Smith
who died Augt the
6th 1776 in the 31st
year of his age

1311 *r*
J. S.
Job son of John J.
& Phebe Smith
died Jany 10th 1800
in the 2^{d} year of
his age

Sleep on dear child
and take thy rest
God called the home
he thought it best

1312 r
J. J. S.
In memory
OF
JOHN J SMITH
who departed
this life
July 9th 1814
Aged 42 years

1313 r
P. S.
In memory of
PHEBE
widow of
John J. Smith,
who departed
this life
Nov. 23d 1835
Aged 61 years

A kind parent, an affectionate
mother

1314 m
IN
MEMORY OF

OGDEN SMITH
WHO DIED
Feb 8th 1851
In the 48th Year
of his age

"Be ye not slothful but followers of
them who through faith and patience
inherit the promises."

By grace are ye saved

1315 r
HERE lies the Body
of Elizabeth Wife of
John Berry, who
departed this Life
Jany ye 15th A. D. 1773
In the 18th Year of
his Age

1316 r
Phebe Daughter of
David & Elizabeth
Thompson. died July
ye 1st 1772. In the 5th
Year of her Age.

1317 m
IN
MEMORY OF
NATHANIEL MILLER
WHO DIED
April 9th 1825
Aged 34 Years
ALSO
NATHANIEL
son of
Nathaniel & Lydia Miller
WHO DIED
July 10th 1842
In the 21st Year of
his age

IF A MAN DIE, SHALL HE LIVE AGAIN?

BEHOLD I SHEW YOU A MYSTERY, WE SHALL NOT
ALL SLEEP, BUT WE SHALL ALL BE CHANGED.
IN A MOMENT, IN THE TWINKLING OF AN EYE AT
THE LAST TRUMP: FOR THE TRUMPET SHALL
SOUND AND THE DEAD SHALL BE RAISED INCOR-
RUPTIBLE AND WE SHALL BE CHANGED
A SON & BROTHERS TRIBUTE

1318 *r*
Come unto me
In Memory of
Nehemiah Wade Esq. who
died Octr ye 19th AD 1776
In the 40th Year of his
Age

And
Abigail his Wife who
died March ye 1st A.D 1783
In the 43^d Year of her
Age

1319 *m*
J. D. W.
Jonathan Dayton Wade
son of
Jonathan & Phebe Wade
died 20th February 1806
aged 10 years

1320 *r*
Benjamin Son of
Nehemiah & Abigai l
Wade died Dece^r
ye 10th 1765 In the
2^d Year of his Age

1321 *r*
In
memory of Jonathan Wade who
died Sept the 10th 1796 in the 35th
year of his age

And of his widow
Phebe Woodruff Wade
who died August 1st 1798
aged 22 years

1322 *m*
WILLIAM WHITEFIELD
DIED
Novr 5th 1839
In the 48th Year
of his age
ALSO
ABIGAIL T.

WIDOW OF
William Whitefield
died July 22^d 1853.
In the 54th Year
of her age
"Blessed are the dead which die in
the Lord,"

FRANK
SON OF
William H. & Sarah Whitefield
died Novr 30th 1855.
aged 2 years 6 months
and 25 days

1323 *m*
[On front side]
ANNIE

[On back side]
ANNIE LOUISE
daughter of
William H. and
Sarah Whitefield
died Decr 5th 1859
aged 1 year 1 month
and 23 days

1324 *m*
ADDIE
DAUGHTER OF
GEORGE & MARY T.
WHITEFIELD
DIED OCT^r 22^d 1877,
AGED 22 YEARS

I LOVE YOU ALL

1325 *r*
In memory of
PHEBE
Relict of
^{Capt} Jonathan Townley;
who died
Jany 25th 1837
in the 70th Year
of her age

INSCRIPTIONS IN FIRST PRESBYTERIAN

The victory now is obtained,
She's gone her dear Saviour to see;
Her wishes she fully has gained,
She's now where she longed to be,
Then let us forbear to complain
That she has now gone from our sight;
We soon shall behold her again,
With new and redoubled delight.

1326 r
J. T.
In memory of
Capt. JONATHAN
TOWNLEY
who died
Septr 29th 1827
in the 61st year
of his age

Determined are the days that fly,
Successive o'er thy head;
The number'd hour is on the wing,
That lays thee with the dead.

1327 r
R. T.
In memory of
RHODA widow of
Richard Townley
who died
July 21st 1823;
in the 80th year
of her age

Let friends no more my sufferings
    mourn
Nor view my relics with concern;
O cease to drop the pitying tear,
I've past beyond the reach of fear.

1328 r
R. T.
In memory of Captn
Richard Townley, died
Augt 4th 1801 In the LXV
year of his age

Rest gentle corpes beneath y^s Clay
Now time has swept your cares away;
For surely now all trouble cease
While in the Grave you rest in peace.

1329 r
IN
memory
three children of
Samuel & Mary C. Pierson
REBEKAH. TOWNLEY
died Augst 16th 1825:
aged 1 year 11 months
& 24 days
AMZI, died Octr 1st 1821;
aged 17 days
PHEBE MAGIE
died Decr 5th 1831
aged 3 years
& 9 days

1330 m
OUR FATHER
DAVID JAQUES
BORN
MARCH 5th 1783
DIED
FEBRUARY 7th 1862

"HE IS NOT DEAD BUT SLEEPETH."

1331 m
OUR MOTHER
MINDWELL MULFORD
WIFE OF
DAVID JAQUES,
BORN
NOVEMBER 27th 1790,
DIED
MARCH 28th 1869.

"HE GIVETH HIS BELOVED SLEEP."

1332 m
IN
Memory of
EDWARD F.
Son of
David and Mindwell
Jaques
who died
August 6th 1823
in the 2nd year of his
age

1333 *m*
IN
Memory of
CHARLOTTE ANN
daughter of
David and
Mindwell Jaques
Died July 13th 1833
aged 8 years and
8 months

My friends forbear to mourn and weep,
My change is for the best ;
For on this earth I ne'er was well,
But now I am at rest,

1334 *r*
W. M.
In memory of
William Marsh, who
died March 16th 1799
in the XXII year
of his age

1335 *r*
In memory of what re-
-mains of 2 children of
Lewis & Mary Mulford
Frankey died Feb. 16th 1795
in the 7th year of her age
Fanne died June 14th 1796
aged 11 months

1336 *r*
L. M.
In memory of
Lewis son of Lewis &
Mary Mulford, who
died Octr 5th 1810 in the
18th year of his age

Farewell O much beloved shade.
The Fathers hope the Mother's prop ;
The God who first our comforts gave,
Demands them & we give them up.

Our loss is great ; we feel the stroke,
And sorely every member moans ;
Sweet consolation in that hope,
That looks beyond these worldly
groans

1337 *m*
IN
Memory of
SARAH
WIDOW OF
John Mulford
who died
Novr 29th 1837
Aged 76 Years

"Take ye heed, watch and pray
for ye know not when the time is."

1338 *m*
IN
Memory of
JOHN MULFORD
WHO DIED
Augst 16th 1815
Aged 58 Years

"I must work the works of him that
sent me while it is day: the night
cometh, when no man can work."

1339 *r*
[Broken]
arth as care
old employ'd ha

1340 *r*
In memory of
Lewis Mulford who
died March the 18th
1790 in the 73 year
of his age

1341 *r*
L. M.
In memory of
LEWIS MULFORD
who died
Feb. 17th 1830
in the 86th year
of his age

With long life will I satisfy him
and show him my salvation
Psalm XCI, 16th

1342 *r*
M. M.
In memory of
MARY, wife of
Lewis Mulford
who died
May 10th 1826;
in the 75th year
of her age

1343 *r*
In memory of
Hannah daughter of
Thomas & Rebekah
Williams, who died
July the 30th 1776 in
the 23d year of her age.

1344 *m*
IN
Memory of
JANE
WIFE OF
ABRAHAM M MULFORD
WHO DIED
May 13th 1850
Aged 62 Years

1345 *m*
IN
Memory of
ABRAHAM M. MULFORD
Born May 8th 1784
Died March 9th 1863

"I shall be satisfied when I arise in
thy likeness."

1346 *m*
IN
Memory of
TOWNLEY MULFORD
WHO DIED
Jan 3d 1857
Aged 73 Years
10 Months and
10 Days

1347 *m*
IN
Memory of
HANNAH
WIFE OF
TOWNLEY MULFORD
who died Feb. 17th 1842
Aged 57 Years
4 Months and
7 Days

1348 *m*
IN
MEMORY OF
ELIZABETH P.
DAUGHTER OF
Townley & Hannah
MULFORD
who died July 24, 1838
Aged 24 Years & 3 days

1349 *r*
In
Memory of
two children of William
& Hannah Mulford
SARAH ANN, died June 17th
1818 Aged 6 years 8 months
& 28 days
SARAH ANN died April 17th
1819 Aged 1 year
& 6 days

Alas how changed these lovely flowers
That bloomed and cheer'd our hearts.

1350 *r*
E. M.
In memory of
EZEKIEL MEEKER
who died
March 10th 1813
Aged 47 years

Dear friends who live to mourn &
weep
Behold the grave in which I sleep
Prepare for death for you must die
And be entomb'd as well as I.

1351 r
P. M.
In memory of
Phebe wife of
Ezekiel Meeker
died July 17th 1808 :
Aged 40 years
3 months & 11 days

also Phebe Spinning, daughter
of Ezekiel and Phebe Meeker
died Octr 20th 1786 aged
7 months and 4 days

1352 m
[Horizontal 2 ft. high]
SACRED
To the Memory of
MOSES AUSTEN
who departed this life July 17th 1827
in the 76th year of his age

ALSO OF
SARAH AUSTEN
Wife of Moses Austen
who departed this life Decr 7th 1776
in the 26th year of her age

ALSO OF
HANNAH AUSTEN
Widow of Moses Austen
who departed this life March 28th 1846
in the 86th year of her age

ALSO OF
AARON
Son of Moses & Hannah Austen
who departed this life April 15th 1823
in the 22nd year of his age

ALSO OF
SUSANNAH
Daughter of Moses & Sarah Austen
who departed this life April 10th 1777
in the 2nd year of her age

AND ALSO OF
SARAH
Daughter of Moses & Hannah Austen
who departed this life Novr 6th 1783
aged 7 months

1353 m
In
Memory
of
OLIVER
son of Oliver
and Mary Pierce
who died
August 25th 1817
Aged 10 months
and 7 days

1354 r
S. H.
In memory of
Samuel son of
Samuel and
Mary Halsey
died April 23d
1805 in the 10th
year of his age

Sleep dear child and take thy rest
You in your maker's arms are blest
A lovely child and active too
Have gone and bid this world adieu

1355 r
P. H. T.
Phebe, daughter of
Lewis & Abbe Terril
died septemr
5th 1801 Aged 12 mo-
nths & 25 days

Rest my dear beneath the
ground. Till the last
trumpet's joyful sound

1356 r
In memory of
Samuel Halsey who
died Feb. the 3d 1797
in the 34th year of his
age

Lord I confess thy sentence just
That all mankind sho'ld turn to dust

1357 *r*
IN
memory of Phebe dau-
-ghter of Daniel & Mary
Halsey died April 5th
1797 aged 6 years 4
months & 10 days

Sleep lovely babe and take thy rest
God call'd thee home he thought it best.

1358 *r*
IN
memory of Anne daugh-
-ter of Daniel & Mary Halsey
died Augt 23^d 1795 aged
1 year 6 months & 2 days

Sleep lovely babe till we do meet
within the gate of Zion sweet

1359 *r*
M. H.
In memory of
MARY HALSEY
who died
July 28th 1833
Aged 73 years

Her soul has now taken its flight
To mansions of glory above
To mingle with angels of light
And dwell in the kingdom of love

1360 *r*
HERE lies interred
the Body of Abigail
Wife of Daniel
Halley, who depart-
-ed this Life Decem^r
the 17th A D 1782
In the 40th Year of her
Age

1361 *r*
D. H.
In Memory of Mr
DANIEL HALSEY
who departed this Life
Novr 16th 1801. In the LXII
year of his Age

Now to the world I bid adieu
Connections dear & all of you
Remember when you pass me by
That you as well as I must die.

1362 *r*
HERE lies interred
what was Mortal—
of Sarah the Wife of
David Spencer, who
departed this Life
Jany the 22^d Anno
Domini 1788 In ye 34th
Year of her Age

1363 *r*
S. O. H.
In memory of
SARAH O.
daughter of
John L, & Sarah
Halsey, who died
Decr 5th 1830;
Aged 12 years

And when our dearest comforts fall
Before his Sovereign will;
He never takes away our all,
Himself—he gives us still.

1364 *m*
J. L. H.
In memory of
JOHN L. HALSEY
who departed this life
November 25th 1833
at Yorkville
South Carolina
in the 39th year
of his age

Into thy hands, my Saviour God,
Did I my soul resign;
In firm dependence on that truth,
Which made salvation mine.

1365 *m*
IN
MEMORY OF
CALEB HALSEY
WHO DIED
Septr 9th 1851
In the 80th Year
of his age

"Blessed are the dead who die in the
Lord. They do rest from their labors
and their works do follow them."

1366 *m*
IN
MEMORY OF
SOPHIA
WIFE OF
Caleb Halsey
who died March 16th 1852
In the 79th Year
of her age

There is rest in Heaven were her
last words
"Mark the Perfect and behold the
upright
For their end is peace."

1367 *r*
IN
memory of
PHEBE W.
wife of Robert Lackey
who departed this life
September the 24th 1798
aged 19 Years & 9 months
Also their Son
WILLIAM PIERSON
who died the same day
aged 1 Year & 10 months.

1368 *m*
IN MEMORY
OF
JOSEPH OGDEN
WHO DIED
AUGUST 28th 1827;
AGED 40 YEARS 7 MONTHS
AND 20 DAYS

ALBERT
SON OF
JOSEPH AND HANNAH OGDEN
DIED OCTOBER 3. 1820
AGED 1 YEAR 1 MONTH
AND 19 DAYS

1369 *m*
IN MEMORY
OF
HANNAH INSLEY
WIFE OF
JOSEPH OGDEN
WHO DIED
SEPTEMBER 13th 1822
AGED 34 YEARS 6 MONTHS
AND 27 DAYS

ALBERT
SON OF
JOSEPH AND HANNAH OGDEN
DIED NOVEMBER 1st 1822
AGED 1 YEAR AND 10 MONTHS

HANNAH
DAUGHTER OF
JOSEPH AND HANNAH OGDEN
DIED SEPTEMBER 12th 1822
AGED 18 DAYS

1370 *m*
IN MEMORY
OF
HANNAH OGDEN
Wife of
STEPHEN MEEKER
BORN
April 30th 1779
DIED
January 10 1863.

"Precious in the sight of the Lord is
the death of his saints."

---

¹³⁶⁸ and ¹³⁷⁰ Son and daughter of Matthias and Margaret Magie Ogden.

1371 *r*
H. I.
In memory of
Henry Insley
who died Decr 20th
1797. in the 51st
year of his
age

1372 *m*
In memory
of
HANNAH DeHART
wife of
Henry Insley
who died
October 24th 1853,
Aged 95 years 3 months
and 22 Days

1373 *m*
In
memory of
HENRY PARSELL
who died Nov 10th 1826
Aged 53 years
Also his Wife
ABIGAIL INSLEY
Died June 12th 1860
Aged 84 years

1374 *r*
IN
Memory of
MARY, Daughter of
David & Ann Burrows
who died Augt 31st 1806,
Aged 10 Months & 19 Days

Also in Memory of
James Caldwell Mulford
Son of David & Ann Burrows
who died Sept 19th 1807
Aged 10 Months & 9 Days

1375 *m*
In
Memory of
LEWIS WATERS
son of
David and Ann Burrows
who departed this life
August 31st 1813
aged 1 year 1 month & 26 days

1376 *r*
Imemory of Fanny
wife of
Waters Burrows
She died Decr 24th 1793
in the 44th year
of her age

1377 *r*
Our Mother
ANNA M.
widow of
DAVID BURROWS
Died Nov. 14th 1860
Aged 74 years & 3 Mo's

Asleep in Jesus blessed sleep,
From which none ever wake to weep;
A calm and undisturbed repose,
Unbroken by the last of foes.

1378 *m*
In
Memory of
HENRY O.
Son of
Oliver C. & Hannah
Washburn
who died Sept 24th 1845
Aged 9 Months & 4 days

(flower
Alas how changed that lovely
Which bloomed and cheer'd my heart
Fair fleeting comfort of an hour
How soon we're call'd to part.

1379 m
IN
Memory of
URIAH
SON OF
Uriah & Jane
WASHBURN
who died March 1st 1847
Aged 22 Years
1 Month and
16 Days

Survey me well ye youthful and believe
The grave may terrify but cant deceive
On beauty's fragile base no more depend
Here youth and pleasure age and sorrow end

1380 m
MARY S.
Born Nov, 10, 1843
Died Oct, 1, 1846

JOSEPHINE Y.
Born July 21 1847
Died Sept. 3, 1849

JONAS W.
Born Jan 12 1852
Died Oct. 23, 1862

Children of Abner W.
& Charlotte S. Parkhurst

1381 m
JOHN S.
Son of Abner W.
& Charlotte S. Parkhurst
Born Dec. 9. 1840
Died Oct 8, 1864.
At Newbern N. C.
A Member of Co. K 9. Reg^t
N. J. Volunteers

1382 m
FATHER
ABNER W. PARKHURST,
Born Aug. 25, 1806,
Died May 22, 1852,

MOTHER
CHARLOTTE S. PARKHURST
Born Dec. 3, 1812
Died Oct, 22. 1854

1383 m
IN MEMORY OF
ELIAKIM,
son of Eliakim &
Susan Marsh
who died Augst 9th 1852
Aged 1 year & 24 days

Now that my journey's just begun,
My road so little trod ;
I'll come before I further run,
And give myself to God.

1384 m
HARRY STEWART,
ONLY SON
OF MARK D. &
HESTER A.
WILSON
DIED
DEC 13, 1870
AGED 6 YRS 5 MO
& 21 DAYS

Not dead but sleeping

1385 m
IN
MEMORY OF
HARRIET ELIZABETH
Daughter of
Mark D. & Helen H.
WILSON
Who died Nov. 14 ; 1856,
Aged 7 years 9 mos,
& 11 days

On the opposite side of this stone is

LIBBIE

We lov'd that tender little one,
And would have wish'd her longer stay
But let our Father's will be done
She reigns in endles day

1386 *m*
HELEN H.
WIFE OF
MARK D WILSON
DIED JUNE 9th 1860
AGED 30 YEARS 2 MO.
& 17 DAYS

BLESSED ARE THE DEAD WHICH DIE
IN THE LORD.

1386½ *m*
ELECTA ANN
DAUGHTER OF
Albert A. and
Joanna B. Bonnell;
died April 15th 1855.
aged 2 years 7 months
and 15 days

Why should I vex my heart or fast
No more she'll visit me
My soul will mount to her at last
And there my child I'll see

1387 *m*
ANN M.
widow of
HARVEY THOMPSON
DIED
November 19th 1865
AGED 75 YEARS

"Blessed are the dead which die
in the Lord."

1388 *m*
IN
Memory of
HARVEY THOMPSON
who died
July 27th 1840,
Aged 53 years
& 2 months

"Be ye also ready for in such
an hour as ye think not, the
Son of man cometh."

1389 *m*
OUR SISTER
MARY ANN
DAUGHTER OF
BENJAMIN & PHEBE
GARTHWAIT
DIED AUG. 29th 1870
AGED 43 YEARS

"I was dumb, I opened not my
mouth: because Thou didst it."

1390 *m*
OUR FATHER & MOTHER
BENJAMIN GARTHWAIT
DIED FEB. 26th. 1876
IN HIS 88th YEAR

with long life will I satisfy him
and show him my salvation
PHEBE CRANE
HIS WIFE
DIED JULY 3rd 1864
AGED 73 YEARS

Earth hath no sorrow that Heaven
cannot heal

1391 *r*
E. G.
In memory of
ESTHER
wife of Benjamin
Garthwait who
died Septr 15th 1824
Aged 30 years
6 months &
15 days

The time is short ye saints rejoice,
The Lord will quickly come;
                                        voice
Soon shall you hear the bridegrooms,
To call you to your home.

1392 r
A. G.
In memory of
ANN, widow of
Anthony Garthwait
who died
May 9th 1826 ;
Aged 64 years

Farewell ye friends whose tender care,
Has long engaged my love ;
Your fond embrace I now exchange,
For better friends above.

1393 r
A. G.
In memory of
Anthony Garthwait
who died May 10th 1806
in the 48 year of
his Age

My glass is run my days are spent,
My life is gone it was but lent ;
And as I am so must you be,
Therefore prepare to follow me.

1394 m
IN
MEMORY OF
JONAS T. MULFORD
WHO DIED
June 7th 1851 ;
In the 30th Year
of his age

Wife Children and friends farewell
 for a while
That tear on thy cheek should give
 place to a smile,
If ye be found faithful the time will
 soon come ;
When Jesus will call you to meet me
 at home.

1395 m
C. T. M.
SACRED
To the memory of
CATHARINE T.
daughter of Abraham
Marsh and wife of
Benjamin W. Mulford
who died Octr 12th 1823
Aged 22 years 5 months
& 5 days

Dear friends who live to mourn and
 weep
Behold the grave in which I sleep
Prepare for death for you must die
And be entombed as well as I

1396 m
IN
MEMORY OF
CATHARINE
WIDOW OF
JONATHAN MULFORD
WHO DIED
SEPTt 18th 1861.
IN THE 84TH YEAR
OF HER AGE

" Blessed are the dead who
 die in the Lord."

1397 m
IN
MEMORY OF
JONATHAN MULFORD
WHO DIED
OCT. 29th 1852
IN THE 80th YEAR
OF HIS AGE

" Watch therefore for ye know not
 what hour your Lord doth come."

1398 r
J. C. M.
In memory of
James Caldwell
son of Thomas &
Phebe Mulford
died June 28 1806
in the 22d year
of his age

Relentless death with indiscriminate
 rage
Will neither spare condition sex nor
 age
The old, the young the middle aged—
 all
Will soon or late unto him victims
 fall

1399 r
T. M.
In memory of
Trembly W. Son of
Jonathan & Catharine
Mulford died Sept^r
27th 1804 Aged 9
months & 27 days

The sweetest babe lies buried here,
The youngest of his Parents care ;
His brothers dear their loss dont know,
To young to feel their parents woe.

1400 r
ANN Daughter of
Thomas & Phebe
April
Mulford died ye 25th
A.D. 1784 In ye 4th
Year of her Age

1401 m
IN
memory of
Capt. THOMAS MULFORD
died
December 31st 1830
in the 81st year
of his age

"There remaineth a rest to the people of God."

1402 m
IN
Memory of
PHEBE
wife of
Capt Thomas Mulford
died
September 18th 1802,
in the 50th year of her age

"Blessed are the dead which die in the Lord."

1403 r
HERE lies y^e Body
of Joanna Wife of
Jonathan Williams
who departed this
Life Feby the 12th
A. D. 1768. In y^e 39th
Year of her Age

1404 r
HERE lies y^e Body o$.$
Ebenezer Williams
who departed this Life
March y^e 31st A.D. 1760
In the 36th Year of his
Age

1405 m
THE GRAVE
OF
JOSEPH BLOOMFIELD
Son of
Maj Charles W. Hunter
who departed this life
August 31st 1831
Aged 15 years

"And the child Samuel grew on and was in favour both with the Lord and also with men."

1406 m
THE GRAVE
OF
MRS ANN WEBSTER
Relict of the late
Capt Rezin Webster
who departed this life
March 20th 1833
Aged 76 years

"For I know that my Redeemer liveth and that he shall stand at the last day upon the earth."

1407 *r*
Here lies the Body of
Benjamin Williams who
Departed this life the 5th
Day of December 1750
In ye 33^d year of his age

1408 *r*
In Memory of
Thomas Williams—
who departed this—
Life July the 21st 1776
In the 52^d Year of his
Age

1409 *r*
In Memory of
Rebekah Wife of
Thomas Williams
who departed this
Life Octr the 5th 1785
In the 57th Year of her
Age

1410 *r*
Caleb son of Thomas
& Rebekah Williams
died Sept ye 23^d 1776
in the 15th year of his
age

1411 *r*
Sarah Daughter of
Aaron and Sarah
Lane departed this
Life April ye 3^d A.D.
1777 aged 4 Years
1 Month & 10 Days

Sleep dear Child, till we do meet
Within the Gates of Sions street

1412 *m*
IN MEMORY OF
HANNAH
WIDOW OF
ICHABOD WILLIAMS
Born May 13th 1766
Died Dec. 31st 1852
Aged 86 Years 6 Months
and 13 Days

1413 *m*
IN MEMORY OF
ICHABOD WILLIAMS
WHO WAS BORN
May 10th 1768 :
AND DIED
Septr 23^d 1837 ;
Aged 68 Years 4 Months
and 13 Days

"An honest man is the
noblest work of God."

1414 *m*
ELIZABETH W.
DAUGHTER OF
Ichabod & Hannah Williams
AND WIDOW OF JACOB D.
HOWELL.
DIED MARCH 15th 1880
IN HER 90th YEAR

1415 *r*
Nancy Daugh^r of
Benjamin & Eliza^h
Williams died Au^t
19th 1793 aged 9
Mos & 3 Days

1416 *r*
Charles son of
Benjamin & Eliza-
-beth Williams di-
-ed Sept ye 4th 1791
aged 3 years & 6
months

1417 *m*
IN
MEMORY OF
FANNY
WIFE OF
CHARLES H HUGHES,
who died July 23d, 1823,
aged 47 years 11 months
& 11 days

"Precious in the sight of the Lord is
the death of his saints."

ALSO
PHEBE
DAUGHTER OF
CHARLES H. & FANNY HUGHES
WHO DIED
Nov 15th 1807
aged 1 year & 11 months

1418 *m*
IN
MEMORY OF
CHARLES H. HUGHES
WHO DIED
August 3d 1855
aged 90 years 7 months
& 12 days

"And I heard a voice from Heaven
saying, write, Blessed are the dead
which die in the Lord."

1419 *r*
M. M.
In memory of
MOSES MEEKER
who died
Octr 12th 1824;
in the 72d year
of his age

Dear friends who live to mourn &
weep
Behold the grave in which I sleep
Prepare for death for you must die
And be entomb'd as well as I.

1420 *r*
In Memory of Ab-
-igail Wife of Moses
Meeker who decea,t
Januay the 30th 1787
In the 31st Year of her
Age

A pale Consumption gave ye fatal Blow
                                           slow
The Stroke was certain but ye Effect was
                                          prest
With wasting pain Death found me long op
Pity'd my Sighs and kindly brought me Rest.

1421 *r*
J. M.
Jonathan son of
William & Hannah Meekr
died septr 5th 1801 aged
8 months & 19 days

Here lies the child that we
did love. In Jesus arm's we
hope above

1422 *m*
IN
Memory of
SUSAN
daughter of William &
Hannah Meeker
who died April 21st 1853
In the 33d year
of her age

1423 m
IN
Memory of
ABBY
daughter of Williams
and Hannah Meeker
who died May 26 1852
In the 42^d Year
of her age

1424 m
IN
Memory of
MARY
daughter of William
& Hannah Meeker
who died Sept. 20, 1830
Aged 30 Years

Also of
MOSES
their son
who died Aug. 20, 1825
Aged 13 Years

1425 m
IN
Memory of
ANN
daughter of
William & Hannah
Meeker
who died Decr 22^d 1844
Aged 26 Years

1426 m
IN
Memory of
HANNAH
WIFE OF
William Meeker
who died Octr 13th 1846
Aged 65 Years

1427 m
IN
Memory of
WILLIAM MEEKER
WHO DIED
Septr 12th 1851 :
In the 75th Year
of his age

1428 r
S. A. M.
In memory of
SALLY ANN
wife of
Robert Meeker
who died
March 30th 1838
in the 35th year
of her age

Also their son
MATTHIAS P. died
April 13th 1842 aged 12 years
4 months & 11 days

1429 r
E. W.
In memory of
ELIZABETH
wife of David
Williams, who
died March 16th
1822 in the 59th
year of her age

Also
OLIVER son of
David and Elizabeth
Williams, who died
April 8th 1791.
Aged 2 years & 9 months.

1430 r
In
Memory of
ELECTA L.
daughter of Samuel
& Nancy Williams
who died Novr 12th
1820 Aged 1 year
1 month & 4 days

1431 *m*
SACRED
TO
THE MEMORY OF
MOSES WILLIAMS
who died
April 21st 1856,
in the 84th year
of his age

"Jesus saith, I am the resurrection
and the life."

1432 *m*
SACRED
TO
THE MEMORY OF
SARAH
WIFE OF
MOSES WILLIAMS
who died
Sept 22nd 1838;
In the 65th Year
of her age

Blessed are the dead that
die in the Lord.   Rev. xiv. 13

1433 *m*
SACRED
TO
THE MEMORY OF
BETSEY
daughter of
Moses & Sarah Williams
who died June 13th 1825:
Aged 19 Years and
2 Months

See here a Youth in all her flow'r
and prime
Snatched from fond life and all the
joys of time
Young friends. & strangers let this
instance show
That there is naught to cleave to here
below
Religion only, makes our sorrows
blest
Fits us for death and gives us Heavenly rest.

1434 *r*
J. W.
In memory of
JOEL
son of Moses
& Sarah Williams
who died Novr 6th 1815,
Aged 15 years,
6 months, &
8 days

Short was thy life, few were thy days,
But they were spent in wisdoms ways;
O may thy death a warning be,
And all prepare to follow thee.

1435 *m*
IN
Memory of
JEMIMA D WILLIAMS
WHO DIED
Nov. 2nd 1842,
In the 34. Year of
her age

Daughter of
Moses & Sarah Williams

1436 *r*
J. B. W.
In memory of
JOHN B WILLIAMS
who died
Augst 25th 1837
in the 69th year
of his age

Unveil thy bosom faithful tomb
Receive this sacred dust
The great the wise they all must
come
When death makes his request.

1437 *r*
M. W.
In memory of
MARY
widow of

CHURCH YARD, ELIZABETH, N. J.   207

John B. Williams
who died
July 3ᵈ 1842
Aged 66 years

A constant wife, a mother dear,
A faithful friend lies buried here ;
Till God shall bid the dead arise,
To meet the Saviour in the skies ;
May she in triumph soar away,
To realms of everlasting day.

1438 *r*
In Memory of
Benjamin Williams
who died Octr 25th
A. D. 1785 in ye 28th
Year of his Age

1439 *m*
IN
MEMORY OF
ELEANOR WILLIAMS
WHO DIED
December 19th 1877
In the 84th Year
of her age

Here's where all sorrow ends,
    No more to weep.
Until the angel calls them forth
    from sleep.

1440 *m*
IN
Memory of
WILLIAM BADGLEY
who departed this life
November 11th 1825
in the
59th Year of his Age

My glass is run, my days are spent,
My life is gone it was but lent ;
As I am now so must you be,
  Oh then prepare to follow me.

1441 *r*
C. H. B.
In memory of
CATHARINE H.
daughter of William
& Rebekah Badgley
who departed this life
June 7th 1817,
in the 21st year
of her age.

Alas how changed that lovely flow'r
Which bloom'd and cheer'd my heart
Fair fleeting comfort of an hour
How soon we're call'd to part

Also ABIGAIL their daughter
who died Feby 12th 1795.
Aged 2 months & 2 days

1442 *r*
In
memory of
Cornelius Badgley who departed
this life June 10th 1794, in the
66th year of his age

Also Elsey, widow of Cornelius
Badgley, who departed this life
July 25th 1809, in the 77th year
of her age

Their days are number'd, and their spirits fled
Their gone, the husband and the wife are dead
Nor weeping friends nor healing art could save
Their bodys from the cold and silent grave.

1443 *m*
R. C. B.
In memory of
RACHEL C.
wife of
Cornelius Badgley
who departed this life
November 28th 1835.
in the 25th year
of her age

Husband and children I must leave.
O, do not mourn, O do not grieve
But strive to gain the happy shore
Where we may meet to part no more
To this sad shrine the relics we com-
  mend
Of once the tender Mother wife and
  friend,
Too soon alas ! those tender ties were
  broke
Friends, husband ; child, all felt the
  fatal stroke.

1444 *m*
H. M. D. B.
In memory of
HENRIETTA McD.
wife of
Cornelius Badgley
who departed this life
May 15th 1840,
in the 22d year
of her age

Thus early in the dawn of day
Thy spirit's call'd to rest
Thy body mould'ring in the clay
Shall be reviv'd and blest

And when the angel's trump shall
  blow
That souls to bodies join
What crow'ds shall wish their lives
  below
Had been as short as thine

1445 *r*
Sacred
To the Memory of
ELIZA BADGLEY wife of
ISAAC BADGLEY:
who departed this life March
the 5th 1811. Aged 31. Years
and 4 Months

When God's decree did call me home
My husband dear was left to moan
My children,—All I left to God,
Then humbly bow'd and kiss'd the rod

Also in memory of
Alice Badgley, who departed this
life August the 6th 1811 Aged 9
Months

1446 *r*
HERE lies ye Body
of Rachel, the Wife
of John Doobs, who
departed this Life
Novr ye 10th AD 1762
In the 29th Year of
her Age

1447 *m*
ABNER BADGLEY
DIED
May 2d 1797,
Aged 38 Years
SARAH
HIS WIFE
died Dec. 19th 1863
Aged 94 Years
and 6 Months

1448 *m*
JANE BADGLEY
wife of
CAPT GILBERT FOWLER
Died Sept 8th 1865
Aged 71 Years 7 Mos
& 21 Days

1449 *m*
IN
MEMORY OF
CORNELIUS BADGLEY
BORN
MAY 3RD, 1802.
DIED
JANUARY 29th 1869.

1450 *r*
HERE lies the Remains of
Joanna the beloved Wife
of John Blanchard, who
departed this Life Septr
the 17th Ano Domini 1786
And in the 52d Year of her
Age

Sacred
to the memory of
JOHN BLANCHARD, who
died March 25th 1811 ;
Aged 81 years.

1451 r
A. V.
To the memory of
Abigail Vergerau,
who departed this
life Augst 30th 1821 :
in the 77th year
of her age

The sweet remembrance of the just
Shall flourish whilst they sleep in dust

1452 r
John Son of John
& Joanna Blanch
-ard died Augt 19th
A. D. 1776. In ye 11th
Year of his Age.

1453 r
James, son of
John & Joanna
Blanchard, who
died Octr ye 3^d
A. D. 1775. aged
5 Months & 11 Days

1454 r
JOHN, son of
John & Joanna
Blanchard, who
died Augt ye 24th
A. D. 1764. In ye 6th
Year of his Age

1455 r
Sacred to the Memory of
ABIGAIL Wife of
Cornelius Hetfield Esq.
and
Daughter of
Benjamin Price Esqr
who died April ye 27th 1781.
Ætat 70.
This excellent Person
was an exemplary Pattern
of Sincere Piety, Charity,
and all other Christian
Virtues.

1456 r
In memory of
Cornelius Hetfield Esq.
who died
March the 20th 1795
in the 86th year
of his age

1457 r
In Memory
of
MARIA, The wife of Doct^r
PAUL MICHEAN, who departed this
life August 15th 1793, Aged twenty years
nine months and eighteen days.

Clos'd are those eyes in endless night
No more to beam with fond delight,
Or with affection roll.
Eternal silence seals that tongue
Where sence and soft persuasion hung
To captivate the soul
that
Oh, she was all thought can paint
The mortal rising to the saint

In every deed of life
At once the fatal arrows end
    the
The fondest child kindest Friend
    And most endearing Wife
Fair as the break of opening day
Calm as the summers evening ray
    Truth, virtue, was her guide
When Sister Spirits call'd her hence
Obedience bow'd at life's expence
    She sigh'd, she sunk, she dy'd
Immortal saint supremely bright
Look down through skies of purest Light
    And bid afflictions cease
Oh, smooth thy Husbands lonely bed
In visions hover round his head
    And hush his mind to peace

1458 *r*

In memory of
Caleb Hetfield
who died
February the 13th 1795
aged
XLVII years

1459 *r*

HERE lies interr'd ye
Remains of Margaret.
Wife of Caleb Hetfield
who departed this Life
Februy ye 12th Anno
Domini 1769. In ye 21st
Year of her Age

1460 *r*

In memory of
Jennet wife of
Caleb Hetfield
who died May 17th 1794
in the 47th year
of her age

1461 *m*

IN
Memory of
HANNAH R. HETFIELD
Daughter of
Caleb & Jennet Hetfield
WHO DIED
July 15th 1845
In the 61st Year
of her age

1462 *m*
[small monument]

[North]	[West]	[South]	[East Side]
SARA ELLA	SHE	ANGELIC	DEAREST
DAUGHTER	WENT HOME	BIRTH	WE SHALL
OF	SEPT 5th	AT 1 YEAR	MEET AGAIN
REV. GEO. W. &	1862	& 4 MONTHS	
S. F. CLARK	——	OF EARTH	

CHURCH YARD, ELIZABETH, N. J.   211

1463 *m*
[Monument]

[East side]
DIED
JUNE 1, 1828
NATHANIEL
MITCHELL
IN HIS 55. YEAR

This Monument of marble
contains all that is dear
And room left for another
That soon must follow here.

DIED APRIL 28 1847
MARY R. WIDOW OF
NATHANIEL MITCHELL
IN HER 72 YEAR

Death is a debt to mortals due
I've paid that debt and so must you

[North side]
DIED
SEPT 6 1837
ALBERT R.

SON OF
Nathaniel & Mary R.
Mitchell
IN HIS 34. YEAR

[West side]
DIED OCT 7 1824
ELIZABETH
WIDOW OF
Ephraim Marsh Dec'd
IN HER 72. YEAR

[South side]
DIED
AUG. 17 1836
CAROLINE M.
WIFE OF
William Donington
DAUGHTER OF
Nathaniel & Mary R.
Mitchell
IN HER 31. YEAR.

1464 *m*
CAROLINE M.
WIFE OF
NOAH STODDARD
Departed this life
October 26, 1857.
Aged 58 Years 4 Mo
& 4 Days
In the hope of a joyful resurrection

Thou art gone dearest sister
To the mansions above,
The palace of angels
The Eden of love.

1465 *m*
IN MEMORY OF
ANN W.
WIFE OF
THOMAS B. MABEE
& DAUGHTER OF
E_D^WD & ANN WELLS
WHO DIED
APRIL 9, 1827,
IN THE 24 YEAR OF
HER AGE

When from the dust of earth I rise
To take my mansions in the skies
Even there shall this be all my plea
Jesus hath lived, hath died for me.

1466 *m*
IN
Memory of
ANN
WIFE OF
Edward Wells
who died Octr 4th 1849 ;
Aged 70 Years
& 9 Months

We hope dear Mother for to meet,
When we with life are done ;
In climes above where friendship
 blooms,
When parting is no more.

INSCRIPTIONS IN FIRST PRESBYTERIAN

1467 *m*
IN
MEMORY OF
PHEBE MUNN
WIFE OF
DANIEL WOODRUFF
DIED JAN. 19, 1887
AGED 80 YEARS 5 MO'S
& 17 DAYS.

1468 *m*
IN
MEMORY OF
DANIEL WOODRUFF
DIED
JUNE 8th 1864,
AGED 59 YEARS 5 MOS.
& 2 DAYS

1469 *m*
IN
MEMORY OF
ROMYNE ADOLPHUS
SON OF
DANIEL AND PHEBE
WOODRUFF
WHO DIED
JULY 31st 1854
AGED 16 YEARS
11 MONTHS AND
8 DAYS.

1470 *m*
IN
MEMORY OF
LAURA ANN
DAUGHTER OF
DANIEL & PHEBE
WOODRUFF
APRIL 21st 1845
AGED 14 YEARS
11 MONTHS AND
17 DAYS.

1471 *m*
THOMAS MULFORD
DIED

in the City of New York
July 26th 1835 :
In the 38th Year
of his age
ALSO
LOCKEY B.
widow of
Thomas Mulford
and Daughter of
Thomas and Hannah Force
died Feby 23d 1842 ;
In the 44th Year
of her age

1472 *r*
Here Lyeth
Interr'd the Body
of JOHN ALLING
who Departed this
life April ye 25th
A D 1734 in ye
65th year of
his age

1473 *r*
r
Mary Haris Daught
Of Georgᵉ and Elen—
Harris Decᴅ Octʳ yᵉ
9th 1728 Aged 1 year
And 3 Months.

Sleep on sweet Babe
Lay still & take thy rest
Thy maker call'd ye home
Therefore it is Best.

1474 *r*
E. S.
In memory of
Elizabeth widow
of Daniel Sale
who died Decʳ
25th 1805 aged
73 years

In faith she lived in dust she lies
But faith foresees that dust shall rise :
When Jesus calls while hope assumes,
And boasts her joy among the tombs,

1475 *r*
IN MEMORY
of Mr. Daniel Sale
who
departed this Life June
the XXIst 1798. In the
LXXIII Year of his Age

As you are now. So once was I,
In Health & Strength, tho here I lie;
As I am now, So you must be.
Prepare for Death & follow me,

1476 *r*
In Memory of
Phebe Wife of Edward
Sale who departed this
Life Febr^y the 11th An^e
Domini 1757. aged LX
Years

Watch & Pray for you know
not the Hour.

1477 *r*
Here lies ye Body
of Elizabeth wife
of Edward Sale
who Died Feb^r y^e
17 173½ in ye 33
year of her Age

1478 *r*
C. D.
Cornelius son of
Isreal & Elizabeth
Disoway died
decem^r 3^d 1800
aged 4 weeks

Happy infant early blest,
Rest in peaceful slumbers rest—
Early rescued from the cares,
Which increase with growing years.

1479 *r*
Daniel son of Edward
& Sarah Sale died Aug^t
the 18th 1796 aged 10 mon^s

Sleep lovely babe and take thy rest
God call'd thee home he thought it best

1480 *r*
S. S.
In memory of
Sarah wife of
Edward Sale
who died Jan^y
20th 1808 in the
35th year of her age

also Edward son of
Edward & Sarah Sale died
Jany 10th 1808 aged 3 months

My glass is run my days are spent
My life is gone it was but lent
And as I am so must you be
Therefore prepare to follow me.

1481 *r*
E. S.
In memory of
EDWARD SALE
who died March 26th
1819; in the 51st year
of his age

Also his son
EDWARD T. died March 7th
1819; Aged 5 months,
& 13 days

1482 *r*
IN MEMORY
of
Benjamin Williams
who died
March the 23^d 1789
In
the XLVIth Year of his
Age

1483 *r*
E. W.
In memory of
Elias son of
Enoch & Joanna
Williams; died
Septr 20th 1796
in the 17th year of
his age

1484 *r*
C M W
In memory of
Charles M. son of
Archibald B. and
Abigail Williams
who died June 26th 1809
aged 1 year & 2 months

1485 *r*
H. W.
In memory of
HANNAH
wife of
Jonathan Williams
who died April 12th 1810
in the 59th year of
her age

But Oh! ye mourners cease to weep,
Receive with joysome cordial charms;
And view her in the world of bliss,
Encircled in her Saviours arms.

1486 *m*
IN
Memory of
ELIZABETH C.
Daughter of
David and Elizabeth
Williams
who died
August 20th 1857
In the 54th Year
of her age

While weeping friends bend O'er
the silent tomb
Recount her virtues and her loss deplore
Faiths piercing eye darts through
the dreary gloom
And hails her blest where tears
shall flow no more

1487 *m*
IN
Memory of
ELIZABETH F
widow of
David Williams
who departed this life
April 28th 1848
In the 86th Year
of her age

"Blessed are the dead which
die in the Lord."

1488 *m*
In
Memory of
DAVID WILLIAMS
A Soldier of the Revolution
who departed this life
Aug 1st 1841
In the 84th Year
of his age.

"Surely I know that it shall be
well with them that fear God."

1489 *m*
The
Grave of
JANE WINANS
Wife of
RICHARD WILLIAMS
who departed this life
the 30th day of
March 1837:
Aged 43 years

1490 *r*
C. W.
Sacred to the memory of
CORNELIUS
son of David & Elizabeth
Williams who died Feby
24th 1811 in the 26th year
of his age

The unremitting paths he trod
That leads to happiness and God
Has run their short and rapid race
E're he was call'd to heavens embrace
The joyful spirit left the clay
Until the everlasting day
And here the precious treasure lyes
Till God shall call it to the skyes

1491 *m*

Sacred
TO THE
Memory
OF
WM W MONROE
who died
Oct. 6. 1842
Aged 35 Years 6 Months
and 3 days

1492 *m*

Sacred
To the
Memory of
JEMIMA
wife of
Jeremiah Monroe
who died
Nov 16, 1840.
In the 58. Year of her age
Also
EDWARD J.
son of
Jeremiah & Jemima Monroe
who died Sept 17. 1817
Aged 1 Year 6 Months and 4 days
Likewise
ELIZABETH W.
their Daughter
who died Oct 13. 1819
Aged 1 Year 10 months and
10 days

1493 *m*

IN
Memory of
LETTE
WIDOW OF
Aaron Lyon
who died
July 29th 1846
In the 75th Year
of her age

Farewell ye friends whose tender care
Has long engaged my love
Your fond embrace I now exchange
For better friends above.

1494 *r*

In memory of
RACHEL widow of
Henry Norris
who died
Novr 16th 1824;
in the 60th year
of her age

Great God I own thy sentence just
And nature must decay
I yield my body to the dust
To dwell with fellow clay.

1495 *r*

H. N.
In memory of
Henry Norris
who died
May 30, 1818
in the 58th year
of his age

Attend my friends as you pass by,
As you are now so once was I ;
As I am now so you must be,
Therefore prepare to follow me.

1496 r
P. N.
In memory of
Phebe Norris
who died
Septr 5th 1837
in the 74th year
of her age

Happy soul thy days are ended,
All thy mourning days below;
Go by angel guards attended,
To the sight of Jesus go.

1497 r
M. N.
In memory of
Mary widow of
Nathanael Norris
who died
Feby 26th 1810
aged 75 years

When I walked thro the shades of
    h
deat.
Thy presence was my stay;   a
One word of thy supporting breth,
Drove all my fears away.

1498 r
N. N.
In memory of
Nathanael Norris
who died
July the 3^d 1798:
in the 67th year
of his age.

The Lord takes pleasure in the just
Whom sinners treat with scorn:
The meek that lie disposed in dust,
Salvation shall obtain.

1499 r
Here lieth the
Remains of Henry
Norris who died
Sepr ye 8th Anno
Domini   1752
And in the 29th
Year of his Age

1500 r
Here lieth the Body
of Samuel Norris who
departed this Life
Augt ye 15th Annoq^e
Domini 1752 In the
34th Year of his Age

1501 m
IN
MEMORY OF
ANN S. WILLIAMS
Daughter of
JOHN & MARY WILLIAMS
WHO DIED
FEBRUARY 12th 1853
AGED 55 YEARS

Watch therefore for in such an hour as ye think not, the Son of man cometh.

1502 r
S. W.
In memory of
Mr. Samuel Williams
who died
October 20th 1801
In the 78th year of
his Age

My friends prepare to follow me.
Both young and old must die you see;
There's no discharge, theres no delay,
When death demands we must obey.

1503 r
Here lies ye Body
of Elenor Wife of
Samuel Williams
who departed this
Life Octr ye 22^d An^o
Dom 1777. In ye 44th
Year of her Age.

1504 r
J. W.
In memory of
Jane widow of
Samuel Williams
died Feby 20th 1807
in the 73^d year
of her age

Return unto thy rest O my soul
for the Lord hath delt
bountifully with the
psalm CXVI. VII.

1505 r
J. H. W.
In memory of
Jane H daughter of
Nathaniel & Ann
Williams, who died
May 27th 1820
Aged 17 years
1 month & 12 days

Died with consumption

Adieu vain world with all your trifling
  toys,
The soul aspires to far superior joys;
My hope it rest with Gods eternal
  love
The great event the judgement day
  will prove.

1506 r
R. W.
In memory of
REZIN
son of Nathaniel
& Ann Williams
who departed this
life July 2nd 1828:
aged 23 years and
6 months

I know that my Redeemer liveth
Job 19th 25th

My flesh and my heart faileth
but God is the strength of my
heart, and my portion forever
Psalm 73rd 26th

Such is the faith of those
That trust and fear the Lord
They live upon his promises
And rest upon his word.

1507 r
J. L. W.
In memory of
John L. Son of
Nathaniel & Ann
Williams, who died
Novr 13rd 1820,
Aged 18 years
& 9 months

Died with consumption

Farewell my relatives so dear,
Improve this solemn call:
Wipe off the precious falling tear,
And make your God your all.

Fear not it will be well he said,
  Prepare to follow me;
And when I'm mingled with the dead,
  You here my change may see.

1508 r
B. B. W.
In memory of
BENJAMIN B.
son of Nathaniel
& Ann Williams,
who departed this
life August 4th 1826
aged 27 years

He's gone! the spirit's fled
Where sin can ne'er annoy,
  His sacred joy,
Nor grief, nor pain, nor anxious
  care   (here
Can reach the peaceful sleeper
While angels watch his soft
  repose

1509 r
D. S.
Sacred to the memory
of
DANIEL SPINNING
who died Novr 3^d 1811
aged 62 years 6
months & 12 days

Go home dear friends and shed no
tears
I must lie here till Christ appears
And at his coming hope to have
A joyful rising from the grave.

1510 r
M. S.
Mary wife of
Daniel Spinning
died March 9th 1802
aged 47 years 3
months & 13 days;

Weep not for me my friends
For why my race is run
It is the will of God
So let his will be done

1511 r
M. S.
Mindwell wife of
Daniel Spinning
died Sept 26. 1783
aged 33 years

Weep not for me my friends,
For why my race is run :
It is the will of God,
So let his will be done.

1512 r
S. S.
of
Sarah daughter
Daniel & Mindwell
Spinning, died
Feb^r 18th 1775 aged
2 months & 29 days

Sleep on dear child and take thy rest
Early you'r call'd God thought it best
Your griefs are done our tears be dry
By the we learn that all must die

1513 r
P. S.
In memory of
Phebe Spinning
who died
Octr 16th 1823 ;
in the 31st year
of her age

1514 m
M. S.
IN MEMORY OF
MARY SPINNING
WHO DEPARTED THIS LIFE
OCTOBER 19th 1823
IN THE 36th YEAR
OF HER AGE

Religion is the chief concern
Of mortals here below
May I its great importance learn
Its sovereign virtue know.

Religion should our thoughts engage
Amidst our youthful bloom.
'Twill fit us for declining age
And for the awful tomb.

1515 r
J. S.
John Spinning
died March 10th 1778
aged 77 years &
4 months

Pray look upon my grave,
All you that passeth by ;
When one lives to such age,
Thousands do younger die.

1516 r
C. S.
Constant wife of
John Spinning sen.
died Sept 9th 1757
aged 51 years

Pray look upon my grave,
All you that passeth by :
Where one lives to such age
Thousands do younger die.

1517 r
W. S.
In memory of
William Stiles
who died
Jan 24th 1781
Aged 47 years
& 4 months

Go home dear friends and shed no tears,
I must lie here till Christ appears;
And at his coming hope to have,
A joyful rising from the grave.

1518 m
IN
Memory of
PHEBE
widow of
William Stiles
who departed this life
Nov 22nd 1822
In the 86th Year
of her age.

Swiftly pass a few fleeting years,
And all that now in bodies live;
Shall quit like me this vale of tears,
Their righteous sentence to receive.

1519 m
In memory of Frances wife of
Joseph Watkins and Daughter
of John Spinning who Departed
This life on the fifth day of July
1787 aged fifty seven years two
months and twenty days

A fabric once on Earth I was
And nothing Else but dust
I'm gone to join the Heavenly tribe
And with my God to Rest.

1520 m
MY MOTHER
PHEBE WOODRUFF
WIDOW OF
DANIEL STILES
DIED DEC. 12th, 1844,
AGED 72 YEARS

She sleeps in Jesus, and is blest;
Calm are her slumbers, sweet her rest.

1521 r
D. S.
In memory of
Daniel Stiles
who died Novr
28th 1810 aged 37
years & 10 months
Also
Abraham his son
died May 6th 1802
aged 4 months
and 22 days

1522 m
SUSAN M.
Daughter of
JOHN & PHEBE STILES
and wife of
Linus Littell,
Died April 11th 1832
Aged 24 years

While weeping friends bend o'er the silent tomb,
Recount her virtues and her loss deplore;
Faith's piercing eye darts through the dreary gloom,
And hails her blest where tears shall flow no more

1523 m
JOHN STILES
Died
Dec. 24, 1857,
In the 91st Year
of his Age

1524 m
IN
Memory of
PHEBE
wife of
JOHN STILES
who departed this life
April 9th 1823;
Aged 52 Years

May her dear friends from tears refrain
Their loss has proved her greatest gain
She dwells with Christ in Heaven above
Where all is harmony and love.

1525 *g*
Luke H Higgins
Born Nov 28th 1809
Died Dec 13th 1884

Harriet S Higgins
Born July 14th 1810
Died May 28th 1848

1526 *m*
Phebe C.
Daughter of
Luke H. and
Harriet Higgins
Died
April 21st 1859,
In the 20th Year
of her age

And now hath thy dust returned to the earth
Thy spirit to god who gave it.
Yet affection shall fondly cherish thy worth
And memory deeply engrave it.
Not here on this tablet of mouldering stone
But on our fond bosoms where best it is known

1527 *m*
IN
memory of
HANNAH
daughter of
the Rev'd E Van Derlip
and Wife of
Morris Stiles
who died
Oct. 5th 1828
Aged 30 years

1528 *m*
IN
Memory of
Our Parents
NEHEMIAH MEEKER
died Septr 12th 1849
Aged 77 Years
HANNAH
his wife died July 23^d 1827
Aged 55 Years
Also
CATHARINE
their daughter died Aug. 4 1849
Aged 52 Years
DAVID T
their son died Oct 23. 1847
Aged 33 Years

1529 *m*
IN
memory of
WILLIAM M WILLIS
who died
Dec. 17th 1837:
In the 64. year
of his age

"And I heard a voice from Heaven saying unto me write. Blessed are the dead which die in the Lord from hencforth; yea saith the spirit that they may rest from their labours and their works do follow them."

1530 *m*
THE GRAVE
OF
JOSHUA O HORTON
who was accidentally
drowned on his passage
to Albany, Dec. 10 1846
Aged 32 years 4 mos.
& 14 days

"Boast not thyself of tomorrow for thou knowest not what a day may bring forth.

CHURCH YARD, ELIZABETH, N. J.   221

1531 r
IN
memory of
MARY P.
Wife of Henry Simmons
Died Oct. 14th 1832;
Aged 23 years 1 month
& 3 days

Also her Brother
JOHN M HORTON
Died May 4th 1835;
Aged 30 years 6 months
& 4 days

A tribute of respect by their
Affectionate brother J. O. Horton.

1532 r
W. H.
In memory of
William Horton
who died
Septr 26th 1831;
in the 58th year
of his age.

1533 m
IN
MEMORY OF
DORCAS OLIVER
wife of
WILLIAM HORTON
WHO DIED
JUNE 9th 1856,
IN THE 83RD YEAR
OF HER AGE

1534 r
In
Memory of Isaac
son of William &
Dorcas Horton who
died July 27th 1819 in
the 4th year of his age

1535 m
Sacred
To the memory of
Mary Earl
Wife of Captain
Samuel D Ellis
Born January 28, 1840
Died March 11. 1858
——o——
Mary thou was mild and lovely
Gentle as the summer breeze
Pleasant as the air of evening
  When it floats among the trees

Peaceful be thy silent slumber
Peaceful in thy grave so low
Thou no more will join our number
Thou no more our songs shall know

Yet again we hope to meet thee
When the day of life is fled
Then in heaven with joy to greet thee
When no farewell tear is shed

1536 m
SOPHIA G. GENUNG
Died
Aug 18th 1858.
Aged 27 years

Dear Sophia thou hast left us.
[the stone has been cut off here and set in base.]

1537 m
In
Memory of
PHEBE CORY
daughter of
Eleazar B. & Nancy Genung
who died May 12. 1842
Aged 21 Years & 6 Months,

Sleep love, and lov'd one sleep
Beneath the quiet sod
And yet with many a tear
We gave you up to God

1538 *m*
In
Memory of
Clifford Austin
Son of
Eleazer & Electa Genung
who died Jan 22 1835
Aged 7 Months & 25 days

This lovely bud so young and fair
Call'd hence by early doom
Just came to show how sweet a flower
In paradise may bloom

1539 *r*
J   F
In memory of
Jacob Foster
who died March 11th
1814 in the 71st year
of his age

My friends prepare to follow me
Both young and old must die you see
There's no discharge there's no delay
When death demands we must obey

1540 *r*
E. T.
In memory of
Elizabeth Todd
who died Augst 24
1810 in the 64th
year of her age

Go home my friends dry up your tears
I must lie here till Christ appears
Repent in time, while time you have
For theres no repentance in the grave

1541 *r*
Here ly ye Remains of

Mrs Hannah Hendr-
-icks Wife of Mr John
Hendricks Obijt Mar
ye 15, 1732. Ætat 39

and David Hend
ricks Son of Mr John
Hendricks Obijt May
29 1732 Ætat 9.

Adieu vain World our dearest Friends farewell
Prepare with us in this dark House to dwell
Till ye last Trump our our ruined Frame repair
                     c
At Christ's Desent to meet him in ye air

1542 *r*
In memory of
two children
of Isaac L &
Catharine Davis
John Jacob
died Jany 26th 1823
aged 1 year 9 months
& 13 days
James Oliver
died Novr 22^d 1824
aged 1 year 3 months
& 17 days

But nature feels—but ah! they're gone
For them our tears have flow'd
It is the Lord, his hand we own
He doth what seems him good.

1543 *m*
In
memory of
Charlotte Farrand
daughter of Isaac and
Margaret Davis who died
August 2″ 1813 aged 1 year
6 months & 2 days

Vain world how transient is its joys,
Its pleasures soon will end in pain ;
But where I'm gone theres no alloy,
Who would not die this bliss to gain.
Then cease ^{t} indulge th falling tear,
I now with Jesus ever dwell ;
If you my praises did but hear,
You^d surely say that all is well

1544 *m*
In
Memory
of
Margaret
Wife of
Isaac L Davis
who departed this life
May 21 1817
Aged 26 years
7 months &
29 Days

She dropt a tear and grasp'd my hand,
And fain she would have spoke ;
But well my heart could understand,
The language of her look.
She rais'd and gently wav'd her hand,
And fill'd me with a joy ;
To which the wealth of sea and land,
Compared, were but a toy.

1545 *m*
IN
memory of
ISAAC L DAVIS
WHO DIED
April 11th 1845 ;
In the 58th Year
of his age

"Boast not thyself of tomorrow for thou knowest not what a day may bring forth."

Friend after friend departs,
Who hath not lost a friend,
There is no union here of hearts
That hath not here an end.

1546 *m*
OUR MOTHER
SARAH C. PRICE
WIFE OF
D. O. PRICE
DIED
SEP'T 23, 1823,
AGED 31 YEARS

Softly her fainting head she lay
Upon her makers breast ;
Her saviour lifted her soul away
And laid her flesh to rest.

1547 *m*
To
THE MEMORY
of
RICHARD PERRIN,
WHO DEPARTED THIS LIFE
APRIL 19th 1813
AGED 45 YEARS

Watch therefore for ye know not
what hour your Lord doth come

1548 *m*
IN
MEMORY OF
MRS LUCRETIA B.
PERRIN
WHO DIED
JANUARY 17, 1850,
Aged 77 Years
Blessed are the dead
which die in the Lord.

1549 *m*
IN
memory of
SOLOMON SLATER
who died
Decr 3^d 1865.
in the 40th year
of his age

JAMES D SLATER
Died March 3^d 1864
Aged 10 Months and 3 Days

EDWARD B SLATER
Died May 11th 1865
in the 4th Year
of his age

1550 r
S. W.
In memory of
SALLY
wife of
Ezekiel Williams
who died
Jan 15th 1828
in the 41. year
of her age

Dear partner of my life
And children whom I love
Remember dying strife
Which you have got to prove.

1551 r
E. W.
In memory of
Ezekiel Williams
who died
Aug. 17th 1830
in the 46th year
of his age

Children 'come view my bed of clay,
This pillow of the ground ;
Here your fair bodies soon must lay,
Till the last trump shall sound.

1552 m
BROTHER
EUGENE A. FAVOR
BORN AUGUST 8. 1856
DIED JUNE 4, 1888.

1553 m
OUR MOTHER
MARY A.
DAUGHTER OF
STEPHEN A. MEEKER
AND WIDOW OF
JOHN J. FAVOR
BORN AUGUST 7, 1837
DIED JUNE 29, 1886

1554 m
IN
Memory of
ALLETTA
WIFE OF
Stephen A. Meeker
who died Sept 5th 1853.
In the 51st Year
of her age

A friend has gone a mother dear,
Whose last remains are resting here ;
Jesus' love whilst here below,
Oft did light her careworn brow.

She oft did speak and feel the words
    so true,
Which is to all and reader you ;
We must enjoy the love divine,
That we may all in glory shine.

1555 m
IN
memory of
STEPHEN A MEEKER
WHO DIED
Augst 22d 1854
In the 55th Year
of his age

He who lies beneath this sod
Whilst here on earth he sought his
    God
The Pearl of greatest price he found
He was filled with joy and peace of
    mind
An interest in Salvation's plan he
    e'er did show
Whilst passing through this world of
    woe.

1556 m
THE GRAVE
OF
ANN
WIFE OF
Nathaniel Williams
who died
Sept 19th 1847
Aged 82 Years

Hers was the life and the death of a
    christian
[The rest of verse too dim to read.]

1557 r
J. L.
In memory
of
MR JOHN LIGHTON,
died Dec 14th 1804
in the 43rd year
of
his age

Death in all his dire array
Has laid the mortal part in dust:
The embodied spirit has wing'd its way
To God the Saviour God the just.
He will his Sovereign power display,
On the great rewarding day.

1558 r
E. L. K.
In memory
of
MRS ELIZABETH L. KEYT
daughter of
Henry & Hannah Weaver:
died March 24th, 1810, in the
22nd year of her age

A faithful wife a mother dear,
A child belov'd a friend sincere;
Consign'd beneath this clod to lay,
Untill the resurrection day:
O then may she in triumph rise,
To join the saints above the skies.

1559 r
W. C. B.
In memory of
two children of Samuel
& Elizabeth Baker,
William died Decr 28th
1808 aged 10 months
& 20 days
Catharine died Octr 7th
1810 aged 1 year 2
months & 21 days

1560 m
SACRED
to the
Memory of
MRS ELIZABETH
relict of
Henry Freeman
who departed this life
March 8th 1835
In the 61st year of
her age

Faith in thy love shall sweeten death
And smooth the rugged way
Smile on me dearest Lord and then
I shall not wish to stay.

1561 m
IN
MEMORY OF
MARY
WIFE OF
MELANTHON FREEMAN
and daughter of
WM & JANE WEIR
WHO DIED JULY 28 1849,
AGED 52 YEARS 4 MO.
& 11 DAYS

Yesterday she clasped my hand
To day she is in the grave

1562 m
MELANTHON FREEMAN SEN.
DIED
April 9th 1858.
IN HIS 75th YEAR

1563 r
E. F.
In memory of
ELIZABETH
wife of
Melanthon Freeman
who died Jany 25 1835
aged 52 years 2 months
& 28 days
Also of
their four children
MATTHEW aged 6 months
& 18 days
CAROLINE aged 11 days
ANSON aged 5 days
JOSIAH aged 8 months
& 5 days.

1564 *r*
In Memory of
three children of
Melanthan & Elizabeth
Freeman
Abigail died April 14th 1810
aged 11 months & 20 days
Rachel died Feby 16th 1812
aged 1 year & 5 days
Henry died Augst 29th 1813
aged 8 months & 13 days

1565 *r*
A. H.
In memory of
ANNA
wife of John C. Hotto
and daughter of
Melanthon & Elizabeth
Freeman : who died
May 20th 1834;
aged 28 years
5 months
& 8 days

1566 *m*
ELIZABETH JANE
WIFE OF
MELANTHON FREEMAN JUN.
Died Nov. 24th 1851
in her 28th year

1567 *m*
In
Memory,
of
ABIGAIL
wife of Jonah Rowland
who departed this life
November 22nd 1806,
In the 46th Year of
her age
Weep not for me, but weep
for yourselves and your children

1568 *r*
J. R.
Jane F. daughr of
Jonah Rowland &
Abigail his wife
died April 20th 1802
aged 11 mons & 27
days
blow
When the archangels trump shall
And souls to bodies join
Millions will wish their time below
Had been as short as thine.

1569 *r*
IN
memory
of
three children of
Michael & Rebecca
Bedell
WM HENRY
died Augt 17th 1822;
Aged 15 months & 7 das :
WM HENRY
died Augt 27th 1829;
Aged 17 months & 9 das :
CAROLINE AMANDA
died Novr 11th 1830
Aged 8 months & 11 das :

1570 *m*
IN
MEMORY OF
MICHAEL BEDELL
WHO DIED
April 11th 1855
AGED 55 YEARS
& 6 MONTHS.

" I know that my Redeemer liveth."

1571 *m*
In memory of
REBECCA
WIFE OF
MICHAEL BEDELL
WHO DIED
May 18th 1868
Aged 71 Years

She sleeps in peace yes sweetly sleeps,
Her sorrows all are oer,
With her the Storms of Life are past
She's gained the Heavenly Shore.

1572 *m*
IN
Memory of
SARAH E.
WIFE OF
GEORGE L. BEDELL,
who died Dec[r] 6th 1857;
Aged 20 Years
and 1 Day

How still and peaceful is the grave
Where life's vain tumults past
The appointed house by heavens decree
Receives us all at last.

1573 *g*
DAVID S. MITCHELL
DIED
MAY 29th 1886
AGED 67 YEARS

MITCHELL

1574 *g*
STEPHEN MAGIE
BORN
MARCH 12. 1807,
DIED
NOV 24. 1874.

MARY S. MAGIE
BORN
NOV. 24, 1799
DIED
MARCH 30, 1881:

MAGIE

1575 *m*
IN
Memory of two children of
Aaron and Ann Pierson
LILLIS
died Nov[r] 21st 1842
aged 4 years 4 months
& 28 days
ALSO
MARY LOUISA
died Jan[y] 3[d] 1848
aged 2 years 5 months
& 16 days

1576 *m*
AARON PIERSON
Died
Jan 11, 1850
Aged
42 years & 6 mos,

And now hath thy dust returned to the
earth
The spirit to God who gave it.
Yet affection shall fondly cherish thy
worth;
And mem'ry deeply engrave it.
Not here on this tablet of mouldering
stone.
But in our fond bosoms where best it
is known.

1577 *m*
IN
MEMORY OF
ABIGAIL
WIDOW OF
Henry D. Woodruff
who died Aug[st] 31st 1850
In the 83[d] Year
of her age.

1578 *m*
IN
memory of
HENRY D. WOODRUFF
WHO DIED
Sept[r] 18th 1849.
In the 81st Year
of his age

1579 *r*
In memory of
Mary wife of
Henry D.
Woodruff
who died Aug[t]
23. 1819;
in the 45th year
of her
age

1580 r
V. W.
In memory of
Vilette wife of Henry
D. Woodruff who died
Dec the 22^d 1797 in
the 24th year of her age.

1581 r
HERE lies interr'd
what was Mortal of
Mr Joseph Woodruff
who died Augt ye 20th
Anno Domini 1778.
In the 76th Year of
his Age

1582 r
Here lies the Body of
Martha Wife of
Joseph Woodruff Dec^d
Octr 13 1757 in the 57
Year of her age

Remember me as you pass by
as you are now so once was I
As I am now so you must be
Therefore prepare to follow me.

1583 r
P. W.
In memory of
Puah Widow of
Joseph Woodruff
who died July 29th
1803 in the 83^d
year of her age

1584 r
Here lies ye Body
of Henry Dusenbar^y
Son of Henry &
Elizabeth Woodruff
Dec^d Sepr 29th 1762
aged 18 Months

1585 r
In memory of
Henry Woodruff
who departed this
Life Septr the 19th
1790 In ye 58th Year
of his Age

1586 r
E. W.
In memory of
Elizabeth Widow of
Henry Woodruff
who died June
the 27th 1804 in
the 70th year of
her Age

1587 r
J. W.
In memory of
JOHN
son of Joseph &
Elizabith Woodruff
who died
April 20th 1817
in the 24th year
of his age

A pale consumption gave the fatal
  blow
The stroke was certain but the effect
  was slow
With wasting pain I long have been
  oppress'd
But in the morn of life I've gone to
  rest.

1588 r
J. W.
In memory of
Joseph Wood-
ruff the third
who died March
6th. 1820. in
the 58th year of
his age

1589 *m*
IN
Memory of
ELIZABETH
widow of
Joseph Woodruff
who died
Novr 17th 1843
In the 81st Year
of her age

Our age to seventy years is set
How short the term how frail the state
And if to eighty we arive
We rather sigh and groan than live

1590 *r*
R. W.
In memory of
RHODA
wife of
James Woodruff
who departed this
life May 15th 1826
Aged 31 years
Also of
ELIZABETH
their daughter who departed
this life Augst 25th 1824
Aged 2 years

1591 *m*
IN
memory of
WILLIAM BAKER
who died April 2^d 1853
aged 9 years 3 months
& 22 days
MARY WHITEHEAD
died Oct 22^d 1852
aged 1 year 8 months
& 16 days
ANNA
died Oct 13th 1841 :
aged 9 months
Children of James and
Jane W Woodruff

1592 *m*
ISREAL M MILLER
DIED
JAN^Y 20th 1850
IN THE 20th YEAR
OF HIS AGE

" Boast not thyself of tomorrow
for thou knowest not what a day
may bring forth."

1593 *m*
IN
MEMORY OF
RICHARD PERRIN
who died March 30th 1844
Aged 43 Years
ALSO
SARAH
WIFE OF
Richard Perrin
died Feby 9th 1841
Aged 41 Years
ALSO
ANN
daughter of
Richard & Sarah Perrin
died May 29th 1845
In the 16th Year
of her age

1594 *r*
M. F.
In memory of
MATILDA
wife of
Jeheil Force
who departed this
life Jany 15th 1818
In the 36th year
of her age

1595 *m*
IN
Memory of
MARIA W.
DAUGHTER OF
Estes & Frances C.
CUMMINGS
who died
Octr 30th 1841
Aged 2 Months

1596 m
HENRIETTA L.
WIFE OF
BENJAMIN J. VRELAND
daughter of
Isaac and Evaline
SPINNING
died Jany 28th 1862
In the 33^d Year
of her age
GEORGE S.
son of Isaac and
Susan P Spinning
died Feby 4th 1862
aged 4 years & 3 months

1597 m
ELVINA
Wife of Isaac Spinning
and Daughter of
Samuel Clark
Died 30th July 1854
Aged 47 Years

Why should our tears in sorrow flow
When God recalls his own
And bids them leave a world of woe
For an immortal crown.

1598 m
IN
MEMORY OF
PHEBE ANN
WIFE OF
JOHN DUNHAM
WHO DIED
DEC 20TH 1831,
AGED 23 YEARS 2 MONTHS & 20 DAYS

Farewell! husband and children dear

Affliction sore long time I bore
  Physicians were in vain
  Till God did please to give me ease
  And free me from my pain

1599 m
IN
memory
of three
children of Asa &
Mary Eliza Vandergrist
HANNAH ANN
died March 21st 1831
aged 5 years, 7 months
& 19 days
HANNAH ANN
died Feb^s 24th 1832.
aged 5 months & 15 days
MAY ELIZABETH
died Feb 12th 1834
aged 1 year & 5 days

Sleep on sweet babes and take your
  rest
You in your Makers arms are blest
And now to you we bid adieu
God fit us all to follow you

1600 m
IN
memory
of
MELSUP HEMING
who died
Jan 21st 1832
aged 54 years
ALSO OF
REBECCA
his wife who died
Octr 27th 1831
aged 56 years

"Prepare to meet thy God."

1601 r
S. T.
In Memory of
Susannah wife of
Ichabod Terrill
who died Feby 6th
1817
in the 50th year of
her age

All we can do is view her tomb
And sorrow o'er her breathless clay
And thus regret the heavy gloom
On us inpends since she's away

1602 *m*
ADELBERT
SON OF
William A. and Rachel E.
FULTON
who died Sept. 29. 1856.
aged 2 months & 22 days

Our darling babe has gone and left us
And his loss we deeply feel
But it's God who hath bereft us
He can all our sorrows heal.

1603 *m*
In Memory of
WILLIAM JAMES MONTGOMERY
who died
March 23 1834;
AGED 35 YEARS
Also AMELIA Dau^r of
WILLIAM & MARY
MONTGOMERY
who died May 29 1838
Aged 4 years

"Thanks be unto God who giveth us the victory through our Lord Jesus Christ."

1604 *m*
IN
Memory of
ELIZA
daughter of
Benjamin & Sarah
ELWOOD
who died
July 30, 1843
In the 2. Year of
her age

Here by my infant home,
The church my childhood blest
My buried sister's sacred dust
Fain would I take my rest.

1605 *m*
IN
Memory of
JOHN JOSEPH
Son of
Johnson & Eliza
SORRELL
who died
April 27. 1837
aged 1 Year 11 Months
and 10 days

1606 *r*
ERECTED
to the Memory of
PETER VAN HORN
who died
October 19th 1840
in the 47th year
of his age

"Come unto me all ye that labour and are heavy laden & I will give you rest."

1607 *r*
IN
memory of   Col'd
LAFAYETTE BOYLESTON
died March 29. 1849
aged 24 years &
6 months

1608
R. C. BRYANT'S
FAMILY VAULT
1845

1609
PETER MASSIE'S
FAMILY VAULT
1840

1610
ELIAS DAYTON'S
FAMILY VAULT
1806

1611
Family Vault
of the
Heirs of Col Gould Phinny

1612
C. O. Halsted's
Family Vault
1838

1613
William Shute's
Family Vault

1614
M. M. Woodruff's
Family Vault
1841

1615 *m*
IN
Memory of
Our Parents,
JOEL BONNEL,
Born Ap'r. 27, 1791.
Died Feb 19, 1880

ARABELLA HALSEY
Born Feb. 23, 1795
Died Dec 2, 1879

There is rest for the weary,

1616 *m*
IN
MEMORY OF
MARY ELISABETH
WIFE OF
JOHN JACOB BAUER
Who departed this life
March 31st 1856
Aged 61 Years & 6 Months

So teach us to number our days, that we may apply our hearts unto wisdom—Ps: 90. Vs: 12.

1617 *m*
IN
Memory of
E V A—D A.
Wife of
PHILLIP KNOEDLER
Who departed this life Oct 29
1852
Aged 35 Years & 1 Month

Also of
HENRIETTE C—.
Daughter of the above
Who died Nov: 7th 1852
Aged 1 Year & 2 Months

For here have We no continuing City but We seek one to come
James 13 : 14.

1618 *m*
IN
Memory of
JOHN G.
son of Jacob and
Mary E. Bauer:
who died July 13th 1850
Aged 21 years &
5 Months

"The lines are fallen unto me in pleasant places yea I have a goodly heritage."

1619 *m*
IN
Memory of
ANNA ROSINA
daughter of Jacob &
Mary E Bauer
who died
Novr 20th 1843 :
Aged 21 Years
& 10 Days

"I know that my Redeemer liveth and he shall at the latter day awake me from the earth."

1620 *m*
EMILY C KNOEDLER
Born March 19th 1837
Died Sept: 29th
1859
My home is in heaven

1621 *m*
A. A. F.

In memory of
ABIGAIL A FAY,
who was born in
Westborough Mass.
Feby 13th 1818
and who died in the
city of New York
May 17 1836

1622 *m*
FREDERICK MERRIAM
only child of
Joseph C &
Anne C. Laughton
died Septr 12th 1836,
aged 10 months
and 6 days

"Of such is the kingdom
of heaven."

1623 *r*
R. P.
In memory of
Rhoda Wife of
John Peet, departed
this life Octr 8th 1803
in the 42d year
of her Age

In faith she liv'd ; in dust she lies :
But faith foresees ; that dust shall
  rise ;
When Jesus calls while hope assumes;
And boasts her joy among the tombs.

1624 *r*
In memory of
RICHARD O JEFFERY
who died
Octr 28th 1833,

aged 44 years
2 months and 13 days

As you are now so I was once
As I am now so you must be
Prepare for Death and follow me.

1625 *r*
S. G.
In memory of
Sarah wife of Joseph
Gorman who died
Augt 3d 1807 in the
56th year of her age
Lie still my dear and take thy rest
God call'd the home he thought it
                                    best

1626 *r*
M. G.
Sacred to the memory
of
Martha wife of John Gal-
-braith a Native of Strabane
Ireland, died June 27th 1812,
Aged 29 years
Lovely in life, serene she welcom'd
  death
Attending seraphs mark'd her latest
  breath
Thou on bright smiles on wings of
  boundless love
Bear her pure spirit to the joys
  above

1627 *g*
[On West side]
MY WORK
IS DONE

NICHOLAS MURRAY
BORN IN IRELAND
Dec 25 1802
PASTOR OF THE 1ST PRESB. CHURCH
ELIZABETH N. J.
FROM JULY 23 1833
UNTIL HIS DEATH
FEB 4th 1861

REMEMBER THE WORDS THAT
I SPAKE UNTO YOU WHILE I
WAS YET WITH YOU

INSCRIPTIONS IN FIRST PRESBYTERIAN

[North side]
THIS MONUMENT
IS ERECTED
BY THE CONGREGATION
TO THE MEMORY OF
A FAITHFUL, AND BELOVED
PASTOR.
A MAN OF GOD,
THOROUGHLY FURNISHED
UNTO ALL GOOD WORKS.

[East side]
ELIZA J RHEES
WIFE OF
REV. NICHOLAS MURRAY
BORN NOV. 30, 1804.
DIED MARCH 7, 1871.
"THERE REMAINETH THEREFORE A
REST TO THE PEOPLE OF GOD."

THOMAS CHALMERS MURRAY
FEB. 1850   MARCH 1879

[South side]
OUR CHILDREN
JOHN MORRISON
WILLIAM WILBERFORCE
ANNA RHEES
MARGARET BRECKENRIDGE
CATHARINE LOXLEY

"OF SUCH IS THE KINGDOM OF
HEAVEN."

ELIZABETH CLARKE
BORN NOV. 1830
DIED JUNE. 1858

"I am
THE RESURRECTION AND THE LIFE"

1628 r

IN
Memory of
THOMAS B.
CAHOW
who
departed
this life
Septr 15th
1810 in the
43^d year of
his age

IN
Memory of
JANE
his widow
who
departed
this life
March 17th
1825 in the
58th year of
her age

1629 r
E. O.
In memory of
Enos Osborn who died
April 18th 1800 in the
75th year of his age

A husband dear a parent kind
A social generous friend
  He's gone to dwell above the skies
Where sorrows ever end

This stone was erected by Thos B
Cahow his son in law as a token of
    his regard

1630 r
In
Memory
of
ELIZABETH
wife of Aaron Ball,
who died Jany 18th 1817
in the 25th year
of her age

Farewell, no more I tread your ground
No more I need the gospel sound
My feet have reach'd the heav'nly
  shore
I know no imperfections more.

CHURCH YARD, ELIZABETH, N. J.   235

Let friends no more my suff'ring
  mourn
Nor view my sorrow's with concern
O cease to drop the pit'ing tear
I've past beyond the reach of fear.

Also of three children of
Aaron & Elizabeth Ball
JAMES T. died May 15th 1815
aged 3 years & 1 day
ABRAHAM S. died Decr 11 1815,
aged 1 year & 1 month
DAVID H. died Decr 13th 1816
aged 2 months & 4 days

1631 *r*
J. H. F.
JAMES HARRIS
son of Richard
R & Mary Ann
Frazee died
Decr 18th 1821 aged
10 months

"The Lord gave and the Lord hath taken away. Blessed be the name of the Lord."

1632 *r*
[Scaled off]
D a i
n & Sa
d may 1st 1801 a
nonth's and 21 d

1633 *r*
G. S.
In memory of
GAVIN SCOTT
from Alnwick,
Northumberland
England who
departed this life
June 27th 1815
Aged 77 years

" Let me die the death of the righteous and let my last end be like his."
  Numb. chap 23^d ver 10

1634 *r*
Mary Wife of
Gavin Scott
from Alnwick
Northumberland
England Died May
1st 1801 Aged 67 Years

Eight years her mortal eyes were
  blind
Not so her faculties of mind
By faith she view'd her Saviour's love
  Much long'd to sing his praise
  above

1635 *r*
M. S.
In memory of
Mather Scott son of
Gavin and Mary Scott
from Alnwick Northum-
-berland England who
died June 7th 1810
aged 40 years

1636 *r*
T. M.
In Memory of
THOMAS MATHER
A native of Northum-
-berland, England,
Who departed this
life May 4th 1815,
in the 84th year
of his age.

Within the compass of this narrow
  span
Lies God's noblest work an honest
  man.

1637 *r*
HERE lies ye Remains
of Mr. Benjamin Thomp-
-son, who died March
the 25th A. D. 1760. In
the 62^d Year of his Age

My Soul, my Body, I will trust
With him who numbers every Dust
My Saviour faithfully will keep
His own for Death is but a Sleep.

INSCRIPTIONS IN FIRST PRESBYTERIAN

1638 *m*
SACRED
to the memory of
ANNE MATILDA
daughter of
Thomas and Phebe
E Gilbert
who departed this life
March 9th 1839
aged 3 years 6 months
and 18 days
"Suffer little children to come unto
me and forbid them not for of such
is the kingdom of Heaven"

1639 *m*
In memory of
Four Children of
Burnet D & Ann Hamilton

SAMUEL F. M.
aged 3 years
3 months &
18 days

GEORGE W.
aged 6 years
2 months &
27 days

LOUISA S.
aged 1 year
& 29 days

WILLIAM M.
aged
2 days

How happy thus to sink to rest
So early numbered with the blest

1640 *m*
IN
MEMORY OF
FRANCIS P HAMILTON
who died March 18th 1864,
Aged 31 Years 9 Mos.
& 15 Days

1641 *m*
IN
MEMORY OF
BURNETT D. HAMILTON
WHO DIED
Feby 22nd 1875,
Aged 63 Years 11 Months
and 8 Days

1642 *m*
IN
MEMORY OF
ANN BRYAN
WIFE OF
Burnet D Hamilton
Died August 13 1887
Aged 76 Years 5 Months
and 17 Days.

1643 *m*
THOMAS PATTERSON
Died
Octr 26th 1852
In the 26th Year
of his age

We meet in Heaven.

1644 *m*
In Memory
OF
UZAL REEVE
who died Jan 23, 1840,
In the 51 Year of
his age
ALSO
JAMES H
SON OF
Uzal & Lucetta Reeve
who died Jan 12 1842
In the 4. Year of his age

How still and peaceful is the grave,
No pain, no grief, no anxious fear,
Invade thy bounds, no mortal woes
Can reach the peaceful sleeper here
———o———

This lovely bud so young and fair
Call'd hence by early doom
Just came to show how sweet a flower
In paradise would bloom

1645 m
In Memory
OF
LUCETTA
widow of
UZAL REEVE
who died June 6th 1847
In the 50th Year
of her age

If a man die shall he live again?
all the days of my appointed time
will I wait till my change come
Job 14. 14.
My flesh shall slumber in the ground
Till the last trumpets joyful sound
Then burst the chains with sweet surprise
And in my Saviours image rise.

1646 m
In Memory
OF
FRANCES H REEVE
who died
April 29th 1845
In the 30th Year of
her age

Sister thou art gone bfore us
And thy saintly soul is flown
Where tears are wip'd from ev'ry eye
And sorrow is unknown

1647 m
MARY MOUNT
DIED
Nov^R 26th 1884
AGED 63 YEARS

1648 m
[On west side]
Ida

[On east side]
Only and beloved
Child of
Thomas T. W. and
Isabel T. Nicholl
died Feby 21st 1860
aged 9 years
and 1 month

1649 r

Here lyeth ye Bo
s
dy of Isaac William
Dec^d Sep^t 22, 1733
Aged 3 days

s
And Joseph William
Died Octr y^e
4th 1728 Aged
10 days

Children of Joseph Williams
Junr

1650 r
In memory of Ann Eliza
Daughter of Joseph and
BETSY WILLIAMS
who departed this life
Septr 2nd 1803
Aged 11 months

Sleep on sweet Babe
And take your peacefull rest
God call'd you hence
Because he saw it best

1651 r
Hannah Daughter of
William & Johannah
Williams died Sept^r
ye 5th 1777 In y^e
2^d year of her age

1652 r
H. W.

In memory of
Hannah daughter
of William and
Johanna Williams
who died Septr 28th
1807 in the 20th
year of her age

My parents dear weep not for me
When in this yard my grave you see
My time was short but blest is he
That call'd me to eternity.

1653 r
W. W.
In memory of
William Williams
who died
April 4th 1816
in the 69th year
of his age

1654 r
[Inscription all gone]

1655 m
IN
Memory of
DANIEL WILLIAMS
Born June 18th 1783
Died July 24th 1825
Aged 42 Years 1 month
& 6 days

1656 m
IN
Memory of
DEBORAH
WIDOW OF
Daniel Williams
who died Octr 18th 1853
Aged 70 years

1657 m
IN
Memory of
THOMAS S.
son of Daniel and
Deborah Williams
who died
July 19th 1847
Aged 26 Years

1658 m
JACOB WILLIAMS JR
D<small>IED</small>
Dec. 21st 1836
in the 32nd year
of his age

1659 r
J. W.
John H. son of Jacob
& Mary Williams
died June 14th 1802
aged 1 year 7 mon^s
& 26 days.

"Except ye be converted and
become as little children ye shall
not enter into the kingdom of
heaven."

1660 r
M. W.
Mary Ann daught^r
of Jacob & Mary
Williams, died June 3^d
1802
aged 4 years 3 mon^s
& 12 days

"suffer little children to come unto
me and forbid them not for of such
is the kingdom of God."

1661 r
In memory of
ELIHU
son of
Jacob and Mary Williams
who departed this life 1st
of Septr 1809 in the 14th
year of his age

Being dead yet speaketh

My glass is run my days are spent
My life is gone it was but lent
And as I am so must you be
O then prepare to follow me.

1662 m
JACOB WILLIAMS SENR
died Nov. 30th 1815
in the 45th year
of his age

ALSO
MARY
his widow
died Aug. 27th 1851
in the 85th year
of his age

"My flesh shall rest in hope."

1663 r
N. M.
In memory of
NATHANIEL
son of Philip and
Sarah Morgan who
died June 21st 1813
in the 17th year of
his age

1664 m
GEO. FORSYTH
CO K
9TH
N. J. INF.

1665 m
In memory of
JAMES DELEREE
son of William &
Sophia E Van Voorhis
who died
July 13 1848
aged 1 year 5 months
& 13 days

And Jesus said suffer little children
to come unto me and forbid them not
for of such is the kingdom of heaven.

1666 r
In
Memory
of
three children of
Edward & Elizabeth
Smith
DAVID died Novr 5th 1813
aged 1 year & 8 months
JOHN W. died Augst 31st 1821
aged 4 months & 9 days
WILLIAM died Oct. 8th 1822
aged 1 month & 5 days

1667 m
THE GRAVE
OF
FRANCIS KING
who died in this Town
July 16th 1837
in the 55th year of his age
He was born in Vernon
Tolland co. Connecticut
where he spent the principal
portion of his life
He was a scholar and a christian
"The memory of the just is bless'd."

1668 m
OUR MOTHER
RACHEL GRIFFITH
Born April 18th 1790.
Died Feb. 24th 1869.

INSCRIPTIONS IN FIRST PRESBYTERIAN

1669 *m*
JOHN GRIFFITH
Born
in New Castle England
and died in this Town
Also
CHARLES W. MOSES
born in Cincinnatti
and   died
in the City of New York
Infant son of Montogue
and Margaret Moses

1670 *r*
In
memory of
Josephine
daughter of John
& Rachel Griffith
who died May 10
1821. Aged 5
months & 23
days

1671 *m*
Capt. FREEMAN DEGROOT
Died
Novr 10th 1856
in the 50th year
of his Age

1672 *m*
Our
Little Hattie
"Of such is the kingdom of heaven."

1673 *m*
ERECTED
in memory
of
MARGARET JANE
Daughter of Robert
And Elizabeth
WALKER
Died July 17th 1850.
Aged 4 years 6. mo
& 17 Days

She was lovely, she was fair
And for a while was given
And angel came, and claimed his own
And bore her home to heaven

1674 *m*
IN
Memory of
JOHN H DUNN
who died
Septr 14th 1853 :
Aged 29 Years

" Unto thee, O Lord do I lift up my soul "

Weep not my Friends
Farewell

1675 *m*
JOHN F. PAULEY
died Aug 2 1854
ag'd 2 y'rs 2 m's
and 17 d's

1676 *m*
HENRY MARTIN
son of
John & Jane
Van Name
died June 5 1841
aged 4 years 11 months
and 14 days
Also
Two infant brothers
of such is the Kingdom
of heaven.

1677 *m*
JANE MATILDA
daughter of
John & Jane
Van Name
died Jan 21 1853
aged 5 years 3 months
and 14 days

Dearest Sister thou hath left us
Here thy loss we deeply feel
But tis God that hath bereft us
He can all our sorrows heal.

1678 *m*
OUR BELOVED SISTERS
FRANCIS WESTERVELT
Born July 15th 1825
Died Jany 19th 1869

ANNA VAN NAME
Born Novr 20th 1839
Died April 11th 1868.

1679 *m*
OUR BELOVED PARENTS
JOHN VAN NAME,
Born October 23d 1800
Died August 30th 1874

JANE TOWNLEY
HIS WIFE
Born February 1st 1803
Died January 9th 1878

They sleep in Jesus

1680 *m*
[Monument. West side]
ELIAS MARSH
Born May 21 1795
Died Dec. 28, 1860

MYRA BUSS
his Wife
Born Oct 14 1790
Died Sept 20 1876
"Blessed are the dead which die in the Lord."

MARSH

[South side]
MARY H MARSH

Born July 12 1820
Died May 8 1839
MARTHA E MARSH

Born Nov. 4. 1821
Died Sept. 8. 1839

[North side]
SOPHRONIA B MARSH
Born Aug. 24. 1823
Died Sept, 25, 1854

MYRA A MARSH
Born March 5, 1834,
Died March 24, 1853,
[East side blank]

1681 *m*
[Monument. North side]
OUR KATIE
DAUGHTER OF
GEO S. AND SARAH M
BADGER
Died May 19th 1858
Aged 19 years

1682 *m*
LIDA C.
DAUGHTER OF
J. W. & MARY C. WILLIAMS
Died May 24th 1875
AGED 9 YEARS

1683 *m*
IN
Memory of
DANIEL HENRY
SON OF
William & Lydia
WILLIAMS
WHO DIED
Feb 24th 1845
Aged 7 Years 7 Months
and 5 days

spirit has gon
Our lovely boy, sleepeth here but his
are unknown
To a climate where sorrow and pain
frame is at rest
His spirit is strengthened his
in the land of the blest
There is health, there is peace

1684 m
In
Memory of
CAROLINE
daughter of
Charles & Elizabeth
DEBO
who died
Aug. 7th 1843
Aged 6 Years 2 months
and 13 days

1685 m
In
Memory of
HENRY
Son of
Samuel and
Catharine Clawson
who died
July 14th 1829
in the 3rd year of his age

This lovely bud so young and fair
Call'd hence by early doom
Just came to show how sweet a flower
In paradise could bloom

1686 r
S. R.
In memory of
SAMUEL RAWL
who died May 27th 1813
aged 19 years 4 months
& 12 days

This stone is placed in
token of the respect justly
due the departed by his
fond Mother

While on the earth I did remain
Was fill'd with sorrow grief & pain
Farewell my friends & foes likewise
My journey is beyond the skies.

1687 r
C R
In Memory of
CATHERINE
widow of
Abraham Roll who
died Augst 9 1814
in the 55th year
of her age

Affliction sore long time I bore
Physician's arts' were vain
Till God did please to give me ease
And free me from my pain

1688 m
JAMES G.
SON OF
Maggie & Tho's Forsyth
Died Dec. 22. 1884
Aged 19 Years
& 9 Months

1689 m
ROBERT J FORSYTH
DIED
May 1st 1881
Aged 35 Years

1690 m
IN
MEMORY OF
MARY SWIFT
wife of
PETER AUSTIN
WHO DIED
MAY 3D 1855
AGED 53 YEARS

Prepare to meet thy God.

1691 m
MARY
daughter of
T & E STREMPEL
Born Aug. 27, 1854
Died Nov. 3. 1855.

A little bud unfolded here
But blossoming now in
heaven

1692 *m*
ANDREW FORSYTH
Sergeant of
Co K 3 Reg N. J. V.
BORN
MAY 12th 1831
Died May 3d 1863
at the fight on Marye's Heights

GEORGE FORSYTH
Co A 1st Reg't N. J. V.
Born July 14 1838
DIED
April 12th 1868.

1693 *m*
IN
MEMORY
OF
ELIZABETH FORSYTH
DIED AUG. 7th
1860
AGED 50 YEARS 2 MO.
& 25 DAYS

SAMUEL FORSYTHE
DIED DEC. 5th
1873
Aged 75 Years

1694 *m*
[Stone broken in three places]
IN
MEMORY
OF
ISABELLA
DAUGHTER OF SAMUEL
AND ELIZABETH
FORSYTH
Died March 5th 1863
Aged 20 Years 11 Mo.
& 18 Days

1695 *m*
IN MEMORY OF
MARY ANN
WIDOW OF
HENRY HAMILTON
who died
February 27th 1850
AGED 68 YEARS

" Blessed are the dead, which die
in the Lord."

1696 *m*
GEORGE
son of
George D & Christian
RANDELL
died Nov 21 1848
aged 6 months

Our beloved and
only son

1697
THE GRAVE
OF
WILLIAM MITCHELL
who died
March 20th 1847
Aged 30 Years

A Native of Ireland

1698 *r*
IN
Memory of
ROBERT McKEE
who died
Septr 18th 1823
Aged 50 years
Also
ELIZABETH
his daughter
who died
Novr 28th 1835
Aged 20 years
2 months
and 22 days

1699 *m*
SACRED
TO THE MEMORY
OF
ALEXANDER PORTER
who departed this life
June 23^d 1851
Aged 37 Years

1700 *m*
THE LAST
Of Her Family
CATHARINE FALCONER
DIED
Dec 4th 1856
aged 34 years

The victory now is obtained
She's gone her Redeemer to see
Her wishes she fully has gained
She's now where she panted to be.

1701 *m*
IN
Memory of
HANNAH
wife of
John I Kopp
who died
April 3rd 1842,
Aged 24 Years 9 Months
and 26 days

No sickness, or sorrow, or pain
Shall ever disquiet her now
For death to her spirit was gain
Since Christ was her life when below

1702 *m*
IN
Memory of
LAVENIA
WIFE OF
JONATHAN SHEPHERD
who died
Jan 14th 1853:
In the 51st Year
of her age

1703 *m*
IN
memory of
ANN MARIA
WIFE OF
WILLIAM J HARRIS
who died
Dec. 30th 1852
In the 21st Year
of her age

1704 *m*
IN
Memory of
CAROLINE POWELL
daughter of
JONATHAN & LAVINA
SHEPHERD
who died
AUG. 17th 1865.
Aged 29 years &
4 months

1705 *m*
SACRED
to the memory of
ELIAS VAN NAME
who departed this life
March 15th 1835
aged 23 years
and 10 months

Pass a few swift and fleeting years
And all who now in bodies live
Shall quit like me this vale of tears
Their righteous sentence to receive

1706 *m*
ANNIE

1707 *m*
MARY JANE
Daughter of
Justus and Mary S. Morris
died Feb 18th 1851
aged 4 years 1 month
and 19 days

CHURCH YARD, ELIZABETH, N. J.   245

This lovely flower e'er it began to
  bloom
was called a tenant for the silent tomb
She lived but to enhance a parents
  heart
And then in sorrow were they doomed
  to part

1708 *m*
WILLIAM RITTER
BORN
AUGUST 28TH 1839
DIED MARCH 6TH 1842

AMELIA RITTER
BORN MARCH 28th 1841
DIED FEB. 28th, 1842.

LOUIS RITTER
BORN JAN 17th 1843
DIED JULY 5th 1843

Children of
J. PETER & AMELIA RITTER

1709 *m*
CHARLES RITTER
BORN & DIED
JULY 10th, 1853.

WILHELMINA RITTER
BORN SEPT. 23RD, 1854.
DIED JUNE 9th 1857.

GEORGE RITTER
BORN JUNE 13th 1857.
DIED AUGUST 13th 1857.

Children of
J PETER & AMELIA RITTER.

1710 *m*
WILLIAM P.
Born June 29th 1848,
Died Dec. 4th 1863.
Aged 15 Years, 5 mos.
& 5 Days

None knew thee but to love
None named thee but to bless

FRANKLIN
Died Oct. 14th 1858.
Aged 3 Mos.

MARY B.
Died Aug 15th 1861
Aged 11 Mos.

Children of
J. P. & Amelia Ritter

1711 *m*
AMELIA R.
WIFE OF
CAPT J. PETER RITTER
Died Sept. 17. 1887
Aged 69 Years 11 Mo's
and 8 Days

At Rest.

1712 *m*
CAPT. J. PETER RITTER
Born
July 16th 1816
Died
Oct. 27th 1872.

1713 *m*
HANNAH
WIDOW OF
JOSIAH MILLER
DIED
March 26th, 1887.
Aged 87 years 6 months
And 22 Days

1714 *m*
JOSIAH MILLER
DIED
FEBRUARY 9th 1866;
AGED 82 YEARS
2 MONTHS
AND 14 DAYS

1715 *m*
ELIZABETH
WIFE OF
JOSIAH MILLER
DIED
SEPTEMBER 1st 1823;
AGED 39 YEARS 3 MONTHS
AND 22 DAYS

1716 *m*
Our Dear Little
CHARLEY
Not lost but
gone before.

1717 *r*
In
memory of
two children
of Obadiah & Mary
Murdoch
James, died Augt 8th
1819; Aged 1 year
& 23 days

Alexander, died
Septr 8th 1828; Aged
7 years 2 months
& 11 days

1718 *m*
OUR MOTHER
CATHARINE TAIT
DIED
JULY 8th 1851
AGED 75 YEARS

She is not dead but sleepeth

1719 *m*
OUR FATHER
WILLIAM TAIT
DIED
APRIL 27 1848,
Aged 67 years

Blessed are the dead
who die in the
Lord

1720 *m*
In
Memory of
Henry William
son of
Erdmann and
Augusta Graef
died Sept 12th 1852
aged 1 month

1721 *r*
In
Memory of
Margaret M.
daughter of Henry
& Sarah Forguson
who died Octr 10th
1828: Aged 7 years
11 months &
5 days

From Ballyhast Ireland

1722 *r*
M. J.
In memory of
Mary wife of
George Janes, born
near Clare Ireland
and died Oct 1 1823
in the 74th year
of her age

There remaineth therefore a rest
to the people of God.

1723 r

In
Memory of
David son of
Joshua & Sarah
Wells who died
June 5th 1818.
Aged 4 years
and 7 months

In
memory of
Louisa A Daughter of
Joshua & Sarah
Wells, who died
Jany 3rd 1819.
Aged 3 years
and 4 months

Tis God that lifts our comforts high
Or sinks them in the grave
He gives and blessed be his name
He takes but what he gave.

1724 m
IN
MEMORY OF
ESTHER
WIFE OF
ROBERT DICKERSON
WHO DIED
SEPTR 16th 1823
IN THE 45th YEAR
OF HER AGE.

1725 m
IN
MEMORY OF
ROBERT DICKERSON
WHO DIED
JANY 2d 1830
IN THE 53d YEAR
OF HIS AGE

1726 m
IN
Memory of
HERMAN DORNBUSH
a native of
Brickhafen Kingdom
of Hanover Germany
WHO DIED
Janr 15th 1845
Aged 28 Years

Hark from the tombs a doleful sound
Mine ears attend the cry
Ye living men come view the ground
Where you must shortly lie

1727 m
IN
Memory of
MGDALENA
WIFE OF
John Geyer
who died
March 26th 1849
aged 57 years

[The two next are unmarked graves. Got record of sexton]

1728
Dr George Summers
Born May 25 1837
Died July 5 1878

Charles Summers
Born March 29 1811
died May 1 1879

1729 m
JOHN M. OGDEN
DIED
APRIL 2d 1834
AGED 50 YEARS

NANCY
WIDOW OF
JOHN M OGDEN
DIED JAN 1st 1855
AGED 66 YEARS

JOANNA T
THEIR DAUGHTER
DIED SEPT 7 1827
AGED 8 MONTHS

1730 *m*
MARY E BEAUMONT
Born Feb. 20, 1861
Died Nov. 7. 1861.

1731 *m*
IN
Memory of
MARGARETTA B.
WIFE OF
Andrew Hoerning
who died
Octr 9th 1853;
Aged 38 Years

Farewell my friends my partner dear
No more I need your tender care;
My groans no more awake your ears
My midnight sigh to rouse your fears

1732 *m*
L. S.
In memory of
LORENZO STEARNS
who was born in
Billerica. Mass.
May 13th 1813:
and died
May 13th 1836;
Aged 23 years

1733 *m*
IN
MEMORY OF
WILLIAM McKAIN SEN^R
WHO DIED
Septr 17th 1849
Aged 90 Years and 3 Months
ALSO OF
WILLIAM McKAIN JUN.
WHO DIED
Octr 24th 1853,
Aged 52 Years

Cheerful I leave this vale of tears,
Where pain and sorrow groan;
Welcome the day that ends my toil,
And every scene of woe.

1734 *m*
THE GRAVE
OF
NOAH BONNELL
WHO DIED
April 3rd 1856
In the 86th Year
of his age
ALSO
HIS FATHER
ISAAC BONNELL
died March 12th 1833
In the 90th Year
of his age

1735
Ballard Vault

1736
Morrell Vault

1737 *m*
N Martin Crane
Died
June 26th 1870,
Aged 34 Years 10 Mo.
& 7 Days

"I will give unto him that is
athirst of the fountains of the
water of life freely."

CRANE.

1738 *m*
IN
MEMORY OF
ELIZA
WIDOW OF THE LATE
GEORGE BLOOM
who died
March 21, 1842
Aged 58 Years

1739 *m*
WILLIAM GIBSON
DIED
Sept. 4, 1853,
Aged 82 Years

1740 *m*
MARY DULONG
BORN
Augst 26th 1839
DIED
Septr 11th 1853

1741 *m*
CATHARINE
WIFE OF
STEPHEN DULONG
died Decr 16th 1854
Aged 62 Years

1742 *m*
CATHARINE
WIFE OF
Jacob Bohnenberger
Died Decr 9th 1856 ;
Aged 30 Years

GEORGE
their son
died Jany 23^d 1857 :
aged 4 months

1743 *m*
IN
Memory of
WILLIAM H.
son of John F. and
Ann Maria Jakle
who died June 12th 1849
Aged 14 Years

1744 *m*
IN
MEMORY OF
EDWARD CARPENTER
WHO DIED
Sept. 17. 1863,
Æ. 28 Y'rs.
& 5 mo.

1745 *m*
IN
memory of
ELLEN CARPENTER
WIFE OF
CHARLES F. DAUCEY
who died
Sept. 21. 1856
Æ. 32 Y'rs &
9 Mo.

1746 *m*
Charlotte Buss
27 y'rs 4 m's
1854

1747 *m*
[Winans monument in Winans plot]
[East side]
SACRED
TO THE MEMORY OF
ELIAS WINANS
WHO DIED
OCT. 1st 1853.
AGED 64 YEARS
AND FOR 23 YEARS
A RULING ELDER
IN THE CHURCH

"HE WAS A GOOD MAN"

[West side]
SACRED
TO THE MEMORY OF
ABBY
WIDOW OF
ELIAS WINANS
WHO DIED
NOV. 5th 1853.
AGED 66 YEARS

"BLESSED ARE THE DEAD
WHO DIE IN THE LORD."

[North side]
JACOB C WINANS
DIED
NOV 12, 1878.
AGED 66 YEARS

"WELL DONE GOOD AND FAITHFUL
SERVANT."

250   INSCRIPTIONS IN FIRST PRESBYTERIAN

SARAH M.
WIFE OF
JACOB C WINANS
Died May 11th 1885
Age 74 Yrs, 2 Months, &
11 Days

[South side]
ELIAS
Died Feb. 1, 1849.

MARY E.
Died Nov. 22, 1872.
Aged 23 Years

Safe within the fold

Children of
Jacob C & Sarah M Winans

1748 *m*
ELIAS
only son of
Jacob C & Sarah M.
Winans
died Feby 1st 1849.
aged 2 years

1749 *m*
In
Memory of
JAMES W. ANGUS
who died Dec. 23rd 1862.
Aged 51 Years, 9 mos,
& 13 days.

The months of affliction are o'er,
The days and the nights of distress ;
We'll see him in anguish no more,
He has gained a happy release.

1750 *m*
Of such is the kingdom of Heaven

JACOB B.
Third son of
James W. & Wealthy Ann Angus
was born in the city of Mexico May 17,
1844 & Died in this town June 8 1850
Aged 6 years & 21 days

We loved, yes no tongue can tell
How much we loved him and how well
God loved him too, and He thought best
To take him home to be at rest.

[The last 4 in Winans plot]

1751
Rest in Heaven
Sacred to the memory of
GEORGE EDWARD,
only son of Matrean R. &
Phebe Ann Livingston
who departed this life
September 5th 1849
aged 1 year & 8 months

Sweet child tho'rt soon released from
earth
From sorrow greif and pain
Why should we greive from thee to
part
Our loss is but thy gain
We trust in God though sad in heart
That we shall meet again

CHURCH YARD, ELIZABETH, N. J.   251

1752 *m*
IN
memory of
MAGDALENA
WIFE OF
Henry Zulanf
who died Feby 7th 1849
aged 27 years
& 2 months
ALSO
MAGDALENA
their daughter
died Jany 2^d 1850
aged 1 year & 13 days

1753 *m*
IN
memory of
ANDREW POST
WHO DIED
Septr 16th 1853
Aged 16 Years

This flower cut down in early bloom
Now sleeps within the narrow tomb.

1754 *m*
IN
Memory of
PHILLIP LUITIG
WHO DIED
Sept 25th 1853
Aged 60 years

Here is the place where you must come
Dear reader when your race is run
Not here to dwell but once to rise
And take your flight beyond the skies

1755 *m*
[Two copies. See 1774]
[West side]
JOSEY
DIED
Sept 22 1864
Aged 18 months
& 12 Days
"Our little lamb is safe
within the fold of God."
[East side]
JOSEPH W.
Son of
J Wilbur & Hannah C.
PRICE

1756 *m*
LILLY   ADA
1886
ELIZA, and her infant MARY. ADA and her infant Frederic.
"is it well with thee? Is it well with the child?
She answered it is well"

1757 *m*
ABIGAIL
Wife of
ARCHIBALD T WOODRUFF
Born Oct. 23 1806.
Died Aug. 24. 1873

1758 *m*
ARCHIBALD S WOODRUFF
Born
November 4. 1811,
Died
June 13, 1878

1759 *m*
THE GRAVE
OF
Andrew McCullum
A Native of Ireland
who died
June 24th 1849
Aged 45 Years

1760 m
IN
memory of
JOHN A HAUCK
WHO DIED
May 29th 1856
In the 56th Year
of his age

Dear Brother thou hast left us
And thy loss we deeply feel
But tis God that has bereft us
He can all our sorrows heal.

1761 m
IN
Memory of
MARGARET
WIFE OF
Adam Hauck
who died Augst 13th 1862
In the 42^d Year
of her age

Our Mother

Dear as thou wert and justly dear
We would not weep for thee
One thought would check the falling tear
It is that thou art free.

1762 r
A. J.
IN
memory of Alexander Jenkins born near Clare parish of Ballymore & county of Armagh Ireland who departed this life July 3^d 1811 in the 50th year of his age

1763
JULIUS C
SON OF
John G and
Catharine Hofmann
died Decr 24th 1853
aged 2 y'rs 8 m'ths
& 22 days

1764 m
CAPT HENRY V DeHART
OF THE
FIFTH REGT U. S. ARTILLERY
BORN JULY 14th 1835.
WOUNDED IN THE BATTLE OF
GAIN'S' MILLS JUNE 27th 1862.
DIED JULY 13th 1862

1765 m
DAVID MEEKER
DIED
NOV^R 5th 1828,
AGED 39 YEARS
ISAAC BLACKFORD,
SON OF
THOMAS MEEKER
DIED SEPT 4th 1851
AGED 4 YEARS

1766 m
FRANCES NESBITT
WIDOW OF
DAVID MEEKER
DIED NOV^R 17, 1861,
AGED 73 YEARS

1767 m
CLARISSA D SPALDING
DIED
SEP^T 19th 1860
IN THE 55th YEAR
OF HER AGE

1768 r
Sacred to
the memory of
John Henry
Williams
Born Oct. 27 1830
Died Jan. 2, 1863

And God shall wipe away all tears from their eyes.

1769 m
IN
Memory of
CHARLOTTE BALDWIN
Infant
daughter of Aaron G.
& Ann Aletta Crane
who died in New York
Dec. 17th 1841
Aged 14 Days

1770 m
IN MEMORY
OF
HENRIETTA
Daughter of
AARON G. & ANN ALETTA
CRANE
BORN DEC. 16th 1842.
DIED APRIL 15th 1871.

1771 m
IN
MEMORY
OF
MARGARET WALDRON
Widow of
E BALDWIN NUTTMAN
Born Oct. 16th 1792
Died May 12th 1871,

1772 g
ANN ALETTA
WIFE OF
A. G. CRANE
BORN DEC. 22nd 1817
DIED DEC 9th 1879

1773 m
CHARLOTTE WALDRON CRANE
WIFE OF
JUDAH L. TAINTOR
BORN APRIL 24, 1848,
DIED MARCH 29, 1886,
"Blessed are the pure in heart for they shall see God."

1774 m
[Two copies. See 1755]
[On West side]
JOSEY
DIED
Sept 22nd 1864
Aged 18 Months
& 12 Days

"Our little lamb is safe within the fold of God."

[On East side]
JOSEPH W.
Son of
J. Wilbur & Hannah C.
PRICE

1775 m
In memory of
JOANNA
youngest daughter of
John & Mertina Cox
who died
Oct 4th 1843
In the 18. Year of
her age

1776 *m*
CHARLOTTE
daughter of
Lewis & Julia
Snider
died April 14th 1856
ag'd 1 y'r & 14 d's

Rest in God.

1777 *m*
WILLIAM A. BOYD M. D.
SON OF
MARY H. & W^M BOYD
BORN JUNE 3. 1820
DIED SEPT. 27, 1860.

1778 *r*
AARON OGDEN BARBER
BORN
January 8. 1820
Died June 17, 1872

1779 *g*

RALPH H. PIERSON
DIED
APRIL 3. 1871
AGED 63 YEARS

SARAH A. PIERSON
HIS WIFE
DIED MARCH 11, 1864
AGED 52 YEARS

"The memory of the just is blessed."

1780 *m*
In memory of
CATHARINE J. E.
daughter of Al^r &
Cecilia Smith
died Jany 15 1850
aged 1 year
& 7 months

1781 *m*
MARY H. ROBERT.
WIDOW OF
WILLIAM BOYD M. D.
BORN MARCH 16, 1792.
DIED MARCH 4, 1866.

1782 *r*
+ In hope of eternal life +
Lucille Dusansay Ogden
Born August 30. 1819.
Entered into rest Oct. 29. 1886.

1783 *r*
In memory of Lucille
Relict of Matthias Ogden
who fell asleep in JESUS
18 Nov A. D. 1861 Aet 67

Them which sleep in JESUS
will GOD bring with Him.

1784 *r*
Mary Henrietta
daughter of
Matthias and Lucille Ogden
Born April 6th 1826.
fell asleep in Christ
April 14th 1871.

"They shall obtain joy and gladness
and sorrow and sighing shall flee
away."

1785 *r*
Ralph Clinton Barber
Born 3. July 1883
Died 29. March 1886

There are they which follow the Lamb whithersoever he goeth.

1786 *r*
In Memory of
Margaretta Chetwood Barber
Born March 20 1878
Died July 17 1879

without fault before the throne of God

1787 *r*
SALLY JELF
DAUGHTER OF
JOSEPH JELF
AND
SUSANNAH HAMPTON
his wife
Born March 29th 1766
Died April 23rd 1870

1788 *r*
CHARLES
HOWARD EDWARDS
Born at Madeira
Aug 30 1813,
Died at Elizabeth
Feb 16 1866

1789 *r*
In memory of
Fanny E Edwards
Born Jan 15, 1880
Died Sept 19. 1881
Blessed forever

1790 *r*
In memory of
FRANCES EDWARDS
Born July 4th 1846.
Died November 12. 1878,
"Until the day dawns."

1791 *m*
IN
Memory of
MARY
daughter of Peter &
Hannah Walker
WHO DIED
June 30th 1839
Aged 7 Years

I bid thee farewell
With Jesus I dwell

1792 *r*
Here lyeth ye Body of
Robeart Morss Junr
Dec^d Novr ye 2^d 1749
in ye 63^d year
of his Age

Here lett him   Sleep in
Undisturbed dust
Until ye Resurrecton of ye Just.

1793 *r*

✵ Mary	Elizabeth
Martin Aged 5 years	Martin Aged 18
& 37 Days Dec'd	Days Dec'd Aug^t
Sepr ye 16 1736	ye 14 1735
ye Children of James & Ann	Martin

Sleep Lovely Babes & take thy Peacefull Rest
God Cal'd ye hence Becaus^e he thought it best.

INSCRIPTIONS IN FIRST PRESBYTERIAN

1794 r

Here Lyes
ye Body of Ann Martin
Aged 11 years & 33 Days
Dec^d Sep^t ye 9th 1736 Dau^r of
James & Ann Martin

here lyes A blooming youth. She
lived in love & Died in Truth

1795 r

Here lyes ye Body
of Mehetabel Littell
wife of Robart
Littell who Departed
this life June ye 22^d
1753 in ye 58
year of his Age

1796 wood

JANE DAVIS
DIED FEB 24th 1881

1797 m

In memory of
ALPHONSO
son of Henry H &
Celia M Fredenburg
died March 24, 1850
aged 5 y'rs 11 mo
& 1 day,

1798 m

IN MEMORY
of
JAMES ROSS
Who departed
this life
April 18th 1870
in the 65th year
of his age

1799 m

THE GRAVE
OF
DELINDA HOPKINS
WIFE OF
JEREMIAH ROSS
WHO DIED
MAY 10th 1855
IN THE 32^d YEAR
OF HER AGE

"HAVING A DESIRE TO DEPART
AND TO BE WITH CHRIST."

1800 m

JEREMIAH ROSS
BORN
MARCH 10 1818
DIED
MARCH 27 1882

1801 m

Here rests the body
of
REBECCA
WIFE OF
James Ross
who died Novr 21 1848
Aged 74 Years

"Precious in the sight of the Lord
is the death of his saints."

1802 m

Here rests the body
of
JAMES ROSS
For many years a Ruling
Elder in this Church
who died Septr 20th 1846
In the 80th Year
of his age

"Blessed are the dead who
die in the Lord."

1803 r
M. R.

In memory of
MARY ROSS
daughter of Andrew
Lougheed near Ballemote
in Ireland, who departed
this life on the 9th of Sep^r
1810 aged 68 years.
Also her sister Martha
Atchison who died on
the 7th June 1797
They lived like Christians
and died in faith

1804 m
WILLIAM ROSS
DIED
June 6th 1871
In the 72^d year
of his age

It is well

1805 m
Sacred to the Memory of
ELIZA CRANE
Beloved Wife of
WILLIAM ROSS
Born March 8, 1809
Died Feb 26, 1881

Asleep in Jesus

1806 m
Here rests
the body of
ELIZA
daughter of William
& Eliza Ross
who died on
Christmas eve 1833
Aged 3 years 1 month
and 16 days

Born in a world where flow'rs of fairest hue
First fade away.
Herself a rose she liv'd as roses do
But for a day.

1807 m
THE MORTAL REMAINS
OF
ALICE
Daughter of
William and Eliza Ross
Rest here
She died in Lambert Ville
Octr 18th 1852
Aged 11 Years 5 Months
and 15 Days

Weep not my Parents weep not I am blest
But must leave Heaven if I come to thee
For I am where the weary are at rest
The wicked cease from troubling
Come to me

1808 m
ELIZA CRANE
WIDOW OF
CALEB CRANE
DIED MARCH 16th 1865,
IN THE 89th YEAR
OF HER AGE

1809 m
[On west side]
WILLIE
[On east side]
W^M HARRISON
Son of
W^M F & MARIA H
GALE
died Nov. 10
1867 Aged 2
weeks

INSCRIPTIONS IN FIRST PRESBYTERIAN

1810 m
[On west side]
FREDERICK MANVEL
Son of
W^m F & Maria H.
GALE,
DIED
Sept, 19th 1866
aged 7 months
& 26 days

OUR
LITTLE
FREDDIE
For us the Cross
For thee, the Crown

1811 m
JOHN GUEST
DIED
March 15, 1864,
Aged 35 Years

Dear husband thou hast left me.
And my loss I deeply feel.

JOHN HENRY
son of John & Kate Guest
died Feb. 29, 1864,
Aged 8 months.
Sleep in Jesus.

1812 m
GEORGE W. REID,
DIED
Feb, 13, 1888,
Aged 72 Years

1813 m
CORNELIA A.
wife of
GEORGE W. REID
DIED
Oct, 15, 1878,
Aged 57 Years

1814 m
JENNIE REID
Daughter of
GEORGE W & CORNELIA
A REID
DIED
Dec. 26th 1872,
Aged 18 Years

1815 m
EMMA REID
Daughter of
GEORGE W & CORNELIA
A REID
DIED
Dec. 12th 1872,
Aged 27 Years

1816 m
MARY
DAUGHTER OF
George W. and
Cornelia A Reid
died Oct. 27, 1856,
aged 1 year
& 2 months

It is well.

1817 m
IN
memory of
JOHN BROOKES
who died Jany 11th 1836
Aged 46 years

Also of ANN, his wife
who died May 5th 1824
aged 35 years
Also five children
ELIJAH
died Augst 1st 1825
THOMAS
died Septr 10th 1826
ELIZABETH
died Augst 26th 1828
WESLEY
died Augst 29th 1830
EZRA C.
died Jan 31st 1835 ;

1818 m
[Monument. North side]
BROWN
[East side]
MRS LUCY M. HARRISON
Wife of
Rev Abraham Brown
DIED
Feb. 11 1843,
Æ 42,

To die is gain
[West side]
REV. ABRAHAM BROWN
DIED
Oct, 15, 1840.
Æ. 45.

His record is on high
[North side blank]

1819 m
IN
MEMORY OF
EMILY F.
WIDOW OF
JAMES W. HARRISON
Born at Litchfield Con.
Decr 10th 1803
Died at Elizabeth N. J.
Novr 15th 1862

1820 m
IN
MEMORY OF
JAMES W. HARRISON
Born at Litchfield Con.
Feby 4th 1803
Died at Elizabeth Port.
May 30th 1849

1821 m
IN
Memory of
FREDERICK PHELPS
Born in Torringford Conn.
Dec 15th 1815.
Died at Elizabeth Port
Augst 22nd 1854
Aged 39 years.

1822 m
IN
Memory of
HENRIETTA
Daughter of
WILLIAM & AVIC INMAN :
who died
Decr 7th 1841
Aged 17 Years 9 Months
and 12 Days
ALSO
SUSAN EMMA
DAUGHTER OF
Lewis & Dorothy W Smith
who died
March 12th 1836 ;
Aged 1 Year 1 Month
and 3 Days

Dearest daughter thou hast left us
Here thy loss we deeply feel
But tis God who has berav'd us
He can all our sorrows heal.

1823 m
GEORGE PETER
son of Martin and
Elizabeth Keller
died March 5th 1853
aged 2 years 4 months
and 3 days

1824 m
IN
memory of
ELIZABETH
WIFE OF
Martin Keller
who died May 2nd 1853
Aged 40 Years 9 Months
and 27 Days

Dearest Mother thou hast left us
Here thy loss we deeply feel
But 'tis God who hath bereft us
He can all our sorrows heal.

1825 m
LUCRETIA VANDERVOORT
Daughter of
John & Mary V
CARPENTER
Born Oct 27 1865
Died Dec 26 1865

Our transplanted Bud

1826 m
IDA RAYMOND
DAUGHTER OF
John & Mary V Carpenter
Died Aug 22 1864
Aged 9 mo- and 17 days

Our transplanted flower

1827 m
ERECTED
to the Memory of
WILLIAM SAYRE
DIED
Nov 25th 1850
Aged 44 yrs & 25
days

1828 m
[Monument. East side]
JOHN SAYRE
DIED JAN 1st 1847
IN HIS 77th YEAR

[East side]
MARY
WIDOW OF
JOHN SAYRE
DIED JUNE 18th 1851
in her 79th year

[West side]
SAMUEL SAYRE
DIED
JAN 16th 1884
AGED 34 YEARS

[North side]
MARGARET JANE
SAYRE
DIED SEPT 21st 1847
IN HER 31st YEAR

MARY ANN
SAYRE
DIED JAN 18th 1852
IN HER 41st YEAR

[South side]
ABIGAIL SAYRE
BORN
JUNE 20th 1804
DIED AUG 21st 1805

HARRIET SAYRE
BORN
OCT 10th 1815
DIED OCT 10th 1816

1829 m
[Small monument. East side]
MARTHA L.
DAUGHTER OF
WALTER F. &
RACHEL SAYRE
DIED
MARCH 5th 1852
AGED
1 YEAR 3 MO.
& 17 DAYS

[West side]
LITTLE
MARTHA

1830 m
WALTER F SAYRE
DIED
Novr 16th 1858,
IN THE 50th YEAR
OF HIS AGE

Dearest one thou hast left us
And thy loss we deeply feel
But 'tis God that hath bereft us
He can all our sorrows heal.

1831 *m*
IN
Memory of
WALTER C.
son of David &
Mary Noe ;
who died
June 28th 1844
Aged 1 Year

Rest here sweet babe

1832 *m*
IN
MEMORY OF
LOUIS F. RANDOLPH
BORN
JULY 11 1796,
DIED
DEC 27, 1858,

ALSO
FRANCES LOUISA
DAUGHTER OF
LOUIS F &
MARY F RANDOLPH
BORN
SEPT. 4 1840
DIED
JAN. 30. 1841.

1833 *g*
MARY A. CAMPBELL
DIED
JULY 24 1885

1834 *m*
Children of
Charles C and Mary Alice Moore

Alice	Genie
Died	Died
Sept 28 1887	July 20, 1875
Aged 6 mo's	Aged 8 mo's

1835 *m*
J. S.
In memory of
JOHN SUTLIF
who departed this life
October 6th 1826 :
Aged 70 Years

Jesus to thy dear faithful hand
My naked soul I trust
And my flesh waits for thy command
To drop into my dust.

1836 *r*
W. S.
Here lies
the body of
WILLIAM SUTLIF
of the City of New York
who departed this life
Septr 24th 1827 :
Aged 39 years
& 4 months

Before I was of age years twenty one
I was call'd to believe in God^s dear son
Now here with dust my body lies
Till my dear saviour shall bid it rise

1837 *m*
IN MEMORY
OF
ISABELLA HAMILL
DIED
OCTO 17, 1877
Aged 59 Years

1838 *m*
JOANNA NELSON
BORN
OCTOBER 28, 1798,
DIED
MARCH 31, 1886

Mother, at Rest,

INSCRIPTIONS IN FIRST PRESBYTERIAN

1839 *m*
SACRED
TO THE
Memory of
JARED NELSON
DIED
May 18th 1842
Aged 54 Years

Happy soul thy days are ended
All thy mourning days below

1840 *m*
OLIVIA A.
Daughter of Jared & Joanna
NELSON
Born March 3rd 1839
Died June 7th 1863

How sweet the hope to mortals given
Of dwelling in the christians heaven.

1841 *m*
IN MEMORY OF
WILLIAM O TOOKER
DIED
July 14th 1872,
Aged 65 yrs. 9
Mos & 26 days.

1842 *m*
IN MEMORY OF
MATILDA
Wife of
WILLIAM O TOOKER
DIED
Sept 7th 1871,
Aged 64 yrs, 4
mos & 17 days

1843 *m*
JAMES C. TOOKER
DIED
Dec 15 1863
Aged 20 yrs,
& 9 months

1844 *m*
IN MEMORY OF
ABBIE E.
Wife of
ROBERT E BARTON
DIED
Dec. 24th 1870
Aged 30 yrs 10
mos & 2 days

1845 *m*
HENRY J BAUER
DIED
June 10th 1863
AGED 28 YEARS, 3 MO'S,
& 2 DAYS

1846 *m*
ANN ELIZABETH TOOKER
DIED
May 31st 1861,
AGED 24 YEARS

1847 *m*
IN
memory of
WILLIAM O TOOKER JR
who died Novr 14th 1856;
Aged 24 Years and
9 Months
DANIEL W TOOKER
died Septr 2d 1832;
aged 3 years & 3 days
Sons of William O. and
Matilda Tooker

1848 *m*
IN
memory of
AUGUSTUS TUCKER
Son of
Benjamin W. & Susan
Tucker
who died
May 9th 1833:
aged 3 years 7 months
and 15 days

1849 *m*
IN
memory of
MARY
wife of
BENJAMIN WHITEHEAD
who died
April 27, 1835
aged 73 years

1850 *m*
IN
memory of
BENJAMIN WHITEHEAD
who died
May 3 1835,
aged 75 years

1851 *r*
S. L. M.
In memory of
Squier L. son of
Squier & Phebe Maurow
died Decr 14th 1810
Aged 3 months & 5 days

Sleep dear babe and take thy rest
God call'd thee home he thought it best.

1852 *r*
M. H.

In memory of
MARY
widow of John Hull
who died July 20th 1811
in the 84th year
of her age

Peace be to her dust & choirs of
Angels sing her to her rest.

1853 *m*
IN
Memory of
GIDEON B. TUCKER
who died Augst 18th 1849
In the 35th Year
of his age

ABNER S. TUCKER
died April 11th 1840
In the 31st Year
of his age

Daniel Tucker
died Dec. 12th 1830
In the 27th Year
of his age

1854 *m*
IN
memory of
MICHAEL WOODRUFF
WHO DIED
Novr 28th 1852;
In the 71st Year
of his age

1855 *m*
IN
MEMORY OF
ESTHER R.
Daughter of
John Zeluf
and wife of
Michael Woodruff
who died Jany 28th 1854
In the 62^d Year
of her age

1856 *r*
A. W.
In memory of
AMELIA
Daughter of John
Zeluff & wife of
Saml R. Winans
who died
Feb 4th 1829
in the 27th year
of her age

Husband and children dear farewell
Kindred and friends adieu
Oft think of me where'er you dwell
Until we meet anew

1857 *r*
J. Z.
In memory of
JOHN ZELUFF
who departed this
life April 17th, 1818
in the 52^d year
of his age

Hark O my soul, he speaks to thee
As he is now so you must be
He sleeps in dust but soon shall rise
Prepare to meet him in the skies

1858 *r*
HANNAH ZELUFF
Widow of
JOHN ZELUFF
Died June 23' 1841,
Aged 69 yrs 4 Mos
and 14 days

1859 *r*
D. W.
To the Memory of
David Woodruff who
died Decr 16th 1795 in
the 75th Year of his Age

John W Zeluff died Nov^r
the 16th 1795 aged 1 Year
and 4 Months.

1860 *r*
Here lyes ye Body of
Sarah wife of David
Woodruff Dec'd Jan^{ry}
ye 25th 1749–50 in ye 29th
year of her Age

1861 *m*
IN
Memory of
PHEBE CRANE
widow of
JOHN JOHNSON
who died
May 9th 1855
aged 88 years 4 months
and 20 Days

1862 *r*
In
Memory of
MARY, WIFE OF
Jesse Toms
who died
Septr 2^d 1820
Aged 35 years

1863 *r*
Here lyeth ye Body of
Elizabeth Lalour
who died Decem^r
ye 17th 1742 in ye 68th
year of her age

1864 *r*
Hear Lyeth ye Bod
y. of Isaac Bonn
el who Dep^d this
Life Feby ye 15th
Anno Dom : 1736
in ye 38th year of
his age

1865 *r*
Here   lyes y^e
Body of   Cornelius
Hetfield who died May y^e
22 A. D. 1718 in ye 52
year of his age
Joanna Daugh^r of Cornelius
& Sarah Hetfield, died
April ye 13th A.D. 1723
Aged 8 years &
5 Months

My weary'd flesh lies here at Rest
My Soul tryumphs beyond ye Skies
Both shall with highest joys be Blest
When Christ shall say you Dead Arise.

1866 *m*
IN
Memory of
MARY B. McGILLIVRAY
daughter of
George & Margaret McGillivray
who died July 3rd 1869
aged 2 Years & 5 Months

Of such is the Kingdom of Heaven

1867 *m*
ELIZABETH B. McGILLVRAY
BORN
April 22d 1868
DIED
August 7 1874
Aged 6 yrs &
3 mos.
———o———
God called the home
he thought it best

1868 *m*
JENNIE McGILLVRAY
BORN
Jan 20' 1870
DIED
August 13 1874
Aged 4 yrs &
6 Mos

Sleep on dear Chil-
-dren and take thy rest

1869 *r*
J. G. W.

In memory of
JONATHAN G.
Son of Michael &
Charlotte Winans:
who died Septr 1st 1840
Aged 17 years
& 4 months

This stone is erected as a tribute
of a mothers affection.

1870 *m*
AARON CRANE
DIED
June 27 1854
Aged 62 years

SARAH
WIDOW OF
AARON CRANE
DIED
Aug, 20, 1869
Aged 74 years

1871 *r*
M. C.
SACRED
To the memory of
MALVINA
daughter of William I.
& Mary Craig:
who departed this life
April 5th 1823
Aged 14 years

1872 *m*
IN
MEMORY OF
THOMAS W.
SON OF WILLIAM I AND
PHEBE C. CRAIG
WHO DIED
July 12th 1841.
Aged 13 Years,
3 Months and
2 Days

There was but a step between
him and Death

1873 *r*
M. C.
SACRED
To the Memory of
MARY, wife of
William I. Craig:
who departed this
life Jany 21st 1822;
Aged 35 years

Also of JULIET
their infant daughter
who departed this life
Augst 5th 1820 ; Aged 4
months & 11 days

1874 *m*
IN MEMORY
OF
W. I. CRAIG
WHO DEPARTED THIS LIFE
SEPT 4th 1858
AGED 73 YEARS

1875 *m*
IN
memory of
SARAH MURDOCK
who died
Dec. 4, 1845 :
Aged 75 years

They who by their steady course
Has happiness insured
When earthes foundation shakes, shall stand
By providence secured

1876 *m*
IN
MEMORY OF
GEORGE W.
Son of
EZRA & MARY DARBY
who died
March 1st A. D. 1843
Aged 5 years 3 months
and 10 days

How short his little feet have trod
Upon the dusty paths of life
His soul has passed away to God
Far, far, from mortal care and strife

1877 *m*
In
memory
of
EZRA DARBY
WHO DIED
FEB^Y 4th 1851
IN THE 34th YEAR
OF HIS AGE

By dint of great perseverance he had surmounted many difficulties and was rapidly rising to a position as a Lawyer and a citizen when struck down by death

I leave the world without a tear
Save for the friends I hold so dear
To heal their sorrows Lord decend
And to the friendless prove a friend.

1878 *m*
IN
memory of
ANNA
WIFE OF
Jacob Courson
WHO DIED
May 8th 1846
In the 76th year
of her age

Tis finish'd the conflict is past
The heaven born spirit is fled
Her wish is accomplished at last
And now she's entombed with the dead.

1879 *m*
IN
memory of
JACOB COURSIN
WHO DIED
Jany 28th 1849.
Aged 81 Years

Receive O Earth his faded form
In thy cold bosom let it lie
Safe let it rest from every storm
Soon must it rise no more to die.

1880 r
JACOB the Son of
Abra^m & Margaret
Marsh, died Sept^r
the 30th 1758, aged
2 Months

1881 m
IN
Memory of
ALFRED BOARD
WHO DIED
Jany 24th 1854.
Aged 46 Years

"Therefore be ye also ready: for
in such an hour as ye think not
the Son of man cometh.

1882 m
ELIZABETH SEABAR
DIED
Aug^st 31st 1853.
In the 21st year
of her age

1883 m
IN
Memory of
MARY
WIFE OF
John Bender
who died Sept 13 1854
Aged 22 years
ALSO
CATHARINE
their daughter
died Sept 12th 1854
aged 1 year and
1 month

1884 m
W. B.
SACRED
To the memory of
of

WILLIAM BUTLER
who departed this
life Feby 5th 1821
in the 32nd year
of his age

1885 m
IN
Memory of
PHEBE H. CRANE
who died
Oct 14th 1862
aged 69 years &
21 days

She was first married to
FRANCIS C. F. RANDOLPH
who died July 11th 1828
and after that, to
GEORGE R. KING
who died Dec 31st 1852

1886 m
SACRED
to the
Memory of
FRANCIS C. F. RANDOLPH Esqr
COUNSELLOR AT LAW, AND LATE
SURROGATE OF ESSEX COUNTY
WHO DEPARTED THIS LIFE
JULY 11th 1828
IN THE 35th YEAR
OF HIS AGE

Stop! passing stranger! drop one
tear
A Husband, Father Friend lies here

1887 m
To the memory of
FRANCIS son of
Francis C. F. Ran-
dolph Esqr and
Phebe H his wife
who died Septr 23
1821: Aged 1 year
9 months &
25 days

1888 *m*
IN
Memory of
ROBERT RANDOLPH
who died
sept^r 25th 1824
aged 1 year 1 month
and 2 days

Also of
MARIA H RANDOLPH
who died
Octr 1st 1826
aged 11 months

CHILDREN OF
FRANCIS C. F. AND
PHEBE H RANDOLPH

1889 *r*
A W
In memory of
ABNER WINANS
who died March
28th 1812 in the 45th
year of his age

1890 *r*
In
Memory of
Gilbert H Son
of Peter & Hannah
Winans who died
July 16 1813 Aged
2 months & 29 days
      rest
Sleep on dear babe & take your
You in your makers arms are blest
And now to you we bid adieu
God fit us all to follow you.

1891 *m*
ERECTED
BY THE CHILDREN OF
PETER WINANS
WHO DIED
IN THE CITY OF NEW YORK
May 10th 1842
Aged 52 years

If ever truth in epetaph was told
Reader for truth this character behold
To act uprightly was through life his
   plan
He lives beloved and dide an honest
   man

1892 *r*
J. W.
Sacred to the memory
of
Isaac Woodruff Esq
Who deceas'd
Octr the 17th 1803
in the 82^d Year
of his Age

A man celebrated for mildness of manners for integrity in his dealings, for faithfulness in public office & for affectionate care for his own Offsprings & for the Church of God

1893 *r*
Sacred to the Memory
of Sarah Woodruff, Wife
of Isaac Woodruff Esqr
who died the Vth day of
September 1799 in the
seventy seventh Year of
her Age

1894 *r*
Here is interred what
Was mortal of Mr
Joseph Woodruff who
Died Septem^r ye 25th
1746 in ye 72^d Year of
his age

Under these clouds in dust and ruin
   ly,
Remains of meekness kindness piety
to be revived when Christ in glory
   come
to raise his Sleeping Saints and call
   em home

CHURCH YARD, ELIZABETH, N. J. 269

1895 r
Here lyeth yᵉ Body
of Mary wife of Joseph
Woodruff who Died
April the 9th 1743
and in the 66th year
of her age

1896 r
Here lyes yᵉ Body of
Jacob Winans Aged
40 years Decᵈ Janʳʸ
yᵉ 4" 1722

1897 r
Here lies yᵉ Body
of Mary Daughʳ
of Jacob & Mary
Winans Died Decᵐʳ
16 1722 Aged 13 yrs

1898 r
[This is a tablet inserted in the rear wall of the church]
[See also 436]
SACRED TO THE MEMORY
Of the Revᵈ James Caldwell & Hannah his Wife
who fell Victims, to their Country's cause
in the Years 1780 & 1781
He was the zealous & faithful Pastor
of the Presbyterian Church in this Town
where, by his evangelical Labours in the
Gospel Vineyard & his early attachment
to the civil Liberties of his Country
He has left in the Hearts of his People
a better Monument than Brass or Marble
Stop Passenger
Here also lies the remains of a Woman
who exhibited to the World
a brigh Constellation of the female Virtues
On that memorable Day, never to be forgotten
when a british Foe invaded this fair Village
and fired even the Temple of the Deity
This peaceful Daughter of Heaven
retired to her hallowed apartment
imploring Heaven for yᵉ pardon of her Enemies
In that Sacred Moment She was
by the bloody Hand of a british Ruffian
despatch'd, like her divine Redeemer
through a Path of Blood.
to her long wish'd for native Skies

1899 r
Here lies yᵉ Body of
Mr Henry Baker who
Died Feb yᵉ 4 : 1734
Aged 76 years

1900 r
In Memory of
Magdalene wife of Isaac
Winans who died Sept
the 12th 1775 in the 58th
year of her age

1901 *r*
IN MEMORY OF
Elias Winans who
died Feb ye 12th 1789
In the XLVIII Year
of his Age

A Loving Husband a
father dear a faithful
friend lies bury'^d here

1902 *r*
E. W.
In Memory of
Esther Winans
Late Wife of Benjamin
Watkins who departed
this life Feb^ry 20th 1807
In the 63^d Year
of her Age

A loving wife a mother dear
A faithful friend lies buried here

1903 *r*
H. W.
Hannah daughter of
Elias & Sarah Winans
who died April the 22^d
1796 in the 30th year
of her age

1904 *r*
IN
memory of
Mary wife of
Wm Dawes
died Jany 28th 1806
in the 52^d year
of her Age

1905 *r*
IN
memory of
William Dawes
who died Aug^st 28th 1811
in the 65th year
of his Age

1906 *m*
S R
In memory of
SARAH
wife of Gilbert Rindell
who departed this life
April 23^d 1833
in the 29th year
of her age

Hosannah to Jesus on high
Another has enter'd his rest
Another has 'scaped to the sky
And lodge'd in Immanuel's breast

The soul of our sister is gone
To heighten the triumph above
Exalted to Jesus's throne
And clasp'd in the arms of his love

1907 *m*
A N
In memory of
ALEXANDER NICOLL
who was born in the
Parish of Fordoun
Kincardenshire Scotland
and died Sept 17th 1834
In the 67th year of his age
Deeply deplored by his bereaved family & the Church
of which he was a ruling
Elder, The benevolent and
religious operations of
the day, have lost in him
a devoted friend
and supporter

No more his prayers shall rise to
bless us
Nor his soul yearn for a closer union
With his God ; Twas not meet
That he should'st longer tarry from
that bliss
Which God reserveth for the pure in
heart

CHURCH YARD, ELIZABETH, N. J.   271

1908 *m*
MARY NICOLL
widow of
ALEXANDER NICOLL
Born in Elizabeth
December 2nd 1777
Died
August 6th 1867

Asleep in Jesus

1909 *m*
AUGUSTUS
Son of
Diego & Hannah I.
McVOY
died Augst 7th 1844
Aged 7 Years
8 Months
& 13 Days

The Lord gave, and the Lord hath taken away: blessed be the name of the Lord

[These stones have been removed since May, 1890, to Evergreen Cemetery]

1910 *m*
John Thomas
Son of
George & Mary E Seaton
died Augst 25th 1849
Aged 1 year 11 months
and 17 days

Sleep on dear babe and take your rest
Since young and old must die
God call'd you home he thought it best
To reign with him on high

1911 *m*
In
Memory of
John Thomas
son of George and
Mary E Seaton
who died Jany 9th 1852
aged 2 years 2 months
and 3 days

Sleep on dear babe and take your rest
God called you home he thought it best

1912 *m*
[Body removed to Evergreen Cemetery]
IN
Memory of
MARY E.
WIFE OF
GEORGE SEATON
Daughter of
Thomas and Mary McCullor
who died April 27th 1852
Aged 24 years
& 9 Months

Friends nor physicians could not save
Her mortal body from the grave
Nor can the grave confine it here
When Christ shall call her to appear
[This stone has been taken up and lies on the ground Feb. 17, 1891]

1913 *m*
MAGGIE
Wife of

THOMAS FORSYTH
DIED
July 28th 1875
Aged 34 yrs
and 10 Months

Her children arise up and
call her blessed : her Husband
also, and He praiseth her

1914 *m*
RICHARD
Son of Richard
and
Sarah Gale
died Dec. 22 1845
aged 22 Days

Sleep on dear child
And take your rest
God called thee home
He thought it best

1915 *m*
WILLIAM EDWARD
INFANT SON OF
JAMES AND CATHARINE A.
GALE
DIED AUG, 17 1852
AGED 3 MONTHS

Ere sin could blight or sorrow fade
Death came with friendly care
The op'ning bud to heaven conveyed
And bid it blossom their

1916 *m*
SARAH MURDOCK
WIFE OF
DR. RICHARD GALE
BORN
April 17 1807
DIED
August 24 1867

"My work is done, I have
left nothing undone"

1917 *m*
RICHARD GALE M.D. U.S.N.
DIED
Octr 4th 1848
Aged 45 Years
and 11 Months

An honest man is the noblest work
of God

1918 *m*
SARAH H GALE
BORN
November 2, 1837
DIED
November 3, 1880
Faithful unto Death

1919 *m*
IN
Memory of
HENRY REILLY
WHO DIED
May 8th 1856
Aged 26 Years
and 10 Months

Gently I laid my treasure down
In faith and holy trust
And sweetly in the green graveyard
Doth sleep his precious dust.

1920 *m*
IN MEMORY OF
HANNAH PHINNEY
LATE WIDOW OF
CAPT. LEWIS WOODRUFF
AND DAUGHTER OF
THE REV. AZARIAH HORTON
who died July 24th 1844
Aged 87 Years

She was a liberal donor of,
and to, this Church ; and one
of its most zealous Members
for nearly 60 Years

"Blessed are the dead
which die in the Lord."
[This is a marble tablet inserted in North wall of church]

1921 *r*
SACRED
to the memory of
ELIZABETH O. BARNET
who departed this life
October 15th 1839
Aged 47 years

The memory of the just is blessed
She's gone the friend and sister dear
We trust where angels ever sing
To mansions in the skies

1922 *r*
Sacred to the memory
of Miss Rachel Daugh-
ter of Joseph & Cath-
erine Barnet, who died
July the 29th 1791 Aged
16 years 11 Months and
29 Days

Death call the aged and the young
From earthly cares from every wrong
His summons seizes on the best
And God the righteous soul hath blest

1923 r
M. B.
In memory of
MARY widow of
Joseph Barnet,
who departed this
life April 16th 1827
Aged 69 years

Affliction sore long time she bore
Physicians skill was vain
Till God in mercy called her home
And eased her of her pain

1924 r
HERE LYETH THE
BODY OF THOMAS
LAWRANCE AIGED
19 YEARS WHO
DEPARTED THIS
LIFE THE 26 OF
OCTOBER
1687

1925 r
J. B.
In memory of
JOSEPH BARNET
who departed
this life
Decr 12th 1816
Aged 70 years

Fear not the terrors of the grave
Or death's tremendous sting
He will from endless wrath pr'serve
To endless glory bring

1926 r
Here lies the body
of Mrs Catharine Wife
of Joseph Barnett who
departed this life may
[Stone defaced]

1927 r
Dedicated to the memory of
Dr. WILLIAM R. BARNET
died Feb 23th 1823
aged 35 years

And lately a Capt in the U. S. Service : who served his country
faithfully through her last bloody
Struggles, then retired, crowned
with laurels of his country and friends
Text, Blessed are the dead &c Rev.
14th 13
Torn from his friends by deaths
bold stroke
[Stone defaced]

1928 m
IN
Memory of
EUNICE WOODRUFF
who died
Jan 22, 1845
In the 64th year of
her age
" Let me die the death of the rightous
and let my last-end be like hers"

1929 r
D. W.
In memory of
DAVID WOODRUFF
who died
Septr 7th 1822
Aged 72 years

As you are now, so once was I
In health and strength though here I lie
As I am now so you must be
Therefore prepare to follow me.

1930 r
E. W.
In memory of
ELIZABETH, wife of
David Woodruff
who died
Decr 28th 1823
Aged 71 years

The year rolls round, and steals away
The breath that first it gave
Whate'er we do where'er we be
We're trav'lling to the grave

1931 *r*
IN
memory of
(WIDOW)
ABIGAIL RICH
who died
May 1ˢᵗ 1831
aged 52 years

Mourn not for me my children dear,
Afflictions long I've borne
Prepare—that you may meet me here
In Heavens eternal home

1932 *r*
Here are interr'd yᵉ Remains of Mrs Hannah
Wife of Mr David
Morehows Dec'd Januʸ
yᵉ 7ᵗʰ A.D. 1733 in yᵉ
35ᵗʰ year of her Age

(fled
Here from all worldly Joys I'm
To yᵉ dark Mansionˢ of yᵉ Dead
Prepare Spectatoʳˢ for you must
Like me be quickˡʸ turned to Dust

1933 *m*
THE GRAVES OF
Three children of
Robert P. & Mary V. Archer
WILLIAM G.
died Augˢᵗ 9ᵗʰ 1844
Aged 6 years
MARY A,
died March 15ᵗʰ 1845.
Aged 3 Years
MARY E.
died April 13ᵗʰ 1846
Aged 1 Year

Of such is the Kingdom of Heaven.

1934 *m*
IN
Memory of
JOANNA
wife of
DANIEL PIERSON

and daughter of
Samuel & Mary Sayre
who died
April 6ᵗʰ 1819
Aged 26 Years & 15 days

write, Blessed are the dead which
die in the Lord   Rev 14c 13v

1935 *m*
IN
Memory of
SAMUEL SAYRE
WHO DIED
Oct. 30ᵗʰ 1838
In the 72ⁿᵈ Year
of his age

How long beneath the law I lay
In bondage and distress
I toil'd, the precept to obey
But toil'd without success

1936 *m*
IN
Memory of
MARY
wife of
Samuel Sayre
WHO DIED
Sept 7ᵗʰ 1828
In the 58ᵗʰ Year of
her age

The victory now is obtain'd
She's gone her dear Savior to see
Her wishes she fulley has gain'd
She's now whare she longed to be

1937 *r*
Mr. Joseph Sayre
departed this Life
Febʸ yᵉ 6ᵗʰ A D. 1757
In the 38ᵗʰ year of
his Age

Weep not for me my Friends
For why? my Race is run
It is the will of God
And let his will be done

1938 *r*
SACRED
to the memory of
ELIZA
wife of
Abraham Craig
who departed this life
June 2ⁿᵈ 1832
aged 40 years

Tis finish'd now the great deciding part
The world subdu'd and Heaven has, all, my, heart
She in a sacred calm resign'd her breath
And as her eyelids clos'd she smil'd in death

1939 *r*
S. R.
In memory of
SOPHIA
daughter of
Gilbert & Sarah
Rindell who died
July 28ᵗʰ 1823
in the 20ᵗʰ year
of her age

when blooming youth is snatch'd away
Our hearts the mournful tribute pay

1940 *r*
J R
In memory of
JOHN
son of Gilbert &
Sarah Rindell
who died May 28ᵗʰ 1811
in the 19ᵗʰ year of
his age

In death lamented, as in life beloved

Also Mary W. daughter of Gilbert & Sarah Rindell, died Janʸ 18ᵗʰ 1804 aged 9 years

We'll cease to mourn for they're at rest

1941 *m*
G. R.
SACRED
To the memory of
GILBERT RINDELL
who departed this life
February 28ᵗʰ 1832
in the 72ᵈ year
of his age

Let friends no more my suff'rings mourn
Nor view my relics with concern
O cease to drop the pitying tear
I've past beyond the reach of fear

1942 *r*
HERE lies the Body
of Timothy Woodruff
who departed this
Life Novemʳ the 15ᵗʰ
Anno Domini 1766
In the 84 Year of
his Age

1943 *m*
IN
Memory of
THOMAS WOODRUFF
who departed this life
April 23ʳᵈ AD. 1805
Aged 71 Years

1944 *m*
M. W.
In memory of
MARY WOODRUFF
widow of
Thomas Woodruff
who departed this life
July 14ᵗʰ 1838
in the 93ᵈ year
of her age

Serene she passed the crumbling verge
Of this terrestrial scene
Breathed soft; in childlike trust
And gave to heaven its own

1945 *r*
Here Lyeth ye Body
of Mrs Sarah Woodruff
Wife of John Woodruff.
Who departed this Life
the 3 of June 1727 in
the 62 year of her age

1946 *r*
Here lies y^e Body of
Hannah Widow of
Thomas Woodruff
who deceas'd y^e 1st of
May Anno Domini 1757
In y^e 66th year of her
Age

1947 *r*
Here lyes y^e Body of
Thomas Woodruf
Dec'd March y^e
25   1752
In y^e 63^d year
of his Age

1948 *r*

Here Lyeth y^e
Body of Matthias
Woodrowfe dec^d
May y^e 22 A$^o{}_o$
1733 in y^e 17
year of his Age

Here Lyeth y^e
Body of Thomas
Thomas Woodrowfe Junr
Dec^d Feb y^e 23
1732 in y^e 20 year
of his Age

1949 *m*
IN
Memory of
ANN ELIZABETH
WIFE OF
Thomas C. Cox
and daughter of
James & Hannah B. Cree
who died Augst 12th 1849
Aged 24 Years and
5 Months
ALSO
CHARLES WILLIAM
their infant son

1950 *m*
IN
Memory of
Robert Porter
who died
Augst 9th 1859
In the 40th Year
of his age

1951 *m*
IN
Memory of
WILLIAM PORTER JR,
who died
March 2^d 1856
Aged 41 Years

1952 *m*
in Memory of
ELIZABETH
WIFE OF
WILLIAM PORTER
WHO DIED
Decr 25th 1843
In the 61st year
of her age

1953 *m*
IN MEMORY
OF
MARGARET PORTER
who died
Augst 5th 1853
Aged 31 Years

We loved her yes no tongue can tell
How much we loved her and how well
God loved her too, and he thought it best
To take her home and be at rest

1954 *r*
Here lyeth the body of
phebe wife of Ephraim
Terrill & daughter of
William & hannah Winan^s
who departed this life
March ye 31st Annoque
Domini 1739 & in ye 19th
year of her age

1955 *r*
Here Lyes Interr'd the Corps
of Experience Winans the
Wife of Josiah Winans Who
Resigned her breath May y^e
23^d Anno Domini 1759. In y^e
37th year of her Age

All Humane Bodies yield to Deaths decree
The Soul survives to all Eternity

1956 *r*
Margaret Daught^r
of James & Jane
Winans,   who
deceas'd July ye 22^d
A. D. 1786. In ye 3^d
Year of her Age

1957 *r*
Here lyes ye Body
of Patience wife of
Jonathan Dayton
Dec^d Jan^{ry} ye 14 1744
In ye 34th year
of her Age

1958 *r*
AS THE TREE FALLS SO IT LIES
SACRED
to the Memory of
Mr Jonathan Dayton
who departed this Life
October ye 4th 1776
in the LXXVI Year of
his Age

1959 *r*
Here lyes ye Body
of Mary wife of
Jonathan Dayton
Dec^d March ye 18 1734
In ye 33^d year
of   her Age

1960 *r*
HERE LYETH THE
BODY OF SAMUEL^L
LAWRENCE AIGED 15
YEARS WHO DEPAR
TED THIS LIFE THE
9 OF AVGVST
1687

1961 *r*
J D
In memory of
Joseph Dayton
who died Septr 22^d
1802 in the 24th year
of his age
Son of Daniel & Hannah
Dayton

                                    trod
        The path which young Josiah walked, he
        And early learned to love, & serve his God
        His days of pilgrimage on earth were few,
        Swift as a chaft, his anxious spirit flew.

1962 r
D. D.
In memory of
Daniel Son of
Daniel & Hannah
Dayton, who
deceas'd Septr 14th
1804 in the 24th
year of his Age

Once more we weep, Once more erect a stone
The last sad office to another son
His bud and blossom promised early fruit
But deaths destroying worm fell at the root

[There's more of this verse but cannot be made out]

1963 r
H. D.
In memory of
Howell son of
Daniel & Hannah
Dayton died Sep^r
27th 1806 in the 32^d
year of his age

O much beloved—much lamented youth
Thy gentle manners—tenderness & truth
Thy filial virtues and thy rising worth
Tho late the bright inhabitants of earth
Are now no more—deaths winged arrow flies
And slays our hopes to raise thee to the skies
Submit our souls to heavens afflictive rod
And yield the sainted spirit to its God

1964 r
HERE   LIES
ye Body of Elizabeth
wife of Jonathan
Daeyton   Dec^d
Octr 17   1766
In the 70 Year
of her Age

1965 r
Here Lyes ye Body of
John Winans Aged
25 years. Dec^d may
ye 22^d 1733. Jacob
Winans Aged 3 years

1966 r
H. D.
Filial respect
has erected this stone
In memory of one
of the best of Mothers
HANNAH DAYTON
relict of
Daniel Dayton
She died March 24th
1816 aged 66 years

Her various virtues as a wife a mother & a christian
Are not recorded on this temporary monument
But in the hearts of her children & friends
As well as in the book of her Saviour and Judge

1967 r
D. D.
In memory of
Daniel Dayton
who died Feby 19th 1808:
Aged 67 years
Also 4 children of
Daniel & Hannah Dayton
Daniel died Septr 17th 1776 in the
5th year of his Age
Abigail died Octr 1st 1776 in
the 9th year of her Age
Daniel died Aug^st 30th 1778
Aged 9 m^o & 11 days
Robert W. died July 1st 1792
in the 6th year of his Age

1968 m
IN
Memory of
DAVID PRICE
who died
Feby 20th 1851
In the 40th Year
of his age

Farewell dear friends I must begone
I have no home nor stay with you
I'll take my staff and travel on
Till I a better world do view

1969 m
HENRIETTA J.
died May 25, 1849,
ag'd 10 Mo. & 9 days
EZRA E.
died Nov. 15. 1852;
ag'd 2 Y'rs & 5 Mo
Children of
Edward W. &
Olivia Price

Dear Children thou hast left us
To the cold and silent tomb
Thy bodies laid beneath the sod
Thy spirits gone away to God.

1970 r
M. P.
Mary
daughter of
Henry & Sarah Post
died May 16th 1813
aged 3 years
& 6 mo.

1971 r
In
Memory of
Mary daughter of
John & Mary Price
who died Novr 4th
1816 Aged 3 months
& 23 days

1972 m
IN
Memory of
JOHN PRICE
who died
Jany 14th 1821
In the 39th Year
of his age

Weep not my friends
Weep not for me
Whilst here beneath the clods I lay
I calmly wait the judgement day.

1973 m
IN
Memory of
MARY P.
WIDOW OF
John Price
who died Nov, 30 1866
In the 78th Year
of her age

My dear friends weep not for me
me
My troubles are o'er, prepare to follow

1974 *m*
IN
memory of
ANN
the 2ⁿᵈ wife of
Daniel Willis
who died
August 13ᵗʰ 1824
In the 54ᵗʰ Year
of her age

Thou art gone to the grave we no
longer behold thee
Nor tread the rough paths of the world
by thy side
But the wide arms of mercy are spread
to enfold thee
And sinners may hope since the Saviour hath died

1975 *m*
IN
Memory of
DANIEL WILLIS
who died
Dec 27ᵗʰ 1845
In the 81ˢᵗ Year
of his age

                                                               thee
Thou art gone to the grave but we will not deplore
Though sorrows and darkness encompass the tomb
The Saviour hath passed through its portals before thee
And the lamp of his love is thy guide through the gloom

1976 *m*
Here lies the Body of
Joshua Marsh who
departed this Life
September yᵉ 21ˢᵗ
Anno Domini 1744
In the 54ᵗʰ Year of
his Age

1977 *r*
I. M.

In memory of
Mr Isaac Marsh who
died Janʸ 30ᵗʰ 1801
in the 48ᵗʰ year of
his age

Children & friends Behold my tomb
This is my home yet there is room
Prepare to die and at a word
To meet your Saviour & your God.

1978 *m*
MARY CUSHING ALLEN
DIED
May 14ᵗʰ 1855
Aged 7 years

1979 *m*
ELIZABETH TREVETTE ALLEN
DIED
April 10ᵗʰ 1864
Aged 18 Years

1980 *r*
William son
of William & Marga-
-ret Ramson, died
augᵗ 17 1800. In
the 2ᵈ year of
his age

1981 *m*
SACRED
to
the memory
of three sons
of Oliver S Halsted &
Mary his wife
CALEB died Octʳ 12ᵗʰ 1827
in the 12ᵗʰ year
of his age
ISAAC WILLIAMSON, died
Novʳ 24ᵗʰ 1828 in the 2ᵈ
year of his age
WILLIS POPE   died at
Chilicothe Augˢᵗ 31ˢᵗ 1823
in his 10ᵗʰ month

Alas they're gone three lovely flow'rs
Which bloomed and cheered our hearts
Fair fleeting comforts of an hour
How soon we're call'd to part.
And shall our bleeding hearts arraign
That God whose ways are love
Or vainly cherish anxious pain
For them who rest above?
No ! let us rather humbly pay
Obedience to his will
And with our inmost spirits say
" The Lord is righteous still."

1982 *m*
To the memory of
CANDACE
widow of
Thomas Steele Jr
Of Lenox Mass—
and daughter of
ELNATHAN BOARDMAN
Born at Rocky Hill Ct
February 3ᵈ 1769
Died
December 1ˢᵗ 1857

1983 *r*
IN MEMORY OF
Mr Caleb Halsted
who departed this
Life June yᵉ 4ᵗʰ Anno
Domini 1784 and
in the 64ᵗʰ year of
his Age

Under these Clouds in Dust & Ruins lie
The Remains of Meekness Kindness Piety
To be reviewed when Christ in glory comes
To wake his sleeping Saints & Call 'em home

1984 *r*
R. H.

In memory of
the widow Rebeccah
relict of Caleb
Halsted who died
March 31ˢᵗ 1806
aged 76 years 9
months & 14 days

The unremitting paths she trod
That leads to happiness and God
Her seventy years had run their race
Ere she was called to heavens embrace
The joyful spirit left the clay
Until the resurrection day
And here the precious treasure lies
Till God shall call it to the skies.

1985 *r*
JACOB, Son of
Caleb & Rebekah
Halsted, deceas'd
May yᵉ 27ᵗʰ 1772
In the 6ᵗʰ Year of
his Age

1986 *r*
In Memory of
William Halsted Esq
who died Novʳ 22ᵈ 1794
in the 47ᵗʰ year
of his age

Firm as the earth thy gospel stands
My lord, my hope my trust
If I am found in Jesus hand,
My soul can ne'er be lost.

1987 r
Elihu O. the Son of
Elihu and Unice
Halsted who died
Octr ye 23^d 1786th
In the 4th Year of
his Age

1988 r
Jane Pierson daugh^r
of Elihu and Eunice
Halsted died April
the 7th 1793, aged
9 Months

1989 r
R. H.

Robert Halsted son of
W^m & Phebe Halsted

died Novr 19th 1801' aged
20 years 4 months &
26 days
Weep not for me my friends
For now my race is run
It is the will of God
So let his will be done

1990 r
S. H.
Samuel, Son of
W^m & Phebe Halsted
died Jany 27 1805.
in the 31st year
of his age
Farewell terrestrial joys
I in the grave must lie
Adieu to glittering toys
Death will not pass me by

1991 m
OLIVER SPENCER HALSTED
Chancellor of New Jersey A.D. 1845-52
Natus. Elizabeth N. J. 1793
Obiit Lyons Farms N. J. 1877, aetat 85.
MARY HETFIELD HALSTED
N. Elizabeth 1795 O. Newark N. J. 1866 ae^t 74
Buried in Hetfield Vault St. Johns E. Church
O. S. HALSTED JUNIOR, (PET)
N. Elizabeth 1818, O. Newark 1871 aet. 53.
"Sleeps near."
ROBERT MORRIS HALSTED
N. Elizabeth 1824 Buried at Sea 1853 aet. 29.
ABEL HETFIELD HALSTED
N. Elizabeth 1825. O. Lyons Farms 1873 aet. 48
"Sleeps near."
FRANCIS WILLIAM HALSTED
Natus Newark 1833
Masters Mate }
Seaman } U S Navy
Acting Ensign } 1861-65
Obiit Minnesota 1876 aetat 43

Sacred to the { Father }
Memory of { Mother & } 1883. G. B. H.
{ Brothers }

1992 *m*
C. H.

In memory of
CALEB HALSTED
born April 24th 1770.
died July 25th 1830
A devoted wife thus
testifies her affectionate
remembrance

"Lean not on earth, 'twill
pierce thee to the heart."

1993 *r*
W. H.
In memory of
DR WILLIAM
HALSTED
who died
June 19th 1828
Aged 49 years
& 4 months

Beneath this stone death's prisoner lies
The stone shall move the prisoner rise
When Jesus with Almighty word
Calls his dead saints to meet their Lord

1994 *r*
P. W.

In memory of
Phebe Wife of
Major John Wiley
died Octr 11th 1795,
in the 38th year
of his Age

1995 *m*
L. B. H.

1996 *m*
IN
Memory of
NATHANIEL N. HALSTED
who departed this life
July 24 1816,
Aged 25 Years
9 Months &
5 Days
Happy are the dead
who die in the Lord.

1997 *m*
[Monument. West side]
IN
MEMORY OF
LUCRETIA B HALSTED
WHO WAS BORN
March 12, 1792
AND DIED
June 27 1860
"Whosoever liveth and believeth
in me shall never die."

[South side]
L. B. H.

[North side]
N. N. H.

[East side]
IN
MEMORY OF
NATHL NORRIS HALSTED
WHO WAS BORN
Octr 19th 1790
AND DIED
July 24th 1816
"Blessed are the dead who
die in the Lord."

1998 *m*
In
Memory of
MATTHIAS HALSTED
who departed this life
17th December 1824
Aged 65 years

1999 *g*
[Horizontal slab]
N. NORRIS HALSTED
1816—1884.
"NOTHING IN MY HAND I
BRING
SIMPLY TO THY CROSS I
CLING."

2000 *r*
C V
In memory of
Cortland Vanaus-
dol who departed
this life June 1st
1796 aged 47
years

2001 *m*
G. P.
In memory of
George Price
who died Jany 31st
1813
aged 77 years

Go home my friends and dry your tear^s
I must lie here till Christ appears
A few more days and you must lie
In the cold grave as well as I.

2002 *r*
P W
In memory of Phebe
daugh^t of George
Price & widow of Sa-
muel Woodruff who
deceased Feby 10th 1797
in the 41st year of her
age

Press'd by the hand of sore disease
In pain I wandered on
Till God my savior armed with love
In murcy called me home

2003 *r*
In Memory of
Joanna the Wife of
Farrington Price
who died Oct ye 16th
A D 1789 In the 31st
year of her Age
and also her two sons
Aaron Price aged
1 year & 9 months &
Benjamin M. Price
aged 6 months

2004 *r*
HERE LIES
ye Body of Elisabeth
Price who deceas'd
Nov ye 27th A. D.
1784 In ye 43^d
year of her
Age

2005 *r*
HERE LIETH
interr'd what was Mortal
of Charity, the Wife of
George Price who died
Octr ye 4th A. D 1776
In the 42^d Year
of her Age

2006 *r*
HERE lyes ye Body of
Benjamin Price Esqr
who died Novr 27th
Anno Domini 1773
In the 97th Year of
his Age

Pray look upon my Grave,
All you that passeth by,
Where one doth live to such an Age
Thousands do younger die.

2007 *r*
HERE LIE'S
the Remains, of M^{rs}
Mary Wife of Mr Ben^j
Price J^r died May
ye 12th A D 1766
Ag^d 48 Years

2008 *r*
HERE LYETH
the Body of Mr
Benjamin Price Jr
who deceas'd Dece^r
the 1st A D 1759
aged 51 years

And his Son John
died 3 week after
him aged 3 months

2009 *r*
HERE lies the Body
of Margaret Price
who departed this
Life April ye 13th An^o
Domini 1777 in ye 32^d
year of her Age

Death like an overflowing stream
Sweeps us away, this Life's a dream

2010 *r*
Here lies the Bodies of 2 Sons of
Anthony & Rebekah Price

William
who died ye 5th of
June A. D. 1783
in the 9th year of
his age

John
who died ye 2^d of
July A. D. 1782
in the 6th year of
his age

2011 *r*
A. P.
Sacred to the memory
of Anthony Price
who died Feb 11th 1807
in the 56th year of
his Age
The years rolls around and steels away
The breath that first it gave
Whate're we do where'er we be
We're travlling to the grave.

2012 *r*
IN
Memory of
REBECCA
WIDOW OF
ANTHONY PRICE
who died
Febuary, —— 1826
Aged 73 years

2013 *r*

Here
Lyes ye Body
of Capt Joseph
Meeker Aged
51 years Dec^d
Decr ye 14th
1731

Here lyes
ye Body of
Elizth Wife of
Benj^m Price
Aged 18 years
Dec^d June y^e
3^d 1731
Dau^r of Capt
Joseph Meeker

2014 *r*
M M
In memory of
Moses Miller
who died Sep^r
24th 1821 aged 80
years 6 mon^s &
22 days

His life was gentle & serene his mind
His morals pure in every action just
Husband dear & as a parent kind
As such he lies lamented in the dust

2015 *r*
IN
Memory of
MARY
wife of
Josiph Meeker
who died
Feby 8th 1834
Aged 72 years

My flesh shall rest in hope

2016 *r*
Sacred
To the Memory of
Joseph Meeker
who departed this
life Oct 23^d 1803
In the 48 year of
his Age

Death calls the aged & the young
From all their cares from every wrong
H His summons seises on the best
Their very pains & deaths are blest

2017 *r*
J S M
In memory of Joseph Steve^ns
Son of Joseph and Mary
Meeker departed this life
June 20th 1784 in the 3^d
year of his age
Likewise Sarah daughter
of Joseph and Mary
Meeker departed this life
July 21th 1803 Aged 12 months

2018 *r*
In memory of
Ezubah Wife of
Moses Miller who
departed this Life
August ye 18 1784
In the 38th year of
her Age

Her weary Body here shall rest
No more by sin nor grief
opprest
Till her dear Saviour bid her
rise
And come to meet him in
the skies

2019 *m*
In
memory of
ABIGAIL
wife of
David Meeker
who died May 14th 1813
aged 25 years

Farewell no more, I tread your ground
No more I need the gospel found
My feet have reach'd the heavenly
throne
I know no imperfection more.

2020 *m*
In
memory
of
ELIZABETH
daughter of David
& Frances Meeker
who departed this life
Septr 19th 1816
Aged 2 months
& 5 days
Also Joseph their son
who departed this life
Septr 18th 1817
Aged 5 months
& 20 days

2021 *m*
In
memory
of
FRANCES
daughter of David
& Frances Meeker
who departed this
life Augst 30 1822
Aged 4 months
& 26 days

2022 *r*
J M M
M A M
In memory of
JOHN M. MEEKER
who died Jan 20 1822
in the 39th year of
of his age

Also of
MARY ANN
daughter of John M.
& Phebe Meeker who
died Sept 22 1825
in the 16 year
of her age

2023 *r*
S M
In memory of
SUSAN
daughter of
John M. and
Phebe Meeker
who died
Jany 22 1833
In the 19th year
of her age

2024 *m*
IN
MEMORY
SUSAN MILLER
DAUGHTER OF
WILLIAM O, & MARY C,
PRICE
WHO DIED
JANUARY 9th 1852
AGED 6 YEARS

2025 *r*
O. P
In memory of Oli-
-ver Son of Farring-
ton Price who de-
ceas'd Octr 3^d 1797
aged 12 years & 11
months

2026 *r*
E P
In memory of
Elizabeth the wife
of
Farrington Price
Who died
Novr 2^d 1800 in the
43^d year of her age

2027 *r*
F P
In memory of
Farrington Price who
deceas'd Decr 18th
1802
in the 45th year of his
age

Thus death you see will not relieve
The bravest men in life
No mortal soul hee'l not retrieve
Beware of worldly strife

2028 *r*
G. F.
In memory of
George Farrington son of
George & Catharine Price
who died June 15th 1810
aged 1 year & 11 months

The Parents wept A last adieu
Upon this beauteous clod
While up to Heaven the seraph flew
To meet A smiling God

2029 *m*
Sacred
to the
memory of
GEORGE PRICE
who departed this life
Febuary the 27 1816
Aged 35 years
Also
to the memory of
JOHN N. O. son of
George & Catharine Price
who departed this life
June the 22^d 1814
Aged 6 days

2030 *m*
IN HONOR OF
CATHARINE OLIVER
RELICT OF
GEORGE PRICE JUN^R
AND WIDOW OF
ISAAC L DAVIS
DIED JUNE 22 AD
1854
AGED 69 YEARS

An Example worthy of all Praise
Rest thou in Peace

2031 *r*
In
Memory of
two children
of George &
Catharine Price
JOHN NICHOLAS
died Novr 3 1816
aged 1 year 3 months
& 15 days
GEORGE FARRINGTON
died July 26 1821
aged 9 years
& 7 Days

Let friends no more our sufferings
  mourn
Nor view our relics with concern
O cease to drop the pitting tear
We've past beyond the reach of fear

2032 *m*
[North side]
JOSEPH O MEEKER
DIED
FEB 17th 1879
AGED 47 YRS

MARY WOODRUFF
WIFE OF
JOSEPH S
MEEKER
DIED APRIL 6th 1853
AGED 60 YEARS

"I am the resurrection
and the life"

[East side]
JOSEPH S MEEKER
DIED
DEC. 8th 1876
AGED 85 Y'RS

Psa   Great peace have they
which love thy law

[South side]
MARY W MEEKER
DIED
APRIL 20th 1881
AGED 64 Y'RS

Isa. 40. 31. They that wait
upon the Lord shall renew
their strength

[West side]
SARAH
DAUGHTER OF
JOSEPH S
AND MARY MEEKER
DIED JULY 1st 1842
AGED 18 YEARS

"In a moment we are cut
down and withered."

MATILDA F. MEEKER
DIED
JAN. 15 1858
AGED 19 Y'RS

ST. JOHNS CHURCH.

Inscribed over South door of
[St. Johns Church in Elizabeth, N. J.]

ST. JOHNS CHURCH

First service Novr 3^d 1703

ENLARGED & REPAIRED

AD 1808

FURTHER ENLARGED

1840

REBUILT

1859

INSCRIPTIONS.

1 *m*
[West side]
JANE D. BUTLER
BORN
JUNE 3rd 1821
DIED
JAN. 15th 1856

[South side]
Her hope

and her glory

2 *m*
IN
Memory of
WILLIAM C. DeHART
A Captain in the Second
Regiment of U. S. Artillery
who whilst on service in
Mexico contracted the
illness of which he died
in this Town April 21st 1848
Aged 48 Years

3 *m*
SACRED
to
the memory of
Capt. CYRUS DeHART
an Officer of the Army
of the Revolution
Born June 17th 1757
Died September 7th 1831

4 *m*
SACRED
to
the memory of

MARY B. CHETWOOD
Consort of
Captain CYRUS DeHART
Born September 21st 1761
Died March 1st 1823

5 *m*
IN
Memory of
SUSANNAH JELF
who died April 27th 1792
in the
57th Year of her Age

6 *m*
J. E. C.
JANE EMOTT
Daughter of William
& Mary Chetwood
died Jany 11th 1829
in the 9th year
of her age

See the lovely blooming flower
Fades and withers in an hour
So our transient comforts fly
Pleasures only bloom to die

7 *m*
SACRED
To the memory
OF
TIMOTHY PHELPS
Son of
Francis B. &
Elizabeth Chetwood
who died Octr 14th 1836
aged 1 year 2 months
and 10 days.

" Of such is the Kingdom of Heaven."

8 *m*	
WILLIAM ASHTON CHETWOOD	September 30th 1809
Born	DIED
	December 8th 1835

---

9 *m*

"Blessed are the pure in heart
for they shall see God." Matt. 5 c. 8 v.
SACRED
to the memory of
CAPT ROBERT EDES
who died at Sea
in sight of the Island of
St. Michals, Aug. 27th, 1836
aged 47 years 5 months
and 16 days

His remains now lie interred in the Episcopal
Burial Ground of that Island.
Here sleeps all that was mortal of his Son
Henry Phelps Edes
who died Aug. 6th 1836
aged 2 years 4 months and 16 days.

Here also sleep another little Son
Robert Henry Edes
who died Dec. 15th 1837
aged 1 year 1 month and 13 days.

E're sin could blight, or sorrow fade
Death came with friendly care
These opening buds to Heaven conveyed
And bade them blossom there.

---

10 *r*	**11** *r*
D. B.	E. B.
In memory of	In memory of
Daniel Barhyt	Elizabeth
who died July 1st 1814	wife of
in the 63^{d} year	Daniel Barhyt
of his age	who died
	Jany 18th 1820
	Aged 62 years

12 *m*

In
Memory of
MARY ANN JELF
CHETWOOD
who died May 29th 1801
Aged
3 years & 7 months

---

13 *m*

SACRED
To the memory of
JOHN CHETWOOD M.D.
who died of Cholera on the
13th of August 1832 in the
64th year of his age
He fell a victim to that
untireing benevolence which
for more than 40 years marked
his professional course.
The meridian Sun found him
ministering to the suffering
poor; its next morning beams
fell upon his grave
"Blessed are the merciful for they
shall obtain mercy."

---

14 *m*

SACRED
To the memory of
GEORGE JELF
Son of John J. &
Margaretta W Chetwood
who was born
July 16th 1836
and died
March 19th 1838

As the sweet flower that scents the
 morn
But withers in the rising day
Thus lovely was this infants dawn
Thus swiftly fled its life away

---

15 *m*

IN MEMORY OF
Mrs. Mary Chetwood
the late amiable Con-
sort of John Chetwood
Esquire. She departed
this Life on Saturday
the 25th of February
A. D. 1786. In the 46th
Year of her Age.

---

16 *r*

IN MEMORY OF
John Ogden
who deceased
September 27th
1817 in the 94th
year of his
Age

---

17 *r*

IN MEMORY OF
Abigail Clark. Wife
of John Ogden
who deceased July
the 29th 1789 In the
LXIV Year of her
Age

---

18 *r*

D. O.
In memory of
Deborough wife
of John Ogden
who deceas'd Octr
6th 1803 in the 53d
year of her age.

Press'd by the hand of sore disease
In pain I wander'd on
Till god my saviour arm'd with love
In mercy call'd me home

---

[16] Son of John Ogden, who was son of Benjamin.

19 r
In Memory of William
Nixon was Born in
Ireland in ye Year 1715
and Departed this Life
Octr 29 1777
Aged 62 Years

20 r
In memory of
ROBERT LEE
who departed
this life
June 19th 1819
in the 71st year
of his age.

21 r
W. L.
In memory of
William Lee who
died Sepr 9th 1799
in the 26th year
of his age

22 m
IN
MEMORY OF
PHEBE
WIFE OF
ANDREW OGDEN
WHO DIED OCT 28th 1847
AGED 83 YEARS AND
2 MONTHS

23 m
IN
MEMORY OF
ANDREW OGDEN
WHO DIED
OCTOBER 10th 1836
AGED 69 YEARS

24 m
IN
MEMORY OF
ISAAC OGDEN
WHO DIED
JULY 11th 1813
AGED 19 YEARS 8 MONTHS
AND 3 DAYS

25 r
SACRED
to
the memory of
MARGARETTA STEWART
BLISS daughter of
B. E. & E. J. Bliss
who died
Octr 17th 1824
Aged 19 years
Life's little lines how short how faint
How fast they fade away,
It's highest hopes its brightest joys
Are compassed in a day

26 r
Sacred to Friendship
This Stone is erected to
the memory of
Capt JOHN RUCASTLE
who died July 16th 1808
in the 55th year of his age
as a testimony of respect
by an unknown Friend
Life & the grave two different lessons
give
Life teaches how to die. Death how
to live

27 r
Sacred
to
the memory of
M^{rs} ANN TIEBOUT
who died Septr 25th 1795. In
the 53^d year of her
AGE
This stone was erected to her memory
(as a token of Filial affection) by
them who knew her worth and
still lament her loss

---

[23] Son of John Ogden, No. 16. [24] Son of Andrew Ogden, No. 23.

28 r
Sacred to the memory of
Edward Thomas Esqr
who died
February 27th 1795
in the
59th year of his age.

Also of
MARY THOMAS his wife
who died February 27th 1824
Aged 86 years

Also of
EDMUND D. THOMAS their son
who died October 15th 1816
Aged 56 years

Also of
PHEBE RUSCASTLE their daughter
who died April 2^d 1817
Aged 53 years.

Also of
SARAH THOMAS their daughter

29 m
GEORGE C. THOMAS
died July 29th 186
Aged 81 Years
ANNA R. THOMAS
HIS WIFE
died Novr 17th 1850
Aged 63 Years

30 m
SACRED
To the memory of
METHETABEL
relict of Capt. Ralph Hylton
who died Octr 15th 1810
Aged 92 years
ALSO
Their daughter
MARY HYLTON
who died Oct 2^d 1831
in the 84th year
of her age

HENRIETTA
Grandaughter of
Capt Ralph & Methetabel Hylton
and wife of James T Johnston
who died Jany 31 1824
in the 24th year
of her age

31 m
HERE REST
The remains of
Mrs RACHEL JOHNSON HYLTON
Widow of the late
William Hylton Junr
Both of the Island of Jamaica
She was born July 17th 1783
And departed this life
Nov 19th 1837
"Blessed are the dead who die in the Lord even so saith the spirit, for they rest from their labours."
This stone is placed here by her children in memory of their Mother

32 *m*
C. P.
SACRED
To the memory of
CATHARINE PROVOOST
who departed
this life
Decr 15th 1835
Aged 72 years

---

33 *m*
H. L. B.
SACRED
To the memory of
Harriet Louisa Bowne
who departed this life
December 8th 1825
Aged 31 years
2 months &
10 days

---

34 *r*
In Memory of
Mrs BELINDA HUNTT
Deceased Septr 16th 1796
Aged 88 Years

---

35 *r*
F. T.
In memory of
Frances Daugh^r of
of Joseph &
Abigail Tooker
who died
Sep 11 1823
in the 4th year
of her age

Also of their son
Charles H. who
died Nov 5 1828
Aged 1 year & 6 D.

---

36 *r*
Here lies interr'd
the Body of Joseph
Tooker who depart
ed this Life Apr^l y^e
13th 1788 In the 69th
Year of his Age

---

37 *r*
Here lies interr'd
the Body of Ann
Wife of Joseph
Tooker who dece^{sd}
Decr ye 20th 1787 In y^e
65th Year of her Age

---

38 *r*
In Memory of Ann
Daughter of Charles
and Mary Tooker &
Wife of Benj^{in} Marsh
who died April the
8th 1789 In ye 19th Year
of her age

---

39 *r*
In memory of
Charles Tooker
who died Jany 15th 1810
in the 66th year of
his age

Go home dear friends & drop no tears
I must lie here 'till Christ appears
And at his coming hope to have
A joyful rising from the grave

---

40 *r*
M. T.
In Memory of
MARY
widow of
Charles Tooker
who died
Octr 14th 1814
Aged 63 years

In faith she liv'd ! in dust she lies !
But faith forsees that dust shall rise
When Jesus calls, while hope assumes
And boasts her joys among the tombs

41 *m*
PETER KEAN
Public spirited as a Citizen
Faithful, affectionate & devoted as a Son Husband & Father
Sincere & firm in his faith as a Christian
Sound & enlightened in his principles as a Churchman
An exemplary & valuable member of this Congregation
With talents & zeal that fitted him for extensive Usefulness
He died deeply & universally lamented Octr 2^d 1828
Aged 40 years

SARAH LOUISA JAY KEAN
Amiable, engaging & affectionate of a spirit too gentle for this world
She was called to a region of love & peace Octr 6th 1828
Aged 10 years

CORNELIA LIVINGSTON KEAN
died April 15th 1829 Aged 5 days

I know that my Redeemer liveth and that he
shall stand at the latter day upon the earth :
And though after my skin worms destroy this
body, yet in my flesh shall I see God.
Parental affection has consecrated this stone

To the memory of
JACOB MORRIS KEAN
who died Decr 23rd 1817 aged 2 years & 8 months
And of
SUSAN MARY KEAN
who died April 21st 1824 aged 2 years & 8 months
And of
HELEN RUTHERFORD KEAN
who died April 3^d 1824 aged 1 year & 5 months
CHILDREN OF PETER & SARAH S KEAN

SUSAN M. NIEMCEWICZ
Obit May 14th 1833
Aged 74 years

The path of the just is as the shining light which shineth more and more
unto the perfect day.

---

42 *m*
IN
Memory
OF
CHRISTOPHER ROBERT
who died
Feb. 27th 1827
in the 79th year
of his age

43 *m*
IN
Memory
OF
JOSEPH ROBERT
who died
June 2^d 1837
in the 38th year
of his age.

His remains were placed under the
Church at the south side of the tower
in 1859 when it was rebuilding.

44 *m*
IN
memory
of
Mary R
daughter of
Charles W & Mary
H Rogers, who
died March 4th 1831
Aged 4 years 2 months
& 3 days

From adverse blasts & low'ring stor^(ms)
Her favor'd soul he bore
And with yon bright angelic forms
She lives, to die no more.

45 *m*
IN
memory
of
Emily Mary
daughter of
Charles W and
Mary H Rogers
who died Jany 7th 1832
Aged 2 years 9 months
& 16 days

Sure when these op'ning blossoms die
And fade in beauty to the eye
None should deplore
For in a clime secure and bright
Sustained by deathless air and light
They pine no more.

46 *m*
W. T.
Sacred
To the momory of
William Townley
who departed this life
February 18th 1835
Aged 51 years
5 months and
27 days

Also of
Cornelia
widow of Wm Townley
who departed this life
April 14th 1840
Aged 55 Years

Sweet is the memory of the just
'Twill flourish when they sleep in dust

47 *r*
G. B.
In memory of
Gabriel Barton
who died Decr 4th
1809 aged 77 years
and 11 months

48 *r*
A, B,
In memory of
Ann widow of
Gabriel Barton
who died March 3^d
1810 aged 68 years
and 6 months

49 *m*
WILLIAM SCUDDER
DIED
July 22^d 1849
Aged 38 years.

Sacred is Memory

ARCHIE

50 *m*
IN
memory of
MARGARET
wife of
Smith Scudder
who died
Novr 27th 1842
Aged 60 years

" How lov'd, how valu'd once
avails thee not."

51 *m*
IN
MEMORY OF
SMITH SCUDDER
BORN Novr 6th 1775
DIED SEPT{r} 26th 1846
AGED 70 YEARS
10 MONTHS AND
20 DAYS.

52 *m*
ISAAC W SCUDDER
DIED SEP 10 1881
AGED 63 YEARS

"AND HE SAID, LET ME GO"
FOR THE DAY BREAKETH

53 *r*
IN
Memory
of
JAMES H
son of Stephen &
Phebe Barton, who
died July 29th 1825
Aged 5 years &
10 months

Alas how chang'd that lovely flower
Which bloom'd and cheer'd my heart
Fair fleeting comfort of an hour
How soon we're call'd to part

54 *r*
IN
Memory
of
WILLIAM S
Son of Stephen &
Phebe Barton who
died June 7th 1807
Aged 1 year &
10 months

God has bereft me of my child
His hand in this I view.

55 *r*
E. B.
In memory of
ELIZABETH
daughter of John
& Catharine Brown
who died
Feb 26th 1811
aged 24 years

I will both lay me down in peace
and sleep, for thou Lord only makest,
me dwell in safety

56 *r*
C. B.
In memory of
CATHARINE
widow of John
Brown who died
Feb 28th 1826
in the 76th year
of her age

Blessed are the dead which die in the Lord from henceforth, yea saith the spirit that they may rest from their labours and their works do follow them.

57 *r*
J. B.
In memory of
JOHN BROWN
who died
March 17th 1810
In the 60th year
of his age

Whatsoever the hand findeth to do, do it with thy might, for there is no work, nor device, nor knowledge, nor wisdom, in the grave whither thou goest.

58 *r*
Phebe daughter
of John & Catharine
Brown died July
the 21st 1792 in ye 11th
year of her age

She liv'd belov'd & dy'd
lamented

59 *m*
IN
MEMORY OF
MY MOTHER
Octr 23dd 1848

60 *r*
IN
Memory of
SARAH widow of
Thomas Tobin
who died Septr 1st 1819;
in the 82d year
of her age
ALSO OF
ANN SALNAVE
who died April 22 1828
in the 84th year
of her age

61 *m*
IN MEMORY OF
BENJAMIN SMITH ESQr
OF ELIZABETHTOWN
who departed this life
October 23d 1824
in the 79th year
of his age.

Lord I have loved the habitations of
thy house, and the place where thine
honour dwelleth.

62 *r*
In Memory
of
John Peter Salnave
who died
Aug'st the 12th 1743
aged XLII Years

63 *r*
J. T.
In memory of
JANE TOBIN
who died
Octr 17th 1831
in the 51st year
of her age

I leave it all with God above
To do his will and show his love,
And when he calls we must obey
To dwell with him in endless day

64 *m*
SACRED
to the memory of
GEORGE TOBIN
who departed this life
Novr 15th 1837
Aged 31 years

Be still my soul the Lord hath call'd
him home
And thy beloved is entered into his
rest.
And of ELIZABETH F. daughter of
George & Nancy K Tobin who
departed this life Septr 20th 1837
Aged 1 month & 23 days

A tender plant too frail for Earths
cold clime
Transplanted to a Heavenly soil, in
beauty there to shine

65 *m*
TO MY
MOTHER
AND
SISTER

66 *m*
LOUIS
died May 8th 1853
Aged 1 yr & 1 mo

LOUISA
died Aug 1st 1853
ag'd 1 yr & 4 mo
Children of Philip
and Catherine Cron

"Verily I say unto you whos
over shall not receive the
kingdom of God as a little
child he shall not enter therein."

67 r
John son of
Joseph & Sarah
Mann died Aug't
the 17th 1792 in
the 4th year of
his age

68 m
NEAR THIS STONE
lies that which was mortal of
JOHN BLACKLEDGE
who departed this lfe
July 19th A. D. 1799
Aged 37 Years

Also his Wife
PHEBE BLACKLEDGE
who departed this life
September 19th A. D. 1827
Aged 66 Years.

How still and peaceful is the grave
When life's vain tumults past
The appointed house by Heaven's
decree
Receives us all at last

69 r
IN
memory
of
GEORGE W.
Son of Joseph &
Mary Whipple
who died Decr 11th 1834
aged 2 years 10 months
and 21 days

This lovely child so early call'd
And hasten'd to the tomb
Just came to show how sweet a flower
In paradise could bloom
Just tasting of life's bitter cup
And now refused to drink it up.

70 r
Elizabeth Damaris
Dautr of John Too
ker Decd July ye
27 1736 aged 1
year 1 month & 0 ds

71 r

HERE
Lyeth ye body of
Abigail wife of
Timothy Hal,
stead, who died
May ye 19th A. D.
1732 and in the
68th year of
Her Age

HERE
Lyeth ye body of
Timothy Hal,
stead who decd
February ye 27th
Anno Domini
1734-5 and in ye
77th year of
His Age

INSCRIPTIONS IN ST. JOHNS

72 r
Here lyes yᵉ Body
of Philip Blacklieg
Decᵈ Augᵗ yᵉ 31
1753 in yᵉ 66ᵗʰ
year of his Age

73 m
In memory of
WILLIAM L
Son of William L
& Margaret R
Rezeau
who died
April 14ᵗʰ 1846
Aged 2 yr's 2 mo
and 14 days

74 m
IN
Memory of
SALLY F
WIFE OF
Comʳ J. D. Williamson
who did
Augˢᵗ 25ᵗʰ 1843
ALSO OF
Comʳ J D WILLIAMSON
who died at Guines
Island of Cuba
April 10ᵗʰ 1844

75 m
ERECTED
to mark the spot
where lie the mortal remains of

ALFRED PARTON
who died Dec 10ᵗʰ 1840
in the 21ˢᵗ year of his age
Summoned hence in the vigor of youth in the very dawn of manhood, he was resigned to the decree of an all wise providence, and departed this life in the assurance of a blessed immortality
"Let me die the death of the rightous and let my last end be like his."

76 r
Beneath this stone
are deposited
the Remains of Margaretta
wife of William Dayton
and Daughter of
Matthias & Susannah Williamson
who died
on the 18ᵗʰ day of April 1794
Aged 28 years

Reader if e'er by tender sorrow led
You trace these silent mansions of the dead
Here solemn pause! the tearful tribute pay
To one alas! too early snatched away.

Dear sainted spirit of our much love'd friend
If from the blest abode thou may'st descend
O! come and teach us nature to subdue
To practice all we saw and loved in you.

77 m
MATTHEW WILLIAMSON

---

78 r
Sacred to the memory of
Mʳˢ Susannah Williamson
wife of
Matthias Williamson Sen.
[Inscription partly scaled off]
The angel   her flight to Heaven
July 11ᵗʰ 1793   7 year of her age

Her clay cold cor   lies here interred
      Remem   reader
that this woman possessed all the amiable virtues of her sex without their
foibles
And has no doubt, received from her Redeemer that well known welcome
"Well done thou good and faithful servant enter thou into the Joy of thy
Lord."

---

79 *r*
THE FAMILY VAULT OF
T. SALTER
1838

80 *m*
J. A. LACHAISE'S
FAMILY VAULT
1849

81 *r*
HERE lies the Body
of Mary Widow of
Boltus De Hart wno
departed this Life
Septr ye 21st A. D. 1779
In the LXIII Year of
her Age.

---

82 *r*
In memory of

WILLIAM F	HENRIETTA	WILLIAM H
Conklin	born April 13th	born March 11th
born July 13th	1823	1825
1821	died Sept 16th	died Sept 12th
died Sept 1st	1824	1826
1823		

Children of Daniel & Sarah S Conklin

Bold infidelity turn pale and Die
Beneath this stone three Infants ashes lie :
  Say are they lost or sav'd ?
If deaths by sin, they sinned, for they are here
If heaven's by works, In heaven they cant appear
  Reason ah how Deprav'd
Revere the Bible's Sacred page ; the knot's untied.
They died for Adams sin'd, they liv'd for Jesus died.

Sleep lovely babes and take thy rest
God call'd thee home he thought it best
Like as the grass is mown,
God has cut our infants down

83
James son of Jeremiah
& Vashti Garthwait
died June yᵉ 12ᵗʰ 1792
aged 3 years and 8
months

---

84 *m*
In Memory of
ELIZABETH
daughter of
Martin & Elizabeth Keller
who died Sept 19 1841
Aged 1 Year 1 Month
& 24 days
"Suffer the little children to come
unto me, and forbid them not, for
of such is the kingdom of God"

---

85 *m*
In memory of
SARAH MARGARET
daughter of George &
Mary Eyre
who died
March 24ᵗʰ 1849
Aged 4 Years and
2 Months

As the sweet flower that scents the
morn
But withers in the rising day
Thus lovely was this infants dawn
Thus swiftly fled its life away

---

86 *m*
In Memory of
MARY JANE
daughter of
Charles & Eleanor Donaghy
who died March 16 1842
Aged 11 Months & 5 days
Also
ELEANOR DONAGHY
who died Aug 1 1843
Aged 12 days

Suffer the little children to come
unto me, and forbid them not for
of such is the kingdom of God.

87

MORRIS HETFIELD
FAMILY VAULT

In memory of
GEORGE BLIGHT
who died on the 28ᵗʰ November
1803

88
M HAMPTON WILLIAMSON'S
FAMILY VAULT.

---

89 *r*
HERE LYES
Interr'd yᵉ Body of
John Dennis who Departed
this Life the 18ᵗʰ Day of July
Annoque Domini 1739
In the 44ᵗʰ Year of his Age
AND
Mrs Mary Dennis who died
Novʳ yᵉ 26ᵗʰ Anno Domini 1777
In the 76ᵗʰ Year of her Age

90
THE FAMILY VAULT OF
EDWARD C MAYO
1850

Hear my prayer O Lord, and with
thine ears consider my calling;
Hold not thy peace at my tears.

91
FILIAL LOVE
Dedicates this Tablet
To the memory of
ISAAC H. WILLIAMSON
who did July 10ᵗʰ 1844
In the 76ᵗʰ Yeaʳ
of his age

92
[Vault]
JAMES & SARAH
RICKETTS

93
O. H. SPENCUS
FAMILY VAULT
1824

94 *r*
In memory of
ELIZABETH
widow of
Jeremiah Garthwait
who died March 26
1817 in the 71st year
of her age

Within thy circling power I stand
On every side I find thy hand
Awake, asleep, at home, abroad
I am surrounded still with God

95 *r*
In
Memory
of
GEORGE S
Son of Henry &
Ann Geiger who
Died Augst 8th 1832
aged 4 years 2 months
and 18 days

This lovely bud so young so fair
Call'd hence by early doom
Just come to show how sweet a flower
In paradise would bloom.

96 *r*
S. G.
In memory of
SUSANNA
wife of
George Geiger
who died April 20th
1823 in the 66th year
of her age

This spirit shall return to him
That heav'nly spark it gave
Yet think not man it shall bedim
When thou art in the grave.

97 *r*
G. G.
In memory of
GEORGE GEIGER
who was born in
Wirtenberg Germany
and who died May 6th
1824 in the 67th year
of his age.

My time is run, my days are spent
My life is gone it was but lent
As I am now so must you be
O then prepare to follow me.

98 *m*
IN
MEMORY OF
HENRY BUTTLE
WHO DIED
on the 27th day of December
1846
Aged 52 Years

Lamented by all who knew his
Worth, Kindness & Integrity

99 *r*
E. B.
In memory of
ELIZABETH BUTTLE
who died
Octr 26th 1823
Aged 67 years

Also of
MARY ANN daughter of
Henry & Hannah Buttle
who died Decr 24th 1828
Aged 3 years & 10 months

This lovely bud so young and fair
Call'd home by early doom
Just came to show how sweet a flower
In Paradise would bloom

100 r
J. S.
In memory of
JOHN
Son of John &
Ann Slater
who died
June 16th 1837
Aged 27 years

Weep not for me my friends
For now my race is run
It is the will of God
So let his will be done.

101 m
IN
memory of
JOHN SLATER
who departed this life
May 19th 1838
in the 61st year
of his age.

Children come view my bed of clay
And pillow of the ground
Where your fair bodies soon must lay
And clods will wrap us round

102 m
ANN SLATER
Wife of JOHN SLATER
died May 1st 1841
aged 75 years

GEORGE HOAGLAND
son of
Cornelius & Esther
HOAGLAND
died June 18 1843
aged 11 months & 17 days

WILLIAM
SLATER HOAGLAND
son of
Cornelius & Esther
HOAGLAND
died June 26 1843
aged 2 years and 10 months

103 r
IN
Memory of
THOMAS SLATER
who died at "Newark"
November 3rd A. D.
1839
aged 31 years
9 months & 27 days

"He shall return no more to his house
neither shall his place know him
anymore"   Job VII. 10

104 m
IN MEMORY
OF
RHODA ANN
WIFE OF
Josiah Beavers &
Daughter of
William and Lucy Ogden
who died
Decr 14th 1843
In the 21st Year
of her age

Tread softly oe'r this hallow'd ground
A kind lamented friend lies here
Ye who have felt misfortune's frown
Come pause, and drop a tear.

105 m
IN
Memory of
LUCY
WIFE OF
William Ogden
who died Decr 17th 1845
Aged 37 Years

106 m
IN
Memory of
WILLIAM OGDEN
WHO DIED
Decr 18 1845
Aged 43 Years

---

[104] Dau. of Wm. Ogden, No. 106.

107 r
Ci-git
Dame Anne Renée desverger de Manpertuis
Veuve de
Marc Antoine Nicolas Gabriel Baron de Clugny
ancien Gouverneur
des isles Guadeloupe et dependances
decédée a Elizabethtown dans le Jersey
le 26th Juillet 1793·
dans la Cinquante troisieme annee de son age
Dieu veuille avoir pitie de son ame !

(translation)
Here lie the remains of
Lady Ann Renie desverger de Manpertuis
the widow of
Mark Antoine Nicolas Gabriel Baron de Clugny
late Governor of the Island of Gaudaloupe
and its dependences
she died at Elizabethtown in New Jersey
the 26th of July 1793
in the fifty third year of her age
The Lord have mercy on her soul.

108 r
CI-GIT
Demoiselle Julie Du Buc de Marcucy
née à la Martinsque le 21 Mai 1750 et
Morte à Elizabeth Town dans l'etat
de New Jersey le 11 Juillet 1799
Son frere Abraham Du Buc de
Marentile recommande le respect et le
soin de cette Tombe aux Hospitaliers
habitans de cette Ville

(translation)
Demoiselle Julie Du Buc de Marcucy
born in the Island of Martinique on the
21st of May 1750 and Deceased at Elizabe
The town in the state of New Jersey on
the 11th of July 1789
Her brother Abraham Du Buc de
Morentille recommends the respect
and the care of this Tomb to the hos-
pitable inhabitants of this Town.

109 r
Sacred to the Memory
of Co^{ll} Jacob Dehart who died
Septr the 21st 1777 In the 78th Year
of his Age
Of Abigail Crane his Wife who
died June the 10th 1770 in the 67th
Year of her Age
Of Do^{ctr} Matthias De Hart their
eldest son who died April the 29th
1766 in the 43^d Year of his Age
Of Capt Jacob Dehart their sec
ond Son who died at Porto Prince
in 1758 In the 31st Year of his Age
Of Joanna Dehart their Daugh
ter who died Octr the 2^d 1735 In y^e
11th Year of her Age

110 r
In memory of
John De Hart Esquire
Counsellor at Law and mayor of
this Borough ;
who departed this life June 1st 1795
aged LXVI years
His worth in private life was
truly great
nor will his public virtues
be forgotten
his name being recorded on that list of
Chosen Patriots
who composed the memoirable
congress of 1775

111 r
HERE
Also lieth the body
of Mrs. Sarah Gildeme
ester Relict of Peter Son
mans Esq. She was
Afterwards married to
Christopher Gildeme
ester Esq Deceas'd. She
Departed this life the 1st
Day of December A. D.
1735 in the 36th year
of her age

HERE
Lieth the body of
Peter Sonmans Esq.
one of ye Proprietors
of this province.
who departed this
Life the 26th day
of march Annoque
Domini 1734 in the
67th year of his age

True Emblem of a hapyy marry'd life
A Tender husband and a loving wife
Lie here interr'd. Reader, behold, and see
How great the difference betwixt them & thee
Yet to this station thou must come at last
When the false pleasures of this life are past
Altho to merit, death hath no Regard
Virtue like theirs will meet its own Reward

112 r
Here lyeth
interr'd the Body of
Captⁿ Peter Margat
who departed this [stone
November ye 19th   scaled off]
1735 in y 50 year of
his Age.

Here also lyeth ye 1 Body of
Mrs Judeth King Relict of
Captⁿ Margat, was afterwards
Married to Robert King Esqr
Dec^d, She Departed this Life
June the 8th A D 1748 in the
61st year of her
Age

113 r
J. G.
In memory of
Jeremiah Garthwait
who died March 19ᵗh 1812
in the 72ᵈ year of his
age

His quivering lips hang feebly down
His pulse is faint and few
Then speechless with a pleasant
     groan
He bids the world adieu
But oh the soul that never dies
At once it leaves the clay
Ye thoughts pursue it where it flies
and track its wondrous way.

114 r
In memory of
JANE
widow of
Henry Garthwait
who died Febʸ 8ᵗʰ
1815 in the 49ᵗʰ year
of her age

Ah! what is human life?
Day after day slides from us unper-
     ceived
Too subtle is the movement to be
     seen
Yet soon the hour is up—and we are
     gone

115 r
H. G.
In memory of
Henry Garthwait
who died
July 20ᵗʰ 1813
in the 5ᵗʰ year
of his
Age

116 r
J. G.
In memory of
JAMES
son of Henry
& Jane Garthwait
who died Decʳ 22ᵈ 1815
in the 18ᵗʰ year of
his age

117 r
I. G.
In memory of Isaac
Garthwait Son of
Jeremʰ & Elizʰ Garth-
wait who died Septʳ
22ᵈ 1808 aged 41
years & 16 days

Death cannot make our souls afraid
If God be with us there
We may walk through the darkesᵗ
     shade
And never yield to fear

118 r
M. G.
In memory of
Mary daugʳ of
Jeremiah & Eliza-
beth Garthwait
who deceas'd Nov.
3ᵈ 1788 in the 19ᵗʰ
year of her age

she was a dutiful daughter she lived
beloved and died lamented by all her
     acquaintances

119 r
HERE lies yᵉ Body
of Henry GARTH-
WAIT who depart-
ed this Life Septʳ
the 8ᵗʰ A. D 1774
In the LXXI Year of
his Age

120 r
Here Lyeth
yᵉ Body of Lydia
Garthwait Wife of
William Garthwait
Deceased January
yᵉ 27ᵗʰ Anno 1729–30

121 r
To the memory of
FRANCISCO HERNANDEZ
SON OF FRANCISCO HERNANDEZ
Merchant in Havana born in
the City of Havana and
died at Elizabeth Town
on the 16th Octr 1812
aged 9 years

122 r
IN MEMORY OF
JONATHAN HAMPTON ESQ^R
who died
Novem^{br} ye 1st A D 1777
In the LXVI Year of his
Age
MARY ANN his first Wife who
died July ye 20th 1746 aged XXXI
Years
HANNAH his Daughter who
died March ye 30th 1768 aged XVI
Years
ANN FRANCES his second Wife
departed this Life Februa^y the
24th 1791. In the 77th Year of her
Age

123 r
HERE
LIETH interr'd the Body
of Mr Charles Townley SON
OF COL^L RICHARD TOWNLEY ESQ^R
who departed this Life Sep
tember ye 2^d Anno Domini
1756. In the 70th Year of his
Age
Likewise The Body of
Abigail his Widow who
deceas'd Decem^r the 31st
A. D. 1759 aged 66 Years

Remember us laid here in Dust
The Grave shall rot off all our Rust
Till ye last Trump shall rend ye Skies
And Christ shall say Ye Dead arise

124 r
Here Lye the
Remains of John, Edwards,
& John Emott ye Sons of John
& Mary Emott of this Town
Who Depated this Life Viz^t
ye Eldest Octr 22^d Aged 7 years
ye Second Novr 30th 4 years
ye youngest Novr 9th 3 Weeks
& 5 D^s Anno Domi^i 1735

Stay and Behold ye mighty force of De ith
Where Three are lay'd who scarce had drawn their ^(Breath)
If Innocents could not escape ye Shock
How should grown Sinners stand Awaiting Look
For ye same Fate its Natures Law they must
E're long be gone & tumble into dust
Let each Observer as he goes a long
Prepare his mind for ye Triumphant Song
of Hallelugahs to ye Lord of Love
With these Blest Angels in ye Quire above
So shall you all be happy in your End
Like them with God through Christ your Life & Friend

125 r
J. B.
Here lies
the body of
JOHN BUTLER
who departed this
life March 15th 1824
in the 78th year
of his age

Weep not for me I'm gone to rest
Prepare to meet your God
I trust in heav'n to meet you there
Through Christ's atoning blood.

126 r
D B
IN
memory of
DANIEL BUTLER
who departed this life
August 21st
1824
aged 57 years

Why should this earth delight us so
Why should we fix our eyes
On these low grounds where sorrows grow
And every pleasure dies

127 r
In memory of
Mr Nicholas Schweighauser
Merchant at New York
Who departed this Life
on the 2^d day of September 1799
in the 33 year of his age
He was a native of Nantes in France

As a Husband, he was affectionate and endearing ;
As a friend, sincere and liberal
As a man, honest and respectable
He died regretted by all who knew him
Peace be to his remains.

128 m
IN
Memory of
MARGARET ELIZABETH
daughter of
Nekolaus & Elizabeth
HATTRCH
who died
Feb. 27th 1844
Aged 2 Years 3 Months
and 17 days

129 *m*
IN
Memory of
GEORGE H DEXTER
WHO DIED
March 3ᵈ 1854
Aged 13 Years
and 4 Months

Dear Mother
once more Good Night
I go and wait your comeing

130 *m*
D S S
SACRED
To the memory of
DEBORAH S
wife of John Stiles
and daughter of
John & Mary Hendricks
who departed this life
Septʳ 21ˢᵗ 1825
Aged 39 Years

The months of affliction are o'er
The days and the nights of distress
We see her in anguish no more
She's gained her happy release

131 *m*
S. H. H.
SACRED
To the memory of
SUSAN H daughter of
John & Mary Hendricks
who departed this life
June 20ᵗʰ 1820;
Aged 36 years

Adieu thou false deluding world adieu
To realms I fly which sorrow never
knew
Where Jesus reigns, where all is joy
and peace
And cares and troubles shall forever
cease

132 *r*
John Son of John &
Mary Hendricks
died Januaʸ the 19ᵗʰ
1792 aged 1 year 10
months 2 weeks and
3 days

Tis God that lifts our comforts high
Or sinks them in the grave
He gives and (blessed be his name)
He takes but what he gave

133 *r*
W. G.
In memory of Wilᵐ
Garthwait Esqʳ who
deceas'ᵈ Septʳ 3ᵈ 1807
in the 76ᵗʰ year of his
age

He was a faithful servent to the
word of God and we have reason
to believe he departed this life a
true christian

How joyful will the christian rise
And rub the dust from of his eyes
My soul my body I will trust
With him that numbers every dust
My saviour he will faithful keep
His own for death is but a sleep.

134 *m*
IN MEMORY OF
ELIZABETH
Widow of
JOSEPH STEVENS
WHO DIED
May 28ᵗʰ 1845
in the 80ᵗʰ year
of her age

ALSO
ELIZABETH
widow of
CALEB BALL
WHO DIED
Aug 7ᵗʰ 1852
in the 63ʳᵈ year
of her age

135 r
V. G.
In memory of
VASHTI
wife of JEREMIAH
C. GARTHWAIT;
who died
Augst 8th 1832
in the 63^d year
of her age

I had my part of worldly care
When I was living as you are
But God from it hath set me free
There fore prepare to follow me

---

136 r
J. C. G
In memory of
JEREMIAH C GARTHWAIT
who died
July 29th 1822
in the 58th year
of his age

He only liv'd on earth to prove
The fulness of a Husband's love
If in thy bosom dwells the sign
Of charity and love divine
Give to this grave a duteous tear
Thy friend, thy Father slumbers here

---

137 r
Here Lyeth ye Body
of William Garthwait
Junr Dec^d April y^e
17th An^o 1730 in y^e
23^d year of his Age

---

138 r
HERE LYETH
the body of William Garth-
wait who departed this life
December the 11th Annoqu
Domini 1738 and in the
Sixty-first year of his
Age

---

139 r
james Son of W^m
& Cordilia Garthwait
Aged 10 months Dec^d
Feb^{ry} ye 12 1717-18

---

140 r
Alis Daug^r of William
Gathwight Dec^d Oct^r
27 1710 in 2 year of
her Age & Mary Dau^r
of Henry Gathwight
Dec^d May 21 1736
Aged 3 years & 3 day^s

---

141 r
Mary Dau^r To Henry
& Rebecca Garthwait
Aged 1 year & 10 Mo
Dec^d Sept 5 1730

---

142 r
P. G.
In memory of
Prudence wife of
WILLIAM GARTHWAIT
who deceas'd Octr 3^d
1802
in the 66th year of
her age

---

143 m
IN
Memory of
MARY
Relict of
WILLIAM BRIEN
who died
Augst 18th 1856
Aged 88 years
and 3 days

144 m
MARY AUSTEN PEIRCE
WIFE OF
W^M M WHITEHEAD M. D.
DIED DEC 12th 1854
AGED 34 YEARS 5 MONTHS
AND 5 DAYS
"Perfect through suffering"
Here also sleep
THEIR INFANT CHILDREN
TOMMY AND WILLIE
"Of such is the Kingdom of heaven"

145 m
A TRIBUTE OF AFFECTION
TO THE MEMORY OF
JANE DE HART
WHO DIED
FEB 21st 1847
AGED 84 YEARS
"She is not dead but Sleepeth"

146 m
H E R E lies the Body of
Mr James Harris, who
departed this Life
April ye 6th A ^x D 1763
In the 63^d Year of his
Age————
And Nathan Poply his
Son, and Elisabeth
his Daughter

147 r
Mattyas D'Hart
of New York aged
84 Years died Oct^r
ye 27th Anno Dom
1751

148 r
Here lies the Body of
Samuel the Son of
Joseph & Susan Bird
who deceas'd Sept^r
the 10th A. D. 1763
In the 6th Year of
His age

149 r
Here Lyes ye Body of
Sarah spining Wife of
Benjamin Spining Dec^d
Sept ye 9 1730 in y^e
37 year of her Age

150 r
HERE LIES the Body
of Susannah Daugh^r
of Joseph & Susannah
Bird who deceas'^d
March ye 14th 1772
In the 10th Year of her
Age

151 r
HERE LYES
Intarr'd the Body of
John Hunt who
Departed this life
April 5 In the
61 Year of his Age
1762

152 m
IN
MEMORY OF
HENRY ECKEL
WHO DIED
July 31st 1845
In the 36th Year
of his age

Affliction sore long time I bore
Physician's art was vain
Till God did please to give me ease
And free me of my pain

153 m
IN
Memory of
NICHOLAS HATTERICK
WHO DIED
March 13th 1846
In the 36th year
of his age

A span is all that we can boast
An inch or two of time
Man is but vanity and dust
In all his flower and prime

154 *m*
ERECTED
to the memory of
ELIZABETH
daughter of
William & Jane
Evans
Died December 11 1845
aged 1 year 8 months
and 16 days

The bud of nature scarce had bloomed
Ere time with ruthless speed
Has laid its beauties in the tomb
But CHRIST shall claim its spirit freed

155 *m*
ERECTED
to the memory of
MARGARET CUMBERSON
daughter of
William & Jane
EVANS
died May 18 1843
aged 3 Years 3 months
and 12 days

Ere sin could blight or sorrow fade
Death came with friendly care
The opening bud to heaven conveyed
And bade it blossom there

156 *m*
In Memory of
JOHN HENDRICKS
who died July 6th 1810
in the 58 year of
his Age

Seeing his days are determined, the number of his months are with thee, thou hast appointed his bounds that he cannot pass.
JOB XIV. 5

To the memory of
MARY the wife of
John Hendricks
who died Septr 26th 1817
in the 52nd year
of her age

Relentless death with indiscriminate rage
Will neither spare conditions sex nor age

Ah ! what is human life ;
Day after day slides from us unpreceived,
Too subtle is the movements to be seen ;
Yet soon the hour is up and we are gone.

There's no discharge there's no delay,
When death demands ; we must obey.

157 *r*
H E R E lies the Body of
William Andarson who
departed this life april
the 13th A ^{x} D 1771 In y^e
42^d Year of his Age

Death's Steps is swift
But yet no noise it makes
It's Hands unseen
Yet all most surely takes

---

158 *r*
H. M.
In memory of
HANNAH Crane
wife of
George Mitchel
died April 4th 1804
in the 60th year
of her age

---

159 *r*
G M
In memory of
George Mitchel
who died
Decr 11th 1820
in the 88th year
of his age

---

160 *r*
H E R E lies y^e Body of
Elizabeth Widow of
Doct^r Briggs, who
departed this Life
Sept$r$ the 28th Anno
Domini 1766 aged 63
Years

---

161 *r*
A T
In memory of
Abner Tooker
who died
Jan. 31 1806
in the 45th Year
of his age

Jesus to thy dear faithful hand
My naked Soul I trust
And my flesh waits for thy command
To drop into my dust

---

162 *m*
Sacred
to the memory of
S U S A N
wife of John Stiles
who died June 5th 1799
aged 59 years

Sacred to the memory of
E L I Z A B E T H
Relict of Alderman
John Bogert of New York
who died Septr 29th 1796
aged 85 years

---

163 *r*
In
memory of
SARAH
wife of
Jeremiah Price who
departed this life Sepr 2nd
1806
in the 22nd year of her age

Weep now for me my friends
For now my race is run
It is the will of God
So let his will be done

---

164 *r*
HERE LIETH
the body of Mr William
Mitchel who departed
this Life Novr ye 18th
Annoq^e Domini 1757
In the 81st Year
of his Age

---

165 *r*
Mary Daughter of
Philip & Abigail
Davis died Decr ye 21st
A. D 1770 In the 11th
year of her Age.

166 *m*
IN
Memory of
ANN
WIFE OF
CHARLES BIFFEN
who died May 27th 1853
In the 38th Year
of her age

---

167 *r*
E. W
In memory of
ELIZABETH
wife of
James Williams
who died Jan^ry 14th 1835
Aged 38 years

Husband and children dear farewell
Kindred and friends adieu
Oft think of me where'er you dwell
Until we meet anew

Also of
ELIZABETH
there daughter who died
at Enmore England
Septr 16th 1836
Aged 16 years

Pause youthful stranger view my doom
Think not that youth can shun the tomb

---

168 *m*
IN
MEMORY OF
ELIHU MITCHEL
WHO DIED
July 8th 1849
In the 79th Year
of his age

"The just man walketh
in his integrity."

169 *r*
In Memory of
Mary the Wife of
George Williams
who died Feb^ry ye 18th
A D 1773 in the 53^d
Year of her Age

---

170 *r*
HERE LIETH
the Body of Elizabeth
Widow of Mr William
Mitchell who died
Feby ye last 1760
aged just 77
Years

---

171 *r*
Here Lieth ye Body
of Jacob Mitchell
Deceased December
the 2^d A° 1730 In the
57th Year of his Age

---

172 *r*
Here Lyeth ye Body
of Mary Mitchell
who departed this
Life August ye 23
An° 1725

---

173 *r*
Elizabeth Daughter
of Ichabod and Mary
Ogden died Nov y^e
16th 1789 in the 3d
Year of her Age

---

174 *r*
IN MEMORY of
Mary the Wife of
Ichabod Ogden
who died Feb. 4th
1789. In the 22^d
Year of her Age

175 r
IN MEMORY
of Ichabod Og-
den, who depart-
ed this Life Feb,
the 11th A D 1789
In ye 24th Year of his
Age

176 r
J P G
John Peter Gouet
son of Peter Louis &
Elizabeth Gouet
died March 27th
1799 in the 2d
Year of his Age

177 r
IN
Memory of
CAROLINE
daughter of
Ceaser & Mary
Alexander; who
died June 12th 1823
Aged 7 years
& 7 months

178 r
E. P.
SACRED
To the memory of
ELIZABETH
widow of
Austin Penny
who departed this
life Novr 7th 1825
Aged 92 years
& 17 days

Our life is ever on the wing
And death is ever nigh;
The moment when our lives begin
We all begin to die

179 r
Here Lyeth ye Body
Of Job Brookfield
who Deped this life
August ye 3rd A. D.
1733 in the 49th year
Of his Age.

180 r
Here Lieth ye Body
of David Joline
Deceased March
ye 9th Anno 1730
in ye 32d Year of
his Age

181 r
In memory of
Daniel Terrill
who died Decr
the 16th 1793 aged
86 years 6 Mons
and 6 days

182 m
There is rest in Heaven.
IN MEMORY
OF
CATHARINE ELEANOR
Eldest daughter of
James & Catharine
M. Moore
who died
Augst 16th 1846;
aged 10 years 11 months
& 13 days.

183 m
CAROLINE MATILDA MOORE
BORN OCTOBER 6 1847
DIED APRIL 18 1850

184 r
Here lies ye Body
of Mary Wife of
Ephraim Terrill died
May ye 3 1733 in ye
49 year of her age

185 r
Here lies yᵉ
Body off Josiah
Terrill Son of
Ephraim Terrill
Junr Who
departed this life
The 5 day of october 1766 in the 16ᵗʰ
year of his age

186 r
Here lies the Body
of ephraim terrill
Who departed this
liefe the 18 day of
June 1761 in 72
yerai of his age

187 r
HERE lies interr'd
what was Mortal of
Ephraim Terrill Esq
who departed this
Life Augᵗ yᵉ 13ᵗʰ Anº
Domini 1786 and in
the LXXIII Year of his
Age

188 r
In memory of
Mʳ John Harriman
who died Septʳ the
9ᵗʰ 1791 in yᵉ 68ᵗʰ year
of his age
Also of Sarah his wife
She died Januarʸ yᵉ 28ᵗʰ
1777 in the 68 year
of her age

189 r
HERE lies interr'd
The Remains of Abel
Hetfield, who departed this Life
January yᵉ 22d Annº
Domini 1782 In yᵉ 31ˢᵗ
Year of his Age.

190 r
Here lyeth yᵉ body of
Mary wife of Joseph
Tooker who Dep'ᵈ this
Life August the 22ᵈ
A. D. 1740 and in yᵉ
21ˢᵗ year of her age

191 r
H. J.
In memory of
Henry, son of Henry
& Jemime Jeffrys
died Febʸ 10ᵗʰ 1807 aged
7 years 1 mº & 5 days

Let all that's hear behºld and see
This child and wonder why
That were alive while he is gone
Into Eternity

192 r
HERE lies the Body of
Martha Wife of Joshua
Jefferys who departed
this Life Novemʳ yᵉ 5ᵗʰ
A. D. 1769 In the 39ᵗʰ
Year of her Age

193 r
HERE lies interr'd
the Body of Joshua
Jeffrys, who died
Janaʸ yᵉ 25ᵗʰ Anno
Dom 1781 In ye 50ᵗʰ
Year of his Age

194 r
Joshua the Son of
Henry & Jamima
Jeffrys died July
the 15ᵗʰ A. D. 1784
In the 3ᵈ Year of
her Age

195 r
Here lyeth y⁰ Body of
Jonathan Son of Caleb Jef-
ferys Born april 16 1715
Decᵈ Novʳ 24 1733
In early Bloom Death me invadeˢ

Translateˢ my Body to theseᵉ shad
Both young & old by thiˢ many see
That they must quickly follow me

196 r
Here lies y⁰ Body of
Elizabeth wife of
William Richardson
Decᵈ March 9ᵗʰ 1723
aged 34 Years

197 r
Here Lieth y⁰ Body
of Jacob Ogden
Deceased July y⁰
31ˢᵗ Ao 1730 Born
Febʳ y⁰ 5ᵗʰ 1722

198 m
GEORGE RHESA
SON OF
Frederick W and
Vashti H Foot;
died March 1ˢᵗ 1852
aged 1 year
& 3 months

199 r
E G H
SACRED
To the memory of
ELIZABETH G.
wife of J. M. Howell
and only daughter
of William Brown
of New York who
died April 23ʳᵈ 1815
Aged 18 Years

Her aching head and fluttering heart
With all their pains and sorrows part
And now we hope her soul doth rest
Upon her dear Redeemer's breast

200 r
IN MEMORY OF
Martha Haviland
who died October
the 19ᵗʰ 1789 In y⁰
XLVI Year of her
Age

She now in pleasant
valies does set down
and for her toil reseiv's
a glorious crown.

201 r
In Memory of Sarah
Widow of Mr Luke
Haviland who deceas'd
Januaʸ y⁰ 30ᵗʰ Anno
Domini 1786 In y⁰ 75ᵗʰ
Year of her Age

She was a patern of her
deceased Husband a
kind Wife a tender &
dear Parent

202 r
Here lies Interr'd the
Body of Luke Haviland
who departed this Life
Janʳʸ 11ᵗʰ 1782 In the
69 Year of his Age

He was a loving & tender Husband
A Kind Father to his Children
He lived Beloved and died
Lamented by his Family
When Death Calls we must Submit

---

¹⁹⁷ Brother of John, No. 16.

203 *r*
HERE LIETH
the Body of Hannah
widow of Jere[h] Crane
who died Jan[y] y[e] 27th
A D 1760 In the
73[d] year of her
Age

204 *r*
Jonathan Son of
Matthias & Susanna
Allen died May y[e] 1st
A. D. 1786 In the 2[d]
Year of his Age

To Gods unerring Will
Be ev'ry Wish resigned

205 *r*
In memory of
Abraham A. Brasher
of New York, He
died Janua[y] the 1st
1793 in the XLIX
year of his age

206 *r*
F P B
In memory of
F P Son of F., P. &
H : Le Breton died
y[e] 8th of aug[t] 1801
aged 3 months

207 *r*
Here lies ye Body
of Joseph Smith
Son of Joseph and
Lucenday Smith
Dec[d] May 25th 1734
In y[e] 22 year of
his Age

208 *r*
Deborah Daughter
of Henry & Sarah
Baker died Nov[r] 4th
A. D. 1774 Aged 4
Yrs 4 M[os] & 25 D[as]

209 *r*
Here lyes y[e] Body
of William Ramsden
Dec[d] Dec[r] y[e] 20th
1758 in y[e] 28th
year of his Age.

210 *r*
Here lies the Remains of
MRS ELIZABETH JONES
WIFE OF JOHN JONES
SCHOOLMASTER
DECESSIT NOV[R] 19 M D C C L X
ANN AETATIS SUA'E XXXI

She all those Qualities possest
That render Matrimony Blest
And constantly did them exert
In Mothers Wifes and Neighbours part

211 *r*
IN MEMORY
OF MR DAVID LEWIS JUN[R]
OF STRATFORD IN CONNECTICUT
Who died of ye Small Pox in this place
March ye 11th A D 1760 Ætatis 24

Whose Memory
Will be ever dear to His Family
and to all who knew Him
Having given singular promising Expectations
of a Life of Comfort to His Friends
of Usefulness to Society.
And of Reputation to Himself Had
Heaven permitted that Life a longer Date

212 r

Christopher
Son of W^m &
Kathern Gardner
Dec'd Jany 12 1732
In ye 21st year
of his Age

Kathern
Gardner Wife of
William Gardner
Dec^d Decr 30th 1732–3
In ye 49th year
of her Age.

Behold the Place Where we do Lie
As you be Now So Once was we
As we be Now So must you be
Prepare for Death & Follow me

213 r

WILIAM
Son of W^m
& Katherine
Gardner Aged
6 Days Dec^d
Feb^ry 14 1717

Henry
Son of W^m
& Katherine
Gardner Aged
18 Months Dec^d
July 15 1725

Sleep Lovley babes
& Take Thy Peacefull Rest
God Call'd ye Heanc
Because he Thought it Best

214 r

Kathern dau^r of
W^m & Kathern
Gardner Dec^d
Jan^ry ye 8th 1732–3
In ye 19th year
of her Age

215 r

HERE lies the
Body of Mary
Jones who deceas'd
Febu^y ye 24th A. D.
1769 In the 72^d
Year of her Age

216 r

HERE lies interr'd
the Body of Margaret
Wife of John Doobs
who departed this
Life July ye 25th 1761
In the 32^d year of her
Age

217 r

HERE lies the Body of
CHRISTOPHER NUT-
TALL Esqr from the
Island of Jamaica who
departed this Life on
Jan. 14th A. D. 1772 In
the XXXIV Years of his
Age

218 r

S P
In memory of
Mrs Sarah Price
who deceas'd
Jany 29th AD 1808
aged 90 Years

CHURCH YARD, ELIZABETH, N. J. 323

219 r
Here Lyeth ye Body
Of James Hampton
Deceased January
Y^e 13th 1732 in ye 40th
year of his Age

220 r
Here lyes ye Body
of Sarah wife of
John Burrowes
Junr Dec^d Novr 22^d
1751 in ye 41
Year of her Age

221 r
In Memory of Mary
Wife of John
Burrowes Aged 37
years Who died
Feb^{ry} ye 11th 1762

O Ses She Death is Com
Prepar and Follow me

222 r
HERE is interr'd
the body of Mr
John Burrowes
who died October
the 10th A D 1785
In the LXXV Year of
his Age

Rest gentle Corpes beneath ye Clay
Now time has swept ye Cares away
For surely now, all Troubles cease
While in the Grave You rest in peace

223 r

H G
1725

W. G
1717

224 r
S M
In memory of
SARAH
daughter of
Isaac and Abigail
Mann ; who died
Jany 20th 1837
in the 59th year
of her Age

225 r
A M
In memory of
ABIGAIL
wife of
Isaac Mann
who died
March 29th 1833
Aged 76 years

226 r
I M
In memory of
ISAAC MANN
who died
Feby 15th 1837
in the 86th year
of his age

227 r
Here lyes ye Body of
Sarah Wife of
David Man Who
died May 12 1760
In ye 34 year
of her Age

228 *r*
M. W. M.
In memory of
Martha Willcox
daughter of Abra
ham and Martha
Mann who died
Augst 8th 1804
in the 15th year
year of her age

---

229 *r*
HERE Lies ye Body
of Mr Samuel Man
who Departed this
Life Febur'y ye 23^d
A. D. 1753 In the 35
Year of his Age

---

230 *m*
SACRED
to the
Memory of
ELIAS MANN
who died
at Elizabeth Town,
September 3rd 1826
Aged 45 years

Also
ELIAS
Son of
Elias & Rebecca Mann
who died
November 20th 1817
aged 1 year

---

231 *m*
SACRED
I H S
To the memory of
ABIGAIL MANN
The fond and affectionate
Mother
of
JACOB M. HETFIELD
who departed this life
in N. York on the
13th Oct 1823
Aged 69 years

The Seraphe's trump shall wake this
sleeping clay
And bid it rise to everlasting day.

---

232 *m*
SACRED
to
the Memory of
MARY
the belov'd consort of
Jacob M Hetfield
who departed this life
in N. York on
March 17th 1812 in
the 25th Y^r of her Age
Also
ALTAMONT MARIUS
Son of
J. M. & Mary Hetfield
who died
Augt 1st 1812
Aged 4 Months and
23 days

Thus to the tomb, in blooming youth
consign'd
A Wife most chaste, most faithful &
most kind—
With her fair form the infant Marius ;
lies
His Spirits soar'd to her's in yonder
Skies

---

233 *r*
Thomas Man Son of
Joseph & Elizabeth
Man Aged 5 years
& 5 Months Dec^d
June ye 25th 1736

234 r
S. H.
I memory of
Sarah wife of
Wil^m Higgins who
died April, 6th 1806
in the 66 year
of her age

Here lies quite free from life's distr
acting care
A tender mother, a friend cincere
Whome death cut down in aged
years we see
Stop our greif we soon shall equal
be
And when the Lord sees fit to end
our time
With thy beloved dust I'le
mingle mine.

235 m
SACRED
TO THE
MEMORY OF
CAPT. ARMSTRONG
Late of the British Army
who departed this life
July 9th 1851
Aged 47 Years

"His end was peace."

236 m
IN
Memory of
FANNY
daughter of
Rev Richard Channing
and Julia Moore
who died June 4 1852
aged 10 months
& 24 days

237 m
IN
Memory of
JULIA GRANT
eldest child of
Rev. Richard Channing
and Julia Moore
who died
March 27th 1847
In the 12th Year
of her age

238 r
J. O.
In memory of
JOHN ODLING
butcher, a native of
England who died
Octr 18th 1836
in the 63^d year
of his age

"Take ye heed, watch and pray
for ye know not when the time is"

239 r
C. O.
In memory of
CHARLES ODLING
who died
June 22^d 1839
in the 36 year
of his age

A loving husband and a tender father
dear
Likewise a sincere friend lies buried
here
Great is the loss to them that's left
behind
But he no doubt eternal bliss will find.

240 m
SACRED
to the
Memory of
GEORGE
son of George W
& Louisa Halsted
who died Dc^r 1st 1825
Aged 2 Years
& 3 months
Also of
MARGARET
their daughter
who died Decr 29th 1825
Aged 3 months
& 19 days

241 *r*
HERE lies the Body of
John Craige who died
Augt ye 22^d A.D. 1758
In the 63^d Year of his
Age.

Weep not for me my Friends
For why? my Race is run
It is the Will of God ;
And let his Will be done.

242 *r*

Here lyeth ye body of
Andrew Craig
Who departed this
Life october ye 6th
Annoque Domini
1739 and in the 77th
Year of his Age

Here lyeth ye body of
Susanna wife of
Androw Craig who
Departed this life
April ye 6th Annoque
Domini 1727 & in ye 59th
Year of her Age

243 *r*
In Memory
of
Captn Isaac Lawrence
who died
April the 2^d A D 1781
aged LII Years

246 *r*
HERE lies ye Body
of Phebe Widow of
James Craig who
departed this Life
Novr ye 25th Anno:
Dominni 1763 In y^e
27th Year of her Age

244 *r*
In memory of
JAMES
son of Elihu and
Abigail Mitchel
who departed this
life August 25th 1797
aged 8 months and
11 days

247 *r*
ISRAEL BEDELL
Aged 80 years

248 *r*
E. S.
In memory of
ELIZABETH SEAMAN
who died
July 13th 1833
Aged 78 Years

245 *r*
HERE lies the Body
of Mrs Hannah Wife
of Mr John Donington
who departed this life
March ye 4th A. D. 1772
In the 44th Year of her
Age

I sleep, I rest, with them thats holy
I liv'd I died prepare to follow

249 *r*
M. S.
In memory of
MARIA SEAMAN
who died
Septr 12th 1832
Aged 46 years

250 r
Sacred
to the
Memory of
CORNELIUS BLANCHARD
who died December the 29th
1801
Aged 48 Years
ALSO SARAH his wife who
died October the 30th 1805
Aged 41 Years

251 r
IN
Memory of
ELIZABETH BEDELL
who died
Septr 10th 1847
In the 72nd Year
of her age

252 r
B R S
In memory of
BENJAMIN R. SEAMAN
who died
May 26th 1844
In the 69th year
of his age

253 r
C. J. S.
In memory of
CATHARINE J SEAMAN
who died
Augst 13th 1848
In the 66th year
of her age

254 r
E. S.
In memory of
ELIZA SEAMAN
who died
July 22, 1856
In the 79th year
of her age.

255 r
In memory of Char
lotte Daughter of
Thomas & Charlotte
Chapman, who died
June the 10th 1796
in the 6th year of her
age

256 r
C. P. S.
CATHERINE PROVOOST SEAMAN
daughter of
Geo. C. T. and Caroline H
SEAMAN
died July 31st 1852
aged 4 months
and 12 days

257 r
M. L.
To the memory of
MARGARET LANDRY
wife of
Francis Chambon

Ducland
who died
on the 7th of Novr 1812
in the 64th year
of her age

258 *m*
SACRED
TO THE
MEMORY OF
ELINOR MARY
infant daughter of
Augustus and
Catharine Yockney
who died May 16 1854
aged 1 year and
7 months.

As the Tree falls so it lies
259 *r*
HERE lies interr'd
the Body of Capt
Baker Hendricks wh°
died Jan^r ye 29th 1789
In the 33^d Year of his
Age
Here lies beneath this Stone repos'd
Patriot Merit, straitly hous'd
His Country call'd he lent an Ear,
Their Battles faught and rested here.

260 *r*

HERE lies Interr'd
the Remains of Mrs,
Phebe, Wife of Mr Baker
Hendricks who died
January the 9th Anno
Domini 1775 In ye 44th
Year of her Age

HERE lies Interr'd
the Remains of Mr.
Baker Hendricks who
departed this Life
January the 9th Anno
Domini 1776 In ye 56th
Year of his Age

261 *m*
THE GRAVE
OF
JOHN PETER
D'ANTERROCHES,
WHO DIED
Decr 24th 1854
Aged 74 Years
IN MEMORY OF
HIS WIFE
ABIGAIL MARSH
WHO DIED
in New York City
April 14th 1825
Age 46 Years

262 *m*
THE GRAVE
OF
MARY
who died July 31st 1844
Aged 86 Years

WIDOW OF
JOSEPH LOUIS
COUNT D'ANTERROCHES
who died in France
Jany 17th 1814 (while on

a visit to his parents)
Aged 60 Years

Also two of their children
ADRIANNE
died Octr 12th 1800
Aged 11 Years

JOSEPH LOUIS
died in New Orleans,
Septr 18th 1819
Aged 20 Years

263 *m*
THE GRAVE
OF
JOHN DeHART
WHO DIED
JAN^Y 26th 1846
AGED 88 YEARS
AND 6 MONTHS

"Tho' lost to sight to memory dear."
AND OF HIS WIFE
JANE F D'ANTERROCHES
WHO DIED
JUNE 18th 1862
IN THE 80th YEAR
of her age

264 *m*

[Horizontal Slab]
SACRED
To the memory of
MARIAH PRISE CAMPBELL
Relict of Mr Prise Campbell
She was born in Switzerland
and was for many Years
a Respectable Member of
St Johns Church at Eliz[th] Town
where she died Nov[r] 29th 1831 ;
Aged 80 years

---

265 *m*
SACRED
To the Memory of
JONATHAN H
LAWRENCE
WHO DIED
June 4th 1844
In the 82nd Year
of his age
ALSO OF .
JOANNA
WIFE OF
Jonathan H Lawrence
who died March 4th 1834
In the 68th Year
of her age

---

266 *m*
[Monument. East side]
SACRED
To the Memory of
JOHN GRAY
who departed this life
April 25th 1777
Aged 54 years

[South side]
SACRED
To the memory of
AMY widow of
John Gray
who departed this life
April 16th 1786
Aged 65 years

[West side]
SACRED
To the Memory of
RICHARDSON Gray Esq
who departed this life
June 21st 1818
in the 65th year
of his age

The sweet remembrance of the just
Shall flourish when they sleep in dust

[North side]
SACRED
to the Memory of
ELIZABETH widow of
Richardson Gray Esq
who departed this life
Jan y[e] 9th 1831
in the 77th year
of her age

While pity prompts the rising sigh
May this dread truth "I too must
    die"

---

267 *m*
SACRED
TO
TO THE MEMORY OF
AMY WALTON
WHO DEPARTED THIS
LIFE
MAY 20th 1826
AGED 74 YEARS 9 MONTHS
AND 26 DAYS

She is made a happy saint above
Who was once a mourner here
And sweetly tastes unmingled love
And joy without a tear
Kind angels watch this sleeping dust
Till Jesus comes to raise the just
Then may she awake with sweet
    surprise
And in her Saviours image rise

INSCRIPTIONS IN ST. JOHNS

268 *m*
To
the memory
of
RICHARD TUITE
HARTMAN
Of the Island of
St Croix
Born
Febuary 7th 1827
Died
April 1st 1828

269 *m*
To
the memory
of
ISAAC HARTMAN
Of the Island of
St Croix
Born
July 13th 1823
Died
January 1st 1828

270 *m*
In memory
OF
Louise Aimée
AND
Fortunée Charlotte Aimée
both daughters of
L. A. B. Terrier de Laistre
& Martha E Deboisville
who departed this life
the 1st
on 20th Feb^{ry} 1802
Aged 1 Month
the 2^{d}
on 16th Augt 1804
Aged 17 Months

271 *m*
SACRED
to the memory of
HOPKIN JONES
A native of Glamorganshire
South Wales
who departed this life
Sept 19th 1831
aged 28 years
ALSO
his daughter
JANUP JONES
who departed this life
June 15th 1831
aged 5 days

272 *m*
In
Memory of
JEAN MARIE
GABRIEL FONTANEILLES
who died
February 3^{d} 1806
aged 22 Months

273 *m*
Little sufferer rest in peace
May we meet the thron'd above

274 *m*
IN
Memory of
HANNAH PAUL
WIDOW OF
Charles Kiggins
who died April 5th 1855
In the 72^{d} Year
of her age
Hear what the voice from heaven
  declares
To those in Christ who die
Released from all their earthly cares
They'll reign with me on high

275 *m*
IN
Memory of
CHARLES KIGGINS
WHO DIED
March 23^{d} 1845
In the 75th Year
of his age
There shall I bathe my weary soul
  In seas of heav'nly rest
And not a wave of trouble roll
  Across my peaceful breast

276 *m*
IN
Memory of
CAROLINE E.
only daughter of
Ogden and Ann C Brown
who died June 15th 1852
Aged 17 Years 6 Months
and 23 Days

How short the race our friend has run
Cut down in all her bloom
The course but yesterday begun
Now finish'd in the Tomb

---

277 *m*
In memory of
ROSE DESIREE
FRANCOISE KORA
daughter of
M. A. TERRIER DELAISTRE
& M. F. P. DEBOISVILLE
who departed this life
September 6th 1808
aged 18 months

---

278 *m*
In Memory
of
ELIZABETH
wife of
Eliphalet Price
and Daughter of
John & Sarah Paul
who departed this life
Dec 10th 1808 in the
23d Year of her age

Blessed are the dead which die in the Lord,

---

279 *m*
A. P.
In memory of
ANDREW PAUL
Son of John and Sarah Paul
who died August 2d 1808
in the 27th year of his age

Press'd by the hand of sore disease
In pain I linger'd on
Till God my Saviour armed with love
In mercy call'd me home

---

280 *m*
S P
In memory of
SARAH wife of
John Paul
who died
Novr 12th 1819
in the 68th year
of her age

Go home dear friends and shed no tears
I must lie here till Christ appears
And at his coming hope to have
A joyful rising from the grave

---

281 *r*
J P
In memory of
JOHN PAUL
who died
July 31st 1819
in the 66th year
of his age

Attend dear friends, as you pass by
As you are now, so once was I
As I am now, so you must be
Therefore prepare, to follow me

---

282 *r*
S. T.
In memory of Sarah
daughr of Richard Townley who deceas'd March
29th 1797 in the 40th year
of her age

---

283 *m*
SACRED
to the Memory of
JOHN DUMONT
who died the
22d day of May 1813
in the 29 Year of
his Age

284 m
IN
MEMORY OF
MRS MARGARET DECKER
WHO DEPARTED THIS LIFE
DEC^R 6th 1853
AGED 63 YEARS

---

285 r
R. T.
In memory of
RHODA
Wife of Effingham
Townly; who died
Octr 26th 1823
in the 58th year
of her age

The months of affliction are o'er
The days and the nights of distress
We see her in anguish no more
She's gained her happy release

JONAS Son of David &
Abigail Smith died May 8th
1827 Aged 4 years 10 months
& 23 days

---

286 r
E. T.
In memory of
EFFINGHAM
TOWNLY
who died
May 2^d 1828
in the 69th year
of his age

Farewell ye friends whose tender care
Has long engag'd my love;
Your fond embrace I now exchange
For better friends above

---

287 r
W. T.
In memory of
WILLIAM
TOWNLY
who died
Augt 13th 1827
in the 35th year
of his age

Farewell farewell my partner dear
My children and my friends
This call of God to you is near
O hear the voice it sends

---

288 r
William, son of
Effingham & Rhoda
Townley died Oct
the 26th 1791 aged
1 year & 3 days

---

289 r
M. T.
In memory of
Mary wife of Edward
Townley who deceas'd
Octr 25th 1794 in the
49th year of her age

Press'd by the hand of sore disease
In pain I wander'd on
Till God my saviour armed with love
In mercy call'd me home

---

290 r
A. T.
In memory of
ABIGAIL
wife of
Edward Townley
who died
Septr 26th 1823
in the 45th year
of her age

---

291 r
E. T.
In memory of
EDWARD
TOWNLEY
who died
March 3^d 1823
in the 84th year
of his age.

292 *r*
W. T.
In memory of
WILLIAM
son of Edward &
Abigail Townly
who died
Septr 9th 1833
in the 22^d year
of his age

293 *m*
IN
Memory
of
OLIVER AUGUS^{tus}
son of
Henry L. &
Eliza Montandon
who died
Augst 27th 1831
Aged 5 years
5 months &
26 days.

INDEX OF INSCRIPTIONS IN FIRST PRESBYTERIAN CHURCH YARD.

Name		Page
Acken	Simeon	638
Albey	Elizabeth	528
Albey	Elizabeth B.	529
Albey	Phebe E.	529
Allen	Charles	1119
Allen	Elizabeth Trevette	1979
Allen	Jonathan	1122
Allen	Mary	1120
Allen	Mary Cushing	1978
Alleson	Mary	611
Alling	John	1472
———	Annie	1706
Angus	Jacob B.	1750
Angus	James W.	1749
Angus	Mary	1249
Archer	Mary A.	1933
Archer	Mary E.	1933
Archer	Wm. G.	1933
Arms	Henry Martyn	1279
Arms	Stilman E.	1279
Armstrong	Catherine	512
Armstrong	Joseph	511
Arnett	Abigail	15
Arnett	Agar	521
Arnett	David, Jr.	521
Arnett	Elizabeth Ann	15
Arnett	Hannah	14
Arnett	Isaac	14
Arnett	John	15
Arnett	William	17
Atchison	Martha	1803
Austen	Aaron	1352
Austen	Hannah	1352
Austen	Moses	1352
Austen	Sarah	1352
Austen	Sarah	1352
Austen	Susannah	1352
Austin	Mary Swift	1600
Badger	Katie	1681
Badgley	Abigail	1441
Badgley	Abner	1447
Badgley	Alice	1445
Badgley	Catherine H.	1441
Badgley	Cornelius	1442
Badgley	Cornelius	1449
Badgley	Eliza	1445
Badgley	Elsey	1442
Badgley	Henrietta McD.	1444
Badgley	Rachel	1443
Badgley	Sarah	1447
Badgley	William	1440
Baker	Catherine	1559
Baker	Ezekiel	670
Baker	Henry	1899
Baker	Phebe	671
Baker	William	1559
Baldwin	Cornelia	524
Baldwin	Elizabeth Thompson	530
Baldwin	Fanny C.	527
Baldwin	Joanna	526
Baldwin	Matthias	525
Baldwin	Peter	531
Baldwin	Phebe	524
Baldwin	William	524
Ball	Abraham S.	1630
Ball	David H.	1630
Ball	Elizabeth	1630
Ball	James T.	1630
Ball	Matilda	200
Ballard	Elizabeth	865
Ballard	Family Vault	1735
Ballard	Jeremiah	1030
Ballard	Mary	1030
Ballard	Rebecca	865
Barber	Aaron Ogden	1778
Barber	Ann	540
Barber	Anna	537
Barber	George C.	538
Barber	George C.	538
Barber	George Clinton	538
Barber	Hannah A.	1211
Barber	Margaretta C.	1786
Barber	Mary	464
Barber	Mary C. Ogden	462
Barber	Phebe A. Ogden	538
Barber	Ralph Clinton	1785
Barnet	Catherine	1926
Barnet	Elizabeth O.	1921
Barnet	Ichabod B.	144
Barnet	Joseph	146
Barnet	Joseph	1925
Barnet	Mary	1923
Barnet	Rachel	1922
Barnet	William R., Dr.	1927
Barnet	William, Dr.	145
Barton	Abbie E.	1844
Barton	Maria M.	1212
Barton	Phebe W.	1213
Barton	Stephen	1214
Bauer	Anna R.	1619
Bauer	Henry J.	1845
Bauer	John G.	1618
Bauer	Mary E.	1616
Baxter	Esther	187
Beaumont	Mary E.	1730
Bedell	Caroline A.	1569
Bedell	Michael	1570
Bedell	Rebecca	1571
Bedell	Sarah E.	1572
Bedell	Wm. Henry	1569
Bedell	Wm. Henry	1569
Berry	Elizabeth	1315
Berry	Georgianna V. W.	773
Bell	Hannah	1196
Bell	Julia Ann D.	1197
Bell	Smith	1198
Bell	Thompson	1199
Bender	Catharine	1883
Bender	Mary	1883
Blakeman	Elizabeth B.	170
Blakeman	Helen Maria	166
Blakeman	Helen R.	169
Blakeman	Isaac Watts	167
Blanchard	James	1453
Blanchard	Joanna	1450
Blanchard	John	1450
Blanchard	John	1454
Blanchard	John	1452
Bloom	Eliza	1738
Board	Alfred	1881
Bohnenberger	George	1742
Bohnenberger	Catherine	1742
Bond	Aaron	156
Bond	Jonathan	158
Bond	Joseph	155
Bond	Maria	155
Bond	Mary	153
Bond	Nathaniel	154
Bond	Robert	160
Bond	Robert	159
Bond	Sarah	158
Bond	Sarah	157
Bonn	Isaac	1864
Bonnel	Arabella Halsey	1615

Bonnell	Electa Ann	1386½	Cahune	Jane	408
Bonnel	Elias	777	Caldwell	Hannah	436
Bonnell	Isaac	1734	Caldwell	James, Rev.	436
Bonnel	James W.	776	Caldwell	Rev. James and wife	1898
Bonnel	Jane	417	Caldwell	John Dickenson	435
Bonnel	Joel	1615	Campbell	Jane Price	532
Bonnell	Nathaniel	311	Campbell	Mary A.	1833
Bonnell	Noah	1734	Cargill	Abigail	301
Boudinot	Catharine	646	Cargill	William	300
Boudinot	Elias	645	Carmichael	Joanna Hetfield	946
Boyd	Mary H. Robert	1781	Carmichael	Mary Badgley	946
Boyd	William A., M.D.	1777	Carpenter	Edward	1744
Boylston	Abby W.	969	Carpenter	Ida R.	1826
Boylston	Caleb	964	Carpenter	Lucretia V.	1825
Boylston	Caleb W.,	966	Carpntr	Mary	274
Boylston	Isaac B.	967	Chandler	Abby	429
Boylston	Isaac W.	415	Chandler	Abigail	364
Boylston	Jemima	963	Chandler	Abigail	494
Boylston	John W.	414	Chandler	Abner	426
Boylston	John W.	965	Chandler	Benjamin	496
Boylston	Lafayette (col'd)	1007	Chandler	Benjamin	423
Boylston	Nathaniel	968	Chandler	Comfort	938
Boylston	Susan W.	965	Chandler	David	493
Boylston	Thomas	960	Chandler	David, Dea.	499
Bradbury	Mary A. Donington	1130	Chandler	Elizabeth	425
Bradbury	Samuel	1130	Chandler	Elizabeth K.	938
Brant	E. W. (Lieut.)	1275	Chandler	Hannah	419
Brittin	Catharine F.	81	Chandler	Henry W.	368
Brittin	Elihu (col.)	86	Chandler	Ichabod	365
Brittin	Eliza A.	80	Chandler	Isaac	939
Brittin	Four Children	82	Chandler	James	888
Brittin	Henry M.	80	Chandler	James, Jr.	887
Brittin	Hugh McBride	81	Chandler	Jemima	886
Brittin	Luna P.	86½	Chandler	Jemima I.	888
Brittin	Maria B. Silvers	85	Chandler	John	885
Brittin	Mary	83	Chandler	John	882
Brittin	Mary	84	Chandler	John	879
Brittin	Mary A.	87	Chandler	Jonathan	889
Brittin	William	84	Chandler	Joseph	884
Brookes	Ann	1817	Chandler	Joseph	883
Brookes	Elijah	1817	Chandler	Mary	890
Brookes	Elizabeth	1817	Chandler	Mary	421
Brookes	Ezra C.	1817	Chandler	Mary	881
Brookes	John	1817	Chandler	Mary	880
Brookes	Thomas	1817	Chandler	Mary	428
Brookes	Wesley	1817	Chandler	Mary	495
Brown	Abraham, Rev.	1818	Chandler	Moses	939
Brown	Benjamin	813	Chandler	Pamelia P.	892
Brown	Benjamin	811	Chandler	Phebe	427
Brown	D. O.	21	Chandler	Prudence	367
Brown	Harriet E.	811	Chandler	Prudence	366
Brown	Jane Magie	1239	Chandler	Samuel	420
Brown	Lucy M.	1818	Chandler	Samuel	424
Brown	Lydia	814	Chandler	Sarah	498
Brown	Mary	164	Chandler	Sarah	497
Brown	Mary Ann	812	Chandler	Stephen	422
Brown	Michael	1239	Chapman	Catharine	1070
Brown	Phebe	163	Chapman	James	340
Brown	William	742	Chapman	Mary	341
Brown	William	162	Charlton	Elizabeth	400
Bryan	James W.	1187	Charlton	Elizabeth	400
Bryan	William H.	375	Charlton	John	400
Bryant	Jane V.	588	—	Charlie	1716
Bryant	John Jay	589	Christy	Ann M.	604
Bryant	Mary Ann	587	Christy	John W.	604
Bryant	R. C.	1608	Clark	Abby	941
Bryant	Sarah Jane	589	Clark	Abigail	1049
Burnet	Mrs. Hannah	143	Clark	Amos	1050
Burnett	Ichabod, Dr.	142	Clark	Anna L.	942
Burnet	John	58	Clark	Cornelius	10
Burrows	Anna M.	1377	Clark	Elizabeth	1084
Burrows	Fanny	1376	Clark	Hannah	69
Burrows	James Caldwell M.	1374	Clark	James B.	791
Burrows	Joanna	1140	Clark	John, Doct.	177
Burrows	Lewis Waters	1375	Clark	John	178
Burrows	Mary	1374	Clark	Margaret B.	791
Russ	Charlotte	1746	Clark	Margaret H.	790
Butler	William	1884	Clark	Mary	180
Cahow	Jane	1628	Clark	Mary Ann	944
Cahow	Thomas B.	1628	Clark	Nancy	10

IN FIRST PRESBYTERIAN CHURCH YARD. 337

Clark	Phebe M.	70	Crane	Elizabeth S.	905
Clark	Robert	943	Crane	Elizabeth S.	905
Clark	Sara Ella	1462	Crane	Eliza	549
Clark	Susan	1270	Crane	Eliza	1808
Clarke	Elizabeth	1627	Crane	Eliza	719
Clarke	Henry	179	Crane	Fanny	897
Clawson	Henry	1685	Crane	Fanny	897
Collet	Joseph F.	299	Crane	George	897
Conditt	Mary H.	613	Crane	George Lewis	955
Conklin	Abigail	1077	Crane	Hannah	896
Conklin	Caleb J.	1072	Crane	Henrietta	1770
Conklin	Catharine H.	1076	Crane	Henrietta M.	955
Conklin	Catharine	1079	Crane	Henry	1031
Conklin	Hannah	1078	Crane	Isaac	1134
Conklin	James	1080	Crane	Isaac	956
Conklin	Jerusha	1074	Crane	Jabez, Esq.	248
Conklin	John	1073	Crane	Jacob	1039
Conklin	John Jr.	1075	Crane	Jacob	150
Conklin	Mary	983	Crane	Jacob	906
Conkling	Joseph	982	Crane	Jacob, 3d	1036
Connet	Betsey	816	Crane	Jacob G.	894
Connet	Moses	816	Crane	James	1054
Connet	Phebe	817	Crane	James	1052
Cooper	Sarah	128	Crane	Jane	480
Cory	Aaron C.	766	Crane	Jane E.	904
Cory	Abigail	757	Crane	Jane Squier	893
Cory	Benjamin, Esq.	763	Crane	Jennet	1037
Cory	Daniel	760	Crane	Jeremiah	1059
Cory	Hannah	764	Crane	Jeremiah B.	1135
Cory	Jonathan	758	Crane	Jeremiah G.	1062
Cory	Joseph	759	Crane	Job	547
Cory	Maria	765	Crane	Job Sayer	910
Cory	Mary	759	Crane	John	833
Cory	Moses	754	Crane	John C.	901
Cory	Mulford	762	Crane	John W.	1195
Cory	Phebe	756	Crane	Jonathan	955
Courson	Anna	1878	Crane	Jonathan E.	1137
Coursin	Jacob	1879	Crane	Jonathan S.	952
Cornwell	Edward	37	Crane	Julia Ann	549
Cornwell	Jane S.	37	Crane	Margaret	1060
Cox	Ann Elizabeth	1949	Crane	Margaret M.	1195
Cox	Charles W.	1949	Crane	Maria	479
Cox	Joanna	1775	Crane	Martha	950
Craig	Eliza	1938	Crane	Mary	1041
Craig	Juliet	1873	Crane	Mary	481
Craig	Malvina	1871	Crane	Mary	1138
Craig	Mary	1873	Crane	Mary	1044
Craig	Thomas W.	1872	Crane	Mary	897
Craig	W. l.	1874	Crane	Mary	832
Crane	Aaron	1870	Crane	Mary	940
Crane	Abigail	895	Crane	Mary B.	548
Crane	Abigail	477	Crane	Mary B. D.	1136
Crane	Abigail	1134	Crane	Mary E.	1134
Crane	Abraham W.	954	Crane	Mary P.	1137
Crane	Ann	1061	Crane	Matthias, Maj.	903
Crane	Anna	958	Crane	Moses M.	1240
Crane	Ann Aletta	1772	Crane	Moses P.	1034
Crane	Alonzo DeLa V.	1133	Crane	Mother	1035
Crane	Benjamin	151	Crane	N. Martin	1737
Crane	Caleb, Jun	1047	Crane	Nathaniel	1043
Crane	Caleb	1136	Crane	Nathaniel	1031
Crane	Caleb	1046	Crane	Nehemiah	1048
Crane	Charles	479	Crane	Nehemiah	949
Crane	Charles Henry	1244	Crane	Noah	953
Crane	Carlotte B.	1769	Crane	Noah	951
Crane	Damaris	1042	Crane	Obediah	1038
Crane	Daniel	474	Crane	Obediah	1038
Crane	Daniel, Jr	474	Crane	Obediah	1038
Crane	David B.	898	Crane	Obediah M.	1033
Crane	David Ross	407	Crane	Phebe	957
Crane	Drake	767	Crane	Phebe	475
Crane	Drake	768	Crane	Phebe	1040
Crane	Edwin B.	901	Crane	Phebe	1057
Crane	Elias S.	1244	Crane	Phebe	473
Crane	Elihu J.	718	Crane	Phebe	899
Crane	Elihu	835	Crane	Phebe H.	1885
Crane	Elihu	1041	Crane	Phebe M.	479
Crane	Elizabeth	1045	Crane	Phebe T.	1241
Crane	Elizabeth	768	Crane	Prudence	902
Crane	Elizabeth	1133	Crane	Rachel	1056

Crane	Robert	897	DeHart	Henry V., Capt.	1764
Crane	Robert M.	1062	Denman	Major	820
Crane	Sarah	479	Denman	Rhoda	819
Crane	Sarah	406	Denman	Wm. H., Capt.	821
Crane	Sarah	1055	Dickerson	Esther	1724
Crane	Sarah Sayre	907	Dickerson	Robert	1725
Crane	Sarah	948	Dickinson	Joanna	507
Crane	Sarah	1053	Dickinson	Joanna	508
Crane	Sarah	1032	Dickinson	Jonathan, Rev.	509
Crane	Sarah	1870	Dill	Margery Ross	214
Crane	Sarah E.	720	Disoway	Cornelius	1478
Crane	Sarah Lum	904	Doane	Eliza	853
Crane	Sarah W.	549	Doane	Henry	855
Crane	Searen	897	Donaldson	Catharine	418
Crane	Stephen	476	Donington	Ann A.	1126
Crane	Stephen	1058	Donington	Caroline wife Wm.	1463
Crane	Stephen, Esq.	472	Donington	Carrie K.	1129
Crane	Susanna	404	Donington	Elizabeth	1126
Crane	Thomas	959	Donington	Elizabeth	1126
Crane	Thomas	1133	Donington	Esther	908
Crane	Thomas O.	1136	Donington	Henry	1126
Crane	William	405	Donington	Jacob	1126
Crane	William, Gen'l	477	Donnington	Jane	900
Crane	Wm. Edwin	720	Donington	John S.	1129
Cree	Frances F.	330	Donington	John	909
Cree	Jane E.	329	Donington	Mary A. Badgley	1126
Cree	John P.	328	Donington	Mary E.	1128
Crowell	Agness	809	Donington	Sarah	1126
Crowell	Christian	809	Donington	Sarah E.	1127
Crowell	Thomas, Capt.	809	Donington	Silas Hays	1127
Crozier	John	752	Donington	William	1126
Cumstick	Ann	55	Doobs	Rachel	1446
Cummings	Maria W.	1595	Dornbush	Herman	1726
Daeyton	Elizabeth	1964	Dow	Elizabeth	926
Darby	Elias	1255	Dow	Samuel	927
Darby	Ezra	1877	Dow	Samuel	928
Darby	George W.	1876	Drake	Mary	471
Darby	Sally	1256	Drewe	John	386
Daucey	Ellen Carpenter	1745	Dunham	Phebe Ann	1598
Davidson	George W.	9½	Dulong	Catharine	1741
Davis	Catharine Oliver	2030	Dulong	Mary	1740
Davis	Charlotte F.	1543	Dunn	John H.	1674
Davis	Elijah	1291	Earl	Jonathan	134
Davis	John J.	1542	Earl	Mary	181
Davis	Isaac L.	1545	Earl	Mary Louisa	135
Davis	James O.	1542	Earl	Sarah Jerusha	135
Davis	Jane	1796	Earl	Susan F.	134
Davis	Margaret	1544	Eaton	Widow	730
Dawes	Mary	1904	Eaton	Albert	725
Dawes	William	1905	Eaton	Maria B.	726
Day	Caroline J.	1110	Eaton	Sarah	727
Day	Eliza B.	1111	Eaton	Samuel W.	728
Day	Foster	1106	Eaton	Susannah	731
Day	Frederick J.	1112	Eaton	Thomas	729
Day	Nancy B.	1108	Edwards	Charles H.	1788
Day	Peter S.	1109	Edwards	David, Capt.	115
Day	Susan R.	1107	Edwards	Frances	1790
Dayton	Abigail	1967	Edwards	Fanny E.	1789
Dayton	Daniel	1967	Edwards	Hannah Elizabeth	913
Dayton	Daniel	1962	Edwards	Jacob	913
Dayton	Daniel	1967	Edwards	Jacob D., Col.	913
Dayton	Daniel	1967	Edwards	Martha	913
Dayton	Elias	1610	Edwards	Mary	115
Dayton	Hannah	1966	Ellis	Mary Earl	1535
Dayton	Howell	1963	Elwood	Eliza	1604
Dayton	Jonathan	1958	Elyea	John	24
Dayton	Jonathan, Dr.	1131	Erwin	Elizabeth	1065
Dayton	Jonathan B.	924	Falconer	Catharine	1700
Dayton	Joseph	1961	Favor	Eugene A.	1552
Dayton	Margaret	1131	Favor	Mary A.	1553
Dayton	Mary	1959	Fay	Abigail A.	1621
Dayton	Patience	1957	Force	Job W.	556
Dayton	Robert W.	1967	Force	Matilda	1594
Dean	Eunice	26	Force	Phebe King	558
Debo	Caroline	1684	Force	Susan Lee	557
Decker	Jane	607	Ferguson	Margaret M.	1721
Decker	Louisa A.	301	Forsyth	Andrew	1692
Decker	Mary A.	523	Forsyth	Elizabeth	1693
Decker	Mary Ann	523	Forsyth	George	1664
Degroot	Freeman, Capt.	1671	Forsyth	George	1692

IN FIRST PRESBYTERIAN CHURCH YARD 339

Forsyth	Isabella	1694	Haines	Elias	227
Forsyth	James G.	1688	Haines	Henrietta B.	232
Forsyth	Maggie	1913	Haines	Joanna	224
Forsyth	Robert J.	1680	Haines	Joanna	225
Forsyth	Samuel	1693	Haines	Job, Capt.	230
Foster	Jacob	1539	Haines	Margaret W.	229
Foster	John, Capt.	692	Haines	Mary	227
Foster	Sarah	692	Haines	Rebekah	30
Fowler	Jane Badgley	1448	Haines	Robert Ogden	231
Frazee	James H.	1631	Haines	Stephen	226
Frazee	Sarah Maria	783	Haines	Stephen	223
Frazee	Susan Ogden	784	Hains	Job	218
Fredenberg	Alphonso	1797	Hanes	Stephen	222
Freeman	Abigail	1564	Hallcy	Abigail	1360
Freeman	Anna	1565	Hallcy	Abigail	877
Freeman	Anson	1563	Hallcy	Joseph	878
Freeman	Caroline	1563	Halsey	Anne	1358
Freeman	Elizabeth	1560	Halsey	Betsey	263
Freeman	Elizabeth	1563	Halsey	Caleb	1365
Freeman	Elizabeth J.	1566	Halsey	Catherine Price	343
Freeman	Henry	1564	Halsey	Damaris	305
Freeman	Josiah	1563	Halsey	Daniel	1361
Freeman	Mary	1561	Halsey	Henrietta Crane	344
Freeman	Matthew	1563	Halsey	Henrietta Perlee	348
Freeman	Melanthon	1562	Halsey	Isaac Crane	343
Freeman	Rachel	1564	Halsey	Jeremiah	307
Fulton	Adelbert	1602	Halsey	Jeremiah	262
Galbraith	Martha	1626	Halsey	John L.	1364
Gale	Charles H.	859	Halsey	Luther	306
Gale	Dolly M.	920	Halsey	Mary	264
Gale	Frederick M.	1810	Halsey	Mary	1359
Gale	Gilbert B.	860	Halsey	Mary	1083
Gale	Lydia	743	Halsey	Mary Chapman	346
Gale	Richard	1914	Halsey	Mary	342
Gale	Richard, M.D. U.S.A.	1917	Halsey	Mary Dayton	925
Gale	Sarah H.	1918	Halsey	Meline W.	347
Gale	Sarah M.	1016	Halsey	Noah Crane	345
Gale	William Edward	1915	Halsey	Phebe	262
Gale	William Harrison	1809	Halsey	Phebe	1357
Gamage	John A.	350	Halsey	Samuel	1354
Garthwait	Ann	1392	Halsey	Samuel	1356
Garthwait	Anthony	1393	Halsey	Sarah	306
Garthwait	Benjamin	1390	Halsey	Sarah	260
Garthwait	Esther	1391	Halsey	Sarah O.	1363
Garthwait	Mary Ann	1389	Halsey	Silas	261
Garthwait	Phebe Crane	1390	Halsey	Sophia	1366
Garthwait	Rebekah	1051	Halsted	Abel Hetfield	1991
Geiger	Abigail T.	1185	Halsted	Caleb	1983
Geiger	Jacob	1184	Halsted	Caleb	1992
Geiger	Sophia C.	1186	Halsted	Caleb	1981
Genung	Clifford A.	1538	Halsted	C. O.	1612
Genung	Phebe Corey	1537	Halsted	Elihu O.	1987
Genung	Sophie G.	1536	Halsted	Francis William	1991
Genung	William Miller	721	Halsted	Isaac Williamson	1991
Geyer	Magdalena	1727	Halsted	Jacob	1985
Gibbons	Ann	1011	Halsted	Jane Pierson	1988
Gibbons	William H.	1011	Halsted	Lucretia B.	1997
Gibson	Jane	362	H.	L. B.	1995
Gibson	William	1730	Halsted	Mary Hetfield	1991
Gilbert	Anne Matilda	1638	Halsted	Matthias	1998
Giles	Jane	173	Halsted	Nathaniel Norris	1997
Gillet	Hannah	403	Halsted	Nathaniel N.	1996
Gorman	Mary	818	Halsted	N. Norris	1999
Gorman	Sarah	1625	Halsted	Oliver Spencer	1991
Graef	Henry W.	1720	Halsted	O. S. Jun. (Pet)	1991
Grier	Margie W.	1194	Halsted	Rebeccah	1984
Griffith	John	1669	Halsted	Robert	1989
Griffith	Josephine	1670	Halsted	Robert Morris	1991
Griffith	Rachel	1668	Halsted	Samuel	1990
Grommon	Bethiah	520	Halsted	William, Esq.	1986
Grumman	Ichabod	519	Halsted	William (Dr.)	1993
Guest	John	1811	Halsted	Willis Pope	1981
Guest	John Henry	1811	Hamill	Isabella	1837
Hainds	Benjamin	29	Hamilton	Ann Bryan	1642
Haines	Catherine	28	Hamilton	Burnett D.	1641
Haines	Benjamin	750	Hamilton	Francis P.	1640
Haines	Benjamin	31	Hamilton	George W.	1639
Haines	Daniel	223	Hamilton	Louisa S.	1639
Haines	David	223	Hamilton	Mary Ann	1695
Haines	Elias	228	Hamilton	Samuel F. M.	1639

340 INDEX OF INSCRIPTIONS

Hamilton	William M.	1639
Hampton	Jeheil	673
Hand	Jane	808
Hand	Jane	808
Hardy	Susanna	430
Harriman	Eaton	666
Harriman	Joanna	664
Harriman	John, Rev.	661
Harriman	Margaret	666
Harriman	Maria	666
Harriman	Samuel, Capt.	665
Harriman	Susan	666
Harriman	Susanna	665
Harriman	Susanna	662
Harriman	William	662
Harland	Betsey	59
Harris	Ann Maria	1703
Harris	Mary	1473
Harrison	Abby W.	834
Harrison	David O.	834
Harrison	Emily F.	1819
Harrison	James W.	1820
Harrison	Stephen	147
Hart	Jason T.	1067
Hatfield	Aaron	259
Hatfield	Charlotte T.	65
Hatfield	Damaris	254
Hatfield	Emily A.	252
Hatfield	Ephraim	675
Hatfield	Harriot N.	257
Hatfield	Harriet C.	63
Hatfield	Jane	253
Hatfield	Job H.	64
Hatfield	Laura D.	251
Hatfield	Mary	1292
Hatfield	Moses	61
Hatfield	Oliver Spencer	253
Hatfield	Sarah	252
Hatfield	Sarah	250
Hatfield	Sarah Barnet	258
——	Hattie	1672
Hauck	John A.	1760
Hauck	Margaret	1761
Haviland	Abigail	799
Haviland	Benjamin	806
Haviland	Isaack	798
Haviland	Jacob	805
Haviland	Luke	804
Haviland	Luke	800
Haviland	Rhode	802
Haviland	Sarah	807
Haviland	Sarah	803
Haviland	Sarah	798
Haviland	Thomas	801
Haviland	William	797
Heming	Melsup	1600
Heming	Rebecca	1600
Hendricks	David	1541
Hendricks	Hannah	1541
Hendry	Phebe Chandler	947
Hetfield	Abigail (Price)	1455
Hetfield	Caleb	1458
Hetfield	Cornelius	1865
Hetfield	Cornelius	1456
Hetfield	Hannah R.	1461
Hetfield	Hannah	148
Hetfield	Isaac	255
Hetfield	Jennet	1460
Hetfield	Joanna	1865
Hetfield	Margaret	1459
Hetfield	Matthias, Dea.	149
Hetfield	Oliver S.	256
Hetfield	Richard S.	647
High	Hannah O.	444
Higgins	Deborah Halsted	932
Higgins	Edmund H.	1124
Higgins	Elizabeth	1012
Higgins	Fanny	1013
Higgins	Gershom	1010
Higgins	Hannah	934
Higgins	Harriet S.	1525
Higgins		933
Higgins	John	1017
Higgins	Joseph T.	1125
Higgins	Luke H.	1014
Higgins	Luke H.	1525
Higgins	Luke T.	1015
Higgins	Nathaniel	1014
Higgins	Nathaniel	1010
Higgins	Phebe C.	1526
Higgins	Sarah B.	1016
Higgings	Susan Hatfield	1017
Higgins	William B.	931
Higgins	William B.	1009
Hines	Sarah	747
Hinds	Abigail	751
Hinds	Abner	746
Hinds	David	749
Hinds	Joseph	748
Hinds	Martha	746
Hinds	Mary	669
Hinds	Mary	755
Hinds	Sarah A. Meeker	669
Hindes	Ann Elizabeth	709
Hindes	Benjamin W.	710
Hindes	Betsey Ann	709
Hindes	Charlotte	633
Hindes	Esther	219
Hindes	Eunice	528
Hindes	Henry	632
Hindes	Henry J.	628
Hindes	Isaac	708
Hindes	Irene	631
Hindes	James	630
Hindes	John	627
Hindes	John J.	629
Hindes	Joseph B.	710
Hindes	Louisa H.	628
Hindes	Margaret A.	624
Hindes	Martha W.	707
Hindes	Mary	220
Hindes	Mary	221
Hindes	Moses W.	709
Hindes	Phebe	220
Hindes	Rachel E.	625
Hindes	Sarah A. D.	626
Hindes	Sarah Jane	707
Hindes	Stephen	221
Hindes	William	634
Hindes	William J.	628
Hinchman	Ann Eliza	851
Hinchman	Maria	847
Hinchman	William H.	852
Hinchman	William O.	850
Hoagland	Susanna W.	416
Hoerning	Margaretta B.	1731
Hofmann	Julius C.	1763
Horton	Dorcas Oliver	1533
Horton	Hannah P.	1920
Horton	Isaac	1534
Horton	John M.	1531
Horton	Joshua O.	1530
Horton	Mary O.	97
Horton	William	1532
Hotto	Anna	1565
Howell	Elizabeth	1414
Huey	Annie E.	56
Huey	Charlotte E.	56
Hughs	Charles H.	1418
Hughs	Fanny	1417
Hughs	Phebe	1417
Hull	Mary	1852
Humes	David L.	303
Humes	Mary E. D.	303
Hunt	Anna D.	864
Hunt	Benjamin	874
Hunt	Davis	789
Hunt	Esther	785
Hunt	Hannah	1276
Hunt	John D.	788

IN FIRST PRESBYTERIAN CHURCH YARD. 341

Hunt	Jonathan D.	788	Latham	Joseph	1019
Hunt	Josiah	788	Latham	Mary Jaquis	1028
Hunt	Josiah	786	Latham	Thomas	1020
Hunt	Sarah	787	Laughton	Frederick M.	1622
Hunter	Joseph Bloomfield	1405	Lawrence	Samuel	1960
Inman	Henrietta	1822	Lawrence	Thomas	1924
Inscription gone		980	Lee	Margaret	309
Insley	Hannah DeHart	1372	Lee	Samuel	310
Insley	Henry	1371	Lighton	John	1557
Jacks	Anzonette P.	704	——	Lilly and Ada	1756
Jacks	Louisa W.	704	Lindsley	Sarah	172
Jakle	William H.	1743	Littell	Aaron	838
Janes	Mary	1722	Littell	Mehetable	1795
Jarvis	Benjamin J.	698	Littell	Sarah	839
Jarvis	Hannah O.	775	Littell	Susan M.	1522
Jarvis	John O.	697	Livingston	George Edward	1751
Jarvis	Margaret M. W.	775	Loach	Edmund	693
Jarvis	Phebe	699	Loach	Harry	693
Jaques	Charlotte Ann	1333	Locker	David C.	891
Jaques	David	1330	Locker	Samuel	891
Jaques	Edward F.	1332	Locker	Samuel M.	891
Jaques	Mindwell Mulford	1331	Lougheed	Mary Ross	1803
Jeffery	Richard O.	1624	Ludlam	Charlott Halsey	1082
Jelf	Jane	1261	Ludlam	Stephen	1082
Jelf	Sally	1787	Luitig	Phillip	1754
Jelf	Sarah	25	Lyon	Aaron	373
Jenkins	Alexander	1762	Lyon	Aaron	275
Jewell	Aaron	72	Lyon	Abe Hendrix	275
Jewell	Betsy L.	840	Lyon	Ann	848
Jewell	Elihu M	72	Lyon	Benjamin	273
Jewell	George M.	123	Lyon	Benjamin	272
Jewell	Mary	124	Lyon	Catherine C.	316
Jewell	Matthew H.	840	Lyon	David	265
Jewell	William	840	Lyon	David	372
Johnson	Abby G.	315	Lyon	David, Capt.	677
Johnson	Elizabeth B.	876	Lyon	Ebenezer, Capt.	431
Johnson	Mary	1081	Lyon	Elizabeth	431
Johnson	Pebe Crane	1861	Lyon	Joanna	374
Johnson	Thomas	876	Lyon	Joanna	278
Joline	Anthony	313	Lyon	Joanna E.	663
Joline	Matthias	313	Lyon	Joseph, Capt.	73
Joline	Phebe	312	Lyon	Joseph, A.B.	74
Jones	Phebe	991	Lyon	Lette	1493
Jones	William R.	990	Lyon	Mary	280
Jousserandot	Louise	304	Lyon	Mary	266
Jousserandot	Laurent	304	Lyon	Matthias, Capt.	268
Keller	Elizabeth	1824	Lyon	Moses	279
Keller	George Peter	1823	Lyon	Moses	281
Kellogg	Amelia	864	Lyon	Obadiah	319
Kellogg	Martha	441	Lyon	Phebe	271
Kellogg	Merritt	440	Lyon	Phebe	276
Kettlewell	George S.	1018	Lyon	Rachel	270
Kettlewell	Sarah W.	1018	Lyon	Samuel	277
Kettlewell	Richard	935	Lyon	Sarah	283
Keyt	Anna	761	Lyon	Sarah	318
Keyt	Benjamin C.	761	Lyon	Sarah Treat	267
Keyt	Elizabeth L.	1558	Lyon	Stephen M.	317
Kiggins	Theodore A.	936	Lyon	Susan	284
Kimball	George Harriman	300	Mabee	Ann W.	1465
Kimball	Kate Nelson	301	Magie	Benjamin	1221
King	Francis	1667	Magie	David	1218
King	Phebe H. Crane	1885	Magie	Elizabeth	1217
Knoedler	Emily C.	1620	Magie	Elizabeth	1222
Knoedler	Eva da	1617	Magie	Ezekiel	1234
Knoedler	Henrietta C.	1617	Magie	Joanna M.	478
Kollock	Elizabeth H.	11	Magie	John	1230
Kollock	Sarah H.	19	Magie	John O.	1232
Kollock	Shepard, Esq.	13	Magie	John, Jr.	1231
Kollock	Shepard K., D.D.	20	Magie	Joseph	1224
Kollock	Susan	13	Magie	Margaret	1223
Kollock	Susan	11	Magie	Mary	1222
Kollock	Wm. M.	11	Magie	Mary	1222
Kopp	Hannah	1701	Magie	Mary	1235
Lackey	Phebe W.	1367	Magie	Mary S.	1574
Lackey	William Pierson	1367	Magie	Phebe	1219
Lambdin	Mary Wilbur	127	Magie	Phebe	1220
Landis	Susan B.	356	Magie	Rachel	1220
Lane	Sarah	1411	Magie	Sophia	1233
Lalour	Elizabeth	1863	Magie	Stephen	1574
Latham	Isaac M.	1020	Marsh	Elizabeth	1463

22

INDEX OF INSCRIPTIONS

Marsh	Chester E.	937	Meeker	Jonathan	1421
Marsh	Eliakim	1383	Meeker	Joseph, Capt.	2013
Marsh	Elias	1680	Meeker	Joseph	2020
Marsh	Evart	937	Meeker	Joseph	2016
Marsh	Evart	937	Meeker	Joseph O.	2032
Marsh	Isaac	1977	Meeker	Joseph S.	2032
Marsh	Jacob	1880	Meeker	Joseph S.	2017
Marsh	John Morse	486	Meeker	Mariah	8
Marsh	Joshua	1076	Meeker	Martha Ann	233
Marsh	Martha E.	1680	Meeker	Mary	826
Marsh	Mary D. C.	937	Meeker	Mary	27
Marsh	Mary H.	1680	Meeker	Mary	2015
Marsh	Myra A.	1680	Meeker	Mary	1300
Marsh	Myra Buss	1680	Meeker	Mary	1424
Marsh	Nathan S.	1025	Meeker	Mary A	1553
Marsh	Phebe	1226	Meeker	Mary Ann	2022
Marsh	Sarah C.	536	Meeker	Mary W.	2032
Marsh	Sophronia B.	1680	Meeker	Mary W.	2032
Marsh	Stephen O.	485	Meeker	Mary (Ogden)	38
Marsh	William	1334	Meeker	Matilda F.	2032
Martin	Ann	1794	Meeker	Matthias P.	1428
Martin	Elizabeth	1793	Meeker	Mickel	112
Martin	Elizabeth	815	Meeker	Moses	1419
Martin	Mary	1793	Meeker	Moses	1424
Massies	Peter	1609	Meeker	Nehemiah	1296
Matteson	Eliza J.	875	Meeker	Nehemiah	1528
Mather	Thomas	1636	Meeker	Noah	1295
Mattison	Abbey	182	Meeker	Obediah, Capt.	237
Mattison	Eliza Johnson	182	Meeker	Phebe	108
Mattison	Julia A.	184	Meeker	Phebe	1351
Mattison	Mary O.	183	Meeker	Phebe Spinning	1351
Maurow	Squier L.	1851	Meeker	Polly	828
McCullum	Andrew	1759	Meeker	Rachel	107
McCullum	Archibald	865	Meeker	Rachel	827
McCullum	Rebecca Ballard	865	Meeker	Rebecca C.	994
McDowell	John, D.D.	152	Meeker	Rebekah	824
McDowell	Matthew	12	Meeker	Sally Ann	1428
McGillivray	Elizabeth	1867	Meeker	Samuel	109
McGillivray	Jennie	1868	Meeker	Sarah	2017
McGillivray	Mary B.	1866	Meeker	Sarah	2032
McKain	William, Jr.	1733	Meeker	Sarah Ann	669
McKain	William, Sr.	1733	Meeker	Sarah E.	995
McKee	Elizabeth	1698	Meeker	Sophia	822
McKee	Robert	1698	Meeker	Susan	2023
McVoy	Augustus	1909	Meeker	Susan	1422
Meeker	Abby	1423	Meeker	Stephen	1299
Meeker	Abigail	1420	Meeker	Stephen	234
Meeker	Abigail C.	825	Meeker	Stephen A.	1555
Meeker	Abigail	2019	Meeker	William	1427
Meeker	Ann	1425	Meeker	Zeruiah	823
Meeker	Anna Halsey	997	Megie	Anna	1225
Meeker	Alletta	1554	Megie	Benjamin	1221
Meeker	Catherine	1528	Megie	Catharine	1237
Meeker	Charity	1298	Megie	Hainds	1237
Meeker	Charlotte	111	Megie	John	1227
Meeker	Charity	110	Megie	John	1223
Meeker	Comfort	236	Megie	Jonathan	1228
Meeker	Daniel	106	Megie	Michael	1236
Meeker	David	1765	Megie	Michael	1237
Meeker	David	235	Megie	Phebe	1238
Meeker	David T.	1528	Melvin	Abigal Ogden	332
Meeker	Elizabeth	2013	Melvin	Harriet	334
Meeker	Elizabeth	2020	Melvin	James	335
Meeeer	Elly	829	Melvin	William, Capt.	331
Meeker	Esther	1297	Michean	Maria	1457
Meeker	Esther	1297	Miller	Abigail	732
Meeker	Ezekiel	1350	Miller	Ann	483
Meeker	Frances	2021	Miller	Anna W.	1243
Meeker	Frances N.	1766	Miller	Anna Irene	1242
Meeker	Hannah	1426	Miller	Benjamin	1204
Meeker	Hannah	216	Miller	Benjamin	1278
Meeker	Hannah	1528	Miller	Elizabeth	1715
Meeker	Hannah Ogden	1370	Miller	Elizabeth	487
Meeker	Henry	9	Miller	Elizabeth	510
Meeker	Isaac R.	1765	Miller	Emeline	490
Meeker	James F.	993	Miller	Esther C.	482
Meeker	James R.	998	Miller	Ezubah	2018
Meeker	John M.	2022	Miller	F. Rossiter	733
Meeker	John T. Halsey	996	Miller	Hannah	873
Meeker	Jonathan	825	Miller	Hannah	1277

IN FIRST PRESBYTERIAN CHURCH YARD. 343

Name		Number	Name		Number
Miller	Hannah	1713	Mulford	Emeline	1288
Miller	Isreal M.	1592	Mulford	Fanne	1335
Miller	Joanna	484	Mulford	Frankey	1335
Miller	John S.	565	Mulford	Hannah	1347
Miller	Jonathan	1202	Mulford	James Caldwell	1398
Miller	Josiah	1714	Mulford	Jane	1344
Miller	Margaret	491	Mulford	Jane H.	1286
Miller	Moses	2014	Mulford	John	1338
Miller	Moses	482	Mulford	Jonas T.	1394
Miller	Nathaniel	1317	Mulford	Jonathan	1397
Miller	Nathaniel	1317	Mulford	Lewis	1336
Miller	Rachel Ann	566	Mulford	Lewis	66
Miller	Richard, Junr.	1201	Mulford	Lewis	1341
Miller	Samuel	489	Mulford	Lewis	1340
Miller	Samuel	492	Mulford	Locky B.	1471
Miller	Samuel, Jr.	488	Mulford	Mary	1342
Miller	Samuel K.	872	Mulford	Mary E.	1287
Miller	Sarah C.	871	Mulford	Mary M.	1286
Miller	Susanna	483	Mulford	Michael	68
Miller	William	482	Mulford	Moses W.	1286
Mills	Mary	439	Mulford	Patience	1289
Mills	William	438	Mulford	Phebe	831
Mitchell	Albert R.	1463	Mulford	Phebe	67
Mitchell	Caroline M.	1463	Mulford	Phebe	1402
Mitchell	David S.	1573	Mulford	Sarah	1337
Mitchell	Mary R.	1463	Mulford	Sarah Ann	1349
Mitchell	Nathaniel	1463	Mulford	Sarah Ann	1349
Mitchell	William	1697	Mulford	Sarah W.	1287
Monroe	Edward J.	1492	Mulford	Thomas	1471
Monroe	Elizabeth W.	1492	Mulford	Thomas, Capt.	1401
Monroe	Jemima	1492	Mulford	Townley	1346
Monroe	William W.	1491	Mulford	Trembly W.	1399
Montgomery	Amelia	1603	Murdoch	Alexander	1717
Montgomery	William James	1603	Murdoch	James	1717
Moore	Alice	1834	Murdock	Sarah	1875
Moore	Catharine	516	Murphy	Sarah Clarke	269
Moore	David	518	Murray	Anna Rhees	1627
Moore	Eliza	89	Murray	Catharine L.	1627
Moore	Genie	1834	Murray	Eliza J. Rhees	1627
Moore	Moses	514	Murray	Elizabeth C.	1627
Moore	Sarah	517	Murray	John M.	1627
Moore	Sarah E.	515	Murray	Margaret B.	1627
Morehous	Phebe	336	Murray	Nicholas	1627
Morehous	Rebecca	337	Murray	Thomas Chalmers	1627
Morehouse	Aaron	781	Murray	William W.	1627
Morehouse	David	394		My Brother	18
Morehouse	David	745	Nelson	Jared	1839
Morehouse	Phebe	778	Nelson	Joanna	1838
Morehouse	Samuel	779	Nelson	Olivia A.	1840
Morehouse	Susannah	780	Nicoll	Alexander	1907
Morehows	Hannah	1932	Nicholl	Ida	1648
Morgan	Nathaniel	1663	Nicoll	Mary	1908
Morrell	Family Vault	1736	No Inscription		591
Morris	Mary Jane	1707	Noe	Jane S. Hatfield	249
Morse	Abby W.	558½	Noe	Walter C.	1831
Morse	Amy	1028	Norris	Catharine M.	640
Morse	Elizabeth	1026	Norris	Cerintha	639
Morse	Isaac, Dr.	1028	Norris	Charles L.	637
Morse	Joanna Brown	1021	Norris	Charlotte	641
Morse	Joseph D.	560	Norris	Elias	642
Morse	Polly	559	Norris	Henry	1499
Morss	Robeart, Jr.	1792	Norris	Henry	1495
Morton	Amelia	864	Norris	Laura A.	639
Morton	Elihu	864	Norris	Mary	1497
Morton	Elvira	864	Norris	Nathaniel	1498
Morton	Lewis M.	864	Norris	Noah	643
Moses	Charles W.	1669	Norris	Phebe	1496
Mount	Hannah	1200	Norris	Rachel	1494
Mount	Mary	1647	Norris	Rebecca	644
Munson	Abby M.	716	Norris	Samuel	1500
Munson	Hallsey	717	Nuttman	A. W.	1003
Mulford	Abraham M.	1345	Nuttman	Elizabeth	1007
Mulford	Ann	1400	Nuttman	James G.	922
Mulford	Anna	1285	Nuttman	James G.	1000
Mulford	Benjamin	1290	Nuttman	John McD.	1004
Mulford	Catharine T.	1395	Nuttman	Lavinia	1001
Mulford	Catharine	1396	Nuttman	Margaret W.	1771
Mulford	Charity	66	Nuttman	Matilda	1001
Mulford	David	753	Nuttman	Matilda G.	999
Mulford	Elizabeth P.	1348	Nuttman	Matilda W.	921

INDEX OF INSCRIPTIONS

Name				Name			
Nuttman		Oliver	1002	Ogden		Samuel	323
Nuttman		Oliver C.	923	Ogden		Sarah W.	349
Nuttman		Oliver C.	1004	Ogden		Sarah Halsey	349
Nuttman		Sarah	1008	Ogden		Sarah Platt	463
Ogden		Aaron, Col.	462	Ogden		Sarah Ross	298
Ogden		Aaron	462	Ogden		Sarah Frazee	784
Ogden		Abigail	140	Ogden		Susan Dayton	461
Ogden		Abraham	36	Ogden		Theodore H.	136
Ogden		Abraham	49	Ogden		Thomas	36
Ogden		Albert	1368	Ogden		Thomas A.	471
Ogden		Albert	1369	Ogden		William	339
Ogden		Benjamin	294	Ogden		William	339
Ogden		Benjamin	402	Ogden		William	326
Ogden		Benjamin, Capt.	399	Ogden		Wm. DeHart	460
Ogden		Charity	293	Ogden		Zurviah	867
Ogden		Charity Ann	325	Ogilvie		Agnes	363
Ogden		David	542	Ogilvie		Alexander	363
Ogden		Dinah	36	Ogilvie		Jane J.	363
Ogden		E. B. Dayton	461	Ogilvie		Jane M.	363
Ogden		E. B. Dayton	462	Oliver		David	567
Ogden		Elizabeth Chetwood	462	Oliver		Hannah	570
Ogden		Elizabeth	395	Oliver		Jacob G.	1193
Ogden		Elizabeth	42	Oliver		James	576
Ogden		Elizabeth	285	Oliver		James	575
Ogden		Elizabeth	393	Oliver		John N.	574
Ogden		Elizabeth	392	Oliver		John Nicholas	578
Ogden		Esther	324	Oliver		Jonathan	571
Ogden		Ezekiel	141	Oliver		Mary	572
Ogden		Ezekiel	41	Oliver		Rhoda	577
Ogden		Hannah	466	Oliver		Samuel	568
Ogden		Hannah	1369	Oliver		Sarah	569
Ogden		Hannah	287	Oliver		Sarah	573
Ogden		Hannah	543	Olliver		Uselna L.	1192
Ogden		Hannah	468	Osborn		Enos	1629
Ogden		Hannah Insley	1369	Osborn		David	930
Ogden		Hatfield	139	Osmun		Martha	691
Ogden		Hetfield	286	Osmun		Stephen T.	690
Ogden		Jacob	396	Pard'w		Martha	1132
Ogden		Jacob	217	Parcell		Andrew	1142
Ogden		Jane Chandler	468	Parcell		Elizabeth	1143
Ogden		Jean	32	Parcell		Elizabeth	1141
Ogden		Joanna T.	1729	Park		Mary Louisa R.	168
Ogden		Joanna	40	Parkhurst		Abner W.	1382
Ogden		John	47	Parkhurst		Charlotte S.	1382
Ogden		John	43	Parkhurst		John S.	1381
Ogden		John M.	1729	Parkhurst		Jonas W.	1380
Ogden		John Robert	462	Parkhurst		Josephine Y.	1380
Ogden		Jonathan	48	Parkhurst		Mary S.	1380
Ogden		Mr. Jonathan	398	Parmalie		George W.	1104
Ogden		Joseph	544	Parmalie		Mary E.	1104
Ogden		Joseph	1368	Parsell		Abigail Insley	1373
Ogden		Joseph G.	338	Parsell		Henry	1373
Ogden		Lewis	291	Passels		Mary	320
Ogden		Lucille	1783	Passel		Phebe	1305
Ogden		Lucille D.	1782	Passel		Price	1306
Ogden		Margaret	290	Passel		Stephen	1305
Ogden		Mary	327	Passel		Stephen	1304
Ogden		Mary	39	Patterson		Thomas	1643
Ogden		Mary Barber	464	Pauley		John F.	1675
Ogden		Mary C. Barber	462	Peach		Jane	173
Ogden		Mary Henrietta	1784	Peason		John	1123
Ogden		Mary J. Magie	137	Peet		Rhoda	1623
Ogden		Matthias, Gen'l	469	Perriam		Elizabeth	244
Ogden		Matthias	462	Perriam		Joseph	245
Ogden		Matthias	292	Perrin		Ann	1593
Ogden		Matthias	289	Perrin		Lucretia B.	1548
Ogden		Moses	539	Perrin		Richard	1547
Ogden		Moses	296	Perrin		Richard	1593
Ogden		Moses	541	Perrin		Sarah	1593
Ogden		Moses Condit	298	Phelps		Frederick	1821
Ogden		Moses H.	297	Phinny		Gould, Col.	1611
Ogden		Nancy	1729	Pierce		Oliver	1353
Ogden		Phebe	465	Pierson		Aaron	1576
Ogden		Phebe Ann	462	Pierson		Abigail	46
Ogden		Rebekah	397	Pierson		Albert R.	989
Ogden		Rhoda	295	Pierson		Albert A.	916
Ogden		Rhoda	138	Pierson		Amzi	1329
Ogden		Robert, Esq.	467	Pierson		Ann B.	985
Ogden		Sally	339	Pierson		Benjamin	186
Ogden		Samuel	288	Pierson		Catharine A.	917

IN FIRST PRESBYTERIAN CHURCH YARD. 345

Surname	Given Name	No.
Pierson	Charlotte	93
Pierson	David	389
Pierson	Elihu	88
Pierson	Elizabeth	387
Pierson	Francis	915
Pierson	Joanna	1934
Pierson	John	45
Pierson	John	91
Pierson	Jonathan	94
Pierson	Jonathan	95
Pierson	Lillis	1575
Pierson	Mary	388
——	——	390
Pierson	Mary Chandler	96
Pierson	Mary Louisa	1575
Pierson	Oliver	98
Pierson	Phebe	92
Pierson	Phebe Magie	1329
Pierson	Prudence	44
Pierson	Ralph H.	1779
Pierson	Rebekah Townley	1329
Pierson	Rhoda	90
Pierson	Sarah A.	1779
Pierson	Stephen	986
Pierson	Stephen E.	987
Pierson	Susan W.	988
Pierson	William	918
Platt	Austin	854
Porter	Alexander	1699
Porter	Elizabeth	1952
Porter	Margaret	1953
Porter	Robert	1950
Porter	William, Jr.	1951
Post	Andrew	1753
Post	Mary	1970
Potter	Hephzibah	609
Potter	John	1068
Price	Aaron	2003
Price	Aaron Ogden	652
Price	Abby W.	130
Price	Abigail	534
Price	Abigail	35
Price	Abigail	1
Price	Abigail	1455
Price	Ann T. (Marsh)	79
Price	Anne	617
Price	Anthony	2011
Price	Benjamin, Esq.	2006
Price	Benjamin Jr.	2008
Price	Benjamin M.	2003
Price	Catharine O.	2030
Price	Celestia	322
Price	Charles Tooker	79
Price	Charity	2005
Price	Children, 5	6
Price	Chloe	623
Price	Cumfort	113
Price	Daniel	197
Price	Daniel	655
Price	Daniel	654
Price	David	1968
Price	David W.	614
Price	Ebenezer	702
Price	Elihu	1293
Price	Elizabeth	3
Price	Elizabeth	369
Price	Elizabeth	2004
Price	Elizabeth	2026
Price	Elizabeth	2013
Price	Elizabeth W.	131
Price	Enos	658
Price	Ephriam	622
Price	Ezra E.	1969
Price	Farrington	2027
Price	George	2029
Price	George	2001
Price	George F.	2031
Price	George F.	2028
Price	Hannah	610
Price	Hedges Ralph	6
Price	Henrietta J.	1969
Price	Jacob	1216
Price	Jane S.	616
Price	Joanna	2003
Price	John	1972
Price	John	2008
Price	John	2010
Price	John	385
Price	John	384
Price	John Nicholas	2031
Price	John N. O.	2029
Price	Jonathan	612
Price	Jonathan	659
Price	Jonathan	648
Price	Jonathan D.	651
Price	Joseph G.	23
Price	Joseph Perriam	653
Price	Joseph W.	1774
Price	Julia Elyea	22
Price	Margaret	2009
Price	Margery	1216
Price	Marian	615
Price	Martha	175
Price	Martha Alice	174
Price	Martha Taylor	199
Price	Mary	660
Price	Mary	2007
Price	Mary	620
Price	Mary	383
Price	Mary	1971
Price	Mary	533
Price	Mary Ann	2
Price	Mary H.	613
Price	Mary P.	1973
Price	Mary W.	1294
Price	Nathaniel	618
Price	Nathaniel	621
Price	Nathaniel	534
Price	Oliver	2025
Price	Pamelia	7
Price	Perriam	649
Price	Phebe	6
Price	Phebe	2002
Price	Phebe	615
Price	Phebe	657
Price	Phebe	198
Price	Phebe Anna	650
Price	Phebe Agnes	174
Price	Puah	6
Price	Rachel	700
Price	Rachel	656
Price	Rachel	132
Price	Ralph	4
Price	Ralph	6
Price	Ralph	6
Price	Rebecca	2012
Price	Robert	5
Price	Sarah	701
Price	Sarah Ann	321
Price	Sarah C.	1546
Price	Simeon	701
Price	Susan	33
Price	Susan Miller	2024
Price	Susan M.	129
Price	Tenrult	34
Price	Thomas	35
Price	Thomas	133
Price	Thomas, Jr.	382
Price	William	2010
Price	Wm. Erastus	534
Price	William Dayton	129
Price	T.	535
Quigley	Daniel	870
Quigley	Elizabeth	868
Quigley	John	869
Quigley	John	869
Quigley	Thomas	870
Radly	John	1121
Ramsden	Boynton	54
Ramsden	Israel Ludlow	53

Ramsden	Martha	50	Ross	John, Esq.	409½
Ramsden	Phebe	54	Ross	Martha	929
Ramsden	William	52	Ross	Mary	1803
Ramsden	William	51	Ross	Rebecca	1801
Ramson	William	1980	Ross	Sarah	410
Randell	George	1696	Ross	William	1804
Randolph	Francis	1887	Ross	William	1263
Randolph	Francis C. F.	1886	Rowland	Abigail	1567
Randolph	Frances Louisa	1832	Rowland	Jane F.	1568
Randolph	Louis F.	1832	Sale	Daniel	1475
Randolph	Maria H.	1888	Sale	Daniel	1479
Randolph	Phebe H.	1885	Sale	Edward T.	1481
Randolph	Robert	1888	Sale	Edward	1480
Rawl	Samuel	1686	Sale	Edward	1481
Red stone cross		21½	Sale	Elizabeth	1477
Reeve	Frances H.	1646	Sale	Elizabeth	1474
Reeve	James H.	1644	Sale	Phebe	1476
Reeve	Lucetta	1645	Sale	Sarah	1480
Reeve	Uzal	1644	Sanderson	Edward	1280
Reid	Cornelia A.	1813	Sanderson	Edward	1283
Reid	Emma	1815	Sanderson	Hannah	1281
Reid	George W.	1812	Sanderson	Mary Chapman	1282
Reid	Jennie	1814	Sanderson	Sarah Bliss	1284
Reid	Mary	1816	Sayre	Abigail	1828
Reilly	Henry	1919	Sayre	Anna	606
Rich	Abigail (wid)	1931	Sayre	Elias R.	605
Richards	Aaron	458	Sayre	Elizabeth P.	238
Richards	Eliza Y.	796	Sayre	Elizabeth P.	242
Richards	John	981	Sayre	Ephriam	1206
Richards	John C.	459	Sayre	Esther	1301
Rindell	Abby W.	1162	Sayre	Ezekiel	1208
Rindell	Gilbert	1941	Sayre	Hannah	1209
Rindell	John	1940	Sayre	Harriet	1828
Rindell	Mary W.	1940	Sayre	James	409
Rindell	Sarah	1906	Sayre	James C.	240
Rindell	Sophia	1939	Sayre	Joanna	1934
Ritter	Amelia	1708	Sayre	Job	830
Ritter	Amelia R.	1711	Sayre	John	1828
Ritter	Charles	1709	Sayre	Joseph	1937
Ritter	Franklin	1710	Sayre	Margaret Jane	1828
Ritter	George	1709	Sayre	Martha L.	1829
Ritter	J. Peter (Capt.)	1712	Sayre	Mary	1207
Ritter	Louis	1708	Sayre	Mary	1210
Ritter	Mary B.	1710	Sayre	Mary	1828
Ritter	Wilhelmina	1709	Sayre	Mary	1936
Ritter	William	1708	Sayre	Mary Ann	1828
Ritter	William P.	1710	Sayre	Noah	1302
Rivers	Jane Eliza	1260	Sayre	Samuel	1935
Rivers	Lewis	1258	Sayre	Samuel	1828
Rivers	Rachel	1259	Sayre	Sidney W.	241
Roberts	Horatio E.	722	Sayre	Theodore J.	239
Roberts	Jesse	724	Sayre	Theodore James	243
Roberts	Lucy M.	723	Sayre	Thomas M.	242
Robertson	Maria Caldwell	166	Sayre	Thomas O.	608
Robertson	Robert Smith	165	Sayre	Walter F.	1830
Rodgers	Margaret M.	437	Sayre	William	1827
Roll	Catherine	1687	Schenck	William	674
Rollo	James	856	Scott	Gavin	1633
Rollo	James S.	849	Scott	Mather	1635
Rollo	Thomas	857	Scott	Mary	1634
Rolston	William R.	919	Scott	Samuel	545
Rosette	Abraham	962	Scudder	Charlot	714
Rosette	Francis Peter	962	Scudder	Eanock	714
Rosette	Furman	1071	Scudder	Isaac	713
Rosette	Louisa	962	Seabar	Elizabeth	1882
Rosette	Lydia	961	Seaton	John T.	1911
Rosette	Susan	961	Seaton	John T.	1910
Ross	Alice	1807	Seaton	Mary E.	1912
Ross	Delinda Hopkins	1799	Seely	Mary	302
Ross	Eliza	1806	Shepherd	Caroline Powell	1704
Ross	Eliza Crane	1805	Shepherd	Lavenia	1702
Ross	Elizabeth	412	Shute	Barnaby	1215
Ross	George, Esq.	1257	Shute	Elizabeth R.	1113
Ross	James	672	Shute	William	1613
Ross	James	672	Simmons	Mary P.	1531
Ross	James	1798	Silvers	Maria B.	85
Ross	James	1802	Slater	Edward B.	1549
Ross	Jane	1262	Slater	James D.	1549
Ross	Jeremiah	1800	Slater	Solomon	1549
Ross	John, Esq.	411	Smith	Abigail	202

IN FIRST PRESBYTERIAN CHURCH YARD. 347

Name	Page	Name	Page
Smith............ Abigail	205	Stackhouse........ Joseph	161
Smith............ Adeline	845	Stagg.............. Henry	1267
Smith............ Anne Halsted	203	Stagg .... Mary	1268
Smith............ Betsy...............	205	Stagg................ Phebe.............	1267
Smith............ Caleb H............	205	Stanbro............. Phebe....	943½
Smith............ Caleb H............	201	Stansbery.......... Harriet A..........	1266
Smith............ Caleb H............	205	Stansbery .... James F.	1266
Smith............ Catharine J. E.....	1780	Stansbery .... William A..........	1266
Smith............ David	1666	Stearns............. Lorenzo	1732
Smith............ Eliza Melvin	333	Steele .... Candace............	1982
Smith............ Elizabeth...........	841	Stiles .... Abraham	1521
Smith............ Fanny..............	205	Stiles .... Daniel.............	1521
Smith............ Hannah	744	Stiles .... Hannah	1527
Smith............ Hannah	211	Stiles .... John	1523
Smith............ Henry	207	Stiles.............. Phebe	1518
Smith............ Henry, Jr...........	208	Stiles.............. Phebe	1524
Smith............ Jacamiah	176	Stiles .... Phebe Woodruff ..	1520
Smith............ James	843	Stiles .... Susan M...........	1522
Smith............ James M............	841	Stiles.............. William	1517
Smith............ Jane...............	619	Stockton .... Mary	470
Smith............ Jeffery	210	Stockton .... Sarah..............	16
Smith............ Joanna	203	Stoddard .... Caroline M.........	1464
Smith............ Job	1311	Stone Cross.......	21½
Smith............ Job................	1310	Stone defaced	1632
Smith............ John J.............	1312	Stone broken off...	1148
Smith............ John W............	1666	Stone broken off	984
Smith............ Julia...............	205	Storm.............. Maria..............	676
Smith............ Margery............	212	Strempel........... Mary...............	1691
Smith............ Mary M............	1308	Summers .... Charles............	1728
Smith............ Moses	215	Summers .... George (Dr.)	1728
Smith............ Ogden	1314	Sutlif .... John...............	1835
Smith............ Oliver	846	Sutlif .... William	1836
Smith............ Phebe	215	Sybrandt .... James	945
Smith............ Phebe	1313	Taintor............. Charlotte W. C. ...	1773
Smith............ Phebe B............	841	Tait .... Catharine	1718
Smith............ Samuel	213	Tait .... William............	1719
Smith............ Samuel O...........	201	Taylor .... Jennet..............	1063
Smith............ Sarah..............	205	Taylor .... Rachel..............	1064
Smith............ Sarah...............	206	Terrill.............. Phebe	1954
Smith............ Sarah...............	1309	Terril .... Phebe	1027
Smith............ Sarah...............	844	Terril .... Phebe H............	1355
Smith............ Sarah H............	205	Terril .... Susanna	1601
Smith............ Susan	842	Tessier .... Susanne	1205
Smith............ Susan Emma	1822	Thane .... Catharine	513
Smith............ Susanna	844	Thompson.......... Abel...............	78
Smith............ Thaddeus M.......	846	Thompson.......... Ann M.............	1387
Smith............ William	209	Thompson.......... Mr. Benjamin......	1637
Smith............ William	1666	Thompson.......... Charles S.	171
Smith............ William	843	Thompson.......... Elias	75
Smith............ William R..........	204	Thompson.......... Fanny..............	76
Snider............ Charlotte	1776	Thompson.......... Harvey.............	1888
Sorrell............ John Joseph	1605	Thompson.......... Henrietta P........	171
Spalding........... Clarissa D.	1767	Thompson.......... Joanna	866
Spencer............ Deborah	1114	Thompson.......... Joann B............	689
Spencer............ Jerusha	635	Thompson.......... John...............	188
Spencer............ Sarah..............	1362	Thompson.......... Martha	546
Spinnage .... Isaac	1150	Thompson.......... Phebe.............	1316
Spinnage .... John	1150	Thompson .... Samuel	689
Spinnage .... Mary..............	1150	Thompson.......... Vashti..............	77
Spinnage .... Mary...............	1151	Thorp............. Baker	60
Spinning .... Abigail	1149	Thorp.............. Henry..............	114
Spinning .... Abraham F.......	1145	Todd .... Elizabeth..........	1540
Spinning .... Benjamin...........	1149	Todd .... Patty Lyon	57
Spinning .... Constant	1516	Toms.............. Mary	1862
Spinning .... Daniel..............	1509	Tooker .... Abram	1105
Spinning .... Elvina Clark	1597	Tooker .... Ann Elizabeth.....	1846
Spinning .... George S...........	1596	Tooker .... Charles............	1092
Spinning .... Hannah	1144	Tooker .... Charles............	1086
Spinning .... Hester M...........	1145	Tooker .... Charles............	1091
Spinning .... John................	1146	Tooker .... Charles............	1102
Spinning .... John................	1515	Tooker .... Daniel W..........	1847
Spinning .... Mary................	1514	Tooker .... Elizabeth..........	1190
Spinning .... Mary................	1510	Tooker .... Elizabeth..........	1102
Spinning .... Mindwell............	1511	Tooker .... Ellen S.	1103
Spinning .... Phebe	1513	Tooker .... Jacob M............	1103
Spinning .... Polly and Abby ...	1149	Tooker .... James C............	1843
Spinning .... Sarah...............	1512	Tooker .... Lewis	1189
Spinning .... Theodore S.........	1146	Tooker .... Lewis	1089
Stackhouse .... Abigail.............	161	Tooker .... Lewis	1088
Stackhouse .... Eliza	715	Tooker .... Mary	1105

Tooker	Matilda	1842	Wade	Nancy	1023
Tooker	Nehemiah W.	1189	Wade	Nehemiah	1318
Tooker	Phebe C.	1093	Wade	Phebe Woodruff	1321
Tooker	Susan M.	1191	Walker	Margaret J.	1673
Tooker	Susanna B.	1090	Walker	Mary	1791
Tooker	Wm. O.	1841	Ward	Elizabeth C.	863
Tooker	William O., Jr.	1847	Ward	Emeline W.	782
Townley	Jonathan, Capt.	1326	Ward	Henrietta M.	782
Townley	Phebe	1325	Ward	Phebe	861
Townley	Rhoda	1327	Ward	Samuel	413
Townley	Richard, Capt.	1328	Ward	Sarah	1118
Trotter	Benjamin	1117	Ward	Silas	862
Trumbull	Ann	636	Washburn	Henry O.	1378
Trumbull	Hannah W.	357	Washburn	Uriah	1379
Trumbull	Joseph	636	Watkins	Esther	1902
Trumbull	Susan Landis	356	Watkins	Frances Spinning	1519
Tucker	Abby	1100	Watson	Elizabeth	1029
Tucker	Abby C.	1098	Webster	Ann	1406
Tucker	Abby W.	1153	Wells	Ann	1466
Tucker	Abner S.	1853	Wells	David	1723
Tucker	Abraham	1085	Wells	Louisa A.	1723
Tucker	Amelia H.	1153	Wells	Sarah	694
Tucker	Augustus	1848	Westervelt	Frances	1678
Tucker	Charles	1094	Whaley	Mehetable	772
Tucker	Daniel	1853	Wheaton	Joseph	308
Tucker	Gideon B.	1853	Whitefield	Abigail T.	1322
Tucker	Henry P.	1100	Whitefield	Addie	1324
Tucker	James H.	1100	Whitefield	Annie Louise	1323
Tucker	Jane	1101	Whitefield	Edward M.	1022
Tucker	Jane	1178	Whitefield	Frank	1322
Tucker	Luke	1099	Whitefield	William	1322
Tucker	Lydia Morrell	1066	Whitehead	Abby	189
Tucker	Margaret	1100	Whitehead	Benjamin	1850
Tucker	Phebe	1095	Whitehead	Children of	194
Tucker	Sarah	1096	Whitehead	David, Dea.	195
Tucker	Wessel	1097	Whitehead	David	193
Tuker	Jonathan Wade	1087	Whitehead	Elizabeth	192
Tunis	Bernadus G.	352	Whitehead	Isaac	401
Tunis	David W.	353	Whitehead	John	190
Tunis	Maria	351	Whitehead	Jonathan M.	189
Tunis	Nehemiah	354	Whitehead	Margaret	196
Tunis	Patience	355	Whitehead	Mary	1849
Vail	Dolly	858	Whitehead	Sarah	191
Van Ausdol	Cortland	2000	Whitehead	Thurston	185
Vandergrist	Hannah A.	1599	Whitlock	Ann	457
Vandergrist	Hannah A.	1599	Whitlock	Ephraim L.	457
Vandergrist	May Elizabeth	1599	Whitlock	Peggy	457
Van Derlip	Hannah	1527	Whitlock	Sarah	457
Van Derveer	Phebe Crane	957	Whitewright	James	992
Van Doren	Margaret H.	711	Whitewright	John	992
Van Doren	Robert H.	712	Whitewright	Susannah	992
Van Horn	Peter	1606	Wilbur	Erastus	125
Van Name	Anna	1678	Wilbur	Joseph	126
Van Name	Elias	1705	Wilbur	Joseph L.	127
Van Name	Henry Martin	1676	Wilbur	Joseph Lyon	125
Van Name	Jane Matilda	1677	Wilbur	Sarah	125
Van Name	Jane Townley	1679	Willcock	Charity	116
Van Name	John	1679	Willcock	Elener	121
Van Pelt	Helen W.	433	Willcock	Elizabeth	117
Van Pelt	Margaret S.	434	Willcock	Samuel	120
Van Pelt	Reuben	432	Willcock	Stephen	122
Van Voorhis	James D.	1665	Wilcox	Elizabeth	118
Vergerau	Abigail	1451	Wilcox	James	71
Vincent	Susanne L.	1205	Wilcox	James, Eld.	119
Vreland	Henrietta L.	1596	Wilcox	Lydia Ross	119
W.	B.	1069	Wiley	Phebe	1994
Wade	Abigail	1318	Willis	Ann	1974
Wade	Benjamin	1320	Willis	Daniel	1975
Wade	David	1271	Willis	James	774
Wade	Elias	1274	Willis	John J.	696
Wade	Francis	213	Willis	Sarah B. Jarvis	774
Wade	Henry Kollock	1273	Willis	Sarah Louisa	695
Wade	James	1023	Willis	William H.	695
Wade	Jane	213	Willis	William M.	1529
Wade	Jane S.	204	Wilson	Elizabeth P.	939
Wade	Jonas H.	1272	Wilson	Harriet Elizabeth	1385
Wade	Jonas H.	1272	Wilson	Harry Stewart	1384
Wade	Jonathan	1321	Wilson	Helen H.	1386
Wade	Jonathan D.	1319	Wilson	James	1139
Wade	Joseph M.	1024	Williams	Ann	1556

IN FIRST PRESBYTERIAN CHURCH YARD. 349

Name		No.	Name		No.
Williams	Ann Eliza	1650	Winans	Benjamin, Jr.	1254
Williams	Ann S.	1501	Winans	Benjamin	1163
Williams	Benjamin	1482	Winans	Benjamin, Jun.	1172
Williams	Benjamin	1407	Winans	Benjamin H.	62
Williams	Benjamin	1438	Winans	Betty	1167
Williams	Benjamin B.	1508	Winans	David R.	1251
Williams	Betsey	1433	Winans	Deborah	973
Williams	Caleb	1410	Winans	Elias	1747
Williams	Charles	1416	Winans	Elias	1747
Williams	Charles M.	1484	Winans	Elias	1748
Williams	Cornelius	1490	Winans	Elias	1901
Williams	Daniel	1655	Winans	Elizabeth	976
Williams	Daniel H.	1683	Winans	Experience	1955
Williams	David	1488	Winans	Fanny	1253
Williams	Deborah	1656	Winans	Frances	506
Williams	Ebenezer	1404	Winans	Gilbert H.	1890
Williams	Elenor	1503	Winans	Hannah	506
Williams	Eleanor	1439	Winans	Hannah	506
Williams	Electa L.	1430	Winans	Hannah	1115
Williams	Elias	1483	Winans	Hannah C.	1246
Williams	Elihu	1661	Winans	Hannah	1157
Williams	Elizabeth	1429	Winans	Hannah	1163
Williams	Elizabeth C.	1486	Winans	Hannah	1903
Williams	Elizabeth F.	1487	Winans	Harriet C. Hatfield.	63
Williams	Elizabeth W.	1414	Winans	Henrietta	1174
Williams	Ezekiel	1551	Winans	Hester	1160
Williams	George	900	Winans	Isaac	1115
Williams	Hannah	1485	Winans	Isaac	977
Williams	Hannah	1652	Winans	Jacob	1896
Williams	Hannah	1412	Winans	Jacob	1166
Williams	Hannah P.	1203	Winans	Jacob	1169
Williams	Hannah	1651	Winans	Jacob	1965
Williams	Hannah	1343	Winans	Jacob C.	1747
Williams	Ichabod	1413	Winans	Jane	1173
Williams	Isaac	1649	Winans	Jane	1179
Williams	Jacob, Senr.	1662	Winans	Joanna	836
Williams	Jacob, Jr.	1658	Winans	Job	554
Williams	Jane	1504	Winans	Job	1156
Williams	Jane H.	1505	Winans	Job	1165
Williams	Jane Winans	1489	Winans	Job R.	1152
Williams	Jemima D.	1435	Winans	Jobe	1164
Williams	Joanna	1403	Winans	John	1303
Williams	Joel	1434	Winans	John	1171
Williams	John B.	1436	Winans	John	1965
Williams	John H.	1659	Winans	John	506
Williams	John Henry	1768	Winans	John	1158
Williams	John L.	1507	Winans	John	1116
Williams	Joseph	1649	Winans	Jonathan	506
Williams	Lida C.	1682	Winans	Jonathan G.	1869
Williams	Mary	1437	Winans	Julia	1171
Williams	Mary	1662	Winans	Magdalene	1900
Williams	Mary Ann	1660	Winans	Magdalene	970
Williams	Moses	1431	Winans	Maline	979
Williams	Nancy	1415	Winans	Margaret	1956
Williams	Oliver	1249	Winans	Mary	1168
Williams	Rebekah	1409	Winans	Mary	668
Williams	Rezin	1506	Winans	Mary	1897
Williams	Sally	1550	Winans	Mary E.	1747
Williams	Samuel	1502	Winans	Mary P.	1170
Williams	Sarah	1432	Winans	Moses	500
Williams	Sarah	1203	Winans	Moses	972
Williams	Thomas	1408	Winans	Moses	974
Williams	Thomas S.	1657	Winans	Nathan M.	553
Williams	William	1653	Winans	Oliver W.	1252
Winance	Phebe	502	Winans	Peter	1891
Winance	Zeruiah	501	Winans	Phebe	667
Winans	Aaron	1245	Winans	Phebe	506
Winans	Aaron	1176	Winans	Phebe	1954
Winans	Aaron T.	1253	Winans	Prudence	1177
Winans	Abby	1747	Winans	Prudence	1177
Winans	Abby	1164	Winans	Remember	1115
Winans	Abner	1889	Winans	Ruth	971
Winans	Amelia	1856	Winans	Samuel	506
Winans	Amelia A.	1251	Winans	Samuel	504
Winans	Amy C.	555	Winans	Samuel	506
Winans	Ann Maria	1170	Winans	Samuel	506
Winans	Annable	1248	Winans	Samuel	503
Winans	Benjamin	1247	Winans	Sarah	1147
Winans	Benjamin, Jun.	1159	Winans	Sarah	1155
Winans	Benjamin, Capt.	1180	Winans	Sarah Ann	837

Winans	Sarah H.	1269		Woodruff	Ezekiel D.	456
Winans	Sarah M.	1747		Woodruff	Fanny	810
Winans	Susan B.	1303		Woodruff	Francis W.	1265
Winans	Susan B. Wood	1303		Woodruff	Hannah	1946
Winans	Susan W.	1170		Woodruff	Hannah Phinney	1920
Winans	Susanna	978		Woodruff	Hannah	600
Winans	Susanna	1161		Woodruff	Hannah E.	913
Winans	Ujenia	1171		Woodruff	Henry	1585
Winans	Wm. O.	1251		Woodruff	Henry D.	1584
Winans	Zeruiah	506		Woodruff	Henry D.	1578
Wood	Ada E.	358		Woodruff	Isaac	376
Wood	Charity	770		Woodruff	Isaac, Esq.	1892
Wood	Clara L.	361		Woodruff	Jabez	585
Wood	Jeremy	550½		Woodruff	Jacob	913
Wood	John	551		Woodruff	Jacob Angus	1250
Wood	John	550		Woodruff	Jacob D. E.	911
Wood	John H.	359		Woodruff	James W., Col.	913
Wood	Jonas	771		Woodruff	Jane	590
Wood	Joseph P.	769		Woodruff	Jane	380
Wood	Louisa M.	358		Woodruff	Jane	739
Wood	Margaret	975		Woodruff	Jane L.	683
Wood	Marietta	360		Woodruff	Joanna	737
Wood	Mary C.	769		Woodruff	Job, Jr.	1265
Wood	Sarah	552		Woodruff	Job	1182
Woodhull	Cornelia	1006		Woodruff	John	1587
Woodhull	Jane Green	1005		Woodruff	Joseph	1581
Woodrowfe	Matthias	1948		Woodruff	Joseph 3d	1588
Woodrowfe	Thomas, Jun.	1948		Woodruff	Joseph	1894
Woodruff	Aaron	443		Woodruff	Laura Ann	1470
Woodruff	Aaron	703		Woodruff	Lewis	579
Woodruff	Aaron	592		Woodruff	Lewis T.	1264
Woodruff	Aaron, Dr.	377		Woodruff	Lizzie B. W.	912
Woodruff	Aaron J.	1188		Woodruff	Louisa	706
Woodruff	Abigail	1757		Woodruff	Louis T.	1183
Woodruff	Abigail	99		Woodruff	Luther	445
Woodruff	Abigail	378		Woodruff	M. M.	1614
Woodruff	Abigail	1577		Woodruff	Margaret	522
Woodruff	Abner	102		Woodruff	Martha A.	913
Woodruff	Abby Meeker	684		Woodruff	Martha	1582
Woodruff	Albert Eaton	725		Woodruff	Mary	1895
Woodruff	Ann	379		Woodruff	Mary	603
Woodruff	Anna	1591		Woodruff	Mary	1579
Woodruff	Anne	740		Woodruff	Mary	735
Woodruff	Archibald S.	1758		Woodruff	Mary	451
Woodruff	Archibald H.	449		Woodruff	Mary	584
Woodruff	Baker	583		Woodruff	Mary	603
Woodruff	Belcher	738		Woodruff	Mary	680
Woodruff	Benjamin	688		Woodruff	Mary	563
Woodruff	Betsey	1154		Woodruff	Mary	1944
Woodruff	Charity	597		Woodruff	Mary	705
Woodruff	Charity	598		Woodruff	Mary	594
Woodruff	Cooper	562		Woodruff	Mary Alice	913
Woodsuff	Damaris N.	1175		Woodruff	Mary Ann	593
Woodruff	Daniel	741		Woodruff	Mary Lyon	1188
Woodruff	Daniel	1468		Woodruff	Mary W.	1591
Woodruff	David	1859		Woodruff	Michael	1854
Woodruff	David	1929		Woodruff	Michael	100
Woodruff	David	736		Woodruff	Morris	101
Woodruff	Elias	247		Woodruff	Nathan	381
Woodruff	Elias George	105		Woodruff	Nathaniel	595
Woodruff	Eliza	734		Woodruff	Ogden	686
Woodruff	Eliza Ann	455		Woodruff	Parsons	679
Woodruff	Elizabeth	1930		Woodruff	Phebe	6.0
Woodruff	Elizabeth	1589		Woodruff	Phebe	914
Woodruff	Elizabeth	454		Woodruff	Phebe	682
Woodruff	Elizabeth	446		Woodruff	Phebe	687
Woodruff	Elizabeth	1586		Woodruff	Phebe wid. of Sam'l.	2002
Woodruff	Elizabeth	685		Woodruff	Phebe Munn	1467
Woodruff	Elizabeth	601		Woodruff	Phebe T.	1181
Woodruff	Elizabeth	453		Woodruff	Phebe T.	442
Woodruff	Elizabeth	1590		Woodruff	Puah	1583
Woodruff	Elizabeth	1182		Woodruff	Rachel	103
Woodruff	Emeline	687		Woodruff	Rachel	104
Woodruff	Emma F.	456		Woodruff	Rhoda	1590
Woodruff	Enos	599		Woodruff	Romyne A.	1469
Woodruff	Esthsr	561		Woodruff	Samuel	378
Woodruff	Esther R.	1855		Woodruff	Sarah	564
Woodruff	Eunice	1928		Woodruff	Sarah	1307
Woodruff	Ezekiel	452		Woodruff	Sarah	1860
Woodruff	Ezekiel	447		Woodruff	Sarah	448

IN FIRST PRESBYTERIAN CHURCH YARD.   351

Woodruff	Sarah	582	Woodruff	William	734
Woodruff	Sarah	1893	Woodruff	William B.	1591
Woodruff	Sarah	1945	Woodruff	William W.	505
Woodruff	Sarah H.	581	Woodward	Harriet V.	371
Woodruff	Seth	596	Woodward	Matthew W.	370
Woodruff	Seth	681	Young	Christian	793
Woodruff	Silas	450	Young	Eliza Voy	792
Woodruff	Stephen H.	683	Young	James	795
Woodruff	Stephen P.	678	Young	Jennet Voy	793
Woodruff	Thomas	1943	Young	Robert	794
Woodruff	Thomas	1947	Zeluf	Amelia	1856
Woodruff	Timothy	602	Zeluf	Esther R.	1855
Woodruff	Timothy	600	Zeluff	Hannah	1858
Woodruff	Timothy	1942	Zeluff	John	1857
Woodruff	Uzal	246	Zeluff	John W.	1859
Woodruff	Vilette	1580	Zulanf	Magdalena	1752
Woodruff	Whitehead	580	Zulanf	Magdalena	1752
Woodruff	Whitehead	586			

INDEX OF INSCRIPTIONS IN ST. JOHNS CHURCH YARD.

Surname	Given Name	Page	Surname	Given Name	Page
Allen	Jonathan	204	Cron	Louisa	66
Alexander	Caroline	177	D'Anterroches	Abigail Marsh	261
Andarson	William	157	D'Anterroches	Adrianne	262
Armstrong	Capt.	235	D'Anterroches	Jane	263
Baker	Deborah	208	D'Anterroches	John Peter	261
Ball	Elizabeth	134	D'Anterroches	Joseph Louis	262
Barhyt	Daniel	10	D'Anterroches	Mary	262
Barhyt	Elizabeth	11	Davis	Mary	165
Barton	Ann	48	Dayton	Margaretta	76
Barton	Gabriel	47	Deboisville	Charlotte	270
Barton	James H.	53	Deboisville	Louise	270
Barton	William S.	54	Deboisville	Rose, D. F. K.	277
Beavers	Rhoda Ann Ogden	104	Decker	Margaret	284
Bedell	Elizabeth	251	DeHart	Abigail Crane	109
Bedell	Israel	247	HeHart	Cyrus	3
Biffen	Ann	166	DeHart	Jacob, Capt.	109
Bird	Samuel	148	DeHart	Jacob, Col.	109
Bird	Susannah	150	DeHart	Jane	145
Blackledge	John	68	DeHart	Jane F.	263
Blackledge	Phebe	68	DeHart	Joanna	109
Blacklieg	Philip	72	DeHart	John	263
Blanchard	Cornelius	250	DeHart	John, Esq.	110
Blanchard	Sarah	250	DeHart	Matthias, Dr.	109
Blight	George	87	D'Hart	Mattvas	147
Bliss	Margaretta S.	25	DeHart	Mary	81
Bogart	Elizabeth	162	DeHart	Mary B. Chetwood	4
Bowne	Harriet Louisa	33	DeHart	William C.	2
Brasher	Abraham A.	205	Dennis	John	89
Briggs	Elizabeth	160	Dennis	Mary	89
Brien	Mary	143	Dexter	George H.	129
Brookfield	Job	179	Donaghy	Eleanor	86
Brown	Caroline E.	276	Donaghy	Mary Jane	86
Brown	Catherine	56	Donington	Hannah	245
Brown	Elizabeth	55	Doobs	Margaret	216
Brown	Elizabeth	199	DuBuc de Marcucy	Julie	108
Brown	John	57	Dumont	John	283
Brown	Phebe	58	Eckel	Henry	152
Burrowes	John	222	Edes	Henry Phelps	9
Burrowes	Mary	221	Edes	Robert Henry	9
Burrowes	Sarah	220	Edes	Robert, Capt.	9
Butler	Daniel	126	Emott	Edward	124
Butler	Jane D.	1	Emott	John	124
Butler	John	125	Emott	John	124
Buttle	Elizabeth	99	Evans	Elizabeth	154
Buttle	Henry	98	Evans	Margaret C.	155
Buttle	Mary Ann	99	Eyre	Sarah Margaret	85
Campbell	Mariah Prise	264	Fontaneilles	Jean Marie	272
Channing	Fanny	236	Foot	George R.	198
Channing	Julia Grant	237	G	H.	223
Chambon	Margaret Landry	257	G	W.	223
Chapman	Charlotte	255	Gabriel	Lady Ann Renie	107
Chetwood	George Jelf	14	Gardner	Christopher	212
Chetwood	Jane Emott	6	Gardner	Henry	213
Chetwood	John, M.D.	13	Gardner	Kathern	212
Chetwood	Mary	15	Gardner	Kathern	214
Chetwood	Mary Ann Jelf	12	Gardner	William	213
Chetwood	Mary B.	4	Gathwight	Alis	140
Chetwood	Timothy Phelps	7	Garthwait	Elizabeth	94
Chetwood	William Ashton	8	Garthwait	Henry	115
Conklin	Henrietta	82	Garthwait	Henry	119
Conklin	William H.	82	Garthwait	Isaac	117
Conklin	William F.	82	Garthwait	James	139
Craig	Androw	242	Garthwait	James	83
Craig	Phebe	246	Garthwait	James	116
Craig	Susanna	242	Garthwait	Jane	114
Craige	John	241	Garthwait	Jeremiah	113
Crane	Agigail	109	Garthwait	Jeremiah C.	136
Crane	Hannah	158	Garthwait	Lydia	120
Crane	Hannah	203	Garthwait	Mary	141
Cron	Louis	66	Garthwait	Mary	140

INDEX OF INSCRIPTIONS

Name		Page	Name		Page
Garthwait	Mary	118	King	Judeth	112
Garthwait	Prudence	142	Lachaise	J. A.	80
Garthwait	Vashti	135	Lawrence	Isaac, Capt.	243
Garthwait	William	138	Lawrence	Joanna	265
Garthwait	William, Esq.	133	Lawrence	Jonathan H.	265
Garthwait	William, Jr.	137	Lebreton	F. P.	206
Geiger	George	97	Lee	Robert	20
Geiger	George S.	95	Lee	William	21
Geiger	Susannah	96	Lewis	David	211
Gildermeester	Sarah	111	Man	Samuel	229
Gouet	John Peter	176	Man	Sarah	227
Gray	Amy	266	Man	Thomas	233
Gray	Elizabeth	266	Mann	Abigail	231
Gray	John	266	Mann	Abigail	225
Gray	Richardson, Esq.	266	Mann	Elias	230
Halstead	Abigail	71	Mann	Elias	230
Halstead	Timothy	71	Mann	Isaac	226
Halsted	George	240	Mann	John	67
Halsted	Margaret	240	Mann	Martha Wilcox	228
Hampton	Ann Frances	122	Mann	Sarah	224
Hampton	Hannah	122	Margat	Judeth King	112
Hampton	James	219	Margat	Peter, Capt.	112
Hampton	Jonathan, Esq.	122	Marsh	Abigail	261
Hampton	Mary Ann	122	Marsh	Ann	38
Harriman	John	188	Maupertuis	Ann Renée	107
Harriman	Sarah	188	Mayo	Edward C.	90
Harris	Elizabeth	146	Mitchel	Elihu	168
Harris	James	146	Mitchel	George	159
Harris	Nathan Poply	146	Mitchel	Hannah Crane	158
Hartman	Isaac	269	Mitchel	James	244
Hartman	Richard Tuite	268	Mitchel	William	164
Hattrch	Margaret E.	128	Mitchel	Elizabeth	170
Hatterick	Nicholas	153	Mitchell	Jacob	171
Haviland	Luke	202	Mitchell	Mary	172
Haviland	Martha	200	Montandon	Oliver Augustus	293
Haviland	Sarah	201	Moore	Caroline Matilda	183
Hendricks	Baker	260	Moore	Catherine Eleanor	182
Hendricks	Baker, Capt.	259	Mother	and Sister	65
Hendricks	Deborah S.	130	Mother	My	59
Hendricks	John	132	Niemcewicz	Susan M.	41
Hendricks	John	156	Nixon	William	19
Hendricks	Mary	156	Nuttall	Christopher	217
Hendricks	Phebe	260	Odling	Charles	239
Hendricks	Susan H.	131	Odling	John	238
Hermandez	Francisco	121	Ogden	Abigail Clark	17
Hetfield	Abel	189	Ogden	Andrew	23
Hetfield	Abigail	231	Ogden	Deborough	18
Hetfield	Altamont M.	232	Ogden	Elizabeth	173
Hetfield	Mary	232	Ogden	Ichabod	175
Hetfield	Morris	87	Ogden	Isaac	24
Higgins	Sarah	234	Ogden	Jacob	197
Hoagland	George	102	Ogden	John	16
Hoagland	William S.	102	Ogden	Lucy	105
Howell	Elizabeth	199	Ogden	Mary	174
Huntt	Belinda	34	Ogden	Phebe	22
Hunt	John	151	Ogden	Rhoda Ann	104
Hylton	Mary	30	Ogden	William	106
Hylton	Mehetable	30	Parton	Alfred	75
Hylton	Rachel Johnson	31	Paul	Andrew	279
Jeffrys	Henry	191	Paul	Elizabeth	278
Jeffrys	Jonathan	195	Paul	John	281
Jeffrys	Joshua	194	Paul	Sarah	280
Jeffrys	Joshua	193	Penny	Elizabeth	178
Jeffreys	Martha	192	Price	Elizabeth	278
Jelf	Susanna	5	Price	Sarah	163
Johnston	Henrietta	30	Price	Sarah	218
Jones	Elizabeth	210	Provoost	Catherine	32
Jones	Hopkin	271	Ramsden	William	209
Jones	Janup	271	Rezeau	William L.	73
Jones	Mary	215	Richardson	Elizabeth	196
Joline	David	180	Ricketts	James and Sarah	92
Kean	Cornelia L.	41	Robert	Christopher	42
Kean	Helen Rutherford	41	Robert	Joseph	43
Kean	Jacob Morris	41	Rogers	Emily Mary	45
Kean	Peter	41	Rogers	Mary R.	44
Kean	Sarah Louisa Jay	41	Rucastle	John, Capt.	26
Kean	Susan Mary	41	Rucastle	Phebe	28
Keller	Elizabeth	84	Salnave	Ann	60
Kiggins	Charles	275	Salnave	John Peter	62
Kiggins	Hannah P.	274	Salter	T.	79

IN ST. JOHNS CHURCH YARD.

Scudder	Isaac W	52
Scudder	Margaret	50
Scudder	Smith	51
Scudder	William	49
Schweighauser	Nicholas	127
Seaman	Benjamin R.	252
Seaman	Catherine J.	253
Seaman	Catherine P.	256
Seaman	Eliza	254
Seaman	Elizabeth	248
Seaman	Maria	249
Slater	Ann Slater	102
Slater	John	101
Slater	John	100
Slater	Thomas	103
Smith	Benjamin, Esq.	61
Smith	Jonas	285
Smith	Joseph	207
Sonmans	Peter, Esq.	111
Sonmans	Sarah	111
Spencer	O. H.	93
Spining	Sarah	149
Stephens	Elizabeth	134
Stiles	Deborah S.	130
Stiles	Susan	162
Sufferer	Little	273
Terrill	Daniel	181
Terrill	Ephriam	186
Terrill	Ephriam, Esq.	187
Terrill	Josiah	185
Terrill	Mary	184
Thomas	Anna R.	29
Thomas	Edmund D.	28
Thomas	Edward, Esq.	28
Thomas	George C.	29
Thomas	Mary	28
Thomas	Phebe Rucastle	28
Thomas	Sarah	28
Tiebout	Ann	27
Tobin	Elizabeth F.	64
Tobin	George	64
Tobin	Jane	63
Tobin	Sarah	60
Tooker	Abner	161
Tooker	Ann	37
Tooker	Ann	38
Tooker	Charles	39
Tooker	Charles H.	35
Tooker	Elizabeth D.	70
Tooker	Frances	35
Tooker	Joseph	36
Tooker	Mary	190
Tooker	Mary	40
Townley	Abigail	290
Townley	Abigail	123
Townley	Charles	123
Townley	Cornelia	46
Townley	Edward	291
Townley	Effingham	286
Townley	Mary	289
Townley	Rhoda	285
Townley	Sarah	282
Townley	William	288
Townley	William	287
Townley	William	292
Townley	William	46
Walton	Amy	267
Whipple	George W.	69
Whitehead	Mary Austen Peirce	144
Whitehead	Tommy	144
Whitehead	Willie	144
Williams	Elizabeth	167
Williams	Elizabeth	167
Williams	Mary	169
Williamson	Isaac H.	91
Williamson	J. D.	74
Williamson	Margaretta	76
Williamson	Matthias	77
Williamson	M. Hampton	88
Williamson	Sally F.	74
Williamson	Susannah	78
Yockney	Elinor Mary	258

ERRATA.

Page 106—No. 725, for Abert read Albert.
" 273—No. 1926, for Barnett read Barnet.
" 286—No. 2015, for Josiph read Joseph.
" 302—No. 77, for Matthew read Matthias.
" 305—No. 93, for Spencus read Spencer.

www.ingramcontent.com/pod-product-compliance
Lightning Source LLC
Chambersburg PA
CBHW070226230426
43664CB00014B/2231